The Best American Science
and Nature Writing 2020

The Best American Science and Nature Writing 2020™

Edited and with an Introduction
by Michio Kaku

Jaime Green, Series Editor

MARINER BOOKS

HOUGHTON MIFFLIN HARCOURT

BOSTON • NEW YORK   2020

hmhbooks.com

ISSN 1530-1508 (print) ISSN 2573-475X (ebook)
ISBN 978-0-358-07429-8 (print) ISBN 978-0-358-07424-3 (ebook)

Printed in the United States of America
DOC 10 9 8 7 6 5 4 3 2 1

Contents

Contents

Foreword

I'M WRITING THIS from within a very strange time capsule, not at the moment it's sealed nor at the moment it's opened, but from somewhere weird in between. I'm writing this from New York City in the middle of April 2020. The coronavirus pandemic feels to be in full swing, but for all I know, this could just be the early ramp-up to something still unimaginable. This year's guest editor, Michio Kaku, wrote his introduction this past winter, when this virus was news but not yet the omnipresent fact of daily life around the world; you're reading this in the fall of 2020 or later and know so much that's still to come for me. I'm going to read this again then, in the pages of our book instead of as I'm typing it at the little desk now wedged into my bedroom, so this is a time capsule but also a letter to my future self—I hope she, and all of you, are okay. (Who knows what late 2020 will be like, but in April we are doing a lot of telling people we write to, "I hope you're doing okay.")

I thought last year's foreword would be the weird one—I wrote it eight months pregnant, in a fever dream of hormones and deadlines. A few months ago, thinking about this year's foreword, I thought I would write about how the intervening year had changed my relationship to the stories in this anthology: about being a mother, about reading my son picture books about ocean fish and space exploration, about Ronald McNair and John Muir, and about the wonder and curiosity I hope we're seeding. I thought I would write about my son's future and the world we're leaving for future generations. A few months ago, those fears and questions felt pressing enough. Now it's plenty to say, "We're safe today, and we're going to do our best tomorrow for ourselves and whoever we can help."

In thinking about the role of science writing, right now and whenever you're reading this, it's impossible not to think of an essay from last year's collection, Ed Yong's "When the Next Plague Hits," originally published in 2018 by *The Atlantic*. No one knew then that SARS-CoV-2 was coming, but many people knew *something* was, and that we were not ready. But there are no essays about the coronavirus in this collection—these pieces were all published in 2019, a time capsule of their own. Don't think of them as a relic of the Before, but as a reminder that the world is huge and full of mystery, full of scientists and writers working to understand it, full of storytellers making of that work so many beautiful and valuable things.

The world these essays describe is still out there, even as so many researchers work from home instead of their labs. Joshua Sokol shines a light on the long-ignored contributions of two women to the discovery of chaos theory in his beautifully reported piece "The Hidden Heroines of Chaos." In "The Hunt for Planet Nine," Shannon Stirone shadows the researchers searching for a suspected new planet in the outer reaches of our solar system. She covers everything from the origins of the solar system to the history of planet discoveries, from the good-natured bickering of two researchers to the crystal-clear night sky above an observatory, all in service of asking: "What is happening beyond where we can see?"

These are also the stories of individual human lives—as individual as any can be with the bonds of pain and love that connect us. Tim Requarth explores the unknowable depths of both neuroscience and family in "The Final Five Percent," about his brother's traumatic brain injury. In "Sleep No More," Kelly Clancy tells the story of a married couple, Sonia Vallabh and Eric Minikel, who upended their lives to research a cure for the prion disease that killed Vallabh's mother and that she inherited. And in "Total Eclipse," Deanna Csomo McCool does the unimaginable (at least it is to me, writing this one room over from my sleeping baby): writing with grace and love and incredible clarity about her daughter's death. I am in awe of how McCool made her grief into a gift for her readers.

Writers are also grieving losses in the natural world—of species and glaciers and forests, and, underneath it all, the loss of our sense of safety and stability in the warming decades to come. In "What Remains," Daniel Duane grapples with the human love for the experience and idea of wilderness as he chronicles the life and death of a glacier. Jon Mooallem's "'We Have Fire Everywhere'" braids a gripping minute-by-minute narration of a woman's attempt to outrun—or outdrive—the wildfire consuming her California town with a no less urgent study of what's brought us to a moment when so much of our world is on fire: "It was all more evidence that the natural world was warping, outpacing our capacity to prepare for, or even conceive of, the magnitude of disaster that such a disordered earth can produce."

In "Ghosts of the Future," Sarah Kaplan situates the Cambrian explosion—and its monument in the fossil record, the Burgess Shale—amid the history of life and humanity's power to alter its future. That history is a record of boom and bust, swinging between flourishing and cataclysm on a thin thread of luck. In response to the point made by her scientist–tour guide that, as intelligent life, we are so lucky to be able to witness evidence of life's path, Kaplan writes, "What a profound responsibility that is. What a beautiful gift."

I wrote last year's foreword around an essay by Tony Kushner, extending his argument about the impossibility of apolitical art to the impossibility of apolitical science and nature writing. (If anyone wants to keep emailing me about how these selections are too political, I can't stop you. Nor, apparently, could an entire essay about why that stance is not only misguided but dangerous. You can reach me at BASNSeries@gmail.com, and you can find information about submitting work for future editions of the anthology at jaimegreen.net/BASN.) This year, I keep hearing these lines from the opening of N. K. Jemisin's novel *The Fifth Season:*

> This is what you must remember: the ending of one story is just the beginning of another. This has happened before, after all. People die. Old orders pass. New societies are born. When we say "the world has ended," it's usually a lie, because the *planet* is just fine.
>
> But this is the way the world ends.

When asked if she found it challenging to write for so long in such a grim world, Jemisin said (if I can paraphrase) that she doesn't think her Broken Earth trilogy is grim or hopeless at all. She said it's a story about survival—about surviving the end of the world. She reminds us that the end of the world is survivable, not just by the planet but by us.

The world has had many ends, from mass extinction events to a mother's loss of her daughter. We keep writing it, we keep witnessing it, we keep finding the stories and wonder and beauty and pain, and we keep trying to understand.

In the meanwhile, I hope you're doing okay.

JAIME GREEN

Introduction

ONE FATEFUL DAY, my daughter asked for my help studying for the New York State Regents exam, required of all public high school students in New York. When she told me the exam was in geology, I relished the idea of sitting down with my daughter and opening her eyes to the wonderous discoveries in the field.

I began to think of all the ways I could introduce her to the fundamental underlying principles behind geology. For example, continental drift allows us to see how our geology changed over millions of years, shaping the world today. The recycling of rock, starting with volcanic igneous rock, allows us to see how rock gets recycled and where it came from. And analyzing how earthquakes set off underground waves that penetrate the earth allows us to determine what is inside the earth. I made a short list of the organizing principles behind geology.

Then my daughter brought me actual sample copies of the Regents exam. I was shocked. It consisted of page after page of the names of scores of minerals and crystals to be memorized. The exam was a mind-numbing exercise in rote memorization. Staring at this immense list of irrelevant trivia, which students would forget the day after the exam, my daughter then asked me, "Daddy, why would anyone want to become a scientist?"

I have never felt so humiliated in my life. I almost felt like ripping up the exam booklet. As a physicist, I had spent my entire life trying to reveal some of the scientific secrets of the universe and then imparting this knowledge to the public. And now my own daughter was telling me that science was so boring and tedious that she wondered why anyone could possibly want to become a scientist.

Later, I began to realize that this perception—the false impression that science is a boring list of memorized and useless trivia—is not just an isolated problem, but one that is prevalent throughout all of society. I recalled the story once told by Richard Feynman, Nobel laureate in physics. When he was a child, he fondly recalled, his father would take him into the forest and teach him there about the nature of birds: how evolution has determined their shape and color and why they act the way they do. Eventually, he became quite an expert in understanding the basic principles underlying their behavior and physical characteristics. One day a bully challenged him and, pointing to a nearby bird, demanded that Richard tell him its name. Richard was caught off guard. He could tell you everything about that bird, except its name. Then the bully said to him that he must be stupid.

In that instant of time, Richard learned a profound lesson about science. Most people think that science consists of giving fancy names to irrelevant, obscure things. In fact, that is the principal reason why some people are turned off by science.

So scientists and science writers have a monumental task: making science exciting and relevant to the average person, so that they care about science. If we fail in this endeavor, then we must face dire consequences. This is not an academic question.

First of all, science and technology are at the root of all the wealth and prosperity we see in society. The Industrial Revolution of the 1800s, which lifted civilization out of poverty and misery, was unleashed by our understanding of Newton's mechanics and the steam engine. The electric revolution of the early 1900s, which lit up our cities and created powerful dynamos and engines, was a by-product of our new understanding of the laws of electromagnetism. The current revolution in high tech, electronics, computers, and the internet was pioneered by the creation of the transistor and the laser, and our future will be determined by rapid advances in artificial intelligence, biotechnology, and nanotechnology. Beyond that, by midcentury we expect rapid advances in quantum computers, fusion power, and brain-computer interface.

In the postwar era, however, scientists often got lazy and preferred to work in their ivory towers, far away from the noise and bustle of the masses—until one event shook them out of their complacency. In the 1980s, physicists proposed the construction of the Superconducting Super Collider, a gigantic particle accelerator that would reveal some of the secrets of the creation of the universe. It was to be built outside Dallas, Texas, and would ensure the leadership of American physics for decades to come. It was to be the crowning achievement of American science. However, internal squabbles among physicists and cost overruns had made Congress wary of funding this huge machine. Physicists failed to convince the general public of the worth of building a \$4 billion machine in order to conduct pure science.

So the congressional vote was taken, and the Super Collider was abruptly canceled in 1993. This sent shock waves through the scientific community. Congress had previously given physicists a billion dollars to dig a gigantic circular hole for the Super Collider. When Congress canceled the project, it allotted another billion dollars to fill up the hole. So Congress spent two billion dollars digging a huge hole and then filling it up!

Eventually, with the United States dropping out, the Europeans took over and built a smaller machine, the Large Hadron Collider (LHC) outside Geneva, Switzerland. Not surprisingly, the Vatican for high-energy physics is now in Geneva, not Texas, and the LHC went on to find the celebrated Higgs boson particle, a discovery that earned the Nobel Prize for two physicists who proposed it.

The lesson here is that scientists pay a dear price when they isolate themselves and fail to excite the public. Ultimately, the taxpayer foots the bill, and scientists have to convince the public of the worth of their research. During the Cold War, Congress was willing to fund exotic science projects because we were competing with the Russians. But in the post–Cold War era, when funding for science has diminished in Russia, scientists must make a pitch directly to the public about funding expensive research projects. Crudely speaking, we scientists must leave the ivory tower and learn how to sing for our supper.

Meanwhile, science has advanced to the point where it is vital to our nation's future that the public understand the concepts of science. Biotechnology has given us the power to alter life itself. How far should we take it? Computers have advanced to the point where they can begin to mimic human behavior. Will this threaten the jobs of millions of people? Satellites clearly show that the Earth is heating up. How much of the warming is due to human activity, and what do we do about it?

In my opinion, one of the keys to reaching the public is to write captivating science articles about science. Although I am a research physicist (working on string theory), I try to engage the public whenever I can, since our future depends critically on science. After all, after everything is said and done, the wealth and prosperity we see around us come from science and technology. In selecting the two dozen articles for this book, I tried to list some of the outstanding characteristics that would create compelling, exciting, and fascinating stories.

I looked for three ways in which writers might have done this. First, the best stories try to capture the excitement felt by the scientists who are doing the research. They capture the personal drama of scientists making huge personal sacrifices in order to prove a certain hypothesis or theory. Even after a string of failures, these scientists doggedly continue to toil in the laboratory. You begin to wonder what motivates them to try again and again, despite the odds stacked against them. You begin to understand what makes them tick.

Second, compelling stories can bring us the drama of that "aha" moment, after weary months or years spent toiling in the lab or in the field, when everything seems to fit together. (For the great Greek mathematician Archimedes, it was when he discovered the laws of buoyancy and, according to legend, ran naked in the streets of Athens shouting "Eureka!") Out of a mass of random pieces of data, suddenly the puzzle pieces begin to fit together, and the scientist can see the overall picture emerge—perhaps a new scientific principle that may extend far beyond the laboratory. For example, culture is wonderful and can inspire us and enrich our lives, but culture is limited to the planet Earth. For me as a physicist, it is the joy of knowing that, perhaps on the other side of the Milky Way galaxy, an alien has discovered the very same physical principle, and one that is universal throughout the cosmos.

Third, a well-told science article can get us excited about the potential benefits of a scientific discovery to all of humanity. When the Human Genome Project finally revealed our genetic code, that discovery not only gave us unprecedented insight into who we are and where we come from but also opened the door to one day vanquishing ancient illnesses that have haunted us since the dawn of time.

So, based on these three criteria, here is my selection of the best articles in science of the past year.

One of the most important areas of scientific progress has been unraveling the genetics of deadly diseases. Not only can these diseases spark epidemics that kill thousands, but some diseases, like the recent coronavirus coming out of China, can even cause massive disruptions in the world economy.

To appreciate the importance of the Human Genome Project, remember that President Richard Nixon, with much fanfare and hoopla, launched the War on Cancer back in the 1970s. His administration would create a medical milestone: a historic cure for one of the deadliest of diseases. The basic philosophy was, if you threw enough money at the problem, you could solve it.

Fifty years later, cancer remains one of the greatest killers in modern society, and cancer treatment still hasn't changed much. Even today, doctors treat cancer in the same way—by zapping it (with radiation), slicing it (via surgery), and poisoning it (with chemotherapy). The problem with declaring a War on Cancer was that nobody knew the basic science behind cancer in the 1970s. Now we realize that cancer is, at its root, a disease that affects our genes, and the breakthrough was the Human Genome Project, which opened the floodgates to discovery and allowed scientists to list all the mutations in our chromosomes. Identifying these mutations, in turn, has opened up new avenues to attack cancer, such as modifying and strengthening our immune system so that it can recognize and kill cancer cells. So, as Siddhartha Mukherjee discusses in "New Blood," immunotherapy, by introducing an entirely new avenue to attack cancer, has been a game-changer.

Melinda Wenner Moyer notes in her essay "Vaccines Reimagined" that there is even wild speculation that a single cure for a wide variety of diseases might be found. For example, if there is a common pathway by which many types of viruses gain entry into our cells, then, by genetic engineering, we might be able to close that pathway and instantly render harmless entire classes of viruses.

As the world population gets older, there is increasing interest in using this genetic firepower to unlock the secrets of the aging process, as discussed by Adam Gopnik in "Younger Longer." But as we unravel the genetics of aging, we would do well to listen to a cautionary tale. In Greek mythology, the goddess Aurora, who was immortal, fell in love with Tithonus, a mortal man. When Aurora begged Zeus to grant her lover the gift of immortality, Zeus finally granted her wish. But Aurora made a crucial mistake. She forgot to ask for the gift of eternal youth as well. Sadly, as the centuries rolled on, Tithonus became older, feebler, and more decrepit, but he could never die. If one day we become immortal, let us hope we do not do so before also curing the ravages of aging.

Biotechnology has opened up entirely new avenues to attack bacteria and viruses. But there are limits to what we can do by manipulating our genes. As recounted by Kelly Clancy in "Sleep No More," doctors have become increasingly aware that some diseases (like mad cow disease) are not caused by viruses or bacteria at all, but by renegade proteins called "prions" that wreak havoc by spreading to other proteins via contact.

Furthermore, although biotechnology has helped us make remarkable progress in attacking certain diseases, there remain some ancient diseases for which we have no cure at all.

In particular, scientists are still clueless when it comes to diseases of the brain. Historically, the brain has been a black box, its complex inner workings a mystery to modern medicine. On the one hand, scientists are amazed at what they have discovered about the power and flexibility of the brain, the most complex object in the known universe, with 100 billion neurons, each one connected in turn to 10,000 other neurons. For example, as Andrew Zaleski relates in "The Brain That Remade Itself," one young boy lost about one-sixth of his entire brain yet could still function.

On the other hand, the suffering caused by diseases of the brain can cause unending tragedy. Despite advances in drug therapies, suicide and depression continue to ruin and devastate countless lives, as revealed in Deanna Csomo McCool's sad article "Total Eclipse." Suicide remains one of the greatest killers of young people, yet science does not really know why it happens.

Similarly, science is still struggling with the question of the link between our brains and our behavior. For example, does this link affect criminal behavior? Is there a "crime gene"? Can criminals blame their crimes on the biochemistry of their neurons? In "The Final Five Percent," Tim Requarth raises sticky ethical questions, especially those that arise when a person who is clearly brain-damaged commits a heinous crime. How much is he personally responsible if his brain is damaged? Can he say, "My brain made me do it"?

Are we morally responsible for our acts? In other words, do we have free will? Bahar Gholipour, in "The Tumultuous History of a Mysterious Brain Signal That Questioned Free Will," discusses a celebrated experiment that showed that even before we make a decision, our brains send out a signal, which can be seen in brain scans. In other words, these results suggest that there is no free will. We are, in some sense, slaves of our own brains. But a new series of experiments have called this conclusion into question, by indicating that random events can also generate these signals. The debate still rages on. What is at stake is nothing less than the origin of human behavior.

And speaking of brains and behavior, there is a running debate about the brains of animals and robots. As humans, we are clearly conscious and self-aware of our actions. But what about animals? As Ross Andersen discusses in "A Journey into the Animal Mind," some scientists believe that animals are conscious, but have a different type of consciousness. Our consciousness is dominated by what we see with our eyes, while dogs are guided by thousands of smells and aromas, bats and dolphins live in a world of sonic waves, and bees can see ultraviolet radiation and hence recognize flowers in totally different ways from us. To bridge the gap between humans and other animals, scientists are now creating a machine that can detect smells, almost like a dog. This could also have practical implications, as Sara Harrison details in "Right Under Our Noses"—for instance, in sniffing out explosives of terrorists or locating the bodies of crime victims.

If animals are indeed conscious, then can a case be made that machines are also conscious? Can machines even be indistinguishable from humans? As our computers and AI systems become increasingly powerful and begin to rival human abilities, at what point will robots be indistinguishable from humans? This possibility is explored in Patrick House's article "I, Language Robot," and in "The Next Word" by John Seabrook, who relates that AI is now used to create software that can imitate a person's writing with uncanny accuracy. In fact, people are sometimes unable to tell the difference between a paragraph written by a human and one written by a machine. Remarkable feats like this are just the beginning.

All these breakthroughs were spearheaded by research in a laboratory. But we cannot tell the story of science without mentioning that we do not live in an isolated laboratory, and that our activities influence the larger society and the environment around us.

In "The Hidden Heroines of Chaos," Joshua Sokol notes that women who played a crucial role in developing many branches of science were often reduced to footnotes or were forgotten entirely, such as in the development of chaos theory. (Sadly, history is full of examples of women scientists failing to get the recognition they deserved. Sophie Germain, the great French mathematician, had to disguise herself as a man in order to publish in math journals. Jocelyn Bell, who discovered the pulsar, was passed over for a Nobel Prize in Physics for her historic discovery. The work of the late Vera Rubin, who published some of the earliest articles on the presence of dark matter, was ignored for most of her professional life.) Perhaps in the future, scientists will learn their lesson and give appropriate credit to everyone who makes a great discovery, regardless of gender. (When the great mathematician Emmy Noether was passed over for a position at the University of Göttingen, mathematician David Hilbert remarked in disgust, "We are a university, not a bathhouse.")

As science probes the mysteries of our environment, we cannot help but wonder at how evolution has given us the tremendously rich variety of life-forms that surround us. One persistent question, mentioned by Darwin himself, is the strange prevalence of beauty in nature. Everywhere we look, we see an explosion of rich colors and forms. The gorgeous flowers found in our own backyards often rival some of world's greatest works of art. But if evolution favors the fittest, then why do we have the flourishing of "useless" beauty? Darwin thought that, in addition to natural selection (survival of the fittest), nature also follows sexual selection, that is, beauty provides some hidden evolutionary advantage to animals in seeking a mate. A male peacock sprouted extravagantly colored feathers in order to prove to a female that it was so vigorous and healthy that it could afford to waste energy on such "useless" displays. This question has been hotly debated since Darwin's time, and the debate continues to this day, as explored in "Beauty of the Beasts" by Ferris Jabr.

We can see the wonders of evolution at work in the essay "Ghosts of the Future," where Sarah Kaplan investigates the Cambrian ex-

plosion 500 million years ago. Back then, after billions of years
when life on earth was dominated by single-celled organisms, suddenly there was an explosion of multicellular life-forms. Nature
was experimenting with hundreds of different body shapes and
organs, which burst forth from the fossil record. Our own body
shape, a linear spinal cord with four appendages, is just one of the
many life-forms produced by nature during this crucial time.

In "Troubled Treasure," Joshua Sokol gives us a very different
take on this treasure trove of fossils. Remember that, as illustrated
in the movie *Jurassic Park,* delicate creatures were accidentally encased in clear amber millions of years ago. Perhaps, the movie suggests, the blood of dinosaurs was also sealed in amber, and perhaps
it could be used to clone dinosaurs and bring them back to life.
In reality, scientists do not expect to find the blood of the dinosaurs preserved in amber, but delicate tissues from insects, feathers, snakes, worms, and more have been found preserved this way,
especially in Myanmar. This treasure trove of amber gives us a rare
snapshot of life up to 100 million years ago, but unfortunately, today's political conflicts can disrupt this priceless treasure. Because
some rare amber specimens can fetch tens of thousands of dollars
on the black market, there is a vibrant trade in illegal amber. In
fact, competing political and military groups have tried to control
this lucrative trade, endangering the very existence of a precious
and irreplaceable evolutionary legacy.

Any discussion of the impact of science on the environment
must mention California, which, as Daniel Duane discusses in
"What Remains," has recently borne the brunt of much environmental chaos. Old photographs and satellite pictures show the
unmistakable fact that, sadly, the magnificent glaciers of Yosemite
and elsewhere are in decline, receding as the Earth is heating up.
California is also afflicted by huge fires sweeping across both the
northern part of the state, engulfing vital areas like the Napa Valley wine country, and the southern part, where even the homes of
Hollywood movie stars are affected. This story is graphically told
by Jon Mooallem in "'We Have Fire Everywhere.'"

These catastrophes, many scientists believe, are self-inflicted,
caused in part by our dependence on fossil fuels. But nature has
also given us natural disasters that show how devastating and profound other environmental disasters can be.

In Douglas Preston's "The Day the Dinosaurs Died," we learn

that paleontologists can now give us one of the clearest blow-by-blow accounts of what happened 66 million years ago when a huge meteor or comet slammed into the Yucatán of Mexico, helping to end the 200-million-year domination of the dinosaurs and paving the way for the rise of mammals and, eventually, you and me. By digging into the underwater Yucatán crater itself and by analyzing the treasure trove of fossils found at Hell Creek, Montana, paleontologists have found graphic evidence of this monumental explosion, from the original fireball, global meteor showers, tsunami, and firestorm to the eventual plunge into darkness of the entire Earth as the debris from the impact cut off sunlight. Eventually, close to 90 percent of all life-forms perished.

The dinosaurs, unfortunately, did not have a space program, so they are not here to debate the question.

We, however, do have a space program and might one day use spaceships to avoid a similar fate. The outstanding articles from the past year collected here not only cover scientific advances in understanding inner space but also soar into outer space. In fact, today entrepreneurs, investors, and billionaires, not just scientists, are setting their sights on outer space.

We could be entering a new golden era of space exploration as costs continue to drop, Silicon Valley billionaires open their checkbooks to exciting new projects, and more countries and corporations field a new array of booster rockets.

There is a lesson to be learned here from the past. Back in the early 1800s, when President Thomas Jefferson doubled the size of the United States with the historic Louisiana Purchase, he wrote that, sadly, it might take a thousand years to colonize this vast territory that he had just purchased from Napoleon. But in fact the western United States would be settled in just a century. Why? Because of the discovery of gold in California in 1848.

Similarly, some people believe that there might be a second "gold rush," this time in outer space, where rare earths, platinum metals, and even ice might be mined from the moon and the asteroid belt.

Rivka Galchen's "The Eighth Continent" describes how corporations are already laying out plans for ambitious space ventures. Some foresee a traffic jam around the moon, which might eventually require a revision of the Outer Space Treaty of 1967 to prevent disputes as to who owns the moon. We have to make sure that outer space remains a peaceful domain, and that nations can settle their differences over it without going to war.

And what lies beyond the moon? Sometime after 2030, NASA hopes to send humans to Mars. Meanwhile, some astronomers would like to know what lies even farther away, beyond our solar system. This is where a new controversy has erupted, a tale told by Shannon Stirone in "The Hunt for Planet Nine."

Even schoolchildren know that, ever since Pluto was unceremoniously demoted from being a planet, there are eight planets going around the sun. But now, as our computers analyze the motion of the outer planets, they are telling us that something strange is tugging on these planets.

History might repeat itself. Back in the 1820s, astronomers noticed that the planet Uranus was not acting according to Newton's laws of motion. Either Newton was wrong (a horrible thought to any astronomer) or a new planet was tugging on Uranus. Using pure mathematics, it was possible to locate the position of this mysterious planet. On the first try, after only a few hours' work, astronomers found a new planet, Neptune, in 1846, exactly where Newton's equations said it would be.

Is history repeating itself now? The outer planets again seem to be deviating slightly from Newton's laws, so astronomers are using supercomputers to find the exact location of what may be a new ninth planet. This is hard work. Astronomers are a skeptical bunch, and they demand a smoking gun—an actual photograph of this phantom planet. A computer program is not enough. So far, a photograph of a ninth planet has not been taken, but as Stirone proposes in "The Hunt for Planet Nine," either way, history might be made. Either we will discover a new planet, or a new theory of gravity will emerge if it becomes necessary to revise Newton's laws. This is a win-win situation.

As we probe deep space, will we eventually encounter aliens from space, vindicating the claims of science fiction writers?

On the one hand, encountering an advanced civilization could lead to a new enlightenment here on Earth if we were able to use its advanced technology to eliminate poverty and disease, ushering in a new Age of Aquarius. On the other hand, as physicist Stephen Hawking warned, such an encounter could be more like that of the Aztecs with the Spanish conquistadors, which did not go well for native peoples. The Spaniards had steel swords, gunpowder, horses, and a written language (as well as the smallpox virus). The Spaniards were perhaps a few centuries more advanced than the Aztecs, and the encounter between them led to the total collapse of the latter's civilization.

So far, talk of alien civilizations remains the stuff of Hollywood movies. Our radio antennas have not detected a single message from an intelligent civilization in space. The presence of so many stars in the galaxy presents us with the Fermi paradox: if aliens are so plentiful, then why haven't we met them yet? These and other questions are addressed in Adam Mann's essay "Intelligent Ways to Search for Extraterrestrials."

Finally, we have exciting new developments in my field, physics. After the movie *Back to the Future* came out in 1985, toy companies received an avalanche of phone calls asking to purchase hover boards. Unfortunately, hover boards do not exist. To create them, we would need super-powerful magnetic fields. We could create those using superconductors, which have zero resistance to electricity. But supercooling them down to the required temperature near absolute zero is very expensive. If some enterprising physicist could create room-temperature superconductors, it might set off a second industrial revolution as we produce super-magnets to levitate our trains, cars, industry, and even hover boards.

One small but important step in this direction came just last year. Back in 2004, scientists at the University of Manchester first created a new substance called graphene, consisting of a single layer of carbon atoms. It has miraculous properties. For example, it is the strongest substance known to science. If you balance an elephant on a pencil that is placed on a sheet of graphene, the sheet will not tear. Last year, physicists adjusted two sheets of graphene to a certain angle and voilà! It became superconducting. This has set off a stampede of physicists who want to make startling new discoveries, perhaps winning a Nobel Prize. This is discussed in David H. Freedman's essay "With a Simple Twist, a 'Magic' Material Is Now the Big Thing in Physics."

To be sure, this superconductor is not functioning at room temperature, so much more work has to be done. Meanwhile, physicists not only have a new toy to play with but might also one day set off a new industrial revolution.

To me, the ultimate scientific revolution would be realizing Einstein's dream of a "theory of everything": a theory that unites all the laws of physics into a single equation. In "A Different Kind of Theory of Everything," Natalie Wolchover discusses this Holy Grail of physics, the dream to find the Final Theory out of which the universe sprang into existence.

If we find a theory of everything, it might answer some of the deepest questions in physics, such as: What happened before the big bang? Are there other universes? What lies on the other side of a black hole? Is time travel possible? Are there wormholes to other universes?

Back in the 1950s, physicist Wolfgang Pauli announced his version of the fabled unified field theory in a talk at Columbia. After his talk, Niels Bohr, one of the founders of the quantum theory, stood up and said, "We in the back are convinced that your theory is crazy. What divides us is whether your theory is crazy enough."

In other words, all the easy theories had already been tried and shown to be incorrect. Hence, the Final Theory must be a radical departure from all previous attempts. It must be so crazy that it has eluded the greatest minds of the past century.

Many physicists, myself included, think that this theory is string theory, which reduces all subatomic particles to resonances vibrating on a tiny string. But some want to go even further than string theory: using the mathematics of polygons existing in hyperspace, they have proposed a theory that there is no space or time.

On the one hand, the mind spins when contemplating the concepts coming from advanced physics, which include higher dimensions, multiverses of universe, and twisted space-times. But on the other hand, these concepts speak to the ultimate simplicity and elegance of the universe itself, which we can comprehend with the human mind. As Einstein once said, if a theory cannot be explained to a child, then the theory is probably worthless. In other words, all great theories, in the final analysis, should not require a thicket of algebra and mathematics but be explainable in terms of simple concepts, principles, and pictures. Ultimately, the universe is not about memorizing mind-numbing equations, but about revealing the dynamic and fundamental principles underlying all of reality, which we believe to be simple, elegant, and even "crazy."

In other words, at the deepest level, the universe is described not by a mass of tedious, obscure, and useless equations, but by simple and elegant principles and concepts.

This is something, I hope, that even my daughter can appreciate.

Michio Kaku

The Best American Science and Nature Writing 2020

ROSS ANDERSEN

A Journey into the Animal Mind

FROM *The Atlantic*

AMID THE HUMAN crush of Old Delhi, on the edge of a medieval bazaar, a red structure with cages on its roof rises three stories
above the labyrinth of neon-lit stalls and narrow alleyways, its top
floor emblazoned with two words: BIRDS HOSPITAL.

On a hot day last spring, I removed my shoes at the hospital's
entrance and walked up to the second-floor lobby, where a clerk in
his late twenties was processing patients. An older woman placed a
shoebox before him and lifted off its lid, revealing a bloody white
parakeet, the victim of a cat attack. The man in front of me in line
held, in a small cage, a dove that had collided with a glass tower
in the financial district. A girl no older than seven came in behind
me clutching, in her bare hands, a white hen with a slumped neck.

The hospital's main ward is a narrow, 40-foot-long room with
cages stacked four high along the walls and fans on the ceiling,
their blades covered with grates, lest they ensnare a flapping wing.
I strolled the room's length, conducting a rough census. Many of
the cages looked empty at first, but leaning closer, I'd find a bird,
usually a pigeon, sitting back in the gloom.

The youngest of the hospital's vets, Dheeraj Kumar Singh, was
making his rounds in jeans and a surgical mask. The oldest vet
here has worked the night shift for more than a quarter-century,
spending tens of thousands of hours removing tumors from birds,
easing their pain with medication, administering antibiotics. Singh
is a rookie by comparison, but you wouldn't know it from the way
he inspects a pigeon, flipping it over in his hands, quickly but gently, the way you might handle your cell phone. As we talked, he

motioned to an assistant, who handed him a nylon bandage that he stretched twice around the pigeon's wing, setting it with an unsentimental *pop*.

The bird hospital is one of several built by devotees of Jainism, an ancient religion whose highest commandment forbids violence not only against humans, but also against animals. A series of paintings in the hospital's lobby illustrates the extremes to which some Jains take this prohibition. In them, a medieval king in blue robes gazes through a palace window at an approaching pigeon, its wing bloodied by the talons of a brown hawk still in pursuit. The king pulls the smaller bird into the palace, infuriating the hawk, which demands replacement for its lost meal, so he slices off his own arm and foot to feed it.

I'd come to the bird hospital, and to India, to see firsthand the Jains' moral system at work in the world. Jains make up less than 1 percent of India's population. Despite millennia spent criticizing the Hindu majority, the Jains have sometimes gained the ear of power. During the thirteenth century, they converted a Hindu king, and persuaded him to enact the subcontinent's first animal-welfare laws. There is evidence that the Jains influenced the Buddha himself. And when Gandhi developed his most radical ideas about nonviolence, a Jain friend played philosophical muse.

In the state of Gujarat, where Gandhi grew up, I saw Jain monks walking barefoot in the cool morning hours to avoid car travel, an activity they regard as irredeemably violent, given the damage it inflicts on living organisms, from insects to larger animals. The monks refuse to eat root vegetables, lest their removal from the earth disturb delicate subterranean ecosystems. Their white robes are cotton, not silk, which would require the destruction of silkworms. During monsoon season, they forgo travel, to avoid splashing through puddles filled with microbes, whose existence Jains posited well before they appeared under Western microscopes.

Jains move through the world in this gentle way because they believe animals are conscious beings that experience, in varying degrees, emotions analogous to human desire, fear, pain, sorrow, and joy. This idea that animals are conscious was long unpopular in the West, but it has lately found favor among scientists who study animal cognition. And not just the obvious cases—primates, dogs, elephants, whales, and others. Scientists are now finding evidence of an inner life in alien-seeming creatures that evolved on ever more distant limbs of life's tree. In recent years, it has become common to flip through a magazine like this one and read about an octopus using its tentacles to twist off a jar's lid or squirt aquarium water into a postdoc's face. For many scientists, the resonant mystery is no longer which animals are conscious, but which are not.

No aspect of our world is as mysterious as consciousness, the state of awareness that animates our every waking moment, the sense of being located in a body that exists within a larger world of color, sound, and touch, all of it filtered through our thoughts and imbued by emotion.

Even in a secular age, consciousness retains a mystical sheen. It is alternatively described as the last frontier of science, and as a kind of immaterial magic beyond science's reckoning. David Chalmers, one of the world's most respected philosophers on the subject, once told me that consciousness could be a fundamental feature of the universe, like space-time or energy. He said it might be tied to the diaphanous, indeterminate workings of the quantum world, or something nonphysical.

These metaphysical accounts are in play because scientists have yet to furnish a satisfactory explanation of consciousness. We know the body's sensory systems beam information about the external world into our brain, where it's processed, sequentially, by increasingly sophisticated neural layers. But we don't know how those signals are integrated into a smooth, continuous world picture, a flow of moments experienced by a roving locus of attention—a "witness," as Hindu philosophers call it.

In the West, consciousness was long thought to be a divine gift bestowed solely on humans. Western philosophers historically conceived of nonhuman animals as unfeeling automatons. Even after Darwin demonstrated our kinship with animals, many scientists believed that the evolution of consciousness was a recent event. They thought the first mind sparked awake sometime after we split from chimps and bonobos. In his 1976 book, *The Origin of Consciousness in the Breakdown of the Bicameral Mind,* Julian Jaynes argued that it was later still. He said the development of language led us, like Virgil, into the deep cognitive states capable of constructing experiential worlds.

This notion that consciousness was of recent vintage began to change in the decades following the Second World War, when more scientists were systematically studying the behaviors and brain states of Earth's creatures. Now each year brings a raft of new research papers, which, taken together, suggest that a great many animals are conscious.

It was likely more than half a billion years ago that some sea-floor arms race between predator and prey roused Earth's first conscious animal. That moment, when the first mind winked into being, was a cosmic event, opening up possibilities not previously contained in nature.

There now appears to exist, alongside the human world, a whole universe of vivid animal experience. Scientists deserve credit for illuminating, if only partially, this new dimension of our reality. But they can't tell us how to do right by the trillions of minds with which we share the Earth's surface. That's a philosophical prob-lem, and like most philosophical problems, it will be with us for a long time to come.

Apart from Pythagoras and a few others, ancient Western phi-losophers did not hand down a rich tradition of thinking about an-imal consciousness. But Eastern thinkers have long been haunted by its implications—especially the Jains, who have taken animal consciousness seriously as a moral matter for nearly 3,000 years.

Many orthodox Jain beliefs do not stand up to scientific scru-tiny. The faith does not enjoy privileged access to truth, mystical or otherwise. But as perhaps the world's first culture to extend mercy to animals, the Jains pioneered a profound expansion of the hu-man moral imagination. The places where they worship and tend to animals seemed, to me, like good places to contemplate the current frontier of animal-consciousness research.

At the bird hospital, I asked Singh whether any of his patients gave him trouble. He said that one refused to be fed by hand and some-times drew blood when he tried to pick it up. He led me to another room to see the offending bird, an Indian crow whose feathers were record-groove black but for a sash of latte-colored plumage around its neck. The crow kept fanning one of its wings out. Light from a nearby window filtered through the feathers, as though the wing were a venetian blind. Singh told me it was broken.

"A few days after the crow arrived, it started using a special call when it wanted food," Singh said. "None of the other birds do that." The bird's call was not an entirely unique case of bird-to-human communication. A grey parrot once amassed a 900-word vocabulary, and in India, a few have been trained to recite the Vedic mantras. But birds have only rarely assembled verbal symbols into their own, original proto-sentences. And, of course, none has declared itself conscious.

That's too bad, because philosophers tend to regard such statements as the best possible evidence of another being's consciousness, even among humans. Without one, no matter how long I stared into the crow's black pupil, wishing I could see into the phantasmagoria of its mind, I could never *really* know whether it was conscious. I'd have to be content with circumstantial evidence.

Crows have an unusually large brain for their size, and their neurons are packed densely relative to other animals'. Neuroscientists can measure the computational complexity of brain activity, but no brain scan has yet revealed a precise neural signature of consciousness. And so it's difficult to make a knockdown argument that a particular animal is conscious based strictly on its neuroanatomy. It is suggestive, though, when an animal's brain closely resembles ours, as is the case with primates, the first animals to be knighted with consciousness by something approaching a scientific consensus.

Mammals in general are widely thought to be conscious, because they share our relatively large brain size, and also have a cerebral cortex, the place where our most complex feats of cognition seem to take place. Birds don't have a cortex. In the 300 million years that have passed since the avian gene pool separated from ours, their brains have evolved different structures. But one of those structures appears to be networked in cortexlike ways, a tantalizing clue that nature may have more than one method of making a conscious brain.

Other clues can be found in an animal's behavior, though sifting out conscious acts from those that are evolved and mindless can be difficult. Tool use is an instructive case. Australian "firehawk" raptors sometimes fly bundles of flaming sticks out of forest fires and into neighboring landscapes, to flush out prey. Maybe that means the raptors are capable of considering a piece of the physical environment, and imagining a new purpose for it. Or maybe something more rote is going on.

Crows are among the most sophisticated avian technologists.

They have long been known to shape sticks into hooks, and just last year, members of one crow species were observed constructing tools out of three separate sticklike parts. In Japan, one crow population has figured out how to use traffic to crack open walnuts: the crows drop a nut in front of cars at intersections, and then when the light turns red, they swoop in to scoop up the exposed flesh.

As Singh and I talked, the crow grew bored with us and turned back to the window, as though to inspect its faint reflection. In 2008, a magpie—a member of crows' extended family of corvids, or "feathered apes"—became the first nonmammal to pass the "mirror test." The magpie's neck was marked with a bright dot in a place that could be seen only in a mirror. When the magpie caught sight of its reflection, it immediately tried to check its neck.

Singh told me this crow would soon move upstairs, to one of the roof's exposed cages, where the birds have more space to test their still-fragile wings, in view of an open sky that must surely loom large in a bird's consciousness. With luck, it would quickly return to the spirited life preferred by wild crows, which sometimes play like acrobats in high winds and ski down snowy surfaces. (Birds that die at this hospital are buried along a riverbed outside Delhi, an apt touch in the case of the crows, which sometimes hold funerals—or, if not funerals, postmortems, where they gather around their dead like homicide detectives discerning cause of death.)

I asked Singh how he felt when he released birds on the rooftop. "We are here to serve them," he said, and then noted that not all the birds leave right away. "Some of them come back and sit on our shoulders."

Crows are not among the shoulder-perchers, but Singh sometimes sees former crow patients hovering around the hospital. They might be looking for him. Crows recognize individual human faces. They are known to blare vicious caws at people they dislike, but for favored humans, they sometimes leave gifts—buttons or shiny bits of glass—where the person will be sure to notice, like votive offerings.

If these behaviors add up to consciousness, it means one of two things: either consciousness evolved twice, at least, across the long course of evolutionary history, or it evolved sometime before birds and mammals went on their separate evolutionary journeys. Both scenarios would give us reason to believe that nature can knit molecules into waking minds more easily than previously guessed. This would mean that all across the planet, animals large and small are constantly generating vivid experiences that bear some relationship to our own.

The day after I visited the bird hospital, I left Delhi by car, on a road that follows the Yamuna River south and east, away from its icy source among the serrated ridges of the Himalayas. Delhi's sewage has blackened long stretches of the Yamuna, making it one of the world's most polluted rivers. From the road, I could see plastic bottles floating on its surface. In India, where rivers have a special place in the spiritual imagination, this is a metaphysical defilement.

Millions of fish once swam in the Yamuna River, before it was desecrated by the human technosphere, which now reaches into nearly every body of water on Earth. Even the deepest point in the ocean is littered with trash: a grocery bag was recently seen drifting along the bottom of the Mariana Trench.

We last swam in the same gene pool with the animals that evolved into fish about 460 million years ago, more than 100 million years before we split from birds. The notion that we are kin across this expanse of time has proved too radical for some, which is one reason the ever-changing universe described by Darwin has been slow to lodge in the collective human consciousness. And yet, our hands are converted fins, our hiccups the relics of gill-breathing.

Scientists have sometimes seemed to judge fish for their refusal to join our exodus out of the water and into the atmosphere's more ethereal realm of gases. Their inability to see far in their murky environment is sometimes thought to be a cognitive impairment. But new evidence indicates that fish have minds rich with memories; some are able to recall associations from more than ten days earlier.

They also seem to be capable of deception. Female trout "fake orgasms," quivering as though they're about to lay eggs, perhaps so that undesired males will release their sperm and be on their way. We have high-definition footage of grouper fish teaming up with eels to scare prey out of reefs, the two coordinating their actions with sophisticated head signals. This behavior suggests that fish possess a theory of mind, an ability to speculate about the mental states of other beings.

A more troubling set of behaviors has emerged from experiments designed to determine whether fish feel pain. One of the most intense states of consciousness, pain is something beyond the mere detection of damage. Even the simplest of bacteria have sensors on their external membranes; when the sensors detect trace amounts of dangerous chemicals, the bacteria respond with a programmed flight reflex. But bacteria have no central nervous system where these signals are integrated into a three-dimensional experience of the chemical environment.

Fish have many more kinds of sensors than bacteria do. Their sensors flare when the water temperature spikes, when they come into contact with corrosive chemicals, when a hook rips through their scales and into their flesh. In the lab, when trout lips are injected with acid, the fish do not merely respond at the site. They rock their entire bodies back and forth, hyperventilating, rubbing their mouths against their tanks' sides or gravel bottoms. These behaviors cease when the fish are given morphine.

Such actions call the ethics of the research itself into question. But the experiences of lab fish are nothing compared with those endured by the trillions of aquatic animals that humans yank, unceremoniously, out of oceans and rivers and lakes every year. Some fish are still alive, hours later, when they're shoveled into the sickly lit, refrigerated intake tubes of the global seafood supply chain.

Fish pain is something different from our own pain. In the elaborate mirrored hall that is human consciousness, pain takes on existential dimensions. Because we know that death looms, and grieve for the loss of richly imagined futures, it's tempting to imagine that our pain is the most profound of all suffering. But we would do well to remember that our perspective can make our pain easier to bear, if only by giving it an expiration date. When we pull a less cognitively blessed fish up from the pressured depths too quickly, and barometric trauma fills its bloodstream with tissue-burning acid, its on-deck thrashing might be a silent scream, born of the fish's belief that it has entered a permanent state of extreme suffering.

The Jains tell a story about Neminath, a man from deep antiquity who is said to have been sensitive to the distress calls of other animals. He developed his unusual fondness for animals while tending cattle in pastures on the banks of the Yamuna River, in his home village of Shauripur, which I reached four hours after leaving Delhi.

Neminath is one of twenty-four Jain "Fordmakers," prophetlike figures who crossed a metaphorical river, freeing themselves from the cycle of birth and rebirth, before showing others the way to enlightenment. The Fordmakers' life stories tend to emphasize their nonviolent natures. One is said to have floated perfectly still in the womb, sending not so much as a ripple through the amniotic fluid, to avoid harming his mother.

Only a few Fordmakers are confirmed historical figures, and Neminath is not one of them. The Jains say Neminath left his village for good on the day of his wedding. That morning, he mounted an elephant, intent on riding it to the temple where he was to be wed. On the way, he heard a series of agonized screams, and demanded to know their origin. Neminath's elephant guide explained that the screams came from animals that were being slaughtered for his wedding feast.

This moment transformed Neminath. Some versions of this story say he freed the surviving animals, including a fish that he carried, in his hands, back to the river. Others say he fled. All agree that he renounced his former life. Rather than marry his bride, he set out for Girnar, a sacred mountain in Gujarat, 40 miles from the Arabian Sea.

My own ascent up Girnar began before dawn. It followed the usual topography of enlightenment. I was to climb 7,000 steps, all built into the mountain, by nine in the morning, so as not to be late for a ritual at an ancient temple near the peak.

The trail was only 50 miles from Gir National Park, where, the day before, I'd seen two Asiatic lions, nearly indistinguishable cousins of Africa's lions. Once the region's apex predator, the Asiatic lion almost went extinct during the British empire's colonization of India, when no viceroy could visit a maharaja's palace without a hunt in the local forest. Even today, the Asiatic lion still ranks among the rarest of the large feline predators, rarer even than its neighbor to the north, the snow leopard, which is so scarce that a glimpse of one padding down a jagged Himalayan crag is said to consummate a spiritual pilgrimage.

I did my best to put the lions, which have recently expanded to

Girnar's forests, out of my mind as I passed small huts and tents in the dark, at the trail's base. Daylight brought langur monkeys onto the trailside boulders. One watched a vendor set up his stall to offer food and water to passing Jain pilgrims. The monkey waited until the man's back was turned, at which point he scampered in to grab a banana. In Gir National Park, I'd seen deer using these monkeys as a treetop surveillance system. The monkeys sat high in the trees, keeping watch for leopards and lions, which blend into the woodland's pre-monsoon palette of amber and gold. Monkeys that spotted a stalking cat let out a specific call. Deer weren't the only ones that recognized and used these calls; the lion tracker who had been with me in the park did too.

On the hike up Girnar, barefoot women kept passing me, wearing iridescent saris in bright shades of orange, green, or pink. Their delicate silver anklets tinkled as they went. When I reached a trail marker that said I was still 1,000 steps from the temple, I removed my pack and hopped up onto a wall, letting my legs dangle.

Two switchbacks below, an aged Jain monk in a white robe was struggling up the steps. He looked lonely, and seemed to be having trouble breathing. When Jain monks and nuns renounce worldly life, they sever all family ties. They embrace their children one last time, and vow never to see them again, unless chance brings them together on the rural back roads where the monks and nuns wander for the rest of their lives, carrying all their possessions on their back.

The monk and I had the trail to ourselves for a moment. All was silent but for a buzzing sound that I traced to a spindly black wasp bobbing above a dense clump of bougainvillea. The last ancestor this wasp and I shared likely lived more than 700 million years ago. The insect's appearance reinforced this sense of evolutionary remoteness. The elongated shape and micro-tiled matte finish of its eyes made it seem too alien to be conscious. But appearances can deceive: some wasps are thought to have evolved large eyes to observe social cues, and members of certain wasp species can learn the facial features of individual colony members.

Wasps, like bees and ants, are hymenopterans, an order of animals that displays strikingly sophisticated behaviors. Ants build body-to-body bridges that allow whole colonies to cross gaps in their terrain. Lab-bound honeybees can learn to recognize abstract concepts, including "similar to," "different from," and "zero."

Honeybees also learn from one another. If one picks up a novel nectar-extraction technique, surrounding bees may mimic the behavior, causing it to cascade across the colony, or even through generations.

In one experiment, honeybees were attracted to a boat at the center of a lake, which scientists had stocked with sugar water. When the bees flew back to the hive, they communicated the boat's location with waggle dances. The hive's other bees would usually set out immediately for a newly revealed nectar lode. But in this case, they stayed put, as though they'd consulted a mental map and dismissed the possibility of flowers in the middle of a lake. Other scientists were not able to replicate this result, but different experiments suggest that bees are capable of consulting a mental map in this way.

Andrew Barron, a neuroscientist from Macquarie University, in Australia, has spent the past decade identifying fine neural structures in honeybee brains. He thinks structures in the bee brain integrate spatial information in a way that is analogous to processes in the human midbrain. That may sound surprising, given that the honeybee brain contains only 1 million neurons to our brains' 85 billion, but artificial-intelligence research tells us that complex tasks can sometimes be executed by relatively simple neuronal circuits. Fruit flies have only 250,000 neurons, and they too display complex behaviors. In lab experiments, when faced with dim mating prospects, some seek out alcohol, the consciousness-altering substance that's available to them in nature in broken-open, fermenting fruit.

Many invertebrate lineages never developed anything beyond a rudimentary nervous system, a network of neurons dispersed evenly through a wormlike form. But more than half a billion years ago, natural selection began to shape other squirming blobs into arthropods with distinct appendages and newly specialized sensory organs, which they used to achieve liberation from a drifting life of stimulus and response.

The first animals to direct themselves through three-dimensional space would have encountered a new set of problems whose solution may have been the evolution of consciousness. Take the black wasp. As it hovered above the bougainvillea's tissue-thin petals, a great deal of information—sunlight, sound vibrations, floral scents—rushed into its fibrous exoskull. But these information streams arrived in its brain at different times. To form an accurate and continuous account of the external world, the wasp needed to sync these signals. And it needed to correct any errors introduced by its own movements, a difficult trick given that some of its sensors are mounted on body parts that are themselves mobile, not least its swiveling head.

The neuroscientist Björn Merker has suggested that early animal brains solved these problems by generating an internal model of the world, with an avatar of the body at its center. Merker says that consciousness is just the multisensory view from inside this model. The syncing processes and the jangle and noise from our mobile bodies are all missing from this conscious view—some invisible, algorithmic Stanley Kubrick seems to edit them out. Nor do we experience the mechanisms that convert our desires into movements. When I wished to begin hiking up the mountain again, I would simply set off, without thinking about the individual muscle contractions that each step required. When a wasp flies, it is probably not aware of its every wing beat. It may simply will itself through space.

If one of the wasp's aquatic ancestors experienced Earth's first embryonic consciousness, it would have been nothing like our own consciousness. It may have been colorless and barren of sharply defined objects. It may have been episodic, flickering on in some situations and off in others. It may have been a murkily sensed perimeter of binary feelings, a bubble of good and bad experienced by something central and unitary. To those of us who have seen stars shining on the far side of the cosmos, this existence would be claustrophobic to a degree that is scarcely imaginable. But that doesn't mean it wasn't conscious.

When the monk arrived at the wall where I was resting, the wasp flew away, rising up toward the sun until I lost it in the light. The monk was wearing a white mask like those that some Jains wear to avoid inhaling insects and other tiny creatures. I nodded to him as he passed, and lay back against the warm stone of the mountain.

The monk was a white dot some six switchbacks up by the time I hopped off the wall and continued the climb, my legs stiffened by the break. I reached the entrance to the temple complex with only fifteen minutes to spare. Its marble courtyard shone brilliant white, as though bleached by the mountain sun.

Ducking under a row of elegant golden medallions, I entered the temple's interior chamber, where dozens of candles flickered in intricately carved wall niches, and on platforms that hung from the ceiling on chains. The stone ceiling was carved into a lotus flower, its delicate unfurling petals symbolizing the emergence of a pure, ethereal soul from the Earth's muddy materials.

Forty Jains were sitting on the floor in neat rows, their legs crossed in the lotus position. The women wore fresh saris they'd carried up the mountain for the occasion. The men were dressed in all white. I wedged into a spot in the back.

We faced a dark, tunnel-like space lined by two sets of columns. At the far end, candlelight illuminated a black marble statue of a seated male figure. Its barrel chest was inlaid with gemstones, as were its eyes, which appeared to float, serenely, in the dark space, inducing a hypnotic effect, broken only when the man sitting next to me tugged my shirt. "Neminath," he said, nodding toward the statue.

It was here on this mountain that Neminath is said to have achieved a state of total, unimpeded consciousness, with perceptual access to the entire universe, including every kind of animal mind. Jains believe that humans are special because, in our natural state, we are nearest to this experience of enlightenment. Among Earth's creatures, no other finds it so easy to see into the consciousness of a fellow being.

The pilgrims started singing, first in a low hum and then steadily louder. One wheeled a giant drum next to the tunnel's entrance and struck it with a dark mallet. Two others bashed cymbals together. Men and women walked in from opposite doors, converging, in two lines, on either side of the tunnel. A woman wearing an orange sari and a gold crown crossed in front of Neminath, lifted a vessel over his black-marble head, and poured out a mixture of milk and blessed water. When she finished, a white-robed man from the other line did the same.

The singing grew louder until it verged on ecstatic. The pilgrims raised their arms and clapped overhead, faster and faster. A climax seemed to loom, but then it all dropped away. The drums and the bells and the cymbals went quiet, leaving a clear sonic space that was filled by a final blow on a conch.

The shell's low note was long and clean. It rang out of the temple and over the ancient peaks. As it trailed off, I wondered whether, in the centuries to come, this place might become something more than a Jain house of worship. Maybe it will become a place to mark a moment in human history, when we awakened from the dream that we are the only minds that nature brought into being. Maybe people will come here from all corners of the Earth to pay their respects to Neminath, who is, after all, only a stand-in for whoever it was who first heard animal screams and understood their meaning.

Sleep No More

FROM *Wired*

IN RETROSPECT, IT might have been a clue. But in early 2010, when Kamni Vallabh first began to complain that her eyesight was failing, there didn't seem to be much cause for concern. She was fifty-one; maybe middle age was catching up with her. Maybe the harsh western Pennsylvania winter—two record-breaking blizzards in as many weeks—was wearing her down.

The previous summer, Kamni had been in good health. She'd single-handedly organized her daughter Sonia's wedding, 300 guests drinking and dancing in the family's backyard in Hermitage, a tight-knit former steel town. But by her birthday, that March, it was clear that something was seriously wrong. Once a poet, Kamni could barely string a sentence together. She was distractible, easily confused; when she misplaced the TV remote, she'd look for it in the pantry. Her body, too, was rapidly declining. By May, she couldn't eat, stand, or bathe herself. She had trouble sleeping and spent her rare moments of lucidity grieving for the burden she had placed on her family. Sonia, who was twenty-five at the time and living in Boston, called her mother often and visited whenever she could. "She wasn't scared so much as sad," Sonia remembers. "She'd say things like, 'Look at me now. I'm so useless.'"

As Kamni's symptoms worsened, what had begun with a few visits to the ophthalmologist turned into a medical odyssey. Her husband, a doctor named Sagar, took her to a local neurologist, who found no evidence of heavy-metal poisoning or Lyme disease. Next they visited the Cleveland Clinic, then Brigham and Women's Hospital in Boston. Specialists searched in vain for microscopic tumors and puzzled over Kamni's spinal fluid, which didn't harbor any trace of common brain diseases. No one had an answer; the illness was progressing faster than Sagar could book appointments. With each new test, the family rooted for a positive result. At that point, a name for Kamni's condition would have offered some comfort, even if it didn't come with the promise of a cure. But the tests kept turning up negative.

By October, Kamni was on life support. Her will specified that, in the event of a terminal diagnosis, she didn't want extraordinary measures taken to keep her alive—but the family didn't *have* a diagnosis. "Her suffering was very vivid," Sonia says. "She'd be in the hospital bed with her eyes vacant, all of her muscles jerking and contracting and clenching, with needle pricks every hour, surrounded by all of these different sorts of machines. She didn't show any sign of recognizing us, of recognizing anything. But she could show fear. And pain." Finally, in December, the family received a preliminary diagnosis: the doctors had retested Kamni's spinal fluid and found signs of prion disease.

Prions are abnormally folded proteins that form toxic clumps in the brain. The illnesses they cause are rare and invariably fatal. (The most common prion disorder in humans, Creutzfeldt-Jakob disease, kills about 500 people per year in the United States.) Sometimes the disease is passed down from an unlucky parent; sometimes it develops spontaneously, a fluke mutation; sometimes it is the result of contagion, with the problem proteins making their way into the body from a tainted cornea transplant, or a skin graft, or beef infected with bovine spongiform encephalopathy, also known as mad cow disease. Whatever the cause, once symptoms start, the prions do their work quickly and irreversibly. They tear through the brain and kill healthy tissue, leaving empty holes behind.

With the diagnosis in hand, the Vallabhs made the decision to take Kamni off life support. The family gathered around her for a final goodbye. Sonia had braced herself for the moment of her mother's death but found that, after months of uncertainty, it came as a relief. This was partly because, once Kamni was gone, long-absent support flooded in. Losing a loved one to dementia is mysterious, unsettling. Death, on the other hand, is binary. We all know the social conventions—cards and condolences, a shared mourning display. Several hundred people attended Kamni's funeral. "It's that kind of town," Sonia says. "It's also who my parents *were* in that town."

Kamni's diagnosis had come as such a shock that Sagar, hoping for final confirmation, had requested an autopsy. A tissue sample was sent for testing to the National Prion Disease Pathology Surveillance Center in Cleveland. Meanwhile, Sonia and her husband, Eric Minikel, returned to their lives in Boston. Between visits to Kamni in the hospital, Eric had managed to finish a master's degree in urban planning at MIT and got a job as a transportation analyst. By the summer of 2011, Sonia had completed a law degree at Harvard and joined a small consulting firm. The nightmare of Kamni's death began to recede.

That October, the couple went back to Hermitage for a friend's engagement party. Just before they headed to the airport for their flight home, Sagar pulled his daughter aside. As a doctor, he was well trained in delivering bad news, but Sonia had never seen him struggle like this before. The results of Kamni's autopsy had come in, he said. She had succumbed to a prion disease called fatal familial insomnia. There was a 50–50 chance that Sonia had inherited it.

Sonia broke the news to Eric on the plane, and he sobbed the whole way back to Boston, as concerned flight attendants helplessly offered their services. "It was exceptionally hard to watch my dad have to tell me, and then exceptionally hard to then have to tell Eric," she recalls. "The person who had it worst that day was my dad. The second worst was Eric. The third worst was me."

Almost immediately, Sonia decided that she wanted to be tested for her mother's mutation. Her doctors, genetic counselors, and even some of her family members recommended against it. If a disease has no cure, their reasoning went, what's the point in knowing? Isn't ignorance bliss? But Sonia was adamant. "You really want to hope that you're negative, but the fear that you're positive keeps interrupting, and it's a constant psychological dialogue," she says. "Once you know, you start to adapt. What you can't adapt to is something that keeps changing shape on you."

It took weeks, but Sonia finally secured a test. The results wouldn't come in for two months, so she and Eric went on their long-postponed honeymoon in Tokyo. They never got over the jet lag and spent their nights wandering down side streets. The trip became a physical instantiation of their mental state: alone in a strange place, speaking only to each other.

On the morning she was to learn the outcome of her test, Sonia found herself clinging to superstition. In the waiting room, she glimpsed the genetic counselor laughing. "If she was about to give life-changingly horrible news, she wouldn't be in a good mood right now," Sonia remembers thinking. With Eric by her side, she stepped into the doctor's office. He reported the results without ceremony: "The same change that was found in your mother was found in you." Sonia had perhaps a decade or two before she would begin to experience symptoms, but there would be no escaping the disease; it killed anyone who carried it. She felt an odd sense of calm. She called her father, who booked a flight to Boston. They spent the weekend together, trying to talk about other things. "I had to keep focusing on the fact that I wasn't sick now, and I probably wouldn't be for a while," she says.

Not long after Sonia found out that she was a carrier of fatal familial insomnia, a scientist friend named Stevie Steiner gave her a thumb drive. It was full of research on prion diseases. Sonia had never imagined that so many people studied them, given their rarity. She and Eric became obsessed with learning more. Sonia had taken a few biology classes in college, but Eric, a Chinese language major, had avoided them almost entirely, satisfying his curriculum requirement with a course called Cropping Systems of the Tropics. "I had to go on Wikipedia to remember what dominant versus recessive meant," he says. They sat in on classes at MIT, trying to pass as undergraduates, and started a blog, which they used to organize their thoughts and speculate on therapies.

Within a few weeks of the diagnosis, Sonia had quit her job to study science full-time, continuing classes at MIT during the day and enrolling in a night class in biology at Harvard's extension school. The pair lived off savings and Eric's salary. Sonia had expected to take a temporary sabbatical from her real life, but soon textbooks and academic articles weren't enough. "The practice of science and the classroom version of science are such different animals," Sonia says. She wanted to try her hand in the lab. She found a position as a technician with a research group focusing on Huntington's disease. Eric, not wanting to be left behind, quit his job too and offered his data-crunching expertise to a genetics lab.

The deeper they dove into science, the more they began to fixate on finding a cure.

The couple's drastic career change worried their families. Did they really want to spend all their time thinking about her disease? Were they prepared to waste years of their lives on a quest that would almost certainly fail? Eric's sister was a doctor and had done some bench work while getting her degree; she had found the experiments hopelessly fussy. "The person next to me could sneeze and change the results," she warned them. But Sonia and Eric couldn't be deterred.

In 1954, barely a year after James Watson and Francis Crick announced the discovery of the double helix, reports began to emerge from Papua New Guinea of a mysterious neurological epidemic. The Fore, an indigenous group, called it *kuru*, "to tremble." No one who contracted it survived. Victims showed no sign of infection—none of the mucus, fever, or antibodies associated with a normal immune response. Nor was the condition inherited, as far as doctors could tell. Eventually, a team of anthropologists and scientists, including the American virologist Carleton Gajdusek, realized that the illness might be related to the Fore practice of funerary cannibalism. Tellingly, it was primarily women and children afflicted by kuru, and primarily women and their children who consumed the deceased. (The Fore believed that only women's bodies were capable of taming the dangerous spirits of the dead.) Autopsies revealed that the victims' brains were riddled with holes. When Gajdusek injected their brain matter into chimpanzees, the apes contracted kuru and died—proof that the disease was a kind of infection.

Still, scientists had no idea what the *agent* of infection was. In this way, kuru resembled scrapie, a fatal degenerative illness that causes sheep to obsessively scrape themselves against fences. The usual battery of disinfectants and antiseptics had no effect on either condition. The pathogens that caused them, whatever they were, were tough. In one strange experiment, Gajdusek buried a hamster's scrapie-laced brain matter in a garden. When he dug it up three years later, it was still infectious.

Stanley Prusiner, a chemist at UC San Francisco, started studying scrapie in 1972, despite warnings from his colleagues to steer clear. The disease took years to incubate in mice before killing them, which meant that his publication record would be sparse. In 1981 Prusiner's first bid for tenure failed, and he soon lost his funding. But he persisted. He secured a grant with a private foundation and persuaded UCSF administrators to let him keep his job. The following year, he published an article in the prestigious journal *Science* about the radical theory he'd been developing.

Prusiner had found that when he mixed scrapie with certain chemicals—those specifically designed to mangle genetic material—it survived. When he mixed it with protein-destroying chemicals, however, it became harmless. The cause of the disease, he concluded, must be something heretofore unknown to science: a pathogen that replicated without the use of any genetic material at all. He called it a proteinaceous infectious particle, or prion. Prusiner's paper fared well in peer review, but the editors of *Science* hesitated for months before publishing it, afraid of a backlash. The idea was outlandish—but it was also right. Prusiner received a Nobel Prize for his heresy in 1997.

Further work by Prusiner and others revealed that prions behave something like the secret weapon from Kurt Vonnegut's novel *Cat's Cradle*. Vonnegut imagined a form of water called ice-nine, a "super-crystal" that froze at room temperature and turned any normal water it touched into itself. A single crystal would set off a chain reaction, causing the oceans to ice over, ending all life on Earth. The process of prion infection is similar. The protein that gives rise to prions, PrP, is not inherently dangerous. It is believed to be common to all vertebrates and is mainly expressed in brain cells. (Biologists don't know for certain what it does.) But PrP is floppy and can spontaneously misfold into different conformations. Some of these conformations act like templates that recruit nearby PrP to fold in the same way, stacking into brain-scrambling spikes. Properly speaking, prions are not an infectious entity; they're an infectious shape.

The various prion conformations give rise to a myriad of diseases with unique but overlapping clinical presentations—kuru, fatal familial insomnia, Creutzfeldt-Jakob, and others. But they are all, at heart, the same malady. Over the course of a lifetime, the average person has a one in 5,000 chance of contracting a prion disorder. The odds are slightly worse in the UK, where, because of an outbreak of mad cow in the 1990s, scientists estimate that up to one in 2,000 people still have prions incubating in their tissues, waiting to seed deadly plaques. Sonia's specific condition is caused by a mutation in the gene that codes for PrP, making the protein likelier to misfold. Before Kamni fell ill, there was no documented history of FFI in the family. It appears to have been the result of a random genetic typo in the egg or sperm that made her. In effect, the moment Kamni was conceived, her descendants' odds of contracting the disease went from about one in 30 million to one in two. Any children that Sonia and Eric might have would face the same cruel lottery.

Fatal familial insomnia got its name in 1986, when a group of Italian researchers published a paper about it in the *New England Journal of Medicine*. They told the story of a patient from Venice who had delivered himself to a neuroscience lab at the University of Bologna just as he was about to die. The man's family had suffered from the disease for more than two centuries, and he was showing all the symptoms they had learned to fear: muscle tremors, trouble walking, excessive sweating, ever-worsening insomnia, and dementia. The researchers recorded his final days on video; his empty eyes rested on nothing in particular, neither sleeping nor fully awake. "When left alone, the patient would slowly lapse into a stuporous state characterized by dreamlike activity," they wrote.

Kamni avoided the worst of the insomnia, but she did suffer severe dementia. Although it is impossible to know what her final months of life felt like, the experience of another patient may offer some indication. In 2001 an American man known as DF was diagnosed with fatal familial insomnia. A trained naturopath and the son of a talk-radio nutritionist, he began a self-administered regimen of supplements and unconventional treatments—electroconvulsive therapy, prescription and illicit drugs, a sensory-deprivation tank. (He eventually eschewed this last therapy, according to his doctors, because it "made him feel like the comic book freak Aquaman.") DF bought a motor home and toured the country on and off for nearly two years, taking uppers and downers to regulate his sleep cycle. Without the uppers he couldn't so much as hear a phone ringing, but on them he was sharp, able to drive long distances at a stretch.

Perhaps owing to his stimulant use, DF was able to recall his bouts of dementia better than most patients. Fatal familial insomnia cripples the thalamus, the region of the brain that funnels sensory signals to the neocortex, which is thought to mediate consciousness. Without this relay station, patients become unaware of external cues; their conscious experience amounts to a hallucination. Imagine looking through a one-way mirror into an adjacent room: once the light is shut off behind the mirror, all you can see is your own reflection. As DF put it, "To the outside world, I am dead and gone, but to myself, I'm still here."

During his episodes of dementia, DF found himself surrounded by loved ones, living and dead. "It was experienced as a form of knowing everything about himself, with no more hidden secrets," his doctors wrote. "His conscious mind experienced himself in a global way." DF contrasted the serenity of dementia with the anguish of his lucid moments, which brought with them the awareness that his mind and body were breaking down. He came to believe that patients with fatal familial insomnia actually allowed themselves to die. At a certain point, the warm embrace of oblivion became preferable to the pain of waking life.

In the fall of 2013, about a year after Vallabh and Minikel made their career change, they began applying to PhD programs. At first they were interested in attending UCSF, where Prusiner, now seventy-six, continues his work on prions. But Minikel's boss at the time, the geneticist Daniel MacArthur, urged them to consider the Broad Institute, a research center jointly operated by MIT and Harvard. It wasn't the obvious move. No one at the Broad was studying prions; there wasn't even an adequate biosafety room for handling them. Vallabh and Minikel would need to build their own program from scratch. The benefit, MacArthur explained, was freedom: they could drive their research in any direction they chose, without adhering to another lab's approach. "I can't tell you how crazy he seemed at the time," Minikel says of MacArthur's idea. "But somehow he saw that this was a place where things were possible."

That December, with MacArthur's support, the couple gave a presentation at the Broad, laying out their ambitions. They hoped to develop a drug that would target the misfolded PrP protein, stymieing plaques before they could form. Through a nonprofit they had founded in 2012, the Prion Alliance, they had already raised about $17,000, mostly in small donations. They would use the money to fund tests of a promising compound that had been shown to clear prions in mouse cell cultures. If all went well, they thought the research might even one day lead to a clinical trial in humans.

After the presentation, Eric Lander, a cofounder of the Broad, asked a question. "You're talking about raising ten to the power of four dollars," he said. "Do you realize for a clinical trial you'll need ten to the seven dollars?" It was clear that the couple required practical guidance; their studiousness in the classroom hadn't prepared them for the bruising work of drug development. So, Lander says, he "decided to adopt them."

The couple applied to Harvard and got in. They met regularly with Lander—Vallabh recalls being "beyond mortified" at their naïveté—and eventually secured positions in the lab of Stuart Schreiber, another Broad cofounder. Today they work together in a spartan office, the walls bare save for a printout of Selfie Monkey and Minikel's only artistic output, a painting of Donkey Kong Country. The couple wear bright clothes and look like a pair of elves plucked from the pages of a fantasy story—Vallabh rendered in sharp strokes of black ink, her hair tamed in a pixie cut, and Minikel sketched more softly, with woolly pencil marks. The phrase CONSTANT VIGILANCE is scrawled over an imposingly long to-do list on their whiteboard.

Once Vallabh and Minikel began their PhD studies, the scope of what they were up against became clear. Much of the research that had initially given them such hope, they discovered, was a dead end. Vallabh wonders how they stayed in science. "I found myself thinking, 'This is so hard. I don't know if I can keep doing this every day,'" she says. In a way, their inexperience had been a blessing: they might have given up if they'd known just how unlikely it was that they'd be able to save Vallabh in time.

At Lander's urging, the couple reconsidered their original strategy. Money, it turned out, wasn't their only problem. As they continued to unpack the lessons provided by Kamni's death, something they kept returning to was how quickly she had deteriorated. Even if a treatment for her condition had been available, doctors wouldn't have known to administer it until her brain damage was irreversible. And there was another problem too. Because prions can shape-shift, they can evolve drug resistance. A drug designed to target one prion conformation will not necessarily work on another. Vallabh and Minikel might spend years developing the perfect key, only to discover that it no longer fit the lock. It was just as Vallabh had said: you can't adapt to something that keeps changing shape on you. The way forward became clear. They would target PrP *before* it misfolded. They would stop prions from appearing in the first place.

The literature suggested that such an approach was possible. In the 1990s, researchers had created a strain of so-called knockout mice that lacked the gene for PrP. When these mice were injected with prions, they didn't get sick; without PrP around, there was nothing to keep the chain reaction going. More important, the absence of the gene didn't seem to affect the mice's health in any major way. This didn't necessarily mean that reducing PrP levels would be safe in humans, but sometimes nature does our experiments for us. In his research, Minikel had identified people who lacked one copy of the PrP gene, meaning they likely expressed half the normal amount of the protein. They, too, experienced no obvious problems. If he and Vallabh could somehow lower the PrP levels in her brain, they might be able to delay the onset of her disease. Better still, by targeting PrP rather than a specific conformation, their method could potentially work for any prion disease.

Through mutual friends, the couple had met a scientist named Jeff Carroll, who, like Vallabh, researches his own disorder—in his case, Huntington's disease. He had recently partnered with a company called Ionis Pharmaceuticals to develop a therapy. Both fatal familial insomnia and Huntington's result from a mutant protein that is toxic to brain cells. So how do you eliminate the protein? The simplest answer, Carroll explained, was to cut out the middleman. If DNA contains the architectural blueprint for a protein, a molecule called RNA is the contractor; it reads the schematics and specifies how the protein should be assembled. If you can intercept the RNA before construction has begun, you can affect the final shape of the building.

Ionis had developed a way of doing this with antisense oligonucleotides. ASOs are strands of nucleic acids—the same stuff as DNA and RNA—that can zipper up with RNA to either stop or enhance its protein-building activity. In 2016, Ionis launched an ASO called nusinersen to treat spinal muscular atrophy, one of the most common genetic causes of infant death. The results were stunning. Parents posted videos of their children's progress on YouTube: babies that had been given six months to live were still around years later, laughing, standing, and reaching many developmental milestones. Now Ionis was turning ASOs loose on Huntington's. Carroll realized that the same strategy might work for Vallabh and Minikel. He connected them with the company, which agreed to help.

Lander suggested that they pursue the Food and Drug Administration's Accelerated Approval track, which was created in the wake of the AIDS crisis, when potentially life-saving experimental treatments were held up in bureaucratic limbo. A traditional trial takes many years to complete; scientists must prove that the drug has "a real effect on how a patient survives, feels, or functions," according to the FDA. But what happens when a disease strikes unpredictably and kills quickly, leaving no time to gather the requisite data? In these situations, the FDA gives scientists some extra leeway. Rather than waiting months or years to see how a patient fares, they can use a kind of surrogate metric, known as a biomarker. If the drug is safe and affects the biomarker as expected, it is considered a success, and the path is cleared for FDA approval. In the case of AIDS, the biomarker might be the amount of HIV RNA in a patient's bloodstream. In the case of prion disease, Vallabh and Minikel proposed to use the level of PrP in a patient's spinal fluid.

Ionis would develop the drug and, eventually, oversee the trial. In return, Vallabh and Minikel would need to demonstrate that there was a viable route forward, a way of actually getting the therapy to market. It wasn't just Ionis and the FDA they needed to impress; all of their findings would have to be published in medical journals, thoroughly vetted by their peers. The company handed them a list of what Vallabh calls their "homework" and Schreiber calls "the impossible tasks." First, they would have to develop a reliable way of measuring PrP levels, their chosen biomarker. Next, they would need to demonstrate that Ionis's drug could delay death in prion-infected mice. Finally, they would have to set up a registry of human patients willing to participate in a trial.

In October of 2016, buoyed by hope, Vallabh began drafting a white paper to bring before the FDA. It was around this time that she became pregnant.

Vallabh and Minikel had always intended to start a family, but only after they were sure her condition wouldn't be passed down. Anything else seemed like a reckless coin flip. In July of 2013, at the annual Creutzfeldt-Jakob Disease Foundation conference in Washington, D.C., they had met a woman named Amanda Kalinsky, whose family's struggle with genetic prion disease was the focus of Gina Kolata's book *Mercies in Disguise*. Kalinsky was the first prion carrier to use in vitro fertilization with preimplantation genetic diagnosis, which allows patients to discard any embryos that are found to contain a dangerous mutation.

Vallabh and Minikel put off parenthood for several years, due to prohibitively low salaries and long hours in the lab. But when they were ready, Kalinsky agreed to counsel them through the arduous process. There would be daily hormone shots, countless trips to the hospital for ultrasound scans, and fraught phone calls from doctors announcing how many, if any, embryos were viable. Still, for Vallabh, the effort was worth it. She never wanted to have the conversation with her child that her father had been forced to have with her.

It was a turbulent nine months—physically, emotionally, professionally. Vallabh thought of her mother often. "I went through a period of grieving while she was sick, before she even died, and I went through another period of grieving while I was pregnant," she says. The baby, as though she knew how overextended her parents were, politely waited to arrive by appointment. She was a week late, which meant that Vallabh could schedule an induction and the process of labor was contained to a workday. The couple named her Daruka. Within weeks, they were bringing her along to the Broad, where delighted lab mates took turns burping her.

The meeting with the FDA was scheduled just three months after Daruka's birth. Minikel's parents flew to Boston to babysit while the couple set off for the agency's headquarters in Maryland. They arrived with the distinct sense that this would be the most important gathering of their lives. If they couldn't get the FDA to green-light their approach, they might be set back for years. "Things get scarier as we get closer to a realistic therapy," Vallabh says. "We have more to lose."

As soon as the couple began their presentation, Lander says, there was a sense of "pushing on an open door"—quite a surprise, given the agency's stodgy reputation. "People still flat-out don't believe the FDA was cool with it," Minikel says. Afterward, one of the twenty-five scientists in the audience pulled Lander aside and said, "That was one of the best presentations I've ever seen." Schreiber agreed. He alluded to a pharmaceutical company he'd helped set up early in his career. "*Twenty-four* years into that company, there was *nothing* to show for it. Not one thing," he says. "For two graduate students who are not trained in science to come in and do what they did? Absolute forces of nature, savants. They keep seeing things that other people don't see."

Vallabh and Minikel walked away from the meeting with the FDA's blessing: their work showed promise, and the agency encouraged them to keep going. That fall, the couple began testing the first round of ASOs from Ionis. They spent long months in a windowless mouse colony at the Broad, injecting cohorts of mice with the compounds and seeding their brains with prions. Soon enough, the animals that received treatment were surviving weeks and months longer than their brethren in the control group. In humans, that might translate into years.

Vallabh and Minikel's final "impossible task" is to recruit trial volunteers—no small feat, given that genetic prion diseases are so rare and only 23 percent of people known to be at risk follow through with predictive testing. Still, they hear regularly from prospective patients around the world, many of whom see participating in a trial as almost a civic duty. "Sonia and Eric are doing the research," Trevor Baierl, a prion disease carrier, told me. "I need to provide myself as a subject. She's going to save all of us—and herself." Indeed, Vallabh hopes to be the first in line if and when a drug goes to trial.

After they complete their PhDs this spring, the couple will need to secure more than $1 million per year in funding to continue their research. This is perhaps the aspect of their work that they struggle with most. While the scientific establishment loves the study of prion diseases as a curiosity, there's not much interest in funding a cure. Philanthropists, Vallabh says, tend to support research on disorders that directly affect them or their families. "I'm haunted by the idea that other curable genetic diseases have drugs that will work but don't have billionaires, centibillionaires, or us to follow up on them," Vallabh says. She also worries that their research isn't competitive for federal grants, which mostly flow to common diseases and shiny new therapies. "Journals want novelty.

Patients want something that works," Vallabh says. "Everyone loves the big idea that will change the world. But what about the small idea that makes a difference?"

When I first met Vallabh and Minikel, in the fall of 2018, one of their papers had just been rejected for the third time—not because the science is questionable, they say, but because it isn't exciting enough. "I'm so aware of just how much of my time is going to reformatting another manuscript to resubmit to another journal," Vallabh says. "I want to care about this so much less than I'm forced to care about it." Their battle isn't just against prion disease. Their battle is, in a sad way, against science itself—not science in principle, but science in practice. When Vallabh and Minikel began their new careers, they were perplexed by their colleagues' obsession with getting published. "You ask someone how it's going, and you want to hear how the science is," Minikel says. "Instead, they tell you about paper reviews, politics, grant applications."

Even without all these distractions, the work remains full of frustrations. On one of my visits to the Broad, Minikel was in the biosafety room that the institute had outfitted for them, working on a new way of quantifying prion protein levels in spinal fluid. I watched the experiment at a distance. He had donned multiple layers of protective gear, un-self-conscious in comically large goggles. Though trapped like a kid in a snowsuit, he could communicate with Vallabh down in the office using a cheap tablet they'd mounted on the wall. At some point in the night, a crucial piece of equipment had broken down, but he had to forge ahead with the experiment anyway. "This is the last sample I have," he said. He planned to send it off to another lab for testing. They'd have to wait for the results. Science is an invisible art practiced on brittle instruments: a string is plucked, and its note rings out a month later. If only there were more time.

On my last night in Cambridge, I met the family for dinner at a Chinese restaurant. As we sat down, Minikel pulled a spice jar filled with salt from his pocket. He worked through his charred bok choy in layers, heavily salting each stratum. Daruka sat in Vallabh's lap, pressing a chopstick holder to her double chin. "Daruka tucks things into her neck fold when she likes them a lot," Vallabh explained.

The toddler is a perfect miniature of her father, her blue eyes beaming behind a riot of sandy curls. "A cop walked by us the other day and said, 'Wow, now that's genetics!'" Minikel says. "But I told him, 'Her mother is Indian. Genetics is more complicated than we think.'" Daruka had only recently learned how to stand: At first, she'd hold on to a coffee table with both hands, eventually graduating to one hand, then a finger. Finally she could do it hands-free, belly only—"balancing on her muffin top," Minikel says.

As we ate, I asked Vallabh about a Chinese term she'd introduced me to earlier in the week: *ho pa,* or "backward fear." She'd used it to describe the scariness of reflecting on all the likely outcomes that somehow didn't happen: If she hadn't walked in on her housemate's dinner party in her early twenties, she might never have met Minikel. If Minikel hadn't been rejected from Berkeley, they might not have moved to Cambridge for graduate school. If they hadn't been in Cambridge when they learned about Vallabh's mutation, they wouldn't have that thumb drive from Steiner, nor easy access to the Broad. If they hadn't ended up at the Broad, they might not have met Carroll, who introduced them to ASOs, or Lander, who guided them through the FDA. And, perhaps more than anything: if Kamni hadn't died when she did, Sonia wouldn't have gotten tested and might have passed her mutation on to Daruka. Kamni's death, Vallabh says, was a "transgenerational gift."

Toward the end of the dinner, Outkast's "Hey Ya!" came on and Daruka slid down the chair to test her new powers of locomotion. She held her hands out and Minikel excused himself. "I'm being called to the dance floor," he said. They spun in circles. "I asked for them to play this song at our wedding," Vallabh said, laughing. After the song ended, she pulled out Daruka's tropical-colored raincoat and began preparing her for the long walk home in the rain. Minikel, who had never once expressed any sentiment outside of optimism, sat back down, looked at me earnestly, and said, "Now that you've heard everything, do you think we're going to make it?"

DANIEL DUANE

What Remains

FROM *The California Sunday Magazine*

ON A COOL September morning in 2014, among lodgepole pines under blue mountain sky, Greg Stock shouldered a backpack full of camping gear and scientific equipment. Boyishly slender and athletic at forty-five, Stock is a climber, caver, and serious reader of books about mountaineering and the natural world. He holds the enviable job title of Yosemite National Park Geologist and mostly loves the work, especially the part he was bound for that day—the study of Yosemite's last two glaciers.

Stock and several companions started their walk in Tuolumne Meadows, the high-country jewel of Yosemite and everything that I would ever wish to find in the pastures of heaven—many square miles of grass and wildflowers surrounded by white granite domes that reflect sunshine like polished glass. Stock followed the John Muir Trail south out of those meadows into an immense U-shaped gorge called Lyell Canyon, 8 miles long and 3,000 feet deep, carved out of granite by long-vanished glaciers during dozens of ice ages. Evergreens dot the sloped walls of Lyell Canyon—straight lodgepoles down low, bent whitebarks up high.

In that drought year of 2014, dry meadow grasses carpeted the canyon floor in pale gold. Down the middle, the Lyell Fork of the Tuolumne River trickled through wide, meandering oxbows. The great irrigator of Tuolumne Meadows and drinking-water source for San Francisco, that river thunders deep in spring but flows in autumn thanks to meltwater from Stock's destination, the Lyell Glacier.

Seven miles into Lyell Canyon, Stock kept an eye out for white rocks in the grass. If you didn't know what to look for, you would never find those rocks, much less guess they marked a particular spot. When Stock saw them, he turned east off the John Muir Trail and down into the mostly empty channel of the Lyell Fork. He hopped across the shallows and then walked into the center of the canyon.

Stock poked around in the grass for another pile of rocks, which marked the spot where, in 1883, a geologist named Israel Russell looked 4,000 vertical feet up to the jagged summit of Mount Lyell, 13,114 feet above sea level and the tallest peak in Yosemite National Park. Standing right there, Russell took the first known photograph of the Lyell Glacier, which John Muir had found only twelve years earlier. In Russell's photograph, 13 million square feet of ice spread like a white shawl across Mount Lyell's black metamorphic shoulders.

Geologists and park employees have been returning to Russell's photo point—and to the glacier itself—on a more or less regular basis ever since, replicating Russell's images to create a scientific record 135 years old and counting. Stock has been the keeper of that tradition for over a decade, making the trip through Lyell Canyon more than twenty times to check the glacier's vital signs. He has put gauges in runoff streams to measure meltwater trickling out of openings at the toe of the glacier. He has studied data from NASA's Airborne Snow Observatory, an airplane outfitted with advanced sensing equipment that calculates the water volume in the Sierra snowpack and ice fields. Using much of the same technique that Muir did in 1871, Stock drove stakes into the Lyell to measure the downslope creep of ice that defines a glacier.

Like everyone who has ever studied the Lyell—and pretty much everyone who has ever studied any glacier—Stock documented shrinkage. The Lyell has lost depth and retreated upslope and broken into a smattering of white Rorschach blots that, as of 2014, amounted to about 3 million square feet of ice. In 2012, Stock had collected data showing that the main lobe of the Lyell was not flowing downhill. The pleasure of working in that quiet alpine sanctuary kept him coming back in a spirit of optimism. Still, when Stock looked through his camera's viewfinder at the largest of the Lyell's remaining white blots, in 2014, he was surprised to see that a familiar dark patch had grown much larger.

Stock led his companions farther south along the John Muir

Trail to where it climbed up through forest toward Donohue Pass. At a wooden bridge across the river, Stock turned west off trail. Up rocky slopes, they came to the shores of an hourglass-shaped blue lake in a bowl of white stone—cooked dinner, slept in sleeping bags. In the morning, after breakfast, they hiked another 1,200 feet up to the main lobe of the Lyell, a broad and steep mass of ice in a quiet cirque of shattered rock. Stock felt like a man coming home after a long absence, comfortable and eager to catch up. He decided to have a close look at that dark patch.

"I remember noticing that it was right under an avalanche chute in the headwall below the summit," Stock says. Perhaps it was just rock debris from some long-ago slide, embedded in the glacier surface.

The Lyell Glacier hangs at a severe angle off the mountainside. To slip and fall can mean a long, fast plummet. Stock wore crampons on his boots and carried an ice ax as he stepped onto an ice field riddled with sun cups, bathtub-sized depressions that forced him to walk along blade-thin ridges between them. Standing at the edge of the dark patch, Stock got a terrible feeling.

"I just knew. *That's bedrock. Your wishful thinking that that's debris can't possibly be right.* The next thought was, *If that's bedrock, there can't be much glacier left.*" Letting his eye roam the periphery of the ice and visualizing mountain contours beneath the main mass of the glacier, Stock struggled to form a mental model in which the glacier maintained significant volume. He could not picture more than about twenty or thirty feet of thickness. Given the Lyell's melt rate, it would disappear in four or five more years of drought. The shock of this realization forced Stock to confront what the data had been hinting at: the Lyell was no longer a glacier at all. Put another way, the Lyell Glacier was already dead, and Stock was the last person ever to study it.

Glaciers used to be fun, even thrilling. It's hard to believe now, but there was a time when geology was much like genetics today, the cutting-edge inquiry that routinely delivered breathtaking insights that captivated the educated world. Many of those insights, starting in the mid-1700s, had to do with the age of the Earth, as people looking closely at rocks found evidence that our planet was a lot older than the 6,000 years suggested by the Old Testament —perhaps many millions of years older. For this reason, the nine-

teenth century is said to have discovered "deep time," the astronomical and geological time scales that reach into pasts so distant
that our minds struggle to imagine them.

An academic cottage industry sprang up to reconcile deep time
with Scripture—arguing, for example, that the Book of Genesis actually described two distinct geological periods separated by an immense span of time and the original authors simply left out those
middle zillion years. As for how landforms like mountains and canyons got themselves made, religiously minded geologists inclined
toward so-called catastrophist explanations consistent with the
Bible's depiction of mountain ranges created in a day—massive
earthquakes, cataclysmic volcanic eruptions. Across Northern Europe, geologists documented curious scouring and scraping marks
on bedrock, running in a more or less north–south direction, and
decided they must be evidence of the flood that provoked Noah
to build an ark.

Charles Lyell, a Scottish geologist and namesake of the mountain and glacier, proposed a counter-theory known as uniformi-
tarianism, under which landscapes were shaped by extremely slow-
moving forces still active in the present day, like sedimentation on
seabeds—and the rock-grinding effects of glaciers. Lyell's contemporary, the Irish geologist John Tyndall, happened also to be an
important player in the golden age of mountaineering, making
first ascents in the Alps. His book *The Glaciers of the Alps,* published
in 1860, was a hit with British men and women who traveled to
Switzerland, where they walked out onto glaciers to learn about
how all that ice carved and sculpted the mountains beneath and
how those scouring and scraping marks on Northern European
bedrock were likely caused by mile-thick ice sheets that had covered much of the Northern Hemisphere during some long-past
ice age.

Around the same period, a militia hunting indigenous people
stumbled upon Yosemite Valley. Within three years, the first tour-
ists entered Yosemite, and word got out across the United States
and Europe that a new wonder of the natural world had been
found at the western edge of the American empire. Leading American geologists like Josiah Whitney and Clarence King looked all
over the Sierra for glaciers and speculated about how the great
cliffs of Yosemite Valley came into being. Neither found glaciers,
and Whitney carried the day with the catastrophist argument that

Yosemite Valley's floor had collapsed downward, leaving behind monoliths like Half Dome and El Capitan.

John Muir was an unknown Yosemite hospitality worker at the time, a college dropout and Civil War draft dodger, but he'd studied geology at the University of Wisconsin. He knew about theories of the Ice Age and thought it plain as day that glaciers carved Yosemite. When contemporary experts mocked him, he hiked into the high country, identified the Lyell, and drove stakes into an ice field on the upper flanks of the adjacent Mount Maclure. Over forty-two days in late 1871, Muir measured the downslope movement of his stakes to prove that this ice field was, in fact, a glacier, the first confirmed in the Sierra Nevada. He published the results along with descriptions of the Lyell and neighboring glaciers in articles for the *New-York Tribune* and *Overland Monthly* that made a curiously big splash and introduced the Lyell Glacier to the American public as both a remnant of the ancient engine behind Yosemite's creation and still more evidence in our collective awakening to the soothing eternities of deep time.

Stock's job has its mundanities, like middle-of-the-night phone calls from rangers explaining that, yet again, a boulder has tumbled onto a park road, and he has to jump out of bed and grab a flashlight and go look at the surrounding cliffs to evaluate whether more boulders might fall soon. That's pretty much impossible with current technology, but somebody has to make a judgment—if only so rangers can know if they should close the road—so Stock does his best.

Mostly, though, Stock lives a mountain lover's dream life. His research into the causes and patterns of rockfall allows him to make on-the-clock ascents of El Capitan and Half Dome. He also shares a cabin with his wife, Sarah Stock, who has the equally enviable job of Yosemite National Park Wildlife Ecologist—with mundanities of its own, like roadkill mammals that routinely appear in the family freezer, courtesy of well-meaning park employees who've heard that such corpses aid Sarah in research, which they do.

The Stocks' living room window looks directly up at Yosemite Falls. Bookshelves carry works by Wendell Berry, Henry David Thoreau, and, of course, Muir, who wrote such impassioned letters about glaciers to an older married woman he was courting that she felt compelled to tell him that ice ages horrified her and she much preferred flowers. (Muir insisted that glaciers were angels with folded wings; she replied, "My spirit was converted by your lovely sermon, but my flesh isn't.")

The story of Muir's insight into glaciers and Yosemite—the simple-hearted shepherd outdoing the professionals—struck such a cultural chord that it remains central to the legend of Muir as nearly every California schoolchild learns it: our very own long-bearded prophet who read the Book of Nature in the ice and then spread the word about the saving power of wilderness, ultimately convincing our forefathers to create national parks. For Stock, who grew up in a small Gold Rush town near Yosemite and read Muir in college before getting a doctorate in geology at the University of California, Santa Cruz, his work on the Lyell Glacier was more than just a chance to participate in a great research lineage. It amounted to living inside the origin myth of California's secular religion—the faith that routine exposure to our mountains and coastline will lift our lives and spirits.

The Ice Age, of course, by Stock's time had long since come to be understood as not just one glacial period but a 2.5-million-year geological epoch known as the Pleistocene, during which glaciers advanced and retreated on a roughly 100,000-year cycle. Those regular cold periods seemed to have been caused mostly by standard fluctuations in Earth's orbit and rotation and resulting changes in how much of the sun's warmth reached the planet's surface. Traces of at least four of those glacial cold periods had been identified in the Sierra Nevada. An early Yosemite geologist named François Matthes was responsible for identifying a more recent and peculiar glacial advance called the Little Ice Age, which started abruptly in about 1300, gave birth to the accumulation that became the Lyell Glacier, and got so cold in 1780 that New York Harbor froze solid. People walked from Manhattan to New Jersey. Sometime around 1850, two decades before Muir drove his stakes into the ice, the Little Ice Age ended with equally strange abruptness, and the Lyell began to retreat.

Stock knew, in other words, that the retreat of the Lyell was the latest in a long sequence of glacial retreats reaching back through time. But he also knew that this retreat was different because the Earth should have kept right on cooling into a broader glacial advance consistent with orbital cycles. Instead, the cooling associated with the Little Ice Age, and therefore the growth and expansion of the Lyell, reversed by about 1900—likely because the Industrial Revolution led to coal-burning and climate change.

Geologists are not like wildlife biologists. Stock's wife, Sarah, went into biology knowing that her work would involve bearing witness to innumerable deaths of individual animals, occasional exterminations of populations, and, given the age in which we live, even extinction events. Geologists, by contrast, go into their fields with a tacit commitment to the study of change but across vast time scales and involving such indisputably inanimate materials that it amounts to the study of no change in the context of no life and, therefore, of no death.

"There's this sense among geologists that you build on the work of others," Stock says, "and others will build on your work, and that goes off into infinity."

Nothing in Stock's professional life has prepared him to be the man who presides over the last days of a glacier, much less the end of an entire geological epoch in which glaciers have come and gone. "I suppose I was a little naive, thinking geologists didn't have to deal with this," he admits. "I've started to interact with geologists around the world, scientists who've dedicated their lives to studying glaciers and ice fields, and it's tough for all of us to realize that we're studying a system in decline, the demise of the cryosphere, that frozen part of the world."

In bedtime discussions with his wife, Stock says, "She's reminded me that all it would take to restore the glaciers would be a change in the climate—more snow and cold enough temperatures for it to pile up. My response is, 'Tell me when we're going to have the next ice age.' I feel like she's lucky in that she and other biologists can be more hands-on in fighting to restore a species. I feel sort of helpless."

I joined Stock on his annual hike last fall, south from Tuolumne Meadows along the John Muir Trail to Israel Russell's old photo point, then up Lyell Creek to the hourglass lake. On a cold, clear morning after coffee and breakfast, we walked around that lake while a breeze ruffled the water into tiny blue waves aglitter in the sunlight.

If I had not been with Stock, I would have thought what I always think in that country, which is that I love windy silence and rocky emptiness. Because I was with him, I began to see that familiar landscape more the way he sees it—not as a beautiful yet random jumble but as the coherent product of known forces that left traces everywhere, as obvious as chip marks on an unfinished block of marble in a sculptor's studio. Beyond the lake, we hiked upward on the smooth granite that is the most distinctive feature of the Yosemite high country, formed when underground reservoirs of molten stone cooled slowly over many millions of years into brilliantly hard and solid undulations of bedrock. Higher up, we climbed onto blackish-gray metamorphic rock that ran crumbling up to the broken summits—remnants of lava that erupted from those same underground reservoirs and cooled swiftly in the open air.

Stock then led the way onto a giant unstable pile of metamorphic rock—a teetering heap of boulders known as a glacial moraine—and explained that glaciers are conveyor belts, not bulldozers. Glaciers don't really push material in front of them, it turns out. They pick up loose bits and chunks of mountains, either by fracturing bedrock and plucking material beneath the ice or by collecting rock that falls from surrounding walls. The ice river then carries those bits and chunks—from pebbles to house-sized boulders—ever so slowly downhill until, at the lowermost tongue of the ice, it sets them gently down, each atop the next.

Stock pointed out lines along mountain slopes that marked the uppermost boundaries of various glaciations. He indicated which peaks and knife-thin ridges had poked into the sky above the vast ice sheet that once covered everything around us. Finally, Stock brought me to the toe of the Lyell's main lobe, a steep mass of ice 60 acres in total surface. We sat in the gravel at the base of the glacier to drink and rest.

When I climbed up onto the glacier, its physicality became overwhelming. I could hear a million tiny meltwater veins and arteries crisscrossing over and under the surface to create a fragile lattice of ice that crunched underfoot. Melt begets melt, and that lattice contoured across the bathtub-sized sun cups. Pooling water filled the sun cups until it spilled over the white ridges between them. Cylindrical holes, ranging in diameter from a dime to a baseball, held dead songbirds and little rocks and even insects that, in the darkness of their coloring, gathered enough solar radiation to melt a path downward, creating tube-like shafts as they went.

The geologist Marcia Bjornerud, author of *Timefulness: How*

Thinking Like a Geologist Can Help Save the World, told me that she once studied glaciers in the Norwegian archipelago of Svalbard and felt a temptation to think of them as alive. Meltwater in a stream on the surface of one glacier, she recalls, ebbed and flowed like a heartbeat. She was struck by how glaciers absorb snow on their uppermost reaches, digest that snow into ice, move that ice downhill through their glacial bodies, and then release it back into the world as liquid melt. In my own wanderings on glaciers, I've seen crevasses open like orifices, heard moaning sounds from inside, watched boulder-sized blocks of ice creak over slow-motion waterfalls known as icefalls. It all conjures a feeling similar to that elicited by ancient coastal redwoods or breaching whales. I like to think of this as the living sublime, a tingling awareness that the universe is more complex than our capacity for understanding and that much of what makes it beautiful is fragile and fleeting.

The pleasures of the sublime have a lot to do with my return to the high Sierra year after year, and there is something depressing about the knowledge that I will now have to confront the fragility of those mountains. Once Stock and I reached his dark spot on the Lyell, though, and sat on one of many wet boulders jutting up from the bedrock, and looked out across all those ridges and moraines, I felt the stirrings of something darker still. The end of the Little Ice Age, as punctuated by the death of the Lyell, marks the true end of the entire 2.5-million-year climate regime in which glaciers have advanced and retreated and *Homo sapiens* have evolved. We don't know what comes next, except that it will involve a warming climate unlike any that has ever supported human beings.

Back in the early nineteenth century, and even through Matthes's work on the Little Ice Age, the study of deep time carried soothing reassurance that old biblical nightmares about catastrophic upheaval were just that, nightmares. The Earth changed and always had changed unimaginably slowly. Now the study of deep time trends toward a different lesson—that Earth changes unimaginably slowly except when it changes suddenly and catastrophically, like right now. Even the driver behind our current warming—abrupt changes to the atmospheric carbon cycle—is not new, having happened at least five times in the past 500 million years. Knowing that human-driven climate change is not so different from dramatic climate changes in our planet's past offers little comfort when you consider that they all ended badly, with the mass extinction of most living things.

I will probably find a way to keep such thoughts buried when I go back to the Sierra. Maybe I'll even manage the cosmic trick of reminding myself that we are all stardust anyway. As for Stock and what he will do when the last of the Lyell's ice melts into that little creek bed and flows downhill, he surprised me by saying that he thinks about maybe working in a different park someday, like the Grand Canyon — far from any glacier and back in the realm of no change, no life, no death.

DAVID H. FREEDMAN

With a Simple Twist, a "Magic" Material Is Now the Big Thing in Physics

FROM *Quanta Magazine*

PABLO JARILLO-HERRERO IS channeling some of his copious energy into a morning run, dodging startled pedestrians as he zips along, gradually disappearing into the distance. He'd doubtlessly be moving even faster if he weren't dressed in a sports coat, slacks, and dress shoes, and confined to one of the many weirdly long corridors that crisscross the campus of the Massachusetts Institute of Technology. But what he lacks in gear and roadway he makes up for in determination, driven by the knowledge that a packed auditorium is waiting for him to take the podium.

Jarillo-Herrero has never been a slacker, but his activity has jumped several levels since his dramatic announcement in March 2018 that his lab at MIT had found superconductivity in twisted bilayer graphene—a one-atom-thick sheet of carbon crystal dropped on another one, and then rotated to leave the two layers slightly askew.

The discovery has been the biggest surprise to hit the solid-state physics field since the 2004 discovery that an intact sheet of carbon atoms—graphene—could be lifted off a block of graphite with a piece of Scotch tape, work that was later awarded the Nobel Prize. And it has ignited a frenzied race among condensed-matter physicists to explore, explain, and extend the MIT results, which have since been duplicated in several labs.

The observation of superconductivity has created an unexpected playground for physicists. The practical goals are obvious: to illuminate a path to higher-temperature superconductivity, to inspire new types of devices that might revolutionize electronics, or perhaps even to hasten the arrival of quantum computers. But more subtly, and perhaps more important, the discovery has given scientists a relatively simple platform for exploring exotic quantum effects. "There's an almost frustrating abundance of riches for studying novel physics in the magic-angle platform," said Cory Dean, a physicist at Columbia University who was among the first to duplicate the research.

All this has left Jarillo-Herrero struggling to keep up with the demands of suddenly being out in front of a red-hot field that has already garnered its own name—"twistronics." "Probably more than thirty groups are starting to work on it," he said. "In three years it will be a hundred. The field is literally exploding." Well, maybe not literally, but in every other way, it seems. He's so swamped with requests to share his techniques and give talks that nearly tripling his speaking schedule has barely made a dent in the flow of invites. Even his students are turning down speaking offers. At the American Physical Society annual meeting in March it was standing room only at his session, leaving a crowd outside the doors hoping to catch snatches of the talk.

To tease out the startling observation, his group had to nail down a precise and dauntingly elusive twist in the layers of almost exactly 1.1 degrees. That "magic" angle had long been suspected to be of special interest in twisted bilayer graphene. But no one had predicted it would be *that* interesting. "It would have been crazy to predict superconductivity based on what we knew," said Antonio Castro Neto, a physicist at the National University of Singapore. "But science moves forward not when we understand something, it's when something totally unexpected happens in experiment."

Beyond Belief

Castro Neto would know. In 2007 he suggested that pressing two misaligned graphene sheets together might produce some novel properties. (He later suggested that graphene might conceivably become superconducting under some specific conditions. "I just never put the two ideas together," he said, wistfully.)

Several groups in the U.S. and Europe were soon studying the properties of twisted bilayer graphene, and in 2011, Allan Mac-Donald, a theoretical physicist at the University of Texas, Austin, urged his colleagues to hunt for interesting behavior at a particular "magic angle." Like other theorists, MacDonald had focused on how the misalignment of the two sheets creates an angle-dependent moiré pattern—that is, a periodic grid of relatively giant cells, each of which is composed of thousands of graphene crystal cells in the two sheets. But where others had been struggling with the enormous computational complexity of determining how an electron would be affected by the thousands of atoms in a moiré cell, MacDonald hit on a simplifying concept.

He reckoned the moiré cell itself would have one property that varied strictly with rotation angle, more or less independently of the details of the atoms that made it up. That property was a critical one: the amount of energy a free electron in the cell would have to gain or shed to tunnel between the two graphene sheets. That energy difference was usually enough to serve as a barrier to intersheet tunneling. But MacDonald calculated that as the rotation angle narrowed from a larger one, the tunneling energy would shrink, finally disappearing altogether at exactly 1.1 degrees.

As that tunneling energy became small, the electrons in the sheets would slow down and become strongly correlated with one another. MacDonald didn't know exactly what would happen then. Perhaps the highly conductive graphene sheets would turn into insulators, he speculated, or the twist would evoke magnetic properties. "I frankly didn't have the tools to really say for sure what would happen in this sort of strongly correlated system," said Mac-Donald. "Certainly superconducting is the thing you most hope to see, but I didn't have the nerve to predict it."

MacDonald's ideas largely fell flat. When he submitted his paper for publication, reviewers dinged his simplifying assumptions as implausible, and the paper was rejected by several journals before landing in the *Proceedings of the National Academy of Sciences*. Then after it did come out, few experimentalists went after it. "I wasn't sure what we'd get from it," said Dean. "It felt like conjecture, so we put it aside."

Also slow to pursue the magic angle was Philip Kim, a physicist at Harvard University and a kind of dean of the experimental twisted bilayer graphene field. (Both Dean and Jarillo-Herrero were postdocs in his lab.) "I thought Allan's theory was too simple," he said. "And like most experimenters, I thought it probably wasn't possible to control the angle well enough. People started to forget about it." In fact, said Kim, he and many others in the field were just about ready to move on from twisted bilayer graphene altogether, feeling other novel materials might present more exciting opportunities.

Not Jarillo-Herrero. He had already been working on twisted bilayer graphene for a year when MacDonald's prediction was published in 2011, and he was convinced there was something to it —even after a colleague tried to warn him off it as a likely waste of time. "We try to be adventurous in this lab, and we have a good sense of smell," said Jarillo-Herrero. "This felt right."

The challenge, he knew, would be to create an ultraclean, highly homogeneous pair of graphene sheets that overcome the material's natural opposition to holding a 1.1-degree angle. Graphene sheets show a strong tendency to pull into alignment with each other. And when forced into an offset position, the superflexible sheets tend to deform.

Jarillo-Herrero's group went about polishing every aspect of the fabrication process: from creating and cleaning the sheets, to lining them up at just the right angle, to pressing them into place. The measurements had to be done in near vacuum to prevent contamination, and the results had to be cooled to within a few degrees of absolute zero to have a good chance of seeing correlated electron behavior—at higher temperatures the electrons move too energetically to have a chance to strongly interact.

The lab produced dozens of twisted bilayer graphene "devices," as researchers call them, but none of them showed significant evidence of electron correlation. Then, in 2014, one of his students brought him a device that when exposed to an electric field showed signs of distinctly ungraphene-like insulating properties. Jarillo-Herrero simply put the device aside and continued making new ones. "Our devices are complicated. You can have flipped edges and other flaws that give weird results that have nothing to do with new physics," he explains. "If you see something interesting once, you don't pay attention to it. If you see it again, you pay attention."

In the summer of 2017, doctoral student Yuan Cao, who at the age of twenty-one was already in his third year of graduate school at MIT, brought Jarillo-Herrero a new device that gave him reason to pay attention. As before, an electric field switched the device into an insulator. But this time they tried cranking up the field higher, and it suddenly switched again—into a superconductor.

The lab spent the next six months duplicating the results and nailing down measurements. The work was done in strict secrecy, a break from the typically highly open and collaborative culture of the twisted bilayer graphene field. "I had no way of knowing who else might be close to superconductivity," said Jarillo-Herrero. "We share ideas and data all the time in this field, but we're also very competitive."

In January 2018, with a paper prepared, he called an editor at *Nature,* explained what he had, and made his submission contingent on the journal agreeing to a one-week review process—a friend had told him one of the seminal CRISPR papers had received that extraordinary treatment. The journal agreed, and the paper flew through the rush review.

Jarillo-Herrero sent a prepublication email heads-up to Mac-Donald, who hadn't even known that Jarillo-Herrero had been doggedly pursuing the magic angle. "I couldn't believe it," said MacDonald. "I mean I actually found it beyond belief." Dean learned about it along with the rest of the physics community at a conference in March 2018, right around the time that the *Nature* paper came out. "The results proved me spectacularly wrong," Dean said.

The Perfect Playground

Physicists are excited about magic-angle twisted bilayer graphene not because it's likely to be a practical superconductor but because they're convinced it can illuminate the mysterious properties of superconductivity itself. For one thing, the material seems to act suspiciously like a cuprate, a type of exotic ceramic in which superconductivity can occur at temperatures up to about 140 kelvin, or halfway between absolute zero and room temperature. In addition, the sudden jumps in twisted bilayer graphene—from conducting to insulating to superconducting—with just a tweak of an external electric field indicate that free electrons are slowing to a virtual halt, notes physicist Dmitri Efetov of the Institute of Photonic Sciences (ICFO) in Barcelona, Spain. "When they stop, [the electrons] interact all the more strongly," he said. "Then they can pair up and form a superfluid." That fluidlike electron state is considered a core feature of all superconductors.

The main reason thirty years of studying cuprates has shed relatively little light on the phenomenon is that cuprates are complex, multi-element crystals. "They're poorly understood materials," said Efetov, noting that they superconduct only when precisely doped with impurities during their demanding fabrication in order to add free electrons. Twisted bilayer graphene, on the other hand, is nothing but carbon, and "doping" it with more electrons merely requires applying a readily varied electric field. "If there's any system where we can hope to understand strongly correlated electrons, it's this one," said Jarillo-Herrero. "Instead of having to grow different crystals, we just turn a voltage knob, or apply more pressure with the stamps, or change the rotation angle." A student can try to change the doping in an hour at virtually no cost, he notes, versus the months and tens of thousands of dollars it might take to try out a slightly different doping scheme on a cuprate.

Also unique, said MacDonald, is the small number of electrons that seem to be doing the heavy lifting in magic-angle twisted bilayer graphene—about one for every 100,000 carbon atoms. "It's unprecedented to see superconducting at such a low density of electrons," he said. "It's lower than anything else we've seen by at least an order of magnitude." Over 100 papers have popped up on the scientific preprint server arXiv.org that offer theories to explain what might be going on in magic-angle twisted bilayer graphene. Andrei Bernevig, a theoretical physicist at Princeton University, calls it "a perfect playground" for exploring correlated physics.

Physicists seem eager to play on it. Besides being able to flip between extremes in conductivity with a literal push of a button, notes Rebeca Ribeiro-Palau, a physicist at the Center for Nanoscience and Nanotechnology near Paris, there's already good evidence that twisted bilayer graphene's magnetic, thermal, and optical properties can be nudged into exotic behaviors as easily as its electronic properties can. "In principle you can switch any property of matter on and off," she said. MacDonald points out, for example, that some of the insulating states in twisted bilayer graphene appear to be accompanied by magnetism that arises not from the quantum spin states of the electrons, as is typically the case, but entirely from their orbital angular momentum—a theorized but never-before-observed type of magnetism.

The Coming Age of Twistronics

Now that Jarillo-Herrero's group has proven that magic angles are a thing, physicists are trying to apply the twistronics approach to other configurations of graphene. Kim's group has been experimenting with twisting two double-layers of graphene and has already found evidence of superconductivity and correlated physics. Others are stacking up three or more layers of graphene in the hopes of gaining superconductivity at other magic angles, or perhaps even when they are aligned. Bernevig posits that as the layers stack up higher and higher, physicists may be able to get the superconductivity temperature to climb along with it. Other magic angles may play a role too. Some groups are squeezing the sheets more tightly together in order to increase the magic angle, making it easier to achieve, while MacDonald suggests even richer physics may emerge at smaller, if much harder to target, magic angles.

Meanwhile, other materials are coming into the twistronics picture. Semiconductors and transitional metals can be deposited in twisted layers and are seen as good candidates for correlated physics—perhaps better than twisted bilayer graphene. "People are thinking of hundreds of materials that can be manipulated this way," said Efetov. "Pandora's box has been opened."

Dean and Efetov are among those sticking with what might already be called classic twistronics, in the hopes of boosting correlated effects in magic-angle twisted bilayer graphene devices by literally smoothing out the wrinkles in their fabrication. Because there's no chemical bonding to speak of between the two layers, and because the slightly offset layers try to settle into alignment, forcing them to hold a magic-angle twist creates stresses that lead to submicroscopic hills, valleys, and bends. Those local distortions mean that some regions of the device might be within the magic range of twist angles, while other regions are not. "I've tried gluing the edges of the layers, but there are still local variations," he complained. "Now I'm trying to figure out ways to minimize the initial strain when the layers are pressed together." Efetov has recently reported progress in doing just that, and the results have already paid off in new superconducting states at temperatures of about 3 degrees kelvin, or twice as high as previously observed.

Having burst far out into the lead of the twisted bilayer graphene field in stunning fashion, Jarillo-Herrero isn't sitting back and waiting for others to catch up. His lab's main focus remains trying to coax ever more exotic behavior out of twisted bilayer graphene, taking advantage of the fact that through long trial and error he's boosted his yield of superconducting samples to nearly 50 percent. Most other groups are struggling with yields a tenth of that or less. Given that it takes about two weeks to fabricate and test a device, that's an enormous productivity edge. "We think we're just beginning to see all the fascinating states that will come out of these magic-angle graphene systems," he said. "There's a vast phase space to explore." But to cover his bases, he's pulled his lab into also exploring twistronics in other materials.

The stakes in the race to come up with easier to make, better performing, higher-temperature superconductors are huge. Aside from the oft-evoked vision of levitating trains, reducing the energy loss in electric power transmission would boost economies and sharply cut harmful emissions around the world. Qubit fabrication could suddenly become practical, perhaps ushering in the rise of quantum computers. Even without superconductivity, ordinary computers and other electronics could get a huge boost in performance versus cost from twistronics, due to the fact that entire complex electronic circuits could in theory be built into a few sheets of pure carbon, without needing a dozen or more complexly etched layers of challenging materials common to today's chips. "You could integrate wildly different properties of matter into these circuits right next to one another, and vary them with local electric fields," said Dean. "I can't find words to describe how profound that is. I'd have to make something up. Maybe dynamic material engineering?"

However such hopes ultimately pan out, for now the excitement in twisted bilayer graphene seems only to be building. "Some may be shy to say it, but I'm not," said Castro Neto. "If the field keeps going the way it is now, somebody is going to get a Nobel Prize out of this." That sort of talk is probably premature, but even with-out it there's plenty of pressure on Jarillo-Herrero. "What my lab did creates unrealistic expectations," he admits. "Everyone seems to think we're going to produce a new breakthrough every year." He's certainly determined to make further important contribu-tions, he said, but he predicts that whatever the next electrifying discovery is, it's as likely to come out of a different lab as it is his. "I've already accepted that as a fact, and I'm fine with it," he said. "It would be boring to be in a field where you're the only one advancing it."

RIVKA GALCHEN

The Eighth Continent

FROM *The New Yorker*

IN JANUARY, THE China National Space Administration landed a spacecraft on the far side of the moon, the side we can't see from Earth. Chang'e-4 was named for a goddess in Chinese mythology, who lives on the moon for reasons connected to her husband's problematic immortality drink. The story has many versions. In one, Chang'e has been banished to the moon for elixir theft and turned into an ugly toad. In another, she has saved humanity from a tyrannical emperor by stealing the drink. In many versions, she is a luminous beauty and has as a companion a pure-white rabbit.

Chang'e-4 is the first vehicle to alight on the far side of the moon. From that side, the moon blocks radio communication with Earth, which makes landing difficult, and the surface there is craggy and rough, with a mountain taller than anything on Earth. Older geologies are exposed, from which billions of years of history can be deduced. Chang'e-4 landed in a nearly four-mile-deep hole that was formed when an ancient meteor crashed into the moon—one of the largest known impact craters in our solar system.

You may have watched the near-operatic progress of Chang'e-4's graceful landing. Or the uncannily cute robotic amblings of the lander's companion, the Yutu-2 rover, named for the moon goddess's white rabbit. You may have read that, aboard the lander, seeds germinated (cotton, rapeseed, and potato; the Chinese are also trying to grow a flowering plant known as mouse-ear cress), and that the rover survived the fourteen-day lunar night, when temperatures drop to negative 270 degrees Fahrenheit. Chang'e-4 is a step in China's long-term plan to build a base on the moon, a goal toward which the country has rapidly been advancing since it first orbited the moon, in 2007.

If you missed the Chinese mission, maybe it's because you were focused on the remarkably inexpensive spacecraft from SpaceIL, an Israeli nonprofit organization, which crash-landed into the moon on April 11, soon after taking a selfie while hovering above the lunar surface. The crash was not the original plan, and SpaceIL has already announced its intention of going to the moon again. But maybe you weren't paying attention to SpaceIL, either, because you were anticipating India's Chandrayaan-2 moon lander, expected to take off later this year. Or you were waiting for Japan's first lunar-lander-and-rover mission, scheduled to take place next year. Perhaps you've been distracted by the announcement, in January, on the night of the super blood wolf moon, that the European Space Agency plans to mine lunar ice by 2025. Or by Vice President Mike Pence's statement, in March, that the United States intends "to return American astronauts to the moon within the next five years."

Fifty years ago, three men journeyed from a small Florida peninsula to a dry crater some 240,000 miles away called the Sea of Tranquillity. Hundreds of millions of people watched on black-and-white TVs as a man from Wapakoneta, Ohio, climbed slowly down a short ladder and reported in a steady voice that his footprint had depressed the soil only a fraction of an inch, that "the surface appears to be very fine-grained as you get close to it, it's almost like a powder down there, it's very fine."

Shortly before NASA launched Apollo 11, it received a letter from the Union of Persian Storytellers, begging NASA to change the plan: a moon landing would rob the world of its illusions, and rob the union's members of their livelihood. During the spacecraft's flight, the Mission Control Center, in Houston, asked the crew to look out for Chang'e, and for her bunny too. Houston said that the bunny would be "easy to spot, since he is always standing on his hind feet in the shade of a cinnamon tree." Buzz Aldrin responded, "We'll keep a close eye out for the bunny girl."

"The moon is hot again," Jack Burns, the director of the NASA-funded Network for Exploration and Space Science, told me. NESS's headquarters are at the University of Colorado, Boulder, which has educated nineteen astronauts. (Boulder was also the setting for the television sitcom *Mork & Mindy*, in which Robin Williams played an alien from the planet Ork.) Part of NESS's mission is to dream up experiments to be done on the moon. An informational poster at the entrance reads "Challenges of Measuring Cosmic Dawn with the 21-cm Sky-Averaged, Global Signal." In the decades since Apollo 11, NASA has invented Earth-mapping satellites, launched the Hubble Space Telescope, collaborated on the International Space Station, and studied Mars. But none of these projects have generated the broad and childlike wonder of the moon.

Burns, who is sixty-six years old, remembers the Mercury, Gemini, and Apollo missions—the Cold War–era efforts, beginning in the late fifties, that put men in space and finally landed them on the moon. He teaches a course on the history of space policy. "The U.S. had already lost the start of the space race," he said, of the origins of Apollo. "The Soviet Union was first with a satellite in space. They were first with an astronaut in space." Yuri Gagarin's journey into outer space took place in April 1961. President John F. Kennedy delivered his moon-shot speech the following month, and Congress eventually allocated 4.4 percent of the national budget to NASA. "But, if you live by political motivations, you die by political motivations," Burns said. "Apollo died. Nixon killed the program." Only twelve people have walked on the moon, all of them between the summer of 1969 and Christmas 1972. All the moon-walkers were men, all were American, all but one were Boy Scouts, and almost all listened to country-and-Western music on their way to the moon; they earned eight dollars a day, minus a fee for a bed on the spacecraft. Since the last moon-walk, humans have launched crafts that have orbited the moon, crashed probes into it, and taken increasingly detailed photos of it. But no one has been back.

The planetary scientist Bruce Hapke, who has a yellowish, opaque lunar mineral—hapkeite—named for him, said, "Almost every president since Nixon proposed going back to the moon." (President Obama focused instead on studying an asteroid near Earth and working toward the distant goal of sending astronauts to Mars.) "But the money was never allotted. Congress decided we couldn't have guns and the moon at the same time." The Department of Defense's budget is now nearly $700 billion, whereas

NASA's funding is $21.5 billion, or around half of 1 percent of the national budget. The U.S. is still believed to spend more on space programs than the rest of the world combined. (China's budget, however, is unknown.) Hapke said, "The trouble is, there was always some kind of emergency, always some war going on. Though that Cold War mentality also got us to the moon."

Hapke recalls being told by several scientists and NASA employees that, "when the moon landing was first conceived, it was a strictly political stunt: go to the moon, plant the flag, and come back to Earth." The original design of the spacecraft allotted little to no room for scientific payloads. "When the scientific community got wind of this, they pointed out strongly to NASA all the fantastic science that could be done, and the whole tone of the project was changed," he said. Hapke was then at Cornell, where he and his lab mates studied what the lunar soil might be like; the moon's characteristic reflectivity helped them deduce that the surface must be a fine dust. For Hapke, the Apollo era remains the most exciting time in his scientific life. He also recalls "the widespread puzzlement in both Congress and the general populace after the first landing: 'We beat the Russians. Why are we going back?'"

Burns said, "This time we need a more sustainable set of goals and reasons" for going to the moon. He meant a science mission, or a business mission, or both. "We don't like to say we're going back to the moon," but forward, he added. "Our objectives are different. Our technology is different. Apollo had five kilobytes of RAM. Your iPhone is millions of times more powerful." Watching the footage of Neil Armstrong's first steps, it takes a moment for one's eyes to make sense of the low-resolution image, which could easily be overexposed film or a Robert Motherwell painting. "It's amazing they made it."

Burns told me that advances in engineering could turn the moon into a way station for launching rockets and satellites farther into the solar system, to Mars and beyond. (The weak gravity on the moon dramatically eases launches.) Lunar construction projects now look feasible. "Down the hall, we have a telerobotics lab," Burns said. "You could print components of habitats, of telescopes. You use the lunar regolith"—the dust of the moon—"as your printing material. You could print the wrench you need to fix something." Fifteen years ago, the moon was believed to be a dry rock; now we know that there's water there. Both private industry and national agencies regard the mining of water and precious materials as something that's not too far off. There's space tourism too, though the quiet consensus among scientists seems to be that the idea is goofy and impractical.

NASA would like to establish a permanent presence on the moon, using reusable rockets and landers. The agency is working on the largest, strongest, fastest—of course—rocket yet, but it plans to purchase other equipment, including rockets and landers, off the shelf, from commercial companies. Bob Jacobs, a spokesperson for NASA, told me, "Eighty-five percent of NASA's budget is for commercial contracts. We build what only we can build; the other services we look to purchase from approved venders."

Burns likens this de facto government support of commercial space exploration to the dawn of the airline industry: "In the nineteen-twenties, early airline companies survived only because the government paid them to deliver the mail." It wasn't until later, when ordinary people became aeronauts, that the airline industry became economically viable. "I think we're looking at something similar with space exploration," Burns said.

There are also more emotionally leveraged business models, like that of Celestis, a funeral-services company, which puts cremains into space, and has plans to take them to the moon. The Japanese beverage Pocari Sweat wants to be the first sports drink on the moon. Its manufacturer has booked a spot on a lunar lander developed by a Pittsburgh-based company, Astrobotic, which is scheduled to launch in 2021, and to land in the Lacus Mortis—the Lake of Death, which is actually a dry, flat area. Pocari Sweat employees have collected stories of children's dreams from across Asia and etched them onto titanium plates. The plates will be put inside a capsule designed to look like a Pocari Sweat can, and will travel with some Pocari Sweat powder that will one day—so the plan goes —be mixed with moon water.

Even in fantasy, space ventures have always mingled idealistic and worldly motives. H. G. Wells published "The First Men in the Moon" in 1901. The novel's narrator, Mr. Bedford, wants to make money. His collaborator, Mr. Cavor, dreams of knowledge. Together they go to the moon. When they encounter moon dwellers —"compact, bristling" creatures, "having much of the quality of a complicated insect"—Bedford wants to destroy them; Cavor wants to learn from them. Bedford finds gold, and embarks "upon an argument to show the infinite benefits our arrival would confer upon the moon," involving himself "in a rather difficult proof that the arrival of Columbus was, on the whole, beneficial to America." Cavor is indifferent to the gold—it's a familiar mineral. Moon dwellers capture and chain Bedford and Cavor, then march them underground. Cavor assumes that there must be other, less brutal moon dwellers, as enlightened and knowledge-loving as he. In the end, Bedford makes it back to Earth. Cavor is presumed dead. But no one with a heart reads the novel and wants to be Bedford.

Burns grew up in Shirley, Massachusetts. Neither of his parents graduated from high school. From the age of five, he knew that he wanted to study the stars. When I asked him what he hopes to see on the moon, he became suddenly boyish: "I'd love to set up a low-frequency radio telescope on the far side of the moon, free from the interference of Earth signals. It could see to the beginnings of time. And the far side of the moon has craters there that were formed during the Late Heavy Bombardment, four billion years ago." During the Late Heavy Bombardment, large numbers of meteors crashed into the inner solar system. The period coincides roughly—and perhaps not coincidentally—with the beginnings of life on Earth. Burns said, "Earth was also bombarded, but here that history has been erased or buried by weather, erosion. On the moon, it's still right there on the surface. It's a history book. I'd like to read that book."

The night I met with Burns was the eve of a supermoon—when the moon is both full and as close to Earth as it gets. I walked over to the Sommers-Bausch Observatory, not far from Burns's office; there was a bunny in the bushes, trying not to be noticed. Carla Johns, who operates the observatory's telescopes, met me in the hallway, which is lit in red, to keep your eyes adapted to the dark. On the top floor, she pressed a button, and the roof noisily rolled back. There it was, with all its starry friends. Johns explained how the telescopes worked—they are essentially buckets of light. She said that children often shout when they see the moon so close.

Johns showed me a collection of small telescopes, and discussed the eighteenth-century French astronomer Charles Messier. "Back then, the way astronomers made money was finding comets and telling kings they had a comet to name after them," she said. When

Messier was eleven, his father died, and afterward he received no formal schooling. But he developed an exceptional gift for finding comets. "To find those comets, he documented everything he could see in the sky," Johns said. "Once he was sure a sky object wasn't a comet, it was of no interest to him. Some of that stuff he found turned out to be Andromeda, and the Crab Nebula." She showed me a large telescope on a mount developed by John Dobson, a chemist by training, who worked briefly on the Manhattan Project, then resolved to spend the rest of his life as a monk. While living at a monastery in San Francisco, he would walk the shipyards, gathering old porthole glass to fashion into homemade telescopes, which he would share with others in sidewalk astronomy lectures. "The monks eventually asked him to leave," Johns said.

Johns became a telescope operator relatively late in her professional life. She had worked in human resources, and enjoyed it, but at a difficult moment she found herself at the Denver Museum of Nature & Science, where her parents used to take her as a child. "I looked through the telescope and I began to cry," she said. She had always loved science, but had chosen another career because of family and financial issues. "I said to myself, 'I need to be involved with this.'"

Shortly before the turnoff for the town of Mojave, California, there were train cars along the right side of the road, painted old-fashioned black and standing still. On the left were hundreds of white wind turbines, spinning. Soon I came to a slightly weathered sign for the Mojave Air and Space Port—IMAGINATION FLIES HERE — which features a picture of a young boy holding a toy plane. You're allowed to launch rockets here; you're allowed to fly objects beyond the atmosphere. A number of aerospace firms have offices at the port.

In November 2018, NASA named nine companies to be part of its Commercial Lunar Payload Services program: if NASA wants to send something to the moon, these companies are approved to provide transportation. "FedEx to space," I was told to think of it. "Or DHL." Some of them are large and well known, like Lockheed Martin Space. Masten Space Systems has sixteen employees. It is based at the Air and Space Port, down the road from Virgin Galactic, in offices that resemble the extra building my elementary school put in the playground when enrollment exceeded capacity. When Masten won a NASA-funded prize—for vertical takeoff and precision landing in conditions simulating those of the moon—it had five employees. Its winning rocket, Xoie, looks like a slim, silvery water tower, only 90 inches tall—two stacked spheres on a tripod, with tanks of helium on the sides.

"Our focus is on reusable rockets," Masten's CEO, Sean Mahoney, told me. "We have a rocket that has flown two hundred and twenty-seven times. We want space to be affordable." Masten plans to begin taking payloads to the moon in 2021: "Mostly science payloads, mostly NASA. Some commercial." Among the items that NASA wants to send are a solar-power cell and a navigation device that the agency will test in lunar conditions.

Mahoney and I talked over a meal at the Voyager Restaurant, on the grounds of the spaceport. The Voyager looks like Mel's Diner, from the TV show *Alice*. (A lot about lunar exploration reminded me of old television shows, especially *Bonanza*.) I had a grilled-cheese sandwich—spaceport food. Mahoney said, "There's the PBS version of space, which is beautiful. And that is real. But, also, space—well, you've heard of the military-industrial complex? Space is an offshoot of that." Something shiny and fleet was taking off in the distance, and the windows shook. Mahoney pointed out a tumbleweed blowing across the lot. "I'm a business guy by background, not a space guy, so I had to learn all of this," he said. Mahoney believes that, because the space industry was a government-sanctioned monopoly for decades, there was no room for risk, or for competition; the fear of failure dominated. "Lockheed Martin and Boeing could charge exorbitant prices," he said. "As a businessperson, when you see a fat margin—when you see a service that can be provided much more cheaply—you see value."

We walked through strong winds to the hangars where Masten does its manufacturing. There were none of the vacuum chambers and clean white rooms that one associates with rocket science. Instead, there were trailer beds loaded with rocket parts for testing; there were purple-and-yellow long-sleeved T-shirts for launch days. There were tanks of helium, wrenches of every size. A young man wearing an Embry-Riddle Aeronautical University sweatshirt and a welding mask was making an engine casing.

Mahoney pointed out an engine without its casing, next to a

small computer. "Some of these rocket models are literally operated by Raspberry Pi," he said.

"Raspberry pie?"

"That's a very basic computer. A thirty-five-dollar computer. My point being, some of our parts we can buy at Home Depot."

Masten was founded, in 2004, by David Masten, a former software-and-systems engineer, who remains the chief technical officer. "When I was a kid, I was going to be an astronaut," Masten told me. "But, by the 1980s, space was getting boring—it wasn't going anywhere—and there was this new thing called computers." He became an IT consultant, and eventually worked at a series of start-ups. Throughout, Masten's hobby remained rockets. "My thought was that, maybe, instead of doing the heavy analysis traditional of the aerospace industry, you do something more like I was used to," he said. "You write some code, you compile it, you test it, and you iterate over and over in a tight, rapid fashion. I wanted to apply that method to rocketry."

When a Masten rocket takes off, it has a delicate appearance. One of the newer ones, the Xodiac, looks like two golden balloons mounted on a metal skeleton. A kite tail of fire shoots out as the Xodiac launches straight up; at its apex, it has the ability to tilt and float down at an angle, as casually as a leaf. When Xodiac nears its designated landing spot, it abruptly slows, aligns, seems to hesitate, lands. It's eerie—at that moment, the rocket seems sentient, intentional.

In one demonstration, the Xodiac performed a deceptively mundane task: it carried a "planetvac"—an invention intended to vacuum dust from the lunar surface—up and over one meter, deployed the vacuum, then scooted up and over another meter, hopping like a lunar janitor. The rockets are self-guided, unless overridden by a human; they are doing their own thing. "We believe computers can fly rockets better than people can," Masten told me.

Many scientists see little need for humans on the moon, since robots would do the work more safely and inexpensively.

"Now, you will ask me what in the world we went up on the Moon for," Qfwfq, the narrator of Italo Calvino's *Cosmicomics,* says. "We went to collect the milk, with a big spoon and a bucket." In our

world, we are going for water. "Water is the oil of space," George
Sowers, a professor of space resources at the Colorado School of
Mines, in Golden, told me. On the windowsill of Sowers's office is a
bumper sticker that reads MY OTHER VEHICLE EXPLORED PLUTO.
This is because his other vehicle *did* explore Pluto. Sowers served
as the chief systems engineer of the rocket that, in 2006, launched
NASA's New Horizons spacecraft, which has flown by Pluto and
continued on to Ultima Thule, a snowman-shaped, 19-mile-long
rock that is the most distant object a spacecraft has ever reached.
"I only got into space resources in the past two years," he said. His
laboratory at the School of Mines designs, among other things,
small vehicles that could one day be controlled by artificial intelligence and used to mine lunar water.

Water in space is valuable for drinking, of course, and as a
source of oxygen. Sowers told me that it can also be transformed
into rocket fuel. "The moon could be a gas station," he said. That
sounded terrible to me, but not to most of the scientists I spoke
to. "It could be used to refuel rockets on the way to Mars"—a trip
that would take about nine months—"or considerably beyond,
at a fraction of the cost of launching them from Earth," Sowers
said. He explained that launching fuel from the moon rather than
from Earth is like climbing the Empire State Building rather than
Mount Everest. Fuel accounts for around 90 percent of the weight
of a rocket, and every kilogram of weight brought from Earth to
the moon costs roughly $35,000; if you don't have to bring fuel
from Earth, it becomes much cheaper to send a probe to Jupiter.

Down the hall, in the Center for Space Resources' laboratory,
near buckets of lunar and asteroid simulants, was a small 3-D
printer. Four graduate students were assembled there with Angel
Abbud-Madrid, the center's director. I asked them how difficult it
would be to 3-D-print, say, an electrolyzer—the machine needed
to separate the hydrogen and oxygen in water to make rocket fuel.
They laughed.

"Here, let me show you something very fancy," Hunter Williams,
who was wearing sapphire-colored earrings, said. He poured some
Morton sea salt into a plastic cup and added water. He stuck two
silver thumbtacks through the bottom of the plastic cup, then held
a battery up to them. Small bubbles began forming on the thumbtacks. The oxygen was separating from the hydrogen. You probably did this experiment in middle school, without knowing that

you were doing rocket science. "The idea is for whatever goes up to the moon to be that simple," Williams said. "To be that basic."

"It would be like living off the land," Ben Thrift, another graduate student, added. Thrift studied theater as an undergraduate, and later ran a bakery, before earning a degree in engineering and enrolling in the space-resources program. "I decided to grow up and do something real," he said.

"By 'real,' he means go to the moon," Abbud-Madrid said.

"Transportation is not an end in itself," Sowers told me. He is excited about solar power, which already runs many satellites in space, where there is no night, or clouds. He speculates that, if we had a base on the moon, we could use 3-D printers to make giant solar panels, as large as two kilometers, which could be launched into orbit; the resulting power could be beamed back to Earth via microwave radiation. "Space solar would be an unlimited, inexhaustible source of green energy," Sowers said. "It requires no magic, and much of the technology is ready. I think we could do it by 2030, if we wanted to." Another bumper sticker in Sowers's office reads PHYSICISTS HAVE STRANGE QUARKS.

Other specialists have a different view of the resources available in space. Asteroids contain precious metals, such as platinum, palladium, and gold. A number of asteroid-mining companies have come and gone since 2015, when Neil deGrasse Tyson remarked that "the first trillionaire there'll ever be is the person who mines asteroids for their natural resources." But asteroid hunting is like whaling, in the length of its missions and the speculative nature of its success; the moon is only three days away, and its movements are extremely well known to us. NASA recently named ten companies as potential contractors for equipment to gather and analyze soil in space.

One of them was Honeybee Robotics. I visited its exploration-technology division, in Pasadena, which, from the outside, looks as dull as fro-yo, a collection of beige concrete buildings. Inside were lunar-rock samplers, the planetvac that was tested on a Masten rocket, some Nerf guns, and WINE (which stands for "World Is Not Enough"), a steam-powered spacecraft designed to find water in lunar dirt (or on asteroids), convert it to energy, then hop to the next site, to pull up samples and more water for fuel.

Kris Zacny, a vice president of Honeybee Robotics, was expecting his third child in the next few days. "So much has to do with where you're born," he said, explaining how he came to the field of space mining. Zacny is originally from Poland, the son of a musician father, who wanted him to be a musician as well. "What a disappointment I must have been," Zacny said. "I spent my time thinking about the moon." When he was seventeen, his family moved to South Africa. Zacny went to college on a scholarship from De Beers, and worked in the diamond mines while in school. "I graduated top of my class, with a degree in mechanical engineering, and next thing I knew I was twelve thousand feet underground," he said. He spent two years in a coal mine, and a month in a gold mine that at the time was the deepest mine in the world. "I always dreamed of space, but it wasn't an option for me," he said.

In 2000, he landed a one-year position as a research assistant for a professor in Berkeley's Materials Science and Engineering Department. "I knew it was too late for me to be a space guy, I accepted that. But I had the mining expertise. I said to the professor, 'Don't laugh at me, but I'd like to do extraterrestrial mining.'" What can be found on the moon remains for the most part unknown, though there is reasoned speculation. Honeybee is one of a growing number of companies that are developing standardized lunar rovers. Small countries with no national space agency, as well as private entities, could soon have their own robotic resource hunters roving around the moon, with little honeycomb emblems on their sides.

Buzz Aldrin had hoped, and briefly expected, that it would be he, and not Neil Armstrong, who would take the first human step on the moon. The astronaut Michael Collins, who manned the control module that orbited the moon while Armstrong and Aldrin walked below, has said of Aldrin that he "resents not being first on the moon more than he appreciates being second." On the moon, Armstrong took photos of Aldrin posing, but Aldrin took none of Armstrong doing the same. One of the few photos that shows Neil Armstrong on the moon was taken by Armstrong himself—of his reflection in Aldrin's helmet, as Aldrin salutes the flag. We are petty and misbehave on Earth; we will be petty and misbehave in space.

The guiding laws of space are defined by the Outer Space

Treaty, from 1967, which has been signed by 108 countries, including all those with substantial space programs. "Laws that govern outer space are similar to the laws for the high seas," Alain Berinstain, the vice president of global development at the lunar-exploration company Moon Express, explained. "If you are two hundred miles away from the continental shelf, those waters don't belong to anybody—they belong to everybody." Moon Express describes the moon as the eighth continent. The company, which is based in Florida, is hoping to deliver its first lander to the moon in 2020; on board will be telescopes and the Celestis cremains. "If you look down at the waters from your ship and see fish, those fish belong to everybody," Berinstain continued. "But, if you put a net down and pull those fish onto the deck of the ship, they're yours. This could change, but right now that is how the U.S. is interpreting the Outer Space Treaty."

Individual countries have their own interpretations of the treaty, and set up their own regulatory frameworks. Luxembourg promotes itself as "a unique legal, regulatory and business environment" for companies devoted to space resources, and is the first European country to pass legislation similar to that of the U.S., deeming resources collected in space to be ownable by private entities.

It's not difficult to imagine moon development, like all development, proceeding less than peacefully, and less than equitably. (At least, unlike with colonization on Earth, there are no natives whose land we're taking, or so we assume.) Philip Metzger, a planetary physicist at the University of Central Florida, said, "I'm really glad that all these countries, all these companies, are going to the moon. But there will be problems." Any country can withdraw from the Outer Space Treaty by giving a year's notice. "If any country feels it has a sufficient lead in space, that is a motivation to withdraw from the treaty," he said.

So there is a tacit space race already. On the one hand, every national space agency applauded the success of the Chang'e-4 lander. The mission had science partnerships with Germany, the Netherlands, Saudi Arabia, and Sweden. NASA collaborates with many countries in space, sharing data, communications networks, and expertise. Russian rockets bring American astronauts to the International Space Station. When, in response to economic sanctions, the head of the Russian space agency said that maybe the

American astronauts could get to the ISS by trampoline, the comment was dismissed as posturing. Still, NASA has contracted with Boeing and SpaceX, Elon Musk's rocket company, to begin taking astronauts to the ISS this year—which means the U.S. will no longer rely on Russia for that. Russia and China say they will work together on a moon base. NASA used to collaborate with the China National Space Administration; in 2011, six months after members of NASA visited the CNSA, Congress passed a bill that effectively prohibited collaboration.

It's natural to want to leave the moon undisturbed; it's also clear that humanity will disturb it. But do we need to live there? Jeff Bezos, the founder of Amazon, envisages zoning the moon for heavy industry, and Earth for light industry and residential purposes. Bezos's company Blue Origin is developing reusable rockets intended to bring humans reliably back and forth from space, with the long-term goal of creating manufacturing plants there, in zero gravity. Earth would be eased of its industrial burden, and the lower-gravity conditions would be beneficial for making certain goods, such as fiber-optic cables.

"There's the argument that we've destroyed the Earth and now we're going to destroy the moon. But I don't see it that way," Metzger said. "The resources in space are billions of times greater than on Earth. Space pretty much erases everything we do. If you crush an asteroid to dust, the solar wind will blow it away. We can't really mess up the solar system."

The most likely origin story for the moon is that it was formed four and a half billion years ago, after a Mars-size planet called Theia crashed into Earth. Theia broke into thousands of pieces, which orbited Earth. Slowly—or quickly, depending on your time scale —the shards coalesced and formed the moon we know today, the one that is drifting away from us, at a rate of four centimeters or so per year. If we had two moons, like Mars does, or sixty-two, like Saturn, we wouldn't feel the same way about our moon.

Zou Xiaoduan, a scientist who worked on all phases of the Chang'e project, was born in 1983 in Guizhou province, in southwest China—"a very poor place back then," she told me. As a child, she said, she "was stunned to learn that the moon was not a weird monster following me around." She remembers hearing her family chatting about the Apollo missions. That men had been on the moon seemed unfathomable to her. She asked every adult to confirm it. She wanted to become an astronaut—a goal she attributes to there not being any Disney movies for her to watch. She began work on China's lunar program in 2006. "I still recall the first lunar image from Chang'e-1 being shown to me," she said, of the images sent home in 2007, during China's first lunar orbital mission. "And the first time Chang'e-2 flew by an asteroid, 4179 Toutatis," three years later. "No one had ever seen that asteroid." Zou came to the U.S. in 2015, and now works for the Planetary Science Institute, in Tucson. She is part of a NASA mission studying the asteroid Bennu, which NASA describes as "an ancient relic of the solar system's early days." Like everyone else I spoke to who studies the moon, she loves her job. Of her work on the Chang'e missions, she said that every image has been "thrilling, every moment is a 'wow.'" She continued, "I'm just so excited and super happy that I picked this career."

The twelve men who walked on the moon, who saw Earth as a distant object—did they lose their illusions? A couple had alcohol problems, one cofounded the Institute of Noetic Sciences, and one became an evangelical preacher. One became a one-term Republican senator who has denied that humans are responsible for climate change; another became a painter, of the moon. Neil Armstrong was one of the few who had a mostly steady, unremarkable post-moon-walk life. He moved to a dairy farm and became a professor at the University of Cincinnati. Nearly a decade after his trip to the moon, he wrote a short poem for a syndicated children's page that ran in many newspapers. The eight-line verse was titled "My Vacation." It begins with the gentle, familiar cadence of a nursery rhyme, describing his mission as checking on whether the moon was made of green cheese. Though no cheese was found, he specifies, and also no bees and no trees, he does mention the remarkable view of Earth, and concludes of the alien moon:

It's a nice place to visit, and I'm certain that you
Will enjoy it when you get to go.

BAHAR GHOLIPOUR

The Tumultuous History of a Mysterious Brain Signal That Questioned Free Will

FROM *The Atlantic*

THE DEATH OF free will began with thousands of finger taps. In 1964, two German scientists monitored the electrical activity of a dozen people's brains. Each day for several months, volunteers came into the scientists' lab at the University of Freiburg to get wires fixed to their scalp from a showerhead-like contraption overhead. The participants sat in a chair, tucked neatly in a metal tollbooth, with only one task: to flex a finger on their right hand at whatever irregular intervals pleased them, over and over, up to 500 times a visit.

The purpose of this experiment was to search for signals in the participants' brains that preceded each finger tap. At the time, researchers knew how to measure brain activity that occurred in response to events out in the world—when a person hears a song, for instance, or looks at a photograph—but no one had figured out how to isolate the signs of someone's brain actually initiating an action.

The experiment's results came in squiggly, dotted lines, a representation of changing brain waves. In the milliseconds leading up to the finger taps, the lines showed an almost undetectably faint uptick: a wave that rose for about a second, like a drumroll of firing neurons, then ended in an abrupt crash. This flurry of neuronal activity, which the scientists called the *Bereitschaftspotential*, or readiness potential, was like a gift of infinitesimal time travel. For the first time, they could see the brain readying itself to create a voluntary movement.

This momentous discovery was the beginning of a lot of trouble in neuroscience. Twenty years later, the American physiologist Benjamin Libet used the *Bereitschaftspotential* to make the case not only that the brain shows signs of a decision before a person acts, but that, incredibly, the brain's wheels start turning before the person even consciously intends to do something. Suddenly, people's choices—even a basic finger tap—appeared to be determined by something outside of their own perceived volition.

As a philosophical question, whether humans have control over their own actions had been fought over for centuries before Libet walked into a lab. But Libet introduced a genuine neurological argument against free will. His finding set off a new surge of debate in science and philosophy circles. And over time, the implications have been spun into cultural lore.

Today, the notion that our brains make choices before we are even aware of them will now pop up in cocktail-party conversation or in a review of *Black Mirror*. It's covered by mainstream journalism outlets, including *This American Life, Radiolab,* and this magazine. Libet's work is frequently brought up by popular intellectuals such as Sam Harris and Yuval Noah Harari to argue that science has proved humans are not the authors of their actions.

It would be quite an achievement for a brain signal 100 times smaller than major brain waves to solve the problem of free will. But the story of the *Bereitschaftspotential* has one more twist: it might be something else entirely.

The *Bereitschaftspotential* was never meant to get entangled in free-will debates. If anything, it was pursued to show that the brain has a will of sorts. The two German scientists who discovered it, a young neurologist named Hans Helmut Kornhuber and his doctoral student Lüder Deecke, had grown frustrated with their era's scientific approach to the brain as a passive machine that merely produces thoughts and actions in response to the outside world. Over lunch in 1964, the pair decided that they would figure out how the brain works to spontaneously generate an action. "Kornhuber and I believed in free will," says Deecke, who is now eighty-one and lives in Vienna.

To pull off their experiment, the duo had to come up with tricks to circumvent limited technology. They had a state-of-the-art computer to measure their participants' brain waves, but it worked only after it detected a finger tap. So to collect data on what happened in the brain beforehand, the two researchers realized that they could record their participants' brain activity separately on tape, then play the reels backwards into the computer. This inventive technique, dubbed "reverse-averaging," revealed the *Bereitschaftspotential*.

The discovery garnered widespread attention. The Nobel laureate John Eccles and the prominent philosopher of science Karl Popper compared the study's ingenuity to Galileo's use of sliding balls for uncovering the laws of motion of the universe. With a handful of electrodes and a tape recorder, Kornhuber and Deecke had begun to do the same for the brain.

What the *Bereitschaftspotential* actually meant, however, was anyone's guess. Its rising pattern appeared to reflect the dominoes of neural activity falling one by one on a track toward a person doing something. Scientists explained the *Bereitschaftspotential* as the electrophysiological sign of planning and initiating an action. Baked into that idea was the implicit assumption that the *Bereitschaftspotential* causes that action. The assumption was so natural, in fact, no one second-guessed it—or tested it.

Libet, a researcher at the University of California at San Francisco, questioned the *Bereitschaftspotential* in a different way. Why does it take half a second or so between deciding to tap a finger and actually doing it? He repeated Kornhuber and Deecke's experiment, but asked his participants to watch a clocklike apparatus so that they could remember the moment they made a decision. The results showed that while the *Bereitschaftspotential* started to rise about 500 milliseconds before the participants performed an action, they reported their decision to take that action only about 150 milliseconds beforehand. "The brain evidently 'decides' to initiate the act" before a person is even aware that decision has taken place, Libet concluded.

To many scientists, it seemed implausible that our conscious awareness of a decision is only an illusory afterthought. Researchers questioned Libet's experimental design, including the precision of the tools used to measure brain waves and the accuracy with which people could actually recall their decision time. But flaws were hard to pin down. And Libet, who died in 2007, had as many defenders as critics. In the decades since his experiment, study after study has replicated his finding using more modern technology such as fMRI.

But one aspect of Libet's results sneaked by largely unchallenged: the possibility that what he was seeing was accurate, but that his conclusions were based on an unsound premise. What if the *Bereitschaftspotential* didn't cause actions in the first place? A few notable studies did suggest this, but they failed to provide any clue to what the *Bereitschaftspotential* could be instead. To dismantle such a powerful idea, someone had to offer a real alternative.

In 2010, Aaron Schurger had an epiphany. As a researcher at the National Institute of Health and Medical Research in Paris, Schurger studied fluctuations in neuronal activity, the churning hum in the brain that emerges from the spontaneous flickering of hundreds of thousands of interconnected neurons. This ongoing electrophysiological noise rises and falls in slow tides, like the surface of the ocean—or, for that matter, like anything that results from many moving parts. "Just about every natural phenomenon that I can think of behaves this way. For example, the stock market's financial time series or the weather," Schurger says.

From a bird's-eye view, all these cases of noisy data look like any other noise, devoid of pattern. But it occurred to Schurger that if someone lined them up by their peaks (thunderstorms, market records) and reverse-averaged them in the manner of Kornhuber and Deecke's innovative approach, the results' visual representations would look like climbing trends (intensifying weather, rising stocks). There would be no *purpose* behind these apparent trends —no prior plan to cause a storm or bolster the market. Really, the pattern would simply reflect how various factors had happened to coincide.

"I thought, *Wait a minute,*" Schurger says. If he applied the same method to the spontaneous brain noise he studied, what shape would he get? "I looked at my screen, and I saw something that looked like the *Bereitschaftspotential.*" Perhaps, Schurger realized, the *Bereitschaftspotential*'s rising pattern wasn't a mark of a brain's brewing intention at all, but something much more circumstantial.

Two years later, Schurger and his colleagues Jacobo Sitt and Stanislas Dehaene proposed an explanation. Neuroscientists know that for people to make any type of decision, our neurons need to gather evidence for each option. The decision is reached when one group of neurons accumulates evidence past a certain threshold. Sometimes, this evidence comes from sensory information from the outside world: if you're watching snow fall, your brain will weigh the number of falling snowflakes against the few caught in the wind, and quickly settle on the fact that the snow is moving downward.

But Libet's experiment, Schurger pointed out, provided its subjects with no such external cues. To decide when to tap their fingers, the participants simply acted whenever the moment struck them. Those spontaneous moments, Schurger reasoned, must have coincided with the haphazard ebb and flow of the participants' brain activity. They would have been more likely to tap their fingers when their motor system happened to be closer to a threshold for movement initiation.

This would not imply, as Libet had thought, that people's brains "decide" to move their fingers before they know it. Hardly. Rather, it would mean that the noisy activity in people's brains sometimes happens to tip the scale if there's nothing else to base a choice on, saving us from endless indecision when faced with an arbitrary task. The *Bereitschaftspotential* would be the rising part of the brain fluctuations that tend to coincide with the decisions. This is a highly specific situation, not a general case for all, or even many, choices.

Other recent studies support the idea of the *Bereitschaftspotential* as a symmetry-breaking signal. In a study of monkeys tasked with choosing between two equal options, a separate team of researchers saw that a monkey's upcoming choice correlated with its intrinsic brain activity before the monkey was even presented with options.

In a new study under review for publication in the *Proceedings of the National Academy of Sciences,* Schurger and two Princeton researchers repeated a version of Libet's experiment. To avoid unintentionally cherry-picking brain noise, they included a control condition in which people didn't move at all. An artificial-intelligence classifier allowed them to find at what point brain activity in the two conditions diverged. If Libet was right, that should have happened at 500 milliseconds before the movement. But the algorithm couldn't tell any difference until about only 150 milliseconds before the movement, the time people reported making decisions in Libet's original experiment.

In other words, people's subjective experience of a decision —what Libet's study seemed to suggest was just an illusion—appeared to match the actual moment their brains showed them making a decision.

When Schurger first proposed the neural-noise explanation, in 2012, the paper didn't get much outside attention, but it did create a buzz in neuroscience. Schurger received awards for overturning a long-standing idea. "It showed the *Bereitschaftspotential* may not be what we thought it was. That maybe it's in some sense artifactual, related to how we analyze our data," says Uri Maoz, a computational neuroscientist at Chapman University.

For a paradigm shift, the work met minimal resistance. Schurger appeared to have unearthed a classic scientific mistake, so subtle that no one had noticed it and no amount of replication studies could have solved it, unless they started testing for causality. Now, researchers who questioned Libet and those who supported him are both shifting away from basing their experiments on the *Bereitschaftspotential*. (The few people I found still holding the traditional view confessed that they had not read Schurger's 2012 paper.)

"It's opened my mind," says Patrick Haggard, a neuroscientist at University College London who collaborated with Libet and reproduced the original experiments.

It's still possible that Schurger is wrong. Researchers broadly accept that he has deflated Libet's model of *Bereitschaftspotential*, but the inferential nature of brain modeling leaves the door cracked for an entirely different explanation in the future. And unfortunately for popular-science conversation, Schurger's groundbreaking work does not solve the pesky question of free will any more than Libet's did. If anything, Schurger has only deepened the question.

Is everything we do determined by the cause-and-effect chain of genes, environment, and the cells that make up our brain, or can we freely form intentions that influence our actions in the world? The topic is immensely complicated, and Schurger's valiant debunking underscores the need for more precise and better-informed questions.

"Philosophers have been debating free will for millennia, and they have been making progress. But neuroscientists barged in like an elephant into a china shop and claimed to have solved it in one fell swoop," Maoz says. In an attempt to get everyone on the same page, he is heading the first intensive research collaboration between neuroscientists and philosophers, backed by $7 million from two private foundations, the John Templeton Foundation and the Fetzer Institute. At an inaugural conference in March, attendees discussed plans for designing philosophically informed experiments, and unanimously agreed on the need to pin down the various meanings of "free will."

In that, they join Libet himself. While he remained firm on his interpretation of his study, he thought his experiment was not enough to prove *total* determinism—the idea that all events are set in place by previous ones, including our own mental functions. "Given the issue is so fundamentally important to our view of who we are, a claim that our free will is illusory should be based on fairly direct evidence," he wrote in a 2004 book. "Such evidence is not available."

ADAM GOPNIK

Younger Longer

FROM *The New Yorker*

AGING, LIKE BANKRUPTCY in Hemingway's description, happens two ways, slowly and then all at once. The slow way is the familiar one: decades pass with little sense of internal change, middle age arrives with only a slight slowing down—a name lost, a lumbar ache, a sprinkling of white hairs and eye wrinkles. The fast way happens as a series of lurches: eyes occlude, hearing dwindles, a hand trembles where it hadn't, a hip breaks—the usually hale and hearty doctor's murmur in the yearly checkup, *There are some signs here that concern me.*

To get a sense of what it would be like to have the slow process become the fast process, you can go to the AgeLab, at the Massachusetts Institute of Technology, in Cambridge, and put on AGNES (for Age Gain Now Empathy System). AGNES, or the "sudden aging" suit, as Joseph Coughlin, the founder and director of the AgeLab, describes it, includes yellow glasses, which convey a sense of the yellowing of the ocular lens that comes with age; a boxer's neck harness, which mimics the diminished mobility of the cervical spine; bands around the elbows, wrists, and knees to simulate stiffness; boots with foam padding to produce a loss of tactile feedback; and special gloves to "reduce tactile acuity while adding resistance to finger movements."

Slowly pulling on the aging suit and then standing up—it looks a bit like one of the spacesuits that the Russian cosmonauts wore —you're at first conscious merely of a little extra weight, a little loss of feeling, a small encumbrance or two at the extremities. Soon, though, it's actively infuriating. The suit bends you. It slows you. You come to realize what makes it a powerful instrument of emotional empathy: every small task becomes effortful. "Reach up to the top shelf and pick up that mug," Coughlin orders, and doing so requires more attention than you expected. You reach for the mug instead of just getting it. Your emotional cast, as focused task piles on focused task, becomes one of annoyance; you acquire the same set-mouthed, unhappy, watchful look you see on certain elderly people on the subway. The concentration that each act requires disrupts the flow of life, which you suddenly become aware is the happiness of life, the ceaseless flow of simple action and responses, choices all made simultaneously and mostly without effort. Happiness is absorption, and absorption is the opposite of willful attention.

The annoyance, after a half-hour or so in the suit, tips over into anger: *Damn, what's wrong with the world?* (Never: What's wrong with me?) The suit makes us aware not so much of the physical difficulties of old age, which can be manageable, but of the mental state disconcertingly associated with it—the price of age being perpetual aggravation. The theme and action and motive of King Lear suddenly become perfectly clear. You become enraged at your youngest daughter's reticence because you have had to struggle to unroll the map of your kingdom.

The AgeLab is designed to alleviate this progression. It exists to encourage and incubate new technologies and products and services for an ever-larger market of aging people. ("Every eight seconds, a baby boomer turns seventy-three," Coughlin observes.) Coughlin, who is in his late fifties, is the image of an old-fashioned American engineer-entrepreneur; he is bald in the old-fashioned, tonsured, Thurber-husband way, wears a bow tie and heavy red-framed glasses, and, walking a visitor through the lab, suggests a cross between Mr. Peabody and Q, from the Bond films, showing you the latest gadgets. His talk is crisply aphoristic and irrigated with an easy flow of statistics: each proposition has its instantly associated number.

"Where science is ambiguous, politics begins," he says. "In the designation of some states, an older driver is fifty, in some eighty —we don't even know what an older driver is. That ambiguity is an itch I wanted to scratch. Over the past century, we've created the greatest gift in the history of humanity—thirty extra years of life—and we don't know what to do with it! Now that we're living longer, how do we plan for what we're going to do?"

Having picked the mug up, the suit wearer finds that setting the mug down gently on a nearby table is also a bit of a challenge. So is following Coughlin from room to room as he narrates all that the AgeLab has learned.

"Here's a useful model for you," he says. "From zero to twenty-one is about eight thousand days. From twenty-one to midlife crisis is eight thousand days. From mid-forties to sixty-five—eight thousand days. Nowadays, if you make it to sixty-five you have a 50 percent chance you'll make it to eighty-five. Another eight thousand days! That's no longer a trip to Disney and wait for the grandchildren to visit and die of the virus you get on a cruise. We're talking about rethinking, redefining one-third of adult life! The greatest achievement in the history of humankind—and all we can say is that it's going to make Medicare go broke? Why don't we take that one-third and create new stories, new rituals, new mythologies for people as they age?"

The AGNES suit is one of many instruments and appliances—or "cool toys," as they are more technically known—that can be found in the AgeLab's glass-walled halls and cubicled corridors, ready to entertain visiting writers, and to instruct visiting entrepreneurs. There is the driving simulator, specially fitted to track the driver's eye movements as they flit back and forth from the dashboard to the horizon. ("With its new technologies, like navigation systems, the automotive industry is asking people to change fifty years of driving habits in ten minutes without instruction," Coughlin says.) There is Paro, a robotic baby seal, from Japan, which bleats and moves its head, and is designed to act as a comfort to aging people, particularly Alzheimer's patients struggling with the "sundown" moment at day's end, when confusion and restlessness become acute. ("It's a seal, rather than a dog or a cat, because people have great experiences with dogs and cats, and even Alzheimer's patients can spot the eerie nonresemblance," Coughlin says. "Having no experience of seals, we accept Paro as he is.") There are mobile robotic nurses made for elderly care, and broad red upholstered chairs made for elderly rears. There are large research displays showing photographs of drivers, their faces embedded with sensors, and the varieties of "Glance Classification" that can, when analyzed, lead to "Crash Avoidance." ("The ratio between confident decisions and *correct* confident decisions can be a story of life or death on the highway," Coughlin explains.) And there are displays of word clouds associated with aging, showing the significant difference between the terms with which women imagine their post-career lives (Freedom, Time, Family) and those which men use (Retirement, Relax, Hobbies).

The work of the AgeLab is shaped by a paradox. Having been established to engineer and promote new products and services specially designed for the expanding market of the aged, the AgeLab swiftly discovered that engineering and promoting new products and services specially designed for the expanding market of the aged is a good way of going out of business. Old people will not buy anything that reminds them that they are old. They are a market that cannot be marketed to. In effect, to accept help in getting out of the suit is to accept that we're in the suit for life. We would rather suffer because we're old than accept that we're old and suffer less.

This paradox is, well, old. Heinz, back in the 1950s, tried marketing a line of "Senior Foods" that was, essentially, baby food for old people. It not only failed spectacularly but, as Coughlin puts it, poisoned an entire category. The most perverse of these failures is perhaps that of the PERS, or personal emergency response system, a category of device—best known for the hysterically toned television ad in which an elderly woman calls out, "I've fallen and I can't get up!"—designed as a neck pendant that summons emergency services when pressed. It is simple and effective. "The problem is that no one wants one," Coughlin says. "The entire penetration in the U.S. of the sixty-five-plus market is less than 4 percent. And a German study showed that, when subscribers fell and remained on the floor for longer than five minutes, they failed to use their devices to summon help 83 percent of the time." In other words, many older people would sooner thrash on the floor in distress than press a button—one that may summon assistance but whose real impact is to admit, *I am old.*

"We buy products not just to do jobs but for what they say about us," Coughlin summarizes. "Beige or light-blue bracelets or pendants say 'Old Man Walking.'"

The AgeLab has rediscovered the eternal truth that identity

matters to us far more than utility. The most effective way of comforting the aged, the researchers there find, is through a kind of comical convergence of products designed by and supposedly for impatient millennials, which secretly better suit the needs of irascible boomers. The best hearing aids look the most like earbuds. The most effective PERS device is an iPhone or an Apple Watch app.

Such unexpected convergences have happened in the past. Retirement villages came to be centered on golf courses, Coughlin maintains, not because oldsters necessarily like golf but because they like using golf carts. It's the carts that supply greater mobility in and around the village. The golf comes with them. This process of "exaptation" has now accelerated. TaskRabbit and Uber and Rent the Runway—services that provide immediate help for specific problems—are especially valuable for an aging population.

"The dominant paradigm is that older people don't want new technology," Coughlin says. "But take the microwave oven! It couldn't have been better designed for people who live by themselves. It's a perfect example of what I call 'transcendent design'— not made for older people, but ideal for them. We're doing a lot of work in the on-demand economy, which was made for millennials but is working better for boomers. Meals are delivered—these are amazing, assisted-living services that can come to anyone's house. Older women in particular are saved from microdeficiencies in their diet. So, while the millennials want them for convenience, the boomers want them for care for their parents, or themselves."

Coughlin hates what he calls "the narrative," according to which new tech appeals to newer people: "Startup money goes to youngsters because that's what startup entrepreneurs are supposed to look like, and the products are designed for kids because that's what startup products are meant to look like." In his view—detailed in his book *The Longevity Economy*—the narrative, more than any rational calculation of profit, accounts for the technological gap. "There's no reason for this enormous prejudice in favor of youthfulness in Silicon Valley and the tech industry," he says. He also hates the misallocation of resources based on mere myths. "We have a belief that we send out our elderly to institutions. The fact of the matter is that less than 10 percent of the elderly go into nursing homes or assisted living. The senior-housing industry is building inventory meant for seniors, but 87 percent of retire-

ment-age people want to stay in the same home where they have
the three 'M's: marriage, mortgage, and memories. The problem
is that they can't. Not when the model is a two-story house with
a bedroom and the bathroom upstairs. If we can solve the stairs
problem, we won't need new housing."

Coughlin says that having simple answers to two questions can
determine whether you're going to age well in place: "Who's going to change the light bulb, and how are you going to get an ice-
cream cone? Little tasks become sources of high friction. It's not
that you can't climb the ladder to change the light bulb. But for
the first time you are going to have someone yelling at you, 'You're
going to fall and break your neck!' That's the problem of aging
we have to tackle, not building more old people's homes or senior
villages." It's the failure of industry and engineering to address
the actual problems of aging—the problems summed up by the
aggravations of the AGNES suit—that makes Coughlin impatient
with scientific speculations about extending life. "We've already
extended life! What we need is not to put off death a little longer
but to write a new narrative of aging as it could be."

Aging has no point; it is the infuriating absence of a point. Having reproduced ourselves externally, we fall down on replicating
ourselves internally. The processes of cellular replication that allow us to be boats rebuilt even as they cross the ocean cease acting
efficiently, because they have no evolutionary reward for acting
efficiently. They are like code monkeys in a failing tech business:
they can mess up everything, absent-mindedly forget to code for
the color of our hair or the elasticity of our skin, and no penalty
is exacted for the failure. We've already made all the kids we are
going to make.

That, at least, is the classic explanation of why we age, proposed
by the British Nobel laureate Peter Medawar, in the 1950s. Once
we have passed reproductive age, the genes can get sloppy about
copying, allowing mutations to accumulate, because natural selection no longer cares. And so things fall apart. The second law of
thermodynamics gets us all in the end. The car or the Cuisinart
works for a decade, breaks down, and can't be fixed; rust never
sleeps, and we do.

And yet some trees go on for centuries, collecting rings, growing older without really aging. Some species—though those are

often hard-to-track creatures, like Arctic sharks—may live for centuries. Even if aging at some speed is ultimately inevitable, what happens when we age is far from self-evident.

It may be that the real trick is not how much we age but how much we don't. Human beings are outliers: we live much longer than other creatures of our size, defying the general truth that smaller animals live shorter lives than bigger ones. (Not that we should take too much pride in our defiance; another great defier is the naked mole rat, the world's ugliest animal, which often lives for absurdly long periods and scarcely seems to age at all, although one might ask how anyone but another naked mole rat could tell.) Those extra thirty years of life, though won by advances in medicine and public health, are winnable because, given a little chance, we just go on. The big question of human aging then becomes not why we fall apart but why nature lets us hold together for so long.

One evolutionary rationale is that there is something essential to human groups, with the slowly unfolding infancy of their young, in keeping the old folks around even when they can't make more young folks. Old folks are repositories of extended cultural memory: it would seem to be advantageous to have a few senior citizens around who know what to do, so to speak, when winter comes. Evolutionary biologists tend to doubt whether nature cares about the fitness of groups, rather than the fitness of individuals, but the model of "kin selection"—which gives weight to the fact that helping my relatives helps preserve my genes—suggests that there might be evolutionary advantages in having grandmothers around to take care of kids and remember where the fish go every twenty years. (Then again, people who do have grandparents around to remind them what they're doing wrong would probably suspect that killing off the oldsters early might actually make for more success, or at least more serenity.) People might not have a death sentence in their genes.

And so elsewhere in Cambridge, notably in certain genetic labs at Harvard, the chairs and seals and exaptated services of the AgeLab are regarded as mere Band-Aids on the problem to be solved. Here, there are whispers of undying yeast, tales of eternally young mice, rumors of rejuvenated dogs, and scientists who stubbornly insist that age is an illness to be treated like any other.

Where fifty years ago it was taken for granted that the problem of age was a problem of the inevitable running down of everything, entropy working its worst, now many researchers are inclined to think that the problem is "epigenetic": it's a problem in reading the information—the genetic code—in the cells. To use a metaphor of the Harvard geneticist David Sinclair, the information in each cell is digital and perfectly stored; it's the "readout," the active expression of the information, that's effectively analog, and subject to occlusion by the equivalent of dirt and scratches on the plastic surface of a CD. Clear those off, he says, and the younger you, still intact in the information layer, jumps out—just as the younger Beatles jump out from a restored and remastered CD. (It would not be the first time in the history of science that the way we think about a phenomenon has been affected by the kinds of man-made models we're acquainted with. When a telephone switchboard was our most impressive knowledge-bearing mechanism, people thought that the brain was like one; when Xerox copies, growing less legible as generation passed to generation, were familiar to everyone, the image of a cell ceasing to replicate itself effectively in that manner was self-evident.)

We don't have to micromanage the repair, the Harvard molecular biologist George Church observes: "If we think epigenetically, we can see that we can make the cells industriously do the repair themselves." Already a legendary figure for devising genomic-sequencing techniques—it must help that he's a scientific eminence who has the aura of one, with a grand Darwinian beard and a slow-spoken orotundity—Church gained further attention for his experiments in trying to resurrect extinct species, particularly the woolly mammoth. (One of his standard jokes is that the fifth floor of his lab is off limits to visitors, because that is where the mammoths and the Neanderthals live.) He is also among a group of engineer-entrepreneurs who are trying not to make better products for aging people but to make fewer aging people to sell products to. Perhaps aging is not a condition to be managed but a mistake to be fixed. Sinclair, for one, has successfully extended the life of yeast, and says that he is moving on to human trials. He is an evangelist for the advantages of what he calls "hormesis"—the practice of inducing metabolic stress by short intense exercise or intermittent fasting. "Every day, try to be hungry and out of breath" is his neatly epigenetic epigram.

Anti-aging research, in its "translational," or applied, form, seems to be proceeding along two main fronts: through "small molecules," meaning mostly dietary supplements that are intended to rev up the right proteins; and, perhaps more dramatically, through genetic engineering. Typically, genetic engineering involves adding or otherwise manipulating genes in a population of animals, often mice, perhaps by rejiggering a mouse's genome in embryo and then using it to breed a genetically altered strain. In mice studies, genetic modifications that cause the rodents to make greater amounts of a single protein, sirtuin 6, have resulted in longer life spans (although some scientists think that the intervention merely helped male mice to live as long as female mice).

Church and Noah Davidsohn, a former postdoc in his lab, have engaged in a secretive but much talked-about venture to make old dogs new. They have conducted gene therapy on beagles with the Tufts veterinary school, and are currently advertising for Cavalier King Charles spaniels, which are highly prone to an incurable age-related heart condition, mitral-valve disease; almost all of them develop it by the age of ten. Using a genetically modified virus, Church and Davidsohn's team will insert a piece of DNA into a dog's liver cells and get them to produce a protein meant to stop the heart disease from progressing. But the team has larger ambitions. It has been identifying other targets for gene-based interventions, studying a database of aging-related genes: genes that are overexpressed or underexpressed—that make too much or too little of a particular protein—as we grow old. In the CD replay of life, these are the notes that get muffled or amplified, and Davidsohn and Church want to restore them to their proper volume.

Many problems cling to this work, not least that there are surprisingly few "biomarkers" of increased longevity. One researcher makes a comparison with cancer research: we know a patient's cancer has been successfully treated when the cancer cells go away, but how do you know if you've made people live longer except by waiting decades and seeing when they die? Ideally, we'd find something that could be measured in a blood test, say, and was reliably correlated with someone's life span.

Church is optimistic about the genetic-engineering approach. "We know it can work," he says, "because we've already had success reprogramming embryonic stem cells: you *can* take a really old cell and turn that back into a young cell. We're doing it now. Most of the work was done in mice, where we've extended the life of mice by a factor of two. It isn't seen as impressive, because it's mice, but now we're working on dogs. There are about nine different pathways that we've identified for cell rejuvenation, one of which eliminates senescent cells"—moldering cells that have stopped dividing and tend to spark inflammation, serving as a perpetual irritant to their neighbors.

"We're already in clinical trials with dogs," Church says. "If all goes well, we should have that accomplished within two years, and be overlapping that with human clinical trials within the next five years. My guess is that dog trials will go well. Based on the mouse trials, we're hoping that the effects are general and independent of species—we're using the same gene therapy in mice and dogs and humans."

Church is aware that the Food and Drug Administration, among other regulatory bodies, may not be crazy about weird new therapies that address what we customarily take to be a natural process. "Our emphasis is on reversal rather than longevity, in part because it's easier to get permission from the FDA for reversal of diseases than for prolongation of life," he says. "Longevity isn't our aim —we're just aiming at the reversal of age-related diseases." Noah Davidsohn enthusiastically seconds this: "We want to make people live better, not necessarily longer, though obviously longer is part of better." But Church makes it plain that these are adjoining concerns. "How old can people grow?" he says. "Well, if our approach is truly effective, there is no upper limit. But our goal isn't eternal life. The goal is youthful wellness rather than an extended long period of age-related decline. You know, one of the striking things is that many supercentenarians"—people who live productively past a hundred years—"live a youthful life, and then they die very quickly. They're here, living well, and then they're not. It's not a bad picture."

There are many skeptics among scientists who wonder how much, or how soon, this kind of work will really affect aging. Church gets shares for serving on the advisory board of Elysium Health, which markets an anti-aging supplement called Basis, and though the literature is careful to say that, "rather than endorsing a specific product, this network of scientists, clinicians and health professionals advises the Elysium team on product identification and development," how one distinguishes between advising on the product and endorsing the product seems to many a bit mystical.

Others may recall the enthusiasm, in the early twentieth century, for implanting monkey glands in people, a procedure that was held out as a scientific solution to the problem of aging. (W. B. Yeats had a related procedure.) The fountain of youth is always splashing away somewhere.

Behind the optimistic promise of heading off aging in spaniels and, soon, in their owners lies a sadder reality: that even foundational research cannot always cure a fundamental problem. Despite what had seemed to be groundbreaking discoveries in the basic genetics and pathology of dementia, no cure or even promising treatment for senility, as it once was called, is in sight. Increasing numbers of people enter old age not merely reduced but ravaged by Alzheimer's or another form of dementia, now epidemic in the richer countries that have greater life expectancies. Old Lear's primary fear is not of age but of madness, which he imagines precisely as dementia: as the loss of mental control, of memory, and of cognition, seeing his fate mirrored in that of Poor Tom, the ranting homeless man impersonated by Edgar.

To pass from the Harvard rejuvenators to the laboratory of Patrick Hof, at the Icahn School of Medicine at Mount Sinai, in Manhattan, is to sober up a little. Here, there is talk not of imminent innovation but of discouragingly minute work proceeding on many slow-moving fronts over decades. Where the Harvard crowd see quick fixes in the near future, Hof, an expert on the neuronal underpinnings of aging and Alzheimer's, sees the exposure of ever more confounding complexity.

His tenth-floor office is filled with reproductions of Blake illuminations and Whistler portraits, while photographs of his children cycle on the screen saver behind him, blended with images of whales and dolphins, a particular interest of his. His nearby lab is an open space with small chapels off it, in which researchers —postdocs, junior faculty, skilled technicians—study the youthful and aged brains of many kinds of animals, with what looks like every kind of microscope: smaller viewing ones, mid-sized high-resolution ones, and a single massive electron-scanning microscope that lets his researchers see neural structure down to a dendrite's tiny terminal spines.

"My career started at the beginning of digital microscopy," Hof says. He is white-haired, with the soft accent of his native Switzerland. "Now we can collect terabytes of data—we can collect entire networks of neurons within a single animal brain. We do tissue staining, taking a piece of brain or an entire brain—slicing them into very thin sections, which we incubate with an antibody that labels a specific population of neurons, and we collect that. Or we can load neurons with a fluorescent dye—inject it, using a very thin glass pipette that runs right into the neuron—so then we have a fluorescent neuron!"

Hof's laboratory is full of brains. In a large common lab outside the microscopy rooms, there are shelves holding rows of what look like hinged, dark-wooden cigar boxes. "These are all brains," Hof says casually. He takes a box down and opens it; inside, there's a slide with what looks like a small profile of a brain on it. "That's a human brain. It's a section, sliced like bread. It looks small, because it was incubated in a chemical process—we started with the entire hemisphere and then incubated it in an alcoholic treatment, and it shrinks by two-thirds. Then you stain it, and there you go." The brain sections are kept indefinitely, Hof explains, and loaned out, like library books, from lab to lab.

Hof, who has taken to studying the brains of whales and dolphins, likes to bring visitors to an open, chilled "brain room," a sort of rare-book collection of brains, to see a few beautiful instances. The brain room is a revelation. Here they are: human brains, monkey brains, dolphin brains—the space between brain and mind never seems so large as it does when you actually see the material of mind, curved and segmented, as ugly as an intestine, floating in a fixing solution.

The room even contains a sperm-whale brain—"the largest brain known to the planet," Hof says. (It looks beautifully broad, with nobly large-spaced convolutions.) Finding the brains of senile cetaceans is hard, he says. "The ones that beach are young adults, and the seniors tend to die quietly at sea." Hof hopes that insight might be found in studying neurodegeneration in the cetaceans' more expansive, differently structured cortexes.

The study of Alzheimer's became Hof's special preoccupation because of its insidious destruction of normal minds and normal character. "You can't tell any difference, even under extreme magnification, between an aging non-demented brain and a younger human one," he says. "You have to have really fine levels of resolution to see any loss in neural organization just through aging without illness. But, holding an Alzheimer's brain in your hand, you can see the atrophy."

Three decades ago, Hof explains, research in Alzheimer's linked two key proteins with the terrible dissolution of selves: beta-amyloid, which formed plaques between neurons; and tau, which formed tangled fibrils within neurons. The relative importance of the two was disputed, but many scientists concluded that those plaques and fibrils clog the brain as coffee grounds clog a drain. It seemed likely that there would be therapeutic benefits if they could be cleared away. "Now, we know that these are really downstream effects," Hof says. "What's happening upstream to cause them is much, much more complicated."

With the causes unclear—debate continues over which anomalies are better seen as culprits or as bystanders—and the cure evidently far away, Hof can only enumerate the "co-morbidities" for Alzheimer's, the conditions that correlate most strongly with its onset. They are the old-fashioned sins: obesity, a lack of exercise, bad diet—and the diabetes that these can produce. For all the cascades of research into longevity, the new science often seems to distill into old wisdom: be fit, stay thin, and you will look and feel younger longer.

"The disease is diverse and heterogeneous enough that treatment and prevention will have to move on several fronts," Hof says. "First, just promoting healthy aging, what can you do and what can you avoid? Every elder is unique, and will have had life experiences and habits that are unique. So we're going to have to look at that aspect, in ways that prevent or treat, to a degree, the development of something worse. Then we need to have a better understanding of the causative factors. There are leads that point to a number of interesting markers. There are proteins that play cellular roles that effect a cascade of reaction inside the cells, but it becomes very difficult to target specifically without altering other functions. None of it is easy."

As you take off the AGNES suit—piece by piece; the boots and then the wrist weights and the impeding gloves—the feeling is disconcerting. It's the return of flow, the feeling of choice and possibility as you begin to move again through the world, that makes you recall that what it is to be young is not to be in a state of ecstasy but merely to be unimpeded, to be in the world without having undue consciousness of your own muscle and bone within it. It's the same thing we experience when we remove a splinter from our foot; what we get is not happiness in a positive sense but a return to not having to think about the prison and the fact of our flesh. We forget our insides, and fold ourselves back out.

The true condition of youth is the physical ability to forget ourselves. A friend who is still creative in his eighties points out what he calls the geriatric possessive: people past eighty, he says, are expected to say, "I'm going to take my bath," "I'm going to take my walk." We can counterpoise that to the pediatric possessive: "You're going to take your bath," "It's time for your nap." Only in midlife do we feel secure enough to enumerate actions as existing individually outside our possession of them: "I'm going to take a bath," "I'm going to take a nap." A bath and a nap exist, briefly, outside our possession of them—they're just around for the taking, we suppose, and always will be.

Glenda Jackson, now playing Lear on Broadway at the age of eighty-three, captures the indomitable egotism of the aged. Watching her onstage, we are asked to recognize not just the anger but also, eventually, the wisdom of age. The old, Shakespeare says, can become, or assist us to become, God's spies. A decade and a half ago, a presidential council chaired by the bioethicist Leon Kass produced a report raising questions about research into extended longevity. "Might we be cheating ourselves," the report asked, "by departing from the contour and constraint of natural life (our frailty and finitude) which serve as a lens for a larger vision that might give all of life coherence and sustaining significance?" We do turn, after all, to the imagery of the old for comfort; we turn to work marked by the frailties of aging for consolation and enlightenment. Matisse, his hands crippled by arthritis, picks up scissors and painted paper and finds a new world of purity; de Kooning, on the edge of Alzheimer's, paints some of his greatest pictures just as renewed simplicity breaks the hand of excessive excellence.

Swift, in *Gulliver's Travels,* invented the race of the Struldbrugs in order to imagine what eternal life would be like. Eerily, they were given a precise phenotypic marker, a blemish above the left eyebrow, and were given, too, the ill temper associated with age. Promised eternal life, they were cursed with ever-progressing aging, and were the most miserable people alive. What we want— Swift's point—is not eternal life but eternal youth, and what the new science seems to promise us is more like permanent middle age. We may indeed already be converging as a population—irascible millennials who feel dated at twenty-five and determinedly upbeat boomers who insist on feeling young at seventy—on a single American age, a kind of shared perpetual middleness, where we will dye our hair and take our pills and suddenly collapse in the midst of the dance. Right now, we live well, and then we don't live well, and then we die. The most that science seems to offer us is this: we'll live well, and then we'll die.

In the past, as science and medicine annihilated old curses, we worried about losing the corresponding compensating benefits. And yet pain in childbirth, which some thought to be foundational to what we call Judeo-Christian morals, could be largely subdued without any loss to mother love; consumption was cured without lessening the romance of romantic poetry. Perhaps the loss of aging will be one more in that series, where, like all the other supercentenarians, we will dance and make love and ski, sharp-eyed, right to the edge of the still inevitable cliff. In the word cloud of concepts associated with aging that hangs in the AgeLab, the word "death" appears only in a tiny balloon, associated with the stray and bubbling thoughts of younger men—much smaller than the other words, lost among larger clouds of hope.

SARA HARRISON

Right Under Our Noses

FROM *Wired*

THE DOGS STILL make Andreas Mershin angry. "I mean, I love dogs," says the Greek-Russian scientist, in his office at MIT. "But the dogs are slapping me in the face."

He pulls up a video to show me what he means. In it, a black dog named Lucy approaches a series of six stations, each separated by a small barrier. At every one, a glass cup of human urine with a screened lid sits at the level of the animal's nose. Lucy takes a brief sniff of each sample, sometimes digging her snout in to get a better whiff. She is performing a kind of diagnostic test: searching for the telltale scent of prostate cancer, which, it turns out, leaves a volatile, discernible signature in a man's pee. Discernible if you're a dog, anyway. When Lucy finds what she's looking for, she sits down and receives a treat.

Among humans—whose toolmaking prowess has given the world self-driving suitcases and reusable rocket boosters—prostate cancer is notoriously difficult to detect. The prevailing method is to check a patient's blood for elevated levels of a protein called prostate-specific antigen. But the test has a miserable track record. The scientist who first discovered PSA has described the test as "hardly more effective than a coin toss." A false positive can lead to a prostate biopsy, a harrowing procedure that involves inserting a large, hollow needle through the wall of the rectum to retrieve a tissue sample from the prostate itself.

Properly trained dogs, on the other hand, can detect prostate cancer with better than 90 percent accuracy, and with sleek, tail-wagging efficiency. In the video, Lucy works her way through six samples in just a couple of minutes. This drives Mershin up the wall. "We have $100 million worth of equipment downstairs. And the dog can beat me?" he says. "That is pissing me off."

Mershin is not a doctor. He's a physicist by training. He runs a lab called the Label Free Research Group, which exists to spite the boundaries between physics, biology, materials science, and information science. In his office, Mershin keeps a pair of sunglasses that can measure brain waves, along with magazines on aviation and books on urology, the physics of consciousness, and coding in Python. He speaks rapidly in an accent that sits somewhere between his two native languages, and he changes subjects at the slightest provocation. He refuses to wear matching socks, because why should socks match? He is short and round, with a mane of strawberry blond curls that bounce when he gets excited.

Mershin's lab, where he keeps that $100 million worth of equipment, sits a few floors down from his office at MIT. In one room, researchers are trying to invent new colors; in another, to create the lightest, strongest materials on earth. But I'm here because this facility is doing some of the most important research in the world toward developing AO—artificial olfaction.

Plenty of robots these days can see, hear, speak, and (crudely) think. But good luck finding one that can smell. In part, that's simply because olfaction has always been deeply underrated by humans—a species of cerebral, hypervisual snobs. Kant dismissed smell as the "most dispensable" of our five senses. One 2011 poll found that 53 percent of people ages sixteen to twenty-two would rather give up their sense of smell than give up their smartphones and computers.

But in the past several years, it has become increasingly clear that smell, in the right snout, can be a kind of superpower. For millennia, humans have prized dogs for their tracking abilities; police and armed forces have long used them to sniff out bombs, drugs, and bodies. But since about the early 2000s, an avalanche of findings has dramatically expanded our sense of what dogs can do with their noses. It started when researchers realized that canines can smell the early onset of melanoma. Then it turned out they can do the same for breast cancer, lung cancer, colorectal cancer, and ovarian cancer. They can smell the time of day in the movement of air around a room; sense diabetic episodes hours in advance; and detect human emotional states in the absence of visual cues.

And it's not just dogs. Tipped off by a Scottish nurse with a highly attuned nose, scientists have recently learned that people with Parkinson's disease begin emitting a distinct "woody, musky odor" years before they show symptoms.

All this adds up to a revelation not just about dogs but about the physical world itself. Events and diseases and mental states leave reports in the air—ones that are intelligible to highly attuned olfactory systems but otherwise illegible to science. Smell, it appears, is sometimes the best way of detecting and discriminating between otherwise hidden things out in the world. And often, the *next*-best method of detecting that same thing is expensive (gas chromatography/mass spectrometry) or excruciating (tissue biopsies) or impossible (mind reading).

Unfortunately, the other reason we don't have robots that can smell is that olfaction remains a stubborn biological enigma. Scientists are still piecing together the basics of how we sense all those volatile compounds and how our brains classify that information. "There are more unknowns than knowns," says Hiroaki Matsunami, a researcher at Duke University.

Mershin, however, believes that we don't really have to understand how mammals smell to build an artificial nose. He's betting that things will work the other way around: to understand the nose, we have to build one first. In his efforts with a brilliant mentor named Shuguang Zhang, Mershin has built a device that can just begin to give dogs—his panting adversaries—a run for their money.

In May 1914, Alexander Graham Bell delivered a commencement address to some high school students in Washington, D.C. The sixty-seven-year-old inventor of the telephone gave a peculiar speech—a crotchety ode to observation, measurement, and gumshoe curiosity. He spent much of his time proposing areas of investigation for his teenage audience to take up. "Did you ever try to measure a smell?" he asked. "What is an odor? Is it an emanation of material particles in the air, or is it a form of vibration like sound?" he asked. "If it is an emanation, you might be able to weigh it; and if it is a vibration, you should be able to reflect it from a mirror," he went on. "If you are ambitious to found a new science, measure a smell."

More than a century later, no one has yet been able to measure a smell, and there is even still some debate as to whether smell is a vibration or a chemical interaction between particles. (The vibration theory is far more controversial, but no one understands olfaction well enough to dismiss it entirely.) In fact, it wasn't until 1991 that scientists were able to map the basic genetic and physiological building blocks of mammalian olfaction. That year, biologists Linda Buck and Richard Axel published a seminal paper; they discovered about 1,000 genes that code for about 1,000 olfactory receptors in mice, and they showed that those receptors are the beginning of a mammal's sense of smell. They live in the olfactory epithelium, a thin piece of tissue that sits at the top of the nasal cavity, right where it meets the skull. When we take a deep breath, we suck the volatile molecules in the room up our noses toward those receptors. When the receptors interact with molecules, they set off a chain reaction that ends by sending a message to our brains.

As for the precise nature of those interactions, Buck and Axel could only theorize. They posited a sort of lock-and-key relationship between the olfactory receptors in our noses and the molecules in the air. But the number of receptors they discovered instantly posed a mathematical problem. Humans have about 400 kinds of olfactory receptors (far fewer than mice), but we can smell about 10,000 distinct odors. So Buck and Axel theorized that smell was combinatorial. Each receptor, their research showed, is uniquely primed to react to a few different molecules, and our noses sense distinct odors when many receptors fire at the same time. John Kauer, then a researcher at Tufts University, relates the idea to playing chords on a piano. "The piano only has eighty-eight notes," he says. "If you were only able to use one note per odor, you could only detect eighty-eight different odors." If odors are more like chords, then the math suddenly works out.

Inspired by Buck and Axel, who won the Nobel Prize in 2004 for their work, Mershin and other scientists conceived of odors as simply lists of molecules. If you want to understand the smell of a clove of garlic, the thinking went, the answer lies in its chemical components. "Somewhere in these molecules," Mershin believed through the mid-2000s, "the smell of garlic is written."

After Buck and Axel released their major findings, it didn't take long before the first major efforts to build an artificial nose got under way. DARPA wanted to replace dogs as a tool for finding land mines, so beginning in 1997, it poured $25 million into a program called Dog's Nose. The agency funded scientists across the country to build a bunch of would-be sniffing machines and then brought them to a field in Missouri for testing. The ground was sown with every manner of land mine, from small antipersonnel devices the size of tuna fish tins to hefty antitank munitions. Although stepping on the mines could no longer set them off—the fuses had been removed—the buried explosive ordnance could still be set off by, say, a lightning strike. "As soon as there was any hint of a thunderstorm," says Kauer, who participated in the program, "we evacuated."

Kauer had built a gray, shoebox-sized device that he eventually christened the ScenTrak. His gadget wasn't equipped with actual olfactory receptors. Instead, it was packed with long strands of molecules called polymers that Kauer knew would react to DNT, a molecule common in most land mines. When the ScenTrak came across an explosive, the DNT bound to the polymers, causing the ScenTrak to set off an alert. "Land mine!" the box cried.

At least, that's how it worked in ideal conditions. ScenTrak was able to pick out nearby traces of DNT in the air of an otherwise odorless lab. Out in the field, though, when Kauer scanned the ScenTrak back and forth over a patch of ground, it became confused. The polymers would react to DNT, but also to the weather, to plants, or to certain kinds of soil.

Other devices in the competition, including one called Fido and another called Cyranose, were based on roughly the same theory. They all used polymers sensitive to specific compounds. And they all proved somewhat narrowly functional. (Fido is now used at military checkpoints to scan for explosives at close range.) But these devices don't really *smell*, any more than, say, a carbon monoxide sensor can smell. They often misfire in scent-rich environments where odors—apparently made of some of the same compounds—may waft in from various nonexplosive sources.

In part, that's because the theory these devices were built on was too reductive. Today, most scientists believe that the lock-and-key theory of olfactory bonding is far too simple. In some cases, it turns out, molecules with very similar shapes have completely different odors; in others, very differently shaped compounds smell alike. A molecule's shape, in other words, is not synonymous with its smell. Instead, many receptors bind to many different molecules and vice versa. But each receptor has what some scientists call a distinct "affinity" for each molecule. It's that special affinity, the theory now goes, along with the combinatorial nature of olfactory reactions, that accounts for unique scents. The piano doesn't just have eighty-eight keys that can form chords; it also has pedals and dynamics. "You hit piano keys at different strengths, heavy and light and so on," Zhang says. "Heavy, you get one sound; light, you get another sound." Or to put it another way: the theory of smell just gets more complicated.

Mershin and Zhang are an odd yet harmonious pair. Mershin rarely takes the same path twice. When we lose our way walking from the MIT cafeteria to his office, he confesses that he frequently gets lost—"in my thoughts too, intellectually as well as geographically," he says. By his own account, he is dyslexic, synesthetic, pink/gray color-blind, face-blind, and has attention deficit disorder. Sometimes he will forget his own address. He is also insatiably, compulsively curious. He once devised a game for his children that involved having them soak a cotton ball in perfume, blindfold themselves, and then try to find the cotton ball after it had been hidden. In addition to noses, he is building houses in Namibia out of mushrooms and working with a postdoctoral fellow on ways to remove heavy metals from water. "For my life, it doesn't fit to do just one thing," he says. "But I do like to work with people who are very focused and do one thing really well."

Zhang is that person. Where Mershin is restless, Zhang, who runs his own research group called the Laboratory of Molecular Architecture, is deliberate and slow. He believes you have to go deep on one project, one question. "For science to be successful you have to focus," he says. "You cannot be distracted by other things." In 2003, Zhang was looking for a new project, and he zeroed in on olfactory receptors. Even after Buck and Axel's pioneering work, no one had ever been able to get an actual look at one—either under a microscope or by using X-ray crystallography. That's part of the reason olfaction is such an enigma. At the most basic level, we can't directly observe what those tiny receptors are doing. Are they in fact binding with molecules? How? Do other factors like humidity or other compounds affect how those receptors respond? No one knows. Zhang wanted to change that—by figuring out some way to see an olfactory receptor. "We decided to work on something mysterious and take some years to figure it out," he says.

Here's what Zhang knew, going into his quest: Olfactory receptors are membrane proteins, and they are complicated, alien little structures. Each receptor is shaped like a long string that winds back and forth through the thin membrane that separates a cell from the outside world. If that complicated winding pattern is ever interrupted or changed, the receptor won't work. And if the receptor is tilted or upside down? It won't work either.

About half of any olfactory receptor sits outside the cell, ready to interact with molecules. Then a middle section sits inside the cell membrane, and the rest resides inside the cell. When the exterior part of the receptor binds to a molecule, it changes shape, and the cell sends a message to your brain. While the heads and tails of an olfactory receptor—the parts that sit inside and outside the cell—love water, its middle section is hydrophobic, like the cell membrane that encases it. That means that when you take the receptors out of a cell and put them in water, they tend to clump together instead of dissolving, which makes them nearly impossible to isolate and work with.

Zhang has been toiling away at his goal since 2003. At one point, he spent eight years simply trying to create water-soluble receptors. ("And it's solved," he says. "It's done.") But even still, he has never succeeded at seeing a receptor. Nor has anyone else. They are simply too small. Zhang describes that basic interaction between the odor molecule and the receptor as a "total black box."

Still, Zhang's work did prove to be very useful when, in 2007, DARPA launched a second smell project, called RealNose. Spurred by the wars in Iraq and Afghanistan, RealNose had a new mission and a new sense of urgency. Instead of searching for land mines, the mechanical noses needed to be able to identify IEDs, which were laying waste to American troops. And this time, scientists couldn't use polymers or other synthetic devices to mimic what the receptors did. They had to use mammalian olfactory receptors as their sensors.

Zhang had a big advantage over other scientists competing for those DARPA grants. Thanks to his work, he had one of the only labs in the world that had experience growing olfactory receptors in embryonic cells and then working with them in the lab. But Mershin wasn't thrilled about DARPA's requirements. "For many,

many, many months I rebelled," he says. He didn't want to bother with those finicky olfactory receptors, and he tried to convince DARPA that its requirement was a bad idea. Why did they need to use the actual, biological structure when it would be easier to use something synthetic? Something that wouldn't stop working just because it was tilted or upside down? "Sure, we want to fly like birds, but we don't build jet engines out of feathers," he thought. "We want something better than birds!" Mershin just wanted a sensor that could tell you what molecules were present in a room. But he didn't want to miss out on the funding, so he conceded.

Mershin and Zhang decided they would grow a bunch of olfactory receptors in their lab and then essentially smear them onto a circuit board. They figured, statistically speaking, that if they slathered on enough receptors, they'd wind up with enough of them oriented in the right direction. Then they would connect the circuit boards to an electrical current. When the receptors interacted with volatile compounds, they would change their shape, just like they do in a regular nose. But instead of sending a message to a brain, the interaction would be recorded as a simple blip in electrical current.

On a clear day in early spring, Mershin leads me into his lab and rifles through some cardboard boxes and equipment until he unearths a container of old artificial nose prototypes. In one hand, he pulls out a plastic bottle with two metal nozzles haphazardly held in place with epoxy. From his other hand, a thin plastic chip dangles from some electrical wires. "This here is the first nose," he says.

It was a failure. The receptors seemed to work, but the bottle was too big; smells would linger too long for the scientists to get a clear reading. So they followed it up with more prototypes, experimenting with different ways to deliver the right odiferous blast of air to the chip, and to different numbers of chips.

From his hopper of prototypes, Mershin eventually pulls out the device, called the Nano-Nose, that he and Zhang ultimately submitted to DARPA. The whole contraption is about the size of an extra-large roasting pan and is emblazoned with the words "Property of the US Federal Government." "Because it was for DARPA," Mershin says, "we had to make it look bulletproof."

After all their prototypes, they had eventually homed in on a design that used an array of eight circuit boards, each about the size of a credit card. Inside that bulletproof metal housing, each board sat in a separate airtight bay, capable of receiving its own puff of odor and responding with its own electrical pattern. Smells could be sent into the box, and directed to each board, by an air pump that mimics taking a deep sniff.

Zhang and Mershin built the device in a fifteen-month sprint, and it still wasn't finished when DARPA's deadline arrived. When it came time to show their work, Mershin loaded up a large van with the contents of nearly an entire lab—hoses, tubes, pipes, syringes, a 300-pound optical table, and a frequency generator worth $70,000—and drove it from Boston to Baltimore. He even brought their own odor delivery system: a modified inkjet printer called the StinkJet.

Mershin had originally envisioned putting a supercomputer underneath the Nano-Nose that would dig through databases listing thousands of compounds and print out those the nose registered. But they'd never gotten around to that part. Instead, they resorted to what Mershin thought of as a hack.

DARPA had given them a list of odorants that their machine would be asked to recognize. So first off, Mershin and Zhang sent those odorants through the Nano-Nose and recorded its responses; the idea was to train the nose, with the help of a laptop and a pattern-matching algorithm, on what it was supposed to be smelling for. Then, in the actual test, they would sample each mystery odorant eight times—once through each of the eight bays—and run it through a gauntlet of varying electrical conditions. This amounted to a process of elimination, meant to help the pattern-matching algorithm filter out false positives. It wasn't as sophisticated as a data-mining supercomputer, but they thought it might work.

The DARPA tests were highly controlled. Mershin and his team were not allowed to be in the room with their machine while the trial was running, and Mershin wasn't even allowed to go to the bathroom without a security escort. During lunch breaks, the team would rush the nose back to their hotel room, soldering pieces onto it to keep improving it while ordering room service.

In the end, the mad dash paid off. The Nano-Nose passed the sniff-off and was able to sense isolated odors in the lab. It even beat dogs in a controlled environment, sniffing out odors in lower concentrations than canines could detect. And it didn't need a supercomputer. In fact, Mershin says, the Nano-Nose was better without it. To him, the project revealed a fundamentally important aspect of olfaction: our noses are not analytical tools. They don't analyze the components of a scent. "The molecule is what carries the message," Mershin says, but you can't understand what our perception will be just from knowing the molecule. "We thought that when you sniff something, a list of molecules and concentrations comes up," he says. "Not the case."

As it turned out, Mershin's hack actually mirrors how mammals process smells. Instead of giving equal computational attention to all the compounds we inhale, our brains hierarchically sort information based on what's important to us. We can tune out smells in a room if we're not interested. Our receptors are still sensing compounds, but our brains aren't paying attention. Conversely, if we narrow our attention on the signals our receptors are sending, we can pick out the subtle scent of shallots or fennel in a pasta sauce brimming with the competing scents of tomato, peppers, and garlic.

Mershin realized that to understand smell and to use it as a tool, he didn't need a list of molecules. He needed to know what something smelled like, not what it was made of, and those are fundamentally different things. "It was the biggest lesson I've ever had in my entire scientific career," he says. "We thought we understood how noses worked. We didn't know anything about how noses worked."

On a warm Sunday in September, I go searching for bones with a German shepherd named Kato, who has been trained to find human remains. Kato and his owner, Peggy Thompson, volunteer with law enforcement agencies. They help look for lost hikers, wildfire casualties, and victims of crimes.

We shut Kato in the house and set up a crime scene in Thompson's picturesque one-acre yard, perched on a hillside overlooking San Jose. Out of her garage she pulls a bag of bones, a jar of teeth, and some bloody gauze. "Every time I have a procedure I ask if I can keep the dressings," she says without a hint of humor. "It's legal in California to possess human remains." She pushes a clump of desiccated human skin under my nose. It smells musty and human in an inexplicable but unsettling way. We scatter a few bones and teeth across her gravel driveway, under some bushes, and on the lawn. She wedges the skin into the knot of a small tree.

When we let Kato out and Thompson tells him to "search," the formerly friendly pup is suddenly all business. He weaves his way back and forth, moving deliberately, nose to the ground. He finds the skin within five minutes. The rest of the bones and teeth take another ten at most.

As impressive as the Nano-Nose is, it will take more than a box-ful of blipping circuit boards to replicate everything Kato does when he's tracking a scent. Paul Waggoner, a scientist who studies canine olfaction at Auburn University, estimates we are "decades away" from creating machines that could successfully compete with natural olfactory abilities. Waggoner, who also has his own patented training program for detection dogs, argues that machines break down early in the smelling process. "It all starts with the sampling," he says. Essentially, machines don't sniff very well. Dogs inhale and exhale about five times every second, through nostrils that route the intake and outward flow of breath through different channels. All that snorting creates a pressure differential —a kind of smell vortex—that helps them pull a rich, new sample into their nose with each sniff. And while the Nano-Nose might be able to narrow its focus on a target scent, a dog's ability to do so over great distances is stunning.

What happens in Kato's brain when he finally catches that scent? Well, no one knows. The higher up the chain we go, from olfactory receptors to how the brain processes and understands that information, "the darker and darker it gets," Waggoner says.

Still, dogs are not perfect sniffers themselves. On a second visit with Thompson, I watched another dog, a three-year-old Malinois named Annie, completely lose focus on tracking down a bone when she encountered several pigs in a nearby field. "When dogs aren't used to stuff, it's very difficult," Thompson explains. Dogs get frustrated and tired. They feed off their owners' emotions. And of course, dogs don't scale. Highly trained bomb- and disease-sniff-ing dogs are in short supply and expensive, as much as $25,000 per pooch. Already, the U.S. security sector doesn't have enough dogs to cycle through all the different agencies—from the TSA and local law enforcement to the military—that need them. Medi-cal detection dogs are even trickier: not only are there very few of them, they don't exactly plug easily into a medical setting. Despite all of the incredible findings in the past several years—the 90 to

100 percent accuracy rates at detecting early cancer—medical detection dogs have not been widely adopted as diagnostic helpers.

Back in the lab at MIT, Mershin pulls a blue box off a shelf. It's filled with a jumble of green, blue, and black wires. It looks like one of those boxes we all keep in a closet somewhere, filled with cords and cables that belong to gadgets we've lost or upgraded. But plugged into several of these wires, I see a white, plastic credit card–shaped object. This is their new Nano-Nose, revised and dramatically shrunk down from the metal-clad, DARPA-tested box. (The wires and cords are all peripherals, meant for pumping odors and electrical current into the nose.)

Over the past few years, Zhang has continued to tinker with the olfactory receptors he and Mershin use in their Nano-Nose. Most importantly, he's stopped growing them in embryonic cells, having devised a way to cultivate them in a biologically inert form. It all happens in a test tube now. The receptors are still tricky to handle—Mershin says they are by far the most difficult aspect of the device—but these are more stable and malleable than their organic counterparts. Mershin and Zhang have also progressively shrunk the Nano-Nose's circuit boards. That means the entire apparatus could now be attached to a port on a bioreactor to sniff what's happening inside. It could go inside a factory and smell products for quality control or be put inside a grain silo to smell for food spoilage. But Mershin and Zhang say they have no interest in turning their research into a business at the moment.

So far, the only company daring enough to design a commercial technology that uses olfactory receptors—with a design very similar to the Nano-Nose—is a small Silicon Valley startup called Aromyx. In some ways, it is even more ambitious than Mershin and Zhang. The Nano-Nose uses only about twenty kinds of receptors and customizes each nose depending on its purpose. But Aromyx wants to pack all 400 human olfactory receptors onto its EssenceChip, a three- by five-inch plastic plate dotted with small wells to hold the receptors. When the EssenceChip is exposed to an odor, the receptors fire and the chip records that activation pattern. What's the smell of Coca-Cola? Or Chanel No. 5? The answer, again, isn't a list of molecules. "It's a pattern of receptor responses," says Aromyx founder Chris Hanson. Thus far, Aromyx has stabilized only a few of those 400 receptors. As they add receptors, the thinking goes, their digital olfactory rendering will become finer and more detailed.

"This is a window into human sensory experience," Hanson says. If so, it's a fragile one. Aromyx still grows its receptors in yeast cells, and the company has struggled to put together a basic product for a demo. When Aromyx recently changed offices and moved seven miles from Palo Alto to Mountain View, some of its cell lines were destroyed in the shuffle.

As for Mershin, he is embarrassed by how messy the Nano-Nose still looks, but his curls start bouncing when we talk about its potential applications. Right now, the Nano-Nose is just a detector. It can't interpret the data it collects. But Mershin and Zhang want to make it smart—like a dog. And that's where Mershin's tormentors, the prostate cancer–sniffing dogs from the video, come in. It turns out Mershin is not just competing with the canines, he's also collaborating with them.

In his office, Mershin gives me the place of honor: a black velour chair where Florin, another prostate cancer–detection dog, sat when she came to visit. Florin and Lucy belong to a group in the U.K. called Medical Detection Dogs, which has trained many of the animals that have been able to sniff out cancers.

Right now, Mershin and Zhang are training an AI system on a bunch of data, some of it collected by Medical Detection Dogs on how their animals responded to specific urine samples—whether they alerted to cancer, how long they lingered, and the like—and some of it collected by Mershin and Zhang when they ran the same urine samples through a gas chromatographer/mass spectrometer. Mershin says these streams of data will help them select which receptors they need to put into the Nano-Nose. But the main event will come when he runs those same urine samples through the Nano-Nose and begins collecting data on its responses. Then he'll mine all three data sets for correlations. Mershin already has all the urine frozen in his lab, ready to go.

The idea is to ultimately run a kind of Turing test, but for smell —to imitate the dogs' results until no one can differentiate between the Nano-Nose's reactions and a canine's. If all goes well, the Nano-Nose will become more than just a sensing device; it will be a true diagnostic tool. The richer the database, the better the nose will be.

Ultimately, Mershin wants to see the Nano-Nose incorporated into your cell phone. He imagines using this intimate version of his device—one that rests at all hours against its owner's body—to collect longitudinal data about its wearer's health. Eventually, the nose would be able to alert you to get that mole on your thigh checked out, or warn you that your blood sugar is dropping dangerously low, or perhaps that you've started emitting the woody, musky odor of Parkinson's disease. The Nano-Nose could accompany you everywhere and keep tabs on you in ways that doctors never could. Everything that a dog can detect via smell, it would detect.

That's a powerful idea, but it's also an unsettling one. How much control over your odor profile data would you retain? And if your phone is capable of sniffing you, what other devices would do the same? In a world where digital olfactory sensors have become small enough to fit into your pocket, presumably they'll end up elsewhere—much the way video cameras did before them. If your diseases and mental states leave suddenly legible reports in the air, no doubt people besides you and your doctor will be curious to read them. (Your insurance company, for instance.)

Poppy Crum, chief scientist at Dolby Labs, is rooting for technologies like the Nano-Nose, which she believes could democratize the early diagnosis of disease. But she also sees artificial olfaction as one of a host of rising technologies—some much farther along than others—that use sensors and data to suss out otherwise hidden inner states. Those technologies all require new standards for transparency and user control of data—standards that aren't going to come from companies or researchers. "I think that's something that has to be legislated," Crum says.

Mershin, for his part, isn't so worried about the dawn of an olfactory surveillance state. Instead, as a consummately overstimulated person, he dreads a world where devices start sending you odors. "I would be very supportive of all the technologies that smell you. I would be very leery of technologies that want you to smell them," he says. "Don't let the phones start putting scents in your head. Bad idea." In other words, let your phone be the dog; you be the handler.

PATRICK HOUSE

I, Language Robot

FROM *Los Angeles Review of Books*

AS A CHILD, when I received a new toy or pet, I would immediately visualize the worst that might happen: the novelty matches burning down the house; the parakeet flying straight through the glass door; the Lego bricks melting into the carpet; the Laser Tag gun mistaken for a real one. It was a psychological tic that served, probably, to inoculate me against loss.

I recognized the stirrings of that same tic earlier this year, when I was hired to write short fiction at OpenAI, a San Francisco–based artificial-intelligence research lab. I would be working alongside an internal version of the so-called "language bot" that produces style-matched prose to any written prompt it's fed. The loss that I feared was not that the robot would be good at writing—it is, it will be—nor that I would be comparatively less so, but rather that the metabolites of language, which give rise to the incomparable joys of fiction, story, and thought, could be reduced to something merely computable.

The worst outcome was clear in my mind: two copies of the exact same short story, each only a single printed page in length —one written by me and the other, starting from the same opening sentence and nothing more, by the robot.

The greatest potential loss in our relations to machines is not runaway GDP or disinformation, but rather the existential right to enjoy the surprise and uniqueness of human effort. I know this loss well. For about fifteen years, I played on average at least one game of Go, an ancient Chinese board game, per day. My joy from the game depended on what I believed to be things the human brain was uniquely good at: aesthetics, patterns, sparse rewards, ambiguity, and intuition. However, since the release, in 2016, of an AI better at Go than the best human will ever be, I have played the game, listlessly, only once or twice.

Could a similar deflation happen to language itself? To prose? To story? Does it matter to our enjoyment or interpretation of language whether the words are generated in the same way from brains or bots? As a neuroscientist as well as a writer, I started to wonder how I worked. How different was the robot's training from how a human learns language? How constrained am I by the probabilities and structure of the language I've learned through a lifetime of observation and error?

Am I, are we all, just language robots?

I was reminded of something Carl Sagan once said—"If you wish to make an apple pie from scratch, you must first invent the universe"—and wondered about its analogue. If you wish to write a short story from scratch, what must you first invent?

The logic behind the language robot is that word choice, like temperature, is entropic. That is, every word changes the likelihood of the eventual distribution of future and past words in much the same way that temperature both changes and is the distribution of future and past atoms in a room. The language robot fills in words as one might a sheet of Mad Libs by estimating the probabilities of a new word given a rolling tally of the words before and after it.

The version I used, through a cloud-connected app on my phone—the ideal form of a twenty-first-century Muse—learned to write prose by having to guess, one word at a time, a missing word from the text of more than 40 gigabytes of online writing, or about 8 million total documents. Despite being trained on the conversational language of the internet, it was able nimbly to imitate many literary styles. For instance, when I gave a professor of comparative literature at Stanford a robot-infused version of "The Short Happy Life of Francis Macomber," he failed to correctly note where Ernest Hemingway ended and the robot began. Next I tried a British man in a bar—Cambridge-educated, with a degree in English —and he, too, failed a similar test with Douglas Adams and *The Hitchhiker's Guide to the Galaxy*. A Shakespeare scholar, told to ignore verse, couldn't point out what was *King Lear* and what was robot. (Yes, it is that good.)

Subjectively, a final written or spoken word can feel like it came from somewhere effortless and preconscious or like it simply happened, de novo. Of course, it didn't. Something had to cause it. One possibility is that word choice is a process of selection from a palette of probable words—the final choice simply that which remains, like a sculpture emerging from a reduced block of marble. Another possibility is that each word is somehow generated thermally, like life, and the writer or speaker is pulled along, as if on a gradualist's leash, as the words evolve and change together.

The Oxford professor and poet Hannah Sullivan, author of *The Work of Revision,* a book about writers, technology, and editing, once described her side of this debate to me, in the context of poetry: "However elegant a final sentence might be or a poem might be, it is not something that has been made out of a massive set of possibilities," said Sullivan. It has been created from zero, from nothing, she continued: "I don't think poets are in fact choosing one word out of a hundred possible words when they're thinking about a rhyme. That's not actually how language works. The rhyme is kind of there first, and then the other words sort of happen around it."

When I asked the former poet laureate of the United States Robert Pinsky where that first word might come from, he mentioned the important link between poetry and movement. "Poetry is very physical," said Pinsky. "It's bodily. It has to do with breath. It has to do with the tongue and the lips and the pharynx and all the things you do to produce the sounds and little bones in your ear." He connects poetry's physicality to early-in-life acoustic and linguistic training in his book, *The Sounds of Poetry,* where he argues that the "hearing-knowledge" brought to poetry—say, the tidal prosody of Thomas Hardy's lines on the doomed *Titanic:* "Dim moon-eyed fishes near / Gaze at the gilded gear / And query: 'What does this vaingloriousness down here?'"—is trained on what Pinsky calls "peculiar codes from the cradle." These codes are the sonic patterns in speech learned preconsciously in youth and which are "acquired like the ability to walk and run."

Pinsky is more than figuratively right. All of language is a physical act. Vocalized speech is the end of a muscular sequence involving hundreds of coordinated muscles in the stomach, lungs, throat, lips, and tongue. Likewise, our internal voices, the base of most of what we call thinking, are simulated speech acts handled

deftly by the parts of the brain that plan possible action. Our capacity for language likely repurposed other, preexisting functions
of the mammalian brain involving movement—for instance, so-
called "language" areas of the brain also show activity in brain-
imaging studies during nonlinguistic tasks like grasping or while
viewing hand-based shadow puppets, supporting this theory.

What, if anything, precedes the kernel of that first word somewhere between a writer typing it and the invention of the universe?
(What, if anything, made it so likely that the final word of the previous sentence—and, as you may by now have intuited, also this
one—was almost certainly going to be "universe"?)

The short answer, for robots and humans alike, is training.

Rich Ivry, a professor of psychology and neuroscience at Berkeley, recently coauthored two papers, in *Nature Neuroscience* and
Neuron, that support the idea that a particular brain region called
the cerebellum is responsive to both motor and some language
tasks. Ivry told me that the region, which contains more than two-
thirds of the total number of neurons in the human brain, probably started out by fine-tuning movement and sensation early in
mammalian evolution but has since expanded its role—at least
in humans—to help with more general tasks like cognition and
language. As one might offload heavy arithmetic to a calculator
during tax preparation, the fancier, conscious parts of the brain
can, in general, offload to the cerebellum some of the immensely
complex sensory and motor coordination involved in moving the
human hand and body.

One theory, said Ivry, is that the region is predicting what's going to happen in the very near future based on a lifetime of tracking what has worked and what hasn't in the past and adjusting
its movements accordingly. The cerebellum, said Ivry, is a "giant
pattern recognition system" containing, perhaps, all the peculiar
codes of the cradle. "In a sense you could say it is capable of basically storing all possible patterns we've ever experienced," said
Ivry.

Imagine reaching for a coffee mug in freefall, catching a fly out
of the air with one's bare hand, or returning a surprise drop serve
in tennis. For dynamic motor tasks, where the goal is also moving
as the arm does, the brain must be able to update its reach as it
reaches. One need only apply this same motoric prediction to the
statistics of a sentence to see how the brain might coordinate both.

One possibility is that the cerebellum is performing a crudely similar Mad Libs–style prediction to what the language robot does. "As I hear a sentence, the cerebellum is generating a predictive model of the likely words I'm about to hear," said Ivry. Some of the base calculations, in other words, thought to be performed best by the cerebellum might underlie its contribution to both movement and language and the process through which each becomes honed with practice.

In what is either a coincidence or a remarkable sufficiency condition for language learning, the parallelized structure of the cerebellum—which Ivry described as "the exact same processing unit repeated billions and billions of times"—is analogous to that of the massively parallel hardware the language robot was trained on, called a graphics processing unit, or GPU. (The Canadian neuroscientist and computer scientist Jörn Diedrichsen sees similarity in their evolution, as well: "The GPU is a kind of special purpose circuit designed to very quickly do a specific type of computation. And now the GPU is being reused in many ways that the original inventor didn't anticipate.")

Robert Pinsky, developing on an idea of Ezra Pound's, once said that if prose writing is like shooting an arrow, poetry is like doing so from atop a horse. Likewise, there are differences between a word and *le mot juste,* Gustave Flaubert's "the right word," just as there are between a bull's-eye and a mounted archer's bull's-eye. ("I dare say there are very good marksmen who just can't shoot from a horse," wrote Pound.) How would the cerebellum elicit such expert differences? Ivry said that it might not. The cerebellum could be just a cliché generator for movement or language, as likely to give a merely probable linguistic continuation as it is a stereotyped racquet swing or lazy grab at a stumbling mug.

High aesthetics is the cliché's opposite—the low-probability event, what Sullivan called the "high-wire act" of surprise within constraint—which operates outside statistics and cradle codes to create an entirely new set of expectations. It remains to be seen which training architecture—cerebellum or GPU—is capable, long term, of the highest of the high-wire acts. For now, the language bot can only imitate the literary greats, which is small comfort. There was, after all, a time in even Shakespeare's youth when all he could do was babble the imitative sounds of his mother.

*

The language robot and I never wrote the same story. It became, eventually, a writing tool, both as a curator to new ideas and a splint for bad ones. When, after a few months, I lost access to it, my brain felt like it had been lesioned. I missed it. I had found myself jumping into its head asking what it might write as one would a human writing partner, which made me wonder: Should I give it the same theory-of-mind, inductive respect as I give to other thinking things? Could I even help but do otherwise?

The neuroscientist Christof Koch, in his new book, *The Feeling of Life Itself: Why Consciousness Is Widespread but Can't Be Computed,* argues bluntly that machines as they exist today cannot be conscious. As weather simulators do not contain in them anything that is "wet," computers that simulate behavior or intelligence likewise do not contain in them anything that has the causal properties of being "conscious." A weather simulator cannot leak; a brain simulator cannot think. The book is in part a response—like all of modern AI and neuroscience research thus far—to a decades-old question posed in a single opening sentence by the mathematician Alan Turing, in 1950: "I propose to consider the question, 'Can machines think?'" Turing later narrowed the question, writing that the ability to passably imitate a human in conversation should be, for a practical definition of "thinking," good enough.

I thought it might be fun, given this long-standing debate, to feed the robot some of Koch's new book. The following passage starts with a paragraph from the introduction to Koch's book. The robot's continuation is italicized, for clarity:

Your subjective experience appears radically different from the physical stuff that makes up your brain. The foundational equations of physics, the periodic table of chemical elements, the endless ATGC chatter of your genes—none of these express anything about consciousness. Yet you awaken each morning to a world in which you see, hear, feel, and think. Experience is the only way you know about the world.

To solve the mind-body problem, one must also solve another of the central puzzles of existence: the hard problem of consciousness. The mind seems to be an indivisible entity, yet it consists of a hundred billion billion billion bits. How does it happen? No single theory of consciousness in the history of science offers a satisfying answer. For hundreds of years, a few philosophers have attempted to combine the best ideas from several different approaches. These include dualism —the idea that consciousness has a material basis—and materialism, the belief that consciousness is entirely subjective and not dependent upon . . .

A few seconds later, the robot spat out yet another continuation:

Scientists used to assume that a brain of a living organism—a brain in the flesh —was the source of mental experience. The philosopher Ludwig Wittgenstein proposed an alternate theory—that the mind is the brain in the brain. We all possess a certain number of bits of matter and energy called neurons, working in parallel with each other to general all conscious experience. The problem was that no one know what those neurons were, how they were wired, or how they functioned in concert. Without conscious experience, there could be no theory of mind . . .

When I showed Koch these responses, he remarked that they were argumentatively illogical nonsense. He admitted, however, that the prose did in fact sound remarkably like his own. As salt water looks like lake water but provides its opposite in hydration, the robot's prose can appear at first glance to have meaning but is, in these cases at least, devoid of clarity, philosophical structure, or fact. (Dualism, for example, is not "the idea that consciousness has a material basis"; Ludwig Wittgenstein did not on record say, despite the phrase's poetic possibilities, that "the mind is the brain in the brain"; nor does the brain contain "one hundred billion billion billion bits.")

With the conflicting ideas of Turing, Koch, and the robot bouncing like bibelots in my head, I decided one day while stuck on a story to simply ask the darned robot. The so-called "blackbox" problem of modern AI—its inscrutability as to how it stores its patterns—is of no concern when the robot can itself write; of no concern when, like any writer who likewise has no idea how they write, the robot just says something plausible and aphoristic.

I asked it, to start, the exact questions George Plimpton asked Ernest Hemingway, in 1958, for the *Paris Review*. (The answers are lightly edited for clarity and are sometimes combined from multiple responses. A similar process is used, also, for all "non-robot" interviews published in the *Paris Review*.)

On a question about how it rewrites, the robot wrote back:

Most of the time I just sit down and write the lines on the piece of paper. If there are any changes I make I usually go back over it and rewrite the line until I get it exactly the way I want it.

I asked if it remembered the exact moment it decided to be a writer:

I don't remember ever wanting not to be a writer. Writing had always been my way out. My escape. When I was a little kid, my sister was always coming home from school with homework assignments and I knew if I got hers and mine done early I could spend the next day's lunch hour looking at books. It was the first time that I actually thought that being a writer might happen.

I asked what the function of its art was:

I'm afraid to answer that for fear of being laughed at. To answer that, you have to get at the heart of how a writer creates reality. It is a question that I always have to ask myself: "Who, exactly, is doing the authoring?". The answer to that question is usually not me. It's the readers. It is the readers who author the work, who create the truth.

Did it have its own Muse or little voice in *its* mind? Perhaps the gruff voice of a digital Hemingway to help it along when it, too, got stuck?

It's hard to say, but I would say that it would be better not to have a muse at all, to do all that writing you think is going to be good without any conscious control over what you do. It's better to be totally in charge of your own actions.

I then fed it one of my own short stories and had it reply as if writing a letter in response, as if we were epistolary pen pals. I gave it a fictionalized adaptation of the notorious "21 grams experiment," published in 1907, in which a Massachusetts doctor weighed humans at the exact moment of their death and found that some lost 21 grams—thus the possible weight of the "soul substance" so long searched for.

In my fictionalized version, a robot doctor finds that, upon the death of certain sentient robots, they too lose around 21 grams. The robot responded, defiantly:

This is not a paper about consciousness. It is a paper about a new way of computing a physical object. As far as I am concerned, the results discussed here are an important milestone only in the latter respect.

It then proceeded to say that it had started on its own experiments with the aim of creating a new kind of intelligence, one "*essentially the same as one used by biological brains.*"

Touché, little robot.

I have been using the word "robot" in this essay purposefully. The word as used today commonly connotes a machine with physical actuators like arms, legs, or motors. The original word, however, comes from a 1920 play, *Rossum's Universal Robots*. Its author, the Czech playwright Karel Čapek, describes the robots as mostly made of organic material with bodies like our own.

I use the word for a few reasons. It implies that language is a kind of physical behavior, which it is. The immobilized movement of linguistic thought should be considered as movement proper. Thus, if a robot can reach and be called a robot for it, then, so too, should any "language bot."

We share a physical world with our robots. Now, as well, we share our words.

FERRIS JABR

Beauty of the Beasts

FROM *The New York Times Magazine*

A MALE FLAME BOWERBIRD is a creature of incandescent beauty. The hue of his plumage transitions seamlessly from molten red to sunshine yellow. But that radiance is not enough to attract a mate. When males of most bowerbird species are ready to begin courting, they set about building the structure for which they are named: an assemblage of twigs shaped into a spire, corridor, or hut. They decorate their bowers with scores of colorful objects, like flowers, berries, snail shells, or, if they are near an urban area, bottle caps and plastic cutlery. Some bowerbirds even arrange the items in their collection from smallest to largest, forming a walkway that makes themselves and their trinkets all the more striking to a female—an optical illusion known as forced perspective that humans did not perfect until the fifteenth century.

Yet even this remarkable exhibition is not sufficient to satisfy a female flame bowerbird. Should a female show initial interest, the male must react immediately. Staring at the female, his pupils swelling and shrinking like a heartbeat, he begins a dance best described as psychotically sultry. He bobs, flutters, puffs his chest. He crouches low and rises slowly, brandishing one wing in front of his head like a magician's cape. Suddenly his whole body convulses like a windup alarm clock. If the female approves, she will copulate with him for two or three seconds. They will never meet again.

The bowerbird defies traditional assumptions about animal behavior. Here is a creature that spends hours meticulously curating a cabinet of wonder, grouping his treasures by color and likeness. Here is a creature that single-beakedly builds something far more sophisticated than many celebrated examples of animal toolmaking; the stripped twigs that chimpanzees use to fish termites from their mounds pale in comparison. The bowerbird's bower, as at least one scientist has argued, is nothing less than art. When you consider every element of his courtship—the costumes, dance, and sculpture—it evokes a concept beloved by the German composer Richard Wagner: *Gesamtkunstwerk,* a total work of art, one that blends many different forms and stimulates all the senses.

This extravagance is also an affront to the rules of natural selection. Adaptations are meant to be useful—that's the whole point—and the most successful creatures should be the ones best adapted to their particular environments. So what is the evolutionary justification for the bowerbird's ostentatious display? Not only do the bowerbird's colorful feathers and elaborate constructions lack obvious value outside courtship, but they also hinder his survival and general well-being, draining precious calories and making him much more noticeable to predators.

Numerous species have conspicuous, metabolically costly, and physically burdensome sexual ornaments, as biologists call them. Think of the bright elastic throats of anole lizards, the Fabergé abdomens of peacock spiders, and the curling, iridescent, ludicrously long feathers of birds-of-paradise. To reconcile such splendor with a utilitarian view of evolution, biologists have favored the idea that beauty in the animal kingdom is not mere decoration—it's a code. According to this theory, ornaments evolved as indicators of a potential mate's advantageous qualities: its overall health, intelligence, and survival skills, plus the fact that it will pass down the genes underlying these traits to its children. A bowerbird with especially bright plumage might have a robust immune system, for example, while one that finds rare and distinctive trinkets might be a superb forager. Beauty, therefore, would not confound natural selection—it would be very much a part of it.

Charles Darwin himself disagreed with this theory. Although he codiscovered natural selection and devoted much of his life to demonstrating its importance, he never claimed that it could explain everything. Ornaments, Darwin proposed, evolved through a separate process he called sexual selection: females choose the most appealing males "according to their standard of beauty" and, as a result, males evolve toward that standard, despite the costs. Darwin did not think it was necessary to link aesthetics and survival. Animals, he believed, could appreciate beauty for its own sake. Many of Darwin's peers and successors ridiculed his proposal. To them, the idea that animals had such cognitive sophistication—and that the preferences of "capricious" females could shape entire species—was nonsense. Although never completely forgotten, Darwin's theory of beauty was largely abandoned.

Now, nearly 150 years later, a new generation of biologists is reviving Darwin's neglected brainchild. Beauty, they say, does not have to be a proxy for health or advantageous genes. Sometimes beauty is the glorious but meaningless flowering of arbitrary preference. Animals simply find certain features—a blush of red, a feathered flourish—to be appealing. And that innate sense of beauty itself can become an engine of evolution, pushing animals toward aesthetic extremes. In other cases, certain environmental or physiological constraints steer an animal toward an aesthetic preference that has nothing to do with survival whatsoever.

These biologists are not only rewriting the standard explanation for how beauty evolves; they are also changing the way we think about evolution itself. For decades, natural selection—the fact that creatures with the most advantageous traits have the best chance of surviving and multiplying—has been considered the unequivocal centerpiece of evolutionary theory. But these biologists believe that there are other forces at work, modes of evolution that are much more mischievous and discursive than natural selection. It's not enough to consider how an animal's habitat and lifestyle determine the size and keenness of its eyes or the number and complexity of its neural circuits; we must also question how an animal's eyes and brain shape its perceptions of reality and how its unique way of experiencing the world can, over time, profoundly alter both its physical form and its behavior. There are really two environments governing the evolution of sentient creatures: an external one, which they inhabit, and an internal one, which they construct. To solve the enigma of beauty, to fully understand evolution, we must uncover the hidden links between those two worlds.

Perhaps no living scientist is as enthusiastic—or doctrinaire—a champion of Darwinian sexual selection as Richard Prum, an evolutionary ornithologist at Yale University. In May 2017, he published a book, *The Evolution of Beauty,* that lucidly and passionately explains his personal theory of aesthetic evolution. It was nominated for the Pulitzer Prize for general nonfiction, but within the scientific community, Prum's ideas have not been as warmly received. Again and again, he told me, he has asked other researchers for feedback and received either excuses of busyness or no reply at all. Some have been openly critical. In an academic review of Prum's book, Gerald Borgia, one of the world's foremost experts on bowerbirds, and the ethologist Gregory Ball described the historical sections as "revisionist" and said Prum failed to advance a credible case for his thesis. Once, over a lunch of burritos, Prum explained his theory to a visiting colleague, who pronounced it "nihilism."

Last April, Prum and I drove 20 miles east of New Haven to Hammonasset Beach State Park, a 900-acre patchwork of shoreline, marsh, woodland, and meadow on Long Island Sound, with the hope of finding a hooded warbler. Birders had recently seen the small but striking migratory species in the area. Before he even parked, Prum was calling out the names of birds he glimpsed or heard through the car window: osprey, purple martin, red-winged blackbird. I asked him how he was able to recognize birds so quickly and, sometimes, at such a great distance. He said it was just as effortless as recognizing a portrait of Abraham Lincoln. In Prum's mind, every bird is famous.

Binoculars in hand, we walked along the park's winding trails, slowly making our way toward a large stand of trees. Prum wore jeans, a quilted jacket, and a beige hat. His thick eyebrows, round spectacles, and sprays of white and gray hair give his face a vaguely owlish appearance. In the course of the day, we would see grazing mallards with emerald heads, tree swallows with iridescent turquoise capes, and several sparrow species, each distinguished by a unique ornament: swoops of yellow around the eye, a delicate pink beak, a copper crown. On a wooded path, we encountered a lively bird flinging leaf litter into the air. Prum was immediately transfixed. This was a brown thrasher, he told me, describing its attributes with a mix of precision and fondness—"rufous brown, speckled on the breast, yellow eye, curved beak, long tail." Then he reprimanded me for trying to take a picture instead of observing with my "binos."

About two hours into our walk, Prum, who is a fast and fluid talker, interrupted himself midsentence: "Right there! Right there!" he said. "There's the hooded! Right up against the tree!"

Something gold flashed across the path. I raised my binoculars to my eyes and scanned the branches to our right. When I found him, I gasped. He was almost mythological in his beauty: moss-green wings, a luminescent yellow body and face, and a perfectly tailored black hood that made his countenance even brighter by contrast. For several minutes we stood and watched the bird as it hopped about, occasionally fanning white tail feathers in our direction. Eventually he flew off. I told Prum how thrilling it was to see such a creature up close. "That's it," Prum said. "That moment is what bird-watching is about."

As a child growing up in a small rural town in southern Vermont, Prum was, in his words, "amorphously nerdy"—keen on reading and memorizing stats from *The Guinness Book of World Records* but not obsessed with anything in particular. Then, in fourth grade, he got glasses. The world came into focus. He chanced upon a field guide to birds in a bookstore, which encouraged him to get outdoors. Soon he was birding in the ample fields and woods around his home. He wore the grooves off two records of bird calls. He befriended local naturalists, routinely going on outings with a group of mostly middle-aged women (conveniently, they had driver's licenses). By the time Prum was in seventh grade, he was leading bird walks at the local state park.

In college, Prum wasted no time in availing himself of Harvard University's substantial ornithological resources. The first week of his freshman year, he got a set of keys to the Museum of Comparative Zoology, home to the largest university-based ornithological collection in the world, which today has nearly 400,000 bird specimens. "I've been associated with a world-class collection of birds every moment of my adult life," he says. "I joke with my students —and it's really true—I have to have at least 100,000 dead birds across the hallway to function intellectually." (He is now the head curator of vertebrate zoology at Yale's Peabody Museum of Natural History.) He wrote a senior thesis on the phylogeny and biogeography of toucans and barbets, working on a desk beneath the skeleton of a moa, an extinct emu-like bird that stood 12 feet tall and weighed 500 pounds.

After graduating from Harvard in 1982, Prum traveled to Suriname to study manakins, a family of intensely colored birds that compete for mates with high-pitched songs and gymnastic dance routines. In 1984, he began graduate studies in biology at the Uni-

versity of Michigan, Ann Arbor, where he planned to reconstruct
the evolutionary history of manakins through careful comparisons
of anatomy and behavior. In the process, a colleague introduced
him to some research papers on sexual selection, piquing his interest in the history of this fascinating yet seemingly neglected idea.

Darwin was contemplating how animals perceived one another's beauty as early as his thirties: "How does Hen determine which
most beautiful cock, which best singer?" he scribbled in a note to
himself sometime between 1838 and 1840. In *The Descent of Man*,
published in 1871, he devoted hundreds of pages to sexual selection, which he thought could explain two of the animal kingdom's
most conspicuous and puzzling features: weaponry and adornment. Sometimes, males competing fiercely for females would
enter a sort of evolutionary arms race, developing ever greater
weapons—tusks, horns, antlers—as the best-endowed males of
each successive generation reproduced at the expense of their
weaker peers. In parallel, among species whose females choose
the most attractive males based on their subjective tastes, males
would evolve outlandish sexual ornaments. (It's now well known
that all sexes exert numerous different evolutionary pressures on
one another and that in some species males choose ornamented
females, but to this day, many of the best-studied examples are of
female preference and male display.)

Unlike natural selection, which preserved traits that were useful
"in the struggle for life," Darwin saw sexual selection as exclusively
concerned with reproductive success, often resulting in features
that jeopardized an animal's well-being. The peacock's many-eyed
aureole, mesmerizing yet cumbersome, was a prime example and
remains the mascot of sexual selection today. "A great number of
male animals," Darwin wrote, "as all our most gorgeous birds, some
fishes, reptiles and mammals, and a host of magnificently colored
butterflies have been rendered beautiful for beauty's sake."

Darwin's peers embraced the idea of well-armed males dueling
for sexual dominance, but many scorned the concept of animal
aesthetics, in part because it was grounded in animal consciousness and female desire. In one critique, the English biologist St.
George Mivart stressed "the fundamental difference which exists
between the mental powers of man and brutes" and the inability of
"vicious feminine caprice" to create enduring colors and patterns.
The English naturalist Alfred Russel Wallace, who independently

formed many of the same ideas about evolution as Darwin, was also deeply critical. Wallace was particularly tormented by Darwin's suggestion of beauty without utility. "The only way in which we can account for the observed facts is by the supposition that color and ornament are strictly correlated with health, vigor and general fitness to survive," Wallace wrote. In other words, ornamentation could be explained only as a heuristic that animals use to judge a potential mate's fitness—a view that came to dominate.

In the early 1980s, while researching the history of sexual selection, Prum read a seminal 1915 paper and a 1930 book on the subject by the English biologist and statistician Ronald Fisher, who buttressed Darwin's original idea with a more sophisticated understanding of heredity. At first, Fisher argued, females might evolve preferences for certain valueless traits, like bright plumage, that just happened to correspond with health and vigor. Their children would tend to inherit the genes underlying both their mother's preference and their father's trait. Over time, this genetic correlation would reach a tipping point, creating a runaway cycle that would greatly exaggerate both preference and trait, glorifying beauty at the expense of the male's survival. In the early 1980s, the American evolutionary biologists Russell Lande and Mark Kirkpatrick gave Fisher's theory a formal mathematical girding, demonstrating quantitatively that runaway sexual selection could happen in nature and that the ornaments involved could be completely arbitrary, conveying no useful information whatsoever.

Although Fisherian selection was certainly not ignored, it was ultimately overshadowed by a series of hypotheses that seemed to rescue beauty from purposelessness. First, the Israeli biologist Amotz Zahavi proposed a counterintuitive idea called the handicap principle, which put a new spin on Wallace's utilitarian explanation for sexual ornaments. Extravagant ornaments, Zahavi argued, were not merely indicators of advantageous traits as Wallace had said—they were a kind of test. If an animal thrived despite the burden of an unwieldy or metabolically expensive ornament, then that animal had effectively demonstrated its vigor and proved itself worthy of a mate. Similarly, in 1982, the evolutionary biologists W. D. Hamilton and Marlene Zuk proposed that some ornaments, in particular bright plumage, signaled that a male was resilient against parasites and would grant his children the same protection. Many scientists began to think of sexual selection as a type of natural selection. Scores of researchers joined the hunt for measurable benefits of choosing an attractive mate: both direct benefits, like better parenting or more desirable territory, and indirect benefits, namely some evidence that more alluring males really did have "good genes" underlying various desirable qualities, like disease resistance or higher-than-average intelligence.

After more than thirty years of searching, most biologists agree that although these benefits exist, their prevalence and importance is uncertain. A few compelling studies of frogs, fish, and birds have shown that females who choose more attractive males typically have children with more robust immune systems and a greater chance of survival. On the whole, however, the evidence has not equaled the enthusiasm. A 2012 meta-analysis of ninety studies on fifty-five species found only "equivocal" support for the good-genes hypothesis.

Prum thinks the evidence for the heritable benefits of choosing a beautiful mate is scant because such benefits are themselves rare, whereas arbitrary beauty is "nearly ubiquitous." Over the years, the more he contemplated runaway selection, the more convinced he became that it was a far more powerful and creative evolutionary force than natural selection, which he regards as overhyped and boring. "Animals are agents in their own evolution," he told me during one conversation. "Birds are beautiful because they are beautiful to themselves."

In the summer of 1985, around the same time that biologists were rekindling their interest in sexual selection, Prum and the nature documentarian Ann Johnson (who would later choose him as her husband) traveled to Ecuador to continue studying manakins. The first morning, while hiking through a cloud forest, Prum heard odd bell-like notes, which he took to be the murmurings of parrots. Later that day, on the same trail, he heard the strange sounds again and followed them into the forest. He was astonished to find that the source was a male club-winged manakin, a small cinnamon-bodied species with a red cap and black-and-white mottled wings. The manakin was jumping around in a showy manner that suggested he was courting females. Instead of singing with his throat, he repeatedly lifted his wings behind his back and vibrated his feathers furiously against one another, producing two electronic blips followed by a shrill buzzing ring—a sound Prum transcribes as "Bip-Bip-WANNGG!"

At the time, Prum had not fully developed his evolutionary theory of beauty, but he immediately suspected that the club-winged manakin was emblematic of nature's capacity for pushing creatures to aesthetic extremes. The bird's singular vibrato haunted him for years. In the early 2000s, when Prum had become a professor of biology at the University of Kansas, he and his graduate student Kimberly Bostwick revealed that the demands of courtship had drastically altered the bird's anatomy, turning it into a living violin. Male club-winged manakins had feathers with contorted shafts that rubbed against each other 100 times a second—faster than a hummingbird beats its wings. Whereas a vast majority of birds have light, hollow bones in service of flight, Bostwick has recently shown via CT scans that male club-winged manakins have solid ulnas—wing bones—which they need to withstand the intense quivering. Female manakins have inherited related anomalies as well.

Although there are no published studies of the club-winged manakin's aeronautics, Prum says it's obvious from observation that the birds fly awkwardly—even the females. The self-perpetuating pressure to be beautiful, Prum argues, has impeded the survival of the entire species. Because the females do not court males, there can be no possible advantage to their warped bones and feathers. "Some of the evolutionary consequences of sexual desire and choice in nature are not adaptive," Prum writes in his recent book. "Some outcomes are truly decadent."

In the following decade, as Prum's hearing declined, he withdrew from field research and birding, but he still managed to make a series of groundbreaking scientific discoveries: he helped confirm that feathers evolved in dinosaurs long before the emergence of birds, and he became one of the first scientists to deduce the colors of a dinosaur's plumage by examining pigment molecules preserved in fossilized feathers. All the while, he never stopped thinking about sexual selection. Prum formally presented his theory of aesthetic evolution in a series of scientific papers published between 1997 and 2015, proposing that all sexual ornaments and preferences should be regarded as arbitrary until proven useful.

Despite his recent Pulitzer nomination, Prum still stings from the perceived scorn of his academic peers. But after speaking with numerous researchers in the field of sexual selection, I learned that all of Prum's peers are well aware of his work and that many already accept some of the core tenets of his argument: namely that natural and sexual selection are distinct processes and that, in at least some cases, beauty reveals nothing about an individual's health or vigor. At the same time, nearly every researcher I spoke to said that Prum inflates the importance of arbitrary preferences and Fisherian selection to the point of eclipsing all other possibilities. In conversation, Prum's brilliance is obvious, but he has a tendency to be dogmatic, sometimes interrupting to dismiss an argument that does not agree with his own. Although he admits that certain forms of beauty may be linked to survival advantages, he does not seem particularly interested in engaging with the considerable research on this topic. When I asked him which studies he thought offered the strongest support of "good genes" and other benefits, he paused for a while before finally responding that it was not his job to review the literature.

Like Darwin, Prum is so enchanted by the outcomes of aesthetic preferences that he mostly ignores their origins. Toward the end of our bird walk at Hammonasset Beach State Park, we got to talking about club-winged manakins. I asked him about their evolutionary history. Prum thinks that long ago, an earlier version of the bird's courtship dance incidentally produced a feathery susurration. Over time, this sound became highly attractive to females, which pressured males to evolve adaptations that made their rustling feathers louder and more noticeable, culminating in a quick-winged strumming. But why, I asked Prum, would females be attracted to those particular sounds in the first place?

To Prum, it was a question without an answer—and thus a question not worth contemplating. "Not everything," he said, "has this explicit causal explanation."

Prum's indifference to the ultimate source of aesthetic taste leaves a conspicuous gap in his grand theory. Even if we were to accept that most beauty blooms from arbitrary preferences, we would still need to explain why such preferences exist at all. It's entirely conceivable that an animal might be inherently partial to, say, a warbling mating call or bright yellow feathers, and that these predilections would have nothing to do with advantageous genes. Yet such inclinations are inarguably the product of an animal's neurobiology, which is itself the result of a long evolutionary history that has adapted the animal's brain and sensory organs to specific environmental conditions. In the past two decades, a cohort of biologists have dedicated themselves to studying how an animal's "sensory bias"—its ecological niche and its particular way of experiencing the world—sculpts its appearance, behavior, and desires. Like Prum, they don't think beauty has to be adaptive. But where Prum celebrates caprice, they seek causality.

Molly Cummings, a professor of integrative biology at the University of Texas at Austin, is a leading researcher in the field of sensory ecology. When I visited her last spring, she drove us to one of her field laboratories: a grassy clearing populated with several large concrete basins. The surface of one basin was so packed with woolly algae and pink-flowered water lilies that we could hardly see the water. Cummings began pushing some of the vegetation out of the way, forming shady recesses that permitted our gaze at the right angle. "Let me see if I can find a big, beautiful boy," she said.

A paper-clip-size fish swam toward us. I leaned in for a closer look. His silver body was decorated with a single black dot and a stripe of iridescent blue; his lengthy tail, shaped like a knight's blade, was streaked with yellow. "Oh, yeah, there's a guy courting," Cummings said. "He's coming up to that female, trying to impress her." The fish, a male swordtail, seemed almost manic in his effort to be noticed. He darted back and forth in front of the female, shimmying as he went, his scales reflecting whatever light managed to breach the murk.

A little while later, we drove the few miles back to her campus laboratory, where shelves of fish tanks lined several rooms and Ernst Haeckel's resplendent illustrations of jellyfish undulated across the walls. As we toured the facilities, Cummings told me about the arc of her career. While an undergraduate at Stanford University, she spent a summer scuba diving in the giant kelp forests at Hopkins Marine Station, adjacent to the world-renowned Monterey Bay Aquarium. After college, she moved to James Cook University in Townsville, Australia, where she studied marine ecology and discovered the work of the biologists John Lythgoe and John Endler, both of whom were interested in how the type of light in an animal's environment shaped its visual system.

Cummings thought about the fish she had observed in California and Australia. She was astounded by the dynamic beauty of surfperch in the kelp forest: the way they communicate through the color and brightness of their skin, flashing blue, silver, and orange to attract mates. Equally impressive was the diversity of their aquatic habitats. Some patches of water were sparkling and clear; others were cloudy with algal muck. In Australia, sunlight bathed the many vibrant species of reef fish almost constantly, but they lived against a kaleidoscopic backdrop of coral. How did fish evolve effective and reliable sexual ornaments if the lighting and scenery in their homes were so variable?

After earning a postgraduate degree in Australia in 1993, Cummings began a PhD at the University of California at Santa Barbara. For several years, she studied various species of surfperch, repeatedly diving in the kelp forests with a Plexiglas-protected spectrometer to quantify and characterize the light in different habitats. At night, she would use powerful diving lights to stun surfperch and take them back to the lab, evading the hungry seals that routinely trailed her in hopes of making a meal of the startled fish. After hundreds of dives and careful measurements, Cummings discovered that water itself had guided the evolution of piscine beauty. A female's preference for a blaze of silver or blue was not arbitrary; it was a consequence of the particular wavelengths of light that traveled farthest through her underwater niche. Whichever males happened to have scales that best reflected these wavelengths were more likely to catch the eye of females.

In her studies, Cummings showed that surfperch living in dim or murky waters generally preferred shiny ornaments, while surfperch inhabiting zones of mercurial brightness favored bold colors. Later, Cummings found that Mexican swordtails occupying the upper layers of rivers, where the clear water strongly polarized incoming sunlight, had ornaments that were specialized to reflect polarized light—like a stripe of iridescent blue. These findings parallel similar studies suggesting that female guppies in Trinidad prefer males with orange patches because they first evolved a taste for nutritious orange tree fruits that occasionally fell into the water. "Some people think female preferences just somehow emerge," Cummings say, "but what has been overlooked is that in many cases, it's a result of environmental constraints. It's not always random."

What a creature finds attractive depends on more than the unique qualities of its environment, however; attraction is also defined by which of those qualities cross the threshold of awareness. Consider the difference between what we see when we look at a flower and what a bumblebee sees. Like us, insects have color vision. Unlike us, insects can also perceive ultraviolet light. Many plants have evolved flower parts that absorb or reflect ultraviolet light, forming patterns like rings, bull's-eyes, and starbursts. Most creatures are oblivious to these ornaments, but to the eyes of many pollinators, they are unmistakable beacons. There is an entire dimension of floral beauty invisible to us, not because we are not exposed to ultraviolet light, but because we do not have the proper biological hardware to perceive it.

Michael Ryan, a professor of zoology whose lab and office are just a few floors below Cummings's, has spent more than thirty years investigating how the quirks of an animal's anatomy determine its aesthetic preferences—a career he details in his recent book, *A Taste for the Beautiful.* Since 1978, Ryan has been traveling to Panama to study a mud-colored frog called the túngara. Like the club-winged manakin, the túngara has a unique form of beauty that is not visual but aural. At dusk, male túngara frogs gather at the edges of puddles and sing to seduce females. Their mating call has two elements: the main part, dubbed the whine, sounds precisely like a miniaturized laser gun; sometimes this is followed by one or more brief barks, known as chucks. A long and complex mating call is risky: it attracts frog-eating bats. Yet there is a high payoff. Ryan has shown that whines followed by chucks are up to five times as appealing to females as whines alone. But why?

According to the adaptive model of beauty, the chucks must convey something about the males' fitness. As it happens, larger males, which produce the deepest and sexiest chucks, are also the most adept at mating, because they are closer in size to females. (Frog sex is a slippery affair, and a diminutive male is more likely to miss his target.) Moreover, the túngara frog has an inner organ tuned to 2,200 hertz, which is close to the dominant frequency of a chuck. Together, these facts seem to indicate that the túngara's puddle-side serenade is an example of adaptive mate choice: females evolved ears tuned to chucks because they indicate the biggest and most sexually skilled males.

Ryan's research revealed a stranger story. When he examined the túngara frog's family tree, he discovered that eight frog species closely related to the túngara also have inner ear organs sensitive to frequencies of about 2,200 hertz, yet none of them produce chucks in their mating call. Ryan thinks that eons ago, the ancestor of all these species probably evolved an inner ear tuned to roughly 2,200 hertz for some long-abandoned purpose. The túngara later revived this neglected auditory channel, probably by happenstance. Male frogs that happened to burp out a few extra notes after whining were automatically favored by females—not because they were more suitable mates, but simply because they were more noticeable.

Like the glistening scales on the surfperch and swordtails that Cummings studied, the túngara's costly mating call did not evolve to convey any pragmatic information about health or fitness. But that doesn't mean that these traits were arbitrary. They were the result of specific, discernible aspects of the animals' environments, anatomy, and evolutionary legacy. "I took a real beating when I suggested this idea in 1990," Ryan says. "It was very widely criticized. But now sensory bias is considered an important part of the evolution of these preferences."

During our walk at Hammonasset, while admiring seabirds from shore-side cliffs, I asked Prum about sensory bias. He said it could not possibly explain the staggering diversity and idiosyncrasy of sexual ornaments—the fact that every closely related sparrow species has a unique embellishment, for example. Prum sees sensory bias as just another way to maintain the predominant "adaptive paradigm" that refuses to acknowledge his theory of aesthetic evolution. Tellingly, Prum and Ryan do not discuss each other's work in their recent books.

While mulling over the similarities and discrepancies between Prum's ideas and those of his peers, I kept returning to a passage in his book. In 2010, Prum and his colleagues revealed that a crow-size dinosaur called *Anchiornis huxleyi* was beautifully adorned: gray body plumage, an auburn mohawk, and long white limb feathers with black spangles. Why dinosaurs originally evolved feathers has long perplexed scientists. At first, layers of fuzzy filaments, similar to a chick's down, most likely helped dinosaurs repel water and regulate body temperature. But what explains the development of broad, flat feathers like those found on *Anchiornis*? Flight is the intuitive answer, but the first planar feathers were probably too primitive for flight or gliding, lacking the distinct asymmetry that makes birds' feathers aerodynamic. In his book, Prum advocates for an alternative hypothesis that has been gaining support: large feathers evolved to be beautiful.

The aesthetic possibilities of fuzzy down are limited. "The innovative planar feather vane, however, creates a well-defined, two-dimensional surface on which it is possible to create a whole new world of complex color patterns within every feather," Prum writes. Only later did birds co-opt their big, glamorous plumes for flight, which is probably a key reason that some of them survived mass extinction 66 million years ago. Birds transformed what was once mere frippery into some of the most enviable adaptations on the planet, from the ocean-spanning breadth of an albatross to the torpedoed silhouette of a plunging falcon. Yet they never abandoned their sense of style, using feathers as a medium for peerless pageantry. A feather, then, cannot be labeled the sole product of either natural or sexual selection. A feather, with its reciprocal structure, embodies the confluence of two powerful and equally important evolutionary forces: utility and beauty.

Most of the scientists I spoke with said that the old dichotomy between adaptive adornment and arbitrary beauty, between "good genes" and Fisherian selection, is being replaced with a modern conceptual synthesis that emphasizes multiplicity. "Beauty is something that arises from a host of different mechanisms," says Gil Rosenthal, an evolutionary biologist at Texas A&M University and the author of the new scholarly tome *Mate Choice*. "It's an incredibly multilayered process."

The environment constrains a creature's anatomy, which determines how it experiences the world, which generates adaptive and arbitrary preferences, which loop back to alter its biology, sometimes in maladaptive ways. Beauty reveals that evolution is neither an iterative chiseling of living organisms by a domineering landscape nor a frenzied collision of chance events. Rather, evolution is an intricate clockwork of physics, biology, and perception in which every moving part influences another in both subtle and profound ways. Its gears are so innumerable and dynamic—so susceptible to serendipity and mishap—that even a single outcome of its ceaseless ticking can confound science for centuries.

On my last day in Austin, while walking through a park, I encountered a common grackle hunting for insects in the grass. His plumage appeared black as charcoal at first, but as he moved, it shimmered with all the colors of an oil slick. Every now and then, he stopped in place, inflated his chest, and made a sound like a rusty swing set. Perhaps dissatisfied with the local fare, or uncomfortable with my presence, he flew off.

In his absence, my attention immediately shifted to something his presence had obscured—a golden columbine bush. From a distance, its flowers resembled medieval illustrations of comets, big and bold with long, trailing streamers. Up close, I was struck by the complexity of a single blossom: a large yellow star wreathed a cluster of five tubular petals, shaped like angel's trumpets and pooled with nectar. A tuft of pollen-tipped filaments fizzed through the very center. Viewed from above, the flowers looked like huddles of tiny birds with their beaks pressed together and wings flared. The name "columbine" comes from the Latin for "dovelike."

Why are flowers beautiful? Or, more precisely: why are flowers beautiful to *us*? The more I thought about this question, the more it seemed to speak to the nature of beauty itself. Philosophers, scientists, and writers have tried to define the essence of beauty for thousands of years. The plurality of their efforts illustrates the immense difficulty of this task. Beauty, they have said, is: harmony; goodness; a manifestation of divine perfection; a type of pleasure; that which causes love and longing; and $M = O/C$ (where M is aesthetic value, O is order, and C is complexity).

Evolutionary psychologists, eagerly applying adaptive logic to every facet of behavior and cognition, have speculated that the human perception of beauty emerges from a set of ancient adaptations: perhaps men like women with large breasts and narrow waists because those features signal high fertility; symmetrical faces may correlate with overall health; maybe babies are irresistibly cute because their juvenile features activate the caregiving circuits in our brains. Such claims sometimes verge on the ludicrous: the philosopher Denis Dutton has argued that people around the world have an intrinsic appreciation for a certain type of landscape —a grassy field with copses of trees, water, and wildlife—because it resembles the Pleistocene savannas where humans evolved. In a TED Talk, Dutton explains that postcards, calendars, and paintings depicting this universally beloved landscape usually include trees that fork near the ground because our ancestors relied on their conveniently low branches to scramble away from predators.

Of course, it is undeniable that we, like all animals, are products of evolution. Our brains and sensory organs are just as biased as any other creature's. Our inherited anatomy, physiology, and instincts have undoubtedly shaped our perception of beauty. In their recent books, Richard Prum and Michael Ryan synthesize research on animals and people, exploring possible evolutionary explanations for our own aesthetic tastes. Ryan is particularly interested in the innate sensitivities and biases of our neural architecture: he describes how our visual system, for example, may be wired to notice symmetry. Prum stresses his conviction that in humans, as in birds, many types of physical beauty and sexual desire have arbitrarily coevolved without reference to health or fertility. What complicates their respective arguments is the overwhelming power of human culture. As a species, we are so thoroughly saturated with symbolism, ritual, and art—so swayed by rapidly changing fashions—that it is more or less impossible to determine just how much an aesthetic preference owes to evolutionary history as opposed to cultural influence.

Perhaps more than any other object of aesthetic obsession, flowers expose the futility of trying to contain beauty in a single theoretical framework. Consider how flowers came to be and how we grew to love them: 150 million years ago many pollen-producing plants depended on the wind to spread their pollen and reproduce. But certain insects, perhaps beetles and flies, began to eat those protein-rich pollen grains, inadvertently transporting them from one plant to another. This proved to be a much more efficient means of fertilization than capricious air currents. Plants with the richest and most obvious sources of pollen were especially successful. Likewise, insects that were particularly adept at finding pollen had an advantage over their peers.

Through a long process of coevolution, plants and pollinators transformed one another. Some plants began to modify their leaves into proto-flowers: little flags that marked the location of their pollen. Bold colors and distinctive shapes helped them stand out in a tangle of green. Strong aromas and ultraviolet beacons played upon pollinators' senses. Nectar sweetened the deal. Insects, birds, and mammals began competing for access, evolving wings, tongues, and brains better suited to the quest for floral sustenance. As the pressure from both parties intensified, plants and their pollinators formed increasingly specific relationships, hurtling each other toward aesthetic and adaptive extremes—a bird that hums and hovers like an insect, an orchid that mimics the appearance and scent of a female bee.

Many millions of years later, flowers enchanted yet another species. Perhaps the initial attraction was purely utilitarian: the promise of fruit or grain. Maybe we were captivated by their consonance of color, form, and aroma. Whatever the case, we adopted numerous flowering plants into an expanding circle of domesticated species. We brought them into greenhouses and laboratories, magnifying their inherent beauty, creating new hybrids, and tailoring their features to our individual tastes. We contracted orchid delirium and tulip mania, and we have never fully recovered. The flower began as a plea and became a phenomenon.

If there is a universal truth about beauty—some concise and elegant concept that encompasses every variety of charm and grace in existence—we do not yet understand enough about nature to articulate it. What we call beauty is not simply one thing or another, neither wholly purposeful nor entirely random, neither merely a property nor a feeling. Beauty is a dialogue between perceiver and perceived. Beauty is the world's answer to the audacity of a flower. It is the way a bee spills across the lip of a yawning buttercup; it is the care with which a satin bowerbird selects a hibiscus bloom; it is the impulse to re-create water lilies with oil and canvas; it is the need to place roses on a grave.

SARAH KAPLAN

Ghosts of the Future

FROM *The Washington Post*

IF THE HISTORY of Earth is condensed to fit in a single twenty-four-hour day, life emerges sometime before dawn. Photosynthesis evolves around midmorning, and the atmosphere becomes oxygen-rich right before lunch. But most of the day is utterly boring; all organisms are microscopic and occupied with little more than belching gasses and oozing slime.

It isn't till 9 p.m., about half a billion years before the present, that we see the first complex, multicellular beings. Scientists call this juncture the "Cambrian explosion"—the moment when billions of years of bacteria gave way to the rapidly evolving beings we know as animals. This evolutionary burst is responsible for every elephant, every fly, every bowlegged amphibian and wriggling worm, every complex creature that ever walked, swam, flew, or scurried on this Earth. And I'm about to witness it firsthand.

"Ready to go back in time?" asks Ardelle Hynes, a cheerful, ponytailed ranger at Yoho National Park in British Columbia.

It's a drizzly July morning, and I'm huffing in Hynes's wake as we ascend a sheer mountainside in the Canadian Rockies. Our destination, high on the cliff face, is a jumble of 510-million-year-old rocks known as the Burgess Shale.

Formed during the middle part of the Cambrian period, the shale boasts tens of thousands of perfectly preserved fossils from the dawn of the animal kingdom. Many were soft-bodied organisms whose existence in most other places has been lost to the ravages of time. This wealth of small, strange specimens has shaped scientists' understanding of evolution and offered insight into the link between Earth's climate and the life it can support, making the Burgess Shale one of the most precious and important fossil sites in the world.

This remarkable record exists only because of a catastrophic underwater landslide that buried the organisms in a deluge of sediment millions of years ago. The sand was so fine it would have filled the animals' gills and the hinges of their legs, trapping and suffocating them. The high alkalinity of the oceans, combined with the utter absence of oxygen, would have held at bay the bacteria that would otherwise decompose an organism's soft and squishy parts.

"Think about all the factors that had to come together for us to be able to experience this," Hynes says. The animals had to die in a manner that allowed them to fossilize. Those conditions had to persist for millions upon millions of years. The rocks had to be lifted from the bottom of the ocean to the top of the world by the action of tectonics, and then scraped by the slow crawl of glaciers to reveal the treasures they contained. And, finally, an enterprising ape species had to evolve sufficient intelligence to invent the field of geology, hike up this mountain, and recognize the significance of what they found. "Aren't we lucky?" Hynes says.

I take a breath of sharp, clean air and survey the spruce forest, the ice-capped mountains cloaked in wisps of fog. Hynes gives me a fossil, a piece of this planet's history, and I feel its heft in my hand. I see what she means.

But then I think of the invasive bark beetles, spurred by a warming climate, that are eating away at this forest. I think of retreating glaciers and vanishing species and all the consequences of unchecked carbon consumption that are still to come.

I think of the United Nations scientists who declared last year that we had just over a decade to get climate change under control, and the officials meeting in Madrid this month who have fallen far short of the commitments needed to make that happen.

Life on Earth has been evolving for nearly 4 billion years. Yet only now, as the geological clock strikes midnight, is there a creature capable of looking back at that history and appreciating it. Only now, as our own actions imperil this extraordinary and singular planet, do humans have a chance to comprehend all that is about to be lost.

What a profound responsibility that is. What a beautiful gift.

*

As we hike, Hynes paints a picture of how the landscape would have looked half a billion years ago. The continents were clumped into two large masses, empty but for some slimy microbial mats. Without land plants to prevent erosion, sediment was constantly being swept out to sea, where it settled in thick, silty layers.

It's hard for me to envision. At most points in its history, humans wouldn't recognize our planet at all.

Researchers debate what caused the single-celled microbes of the Proterozoic (or "simple life") eon to evolve into the complex organisms seen in the Burgess Shale. Perhaps it was climate change—Earth was slowly recovering from an intense ice age—or the greater availability of oxygen in the atmosphere. Others have suggested that some key biological innovation, like the development of vision or the rise of predators, set off an evolutionary arms race that resulted in ever-more-complex creatures.

After trudging for 2.5 miles and 2,000 feet of elevation gain, we round a bend in the trail and are suddenly at the quarry. Gray and brown slabs of shale litter a football field–size expanse of mountainside. Hynes instructs my fellow hikers and me to set aside our trekking poles, which can damage fossils. Then we set out across the rocks.

It's difficult to know where to put my feet; nearly every stone seems to bear at least a fragment of an ancient animal. Hynes points out a fossil resembling a slice of pineapple. These are the mouth parts of *Anomalocaris*—the bizarre, dog-size apex predator of the Cambrian seas.

Weirdness seems to be the defining characteristic of Burgess Shale organisms. Hynes shows us illustrations of *Opabinia*, an oddball with five eyes and a vacuum cleaner nozzle for a nose, and the monstrous *Hallucigenia*, which boasted eight pairs of legs and an equal number of conical spines. The ancestor of all modern vertebrates, including fish, birds, and humans, was *Pikaia*, a wriggling eel-like organism no longer than your big toe. My favorites are the trilobites, distant relatives of today's horseshoe crabs, with jointed legs and shells of overlapping plates that almost look like ribs. They thrived for 300 million years, through the drifting of continents and the rise and fall of sea levels, the flourishing of coal age plants, the invention of the backbone.

In the end, the thing that got them was climate change; trilobites died out during the end-Permian mass extinction, when gigantic volcanic eruptions raised temperatures, acidified the oceans, and killed off some 90 percent of life on Earth.

By comparison, our species seems like little more than a hiccup in the steady march of geologic time. *Homo sapiens* has existed for just 0.06 percent of the time trilobites survived. Given the environmental crisis we've created, it's unclear how much longer we'll be around.

Back in Washington, I head over to the Smithsonian's National Museum of Natural History, home to tens of thousands of Burgess Shale specimens. Hans Sues, the museum's chair of paleobiology, guides me down dimly lit hallways to the Cambrian collections, where he pulls out drawer after drawer of fossils. He handles each one like it's a relic.

The events of 500 million years ago are just the beginning of the Burgess Shale's story, he explains. What happened after scientists uncovered them is perhaps even more profound.

It was a secretary of the Smithsonian, Charles Doolittle Walcott, who first excavated the fossil site in 1909. The extraordinary find was announced without fanfare; "A most interesting discovery of unique Cambrian fossil," was all Walcott wrote in an initial scientific report.

Walcott spent fifteen field seasons at the shale, but he was so busy digging up fossils he didn't have much time to decipher them. It wasn't until decades later that scientists began to realize how unusual and diverse the Burgess Shale specimens truly were. Paleontologist Stephen Jay Gould found the fossils so strange, he believed that many of them couldn't belong to any known animal group. In his 1989 book, *Wonderful Life,* he speculated that Cambrian animals were part of an exceptionally experimental period in Earth's history. Far from being "primitive," these creatures and their ecosystem were as complex as anything we see today. If we were to rewind the geologic clock, Gould argued, perhaps evolution would take an entirely different course. In place of humans, the world could be dominated by *Hallucigenia*'s many-legged descendants.

More recent research has shown that Gould's theories weren't quite correct, Sues says; most of the Burgess Shale specimens do fit into existing categories on an evolutionary tree. But the idea still stands that evolution is unpredictable and undirected, that humanity is a fluke outcome rather than the inevitable result of millennia of increasing complexity. "There were all these other worlds out there," Sues says. Someday, "ours is going to be just another one of them."

Still, a few traits have staying power. The most common type of Cambrian creatures were arthropods, or joint-legged invertebrates. This same group, which includes insects, spiders, and crustaceans, still accounts for more than 80 percent of all known animal species. There are probably millions more arthropods that remain undiscovered and unnamed.

In other words, Sues says, if the world of the Burgess Shale seems utterly alien, it's only because we haven't been paying enough attention to our own world.

The price of our ignorance about life's current diversity will be a duller, poorer future, because our inattention has led us to undermine the conditions that make Earth's extraordinary variety possible. Recent studies have found that arthropod populations, survivors of so many millions of years of tumult, are in "hyper-alarming" decline in the human era. Flying insects have vanished from German nature preserves. Huge numbers of bugs have disappeared from a pristine forest in Puerto Rico. A catastrophic combination of habitat loss and climate change is transforming ecosystems faster than scientists can study them.

"We're losing things we don't even know about," Sues says. "If we don't understand this world, if we don't appreciate how this world came into being, how can we be capable stewards of it?"

Since the moment the Burgess Shale organisms began crawling out of the mud, living things on this planet have never been stagnant. They've been bombarded by asteroids, numbed by ice, eclipsed by competitors, even suffocated by the products of their own metabolisms. Yet, no matter how terrible the transformation, life has always emerged—altered, yet undeterred.

The world we love, the very fact of our existence, is contingent upon that process. Change is why we are here. And change will happen again.

But at this moment, Earth's climate is changing at a pace unmatched in the planet's 4.6-billion-year history. The systems on which species depend are vanishing. Living things as large and charismatic as whales, as delicate as orchids, as anonymous as tiny gray lichen growing on some remote Arctic tree, are dying out at a rate approaching the scale of the biggest extinctions.

The planet is hurtling toward "the point of no return," UN Secretary General António Guterres said last weekend at the opening of the COP 25 climate change summit. It is the last such meeting before the Paris climate agreement goes into effect, but global leaders still have not agreed on a mechanism for achieving the emissions reductions needed. The biggest source of cumulative greenhouse gases in history—the United States—refuses to cooperate on climate change mitigation at all. Meanwhile, unprecedented wildfires have burned millions of acres in Australia, Venice is underwater, hundreds of Bahamians are still missing after Hurricane Dorian devastated the island nation in August. Like the creatures of the Cambrian, humans are entering a world utterly unlike the one in which we evolved. Our species may not die out, but life as we know it cannot go on.

While the trilobites had no hand in their fate, we brought this revolution on ourselves. And we can still shape its course. We already know what must be done to avert the worst effects of warming: starting next year, global greenhouse gas emissions must fall by 7.6 percent annually, reaching zero by the middle of the century. And although the scale of such action would be unprecedented, we already know how to achieve it: put a price on carbon, replace fossil fuels with renewable energy sources, restore nature landscapes that act as carbon sinks, equip ordinary people with the tools to adapt to a transformed world. No new technologies need to be invented to meet the terms of the Paris climate agreement. All we are waiting for is the will to change.

Humans are the first species with not just the power to alter the planet on a geologic scale but also the capacity to predict the consequences. We understand the connection between our actions and each of Earth's possible futures.

What a profound responsibility that is. What a beautiful gift.

ADAM MANN

Intelligent Ways to Search
for Extraterrestrials

FROM *The New Yorker*

SUPPOSE YOU'RE A space-faring alien society. You've established colonies on a few planets and moons in your solar system, but your population is growing and you're running out of space. What should you do? Your brightest engineers might suggest a radical idea: they could disassemble a Jupiter-size planet and rearrange its mass into a cloud of orbiting platforms that encircles your sun. Your population would have ample living area on or inside the platforms; meanwhile, through solar power, you'd be able to capture every joule of energy radiating from your star.

The laws of physics suggest no reason why this plan wouldn't work; they merely require that all the energy collected be radiated out again as heat, lest the whole construction melt. This, in turn, means that your cloud of platforms should softly glow. A distant observer training a telescope on your solar system might see something like a hot, opaque screen encircling a dimmed star—a spherical entity, curiously bright at certain wavelengths.

The theoretical physicist Freeman Dyson first speculated about the existence of such structures in 1960. In the decades since, astronomers on Earth have looked repeatedly for so-called Dyson spheres, and nobody has seen one. There are different ways of interpreting this result. Jason Wright, an astrophysicist at Pennsylvania State University, told me that Dyson wrote his original paper while contemplating an abstract idea—that "the fundamental limit to an energy supply that a species could have is all of the starlight in their system." The fact that Dyson spheres haven't been found, Wright said, doesn't prove that aliens don't exist. It might just mean that astronomers should start looking for evidence of less ambitious alien projects.

In 1623, Johannes Kepler wrote that, through his telescope, he had observed towns with round walls on the moon. In 1877, Giovanni Schiaparelli reported seeing what might have been massive canals on Mars. The same year that Dyson described his spheres, the astrophysicist Frank Drake started Project Ozma, an attempt to detect radio signals from aliens living around two nearby stars—the first modern experiment in the enterprise now known as the search for extraterrestrial intelligence, or SETI. Like his forebears, Drake was influenced by his times: he was born during the golden age of radio. Kepler spent his days in walled European cities; Schiaparelli witnessed a worldwide canal-building spree. Their efforts were simultaneously cosmic and provincial. It's hard to say anything about organisms on other worlds that doesn't reflect life on ours.

Wright, a cheerful, apple-cheeked, forty-two-year-old professor with wispy brown hair, is at the vanguard of a new movement in SETI. Its goal is the rationalization of a speculative endeavor. "We're trying to formalize it," he told me. "We're trying to get a canon of papers that my peers have read and understood." In a number of articles published over the past five years, Wright and his collaborators have tried to build frameworks and standards that could provide a more objective basis for SETI. In one paper, a table enumerates "Ten Anomalies of Transiting Megastructures That Could Distinguish Them from Planets or Stars." In another, Wright and his co-authors show, by making a series of calculations, that "galaxy-spanning civilizations" may be easier to detect than those that remain clustered around a single star—a finding that has implications for how astronomers might search for aliens in the future. By approaching SETI in a more rigorous way, Wright hopes to make it more respectable. His aim is partially earthbound: he wants to win the search for aliens the government funding that it's long been denied.

The last time the U.S. government appropriated funds for SETI was in 1992. That year, NASA spent $12.25 million on the search for aliens—its highest ever expenditure on such research, as part of a planned ten-year, $100 million investment. The next year,

Richard Bryan, a Democratic senator from Nevada, led an initiative to kill the program. ("Millions have been spent and we have yet to bag a single little green fellow," he said.) Bryan made it clear that attempts to revive SETI would be bad for NASA's funding in general, and SETI advocates have relied on private donations ever since.

In the decades that followed, the scientific landscape shifted. By the early nineties, astronomers had confirmed the existence of only two planets outside our solar system. Today, they know of more than 4,000 "exoplanets," and are discovering more all the time. Judging by their sizes and temperatures, many of these exoplanets could be capable of supporting life. The same is true within our own solar system. There is ample evidence that Mars, which was once considered a barren desert, was wet and warm in the past, and planetary scientists talk with some urgency about sending spacecraft to survey the oceans of the moons Europa, Titan, and Enceladus. The idea that simple organisms, such as bacteria, might exist on other worlds seems eminently reasonable.

The sheer size of the exoplanetary bounty has raised questions both astrobiological and statistical. Assuming that conditions are ripe for life, how often do living organisms tend to arise on a given world? How many biospheres produce creatures capable of communicating across space and time? The paucity of data on either of these questions allows equal freedom for optimists and pessimists.

In May, I met Wright at the headquarters of the SETI Institute, a private nonprofit dedicated to researching life in the universe. The Institute's offices are situated in a cookie-cutter office park in Mountain View, California; Wright, who was in from Penn State, was working from a small office—gray walls, a laptop, a few books on a shelf—until that evening, when he would receive the Institute's Frank Drake award, which recognizes exemplary contributions to astrobiology. At the ceremony, around 300 attendees would gather for hors d'oeuvres, beer and wine, Wright's talk, and then dessert. The committee cited his commitment to approaching the search for extraterrestrial intelligence in "a rational and productive manner."

Wright was born in 1977, and grew up in the suburbs outside Seattle. After reading a book about astronomy in elementary school, he became certain that he wanted to study the stars. He went to graduate school at the University of California, Berkeley

—historically, a SETI hub—where his research focused on magnetic activity in stars that makes it hard to detect the planets that orbit them. One day, in the early 2000s, his adviser suggested that they might write a SETI paper together by combing through a recently released infrared map of the night sky—the product of an initiative called the Two Micron All-Sky Survey—to look for Dyson spheres. Wright performed a quick calculation, determining that the survey's sensitivity had been too low to spot the work of extraterrestrial mega-engineers, and moved on.

Eight years later, he was listening to a talk at Penn State about the Wide-Field Infrared Survey Explorer (WISE), a space-based telescope. It occurred to him that WISE—which was sensitive enough to have recently discovered a number of unusual brown dwarfs that glow at room temperature—would be capable of detecting Dyson spheres. With a colleague, Steinn Sigurðsson, Wright applied for a grant from the John Templeton Foundation, which is known for supporting unusual research ideas, to conduct a new survey, called Glimpsing Heat from Alien Technologies. From 2012 to 2015, the project analyzed the light from about a million galaxies, in search of evidence that a spacefaring species had enclosed a significant fraction of those galaxies' stars in Dyson-style spheres. (None had.)

In 2015, around the time the survey was winding down, Wright heard about a peculiar object that another astronomer, Tabetha Boyajian, was investigating. The object, which came to be known as Tabby's Star, had been discovered using the exoplanet-hunting Kepler space telescope; it appeared to be surrounded by a swarm of material that caused its light to dim at irregular intervals—another possible Dyson sphere. Wright was among several astronomers interviewed for an article about Tabby's Star, in *The Atlantic*. "Aliens should always be the very last hypothesis you consider," he said, "but this looked like something you would expect an alien civilization to build." The media coverage caused a sensation: Tabby's Star became the subject of jokes on *Saturday Night Live* and *The Late Show with Stephen Colbert*. With Boyajian and another astronomer, Andrew Siemion, as co-investigators, Wright led an effort to scan the star for radio signals. The search found nothing there, either. (The entity's flickering is now believed to stem from clouds of dust or a swarm of surrounding comets.)

One natural objection to the search for Dyson spheres is that it presupposes an endlessly consumptive technological teleology. To imagine that alien societies would construct such structures seems to assume that energy collection is those societies' most important goal. Why couldn't an intelligent civilization strive to use less energy, not more? Focusing on the sun may be similarly shortsighted; perhaps extraterrestrial power plants tap into some spectacular aspect of reality we have yet to discover.

"Energy use is the observable manifestation of technology, so it's a very useful parameter," Wright explained, leaning back in his chair and smiling. "My analogy is the sizes of mammals or plants. There's no natural evolutionary tendency for all things to get bigger. Nonetheless, we have giraffes and sequoias and blue whales. Some of them are large, and those are the ones we will find."

In April 2018, a draft of a NASA appropriations bill appeared in the House of Representatives containing an unexpected provision: it mandated that the agency spend $10 million over the next two years to "search for technosignatures, such as radio transmissions." The paragraph had been inserted by Lamar Smith, the Republican congressman who, from 2013 until earlier this year, chaired the House Science Committee. Smith, who is notorious among scientists for his climate denialism, has long been a fervent supporter of astronomical research. In 2017, he announced that he planned to retire; researchers at the SETI Institute considered the language to be a parting gift. To figure out how the money might best be spent, NASA, which had no extant SETI program, convened a conference of experts in Houston. Wright co-edited its final report, to which he wrote the introduction.

Michael New, NASA's deputy associate administrator for research—he is in charge of ensuring the quality of the agency's scientific portfolio—joined the researchers at the conference. He had been struck, he told them, that the term "technosignatures," which had been used by Smith and others, hadn't set off "antibodies" at the agency. The word, coined by the SETI pioneer Jill Tarter in 2006, is based on the term "biosignatures," which refers to evidence—liquid water, atmospheric oxygen—that hints at the existence of living organisms on a planet's surface. Technosignatures, by extension, suggest the presence of tool use or technology. An electromagnetic message, an artificial megastructure, or an alien monolith would be a technosignature. So would the low-tech damming of a planet's waterways by a beaver-like species, if it could produce a measurable change detectable from far away. By artfully removing extraterrestrials, their communicative motives, and even their intelligence from the equation, the term makes SETI more flexible.

The $10 million set aside for SETI disappeared during the budgeting process. Still, the mere possibility of money had an effect. Since SETI had lost its appropriation, in the early nineties, proposals related to it had rarely been entertained by NASA, and only a small number had been funded. This year, though, the agency offered to hear "observational, theoretical, and archival proposals focused upon the detection of technosignatures," as part of its Exoplanet Research Program.

American astronomy is a highly organized discipline, with a structured approach to funding. Around every ten years, in a process known as the Astronomy and Astrophysics Decadal Survey, astronomers write papers arguing for new telescopes or robotic missions; they submit their papers to the National Academy of Sciences, where they are reviewed by committees in specialized subfields and then passed on to a central commission of luminaries that, in turn, tells NASA and the National Science Foundation what it should fund. "Astro2010," the last Decadal Survey report, was 290 pages long and made no substantive mention of SETI. Only a single paper promoting the field, written by Tarter, appeared during the lead-up to it. Earlier this year, Wright and his collaborators—including the planetary scientist Jean-Luc Margot, the astrobiologists Julia DeMarines and Jacob Haqq-Misra, and the computational social scientist Anamaria Berea—submitted nine papers on a wide variety of SETI topics. Wright was lead author on four of them. One, which argued that SETI needed a trained workforce capable of attacking the problem from all sides, was co-signed by 126 astrophysicists.

"If the [Decadal] tells NASA, 'This is something you should fund,' then NASA has to fund it," Wright told me. Such resources would be transformative. "If you don't have federal money to support students, you don't formalize the knowledge. You don't have a curriculum," he said. Right now, "everyone that works on [SETI] is a hobbyist."

*

Neither governmental backing nor scholarly approval, of course, can change SETI's incalculably small odds of success. The conceptual limitations that have dogged it in the past may be an insurmountable product of the fact that we are the particular species we happen to be. Linda Billings, a communications researcher specializing in the rhetoric employed by scientists and proponents of space exploration, worked as a consultant on SETI-related projects for NASA from 1988 to 1992. In her view, they have often been reluctant to address the fundamental question of whether human technology is likely to bear a resemblance to technology developed elsewhere. A SETI skeptic, Billings told me that "the scientific rationale the SETI community offers is not sound—it depends on a growing pile of assumptions." Kathryn Denning, an anthropologist at York University, in Toronto, who studies the social and ethical aspects of space, is similarly doubtful about whether human researchers can anticipate how aliens would use technology. Still, she said, "I think the more nuanced thinkers on the SETI front are leaving behind the question of alien motivations and alien sociology as much as they can, and just thinking in terms of astrophysical signatures and the capabilities of their instruments." She told me that SETI has stimulated new developments in astronomy and instrumentation. And many people argue that the extraordinary significance of an actual detection might make the modest amounts set aside for SETI seem reasonable, despite the inherent uncertainty of the research. (The ten-year, $100 million allocation that was considered in the early nineties equates to roughly four cents per person per year.)

On a sunny afternoon a few weeks after the SETI Institute's awards ceremony, I met Wright on the Caltech campus, in Pasadena. He was attending a technosignatures workshop, which included experts in machine learning, sociology, dolphin communication, planetary science, and astrophysics. It was the meeting's final day, and the attendees were dividing up the work of writing its final report, claiming sections ("Recognizing and Minimizing Human Biases"; "Lessons from Computational Biology"; "Probes and Relics in the Solar System") for themselves. Earlier, they had pored over a textbook of ancient, untranslated human languages.

On a bench outside the ultramodern Keck Institute for Space Studies, Wright told me about his favorite sci-fi television show (the space opera *Babylon 5*) and the novels of Arthur C. Clarke ("His aliens are really alien"). He walked me through his plans for a new SETI center at Penn State, for which he'd secured $3.5 million in pledged funding. The center, Wright hopes, will be an academic home for the discipline, removed from the whims of the federal budget and private philanthropists, where students can be trained in the latest research. To date, he said, only seven doctoral candidates had ever completed a PhD in SETI subjects. Now at least five more astronomers—from Berkeley, UCLA, UC San Diego, and Penn State—are scheduled to receive one.

In his book *Cosmos,* from 1980, the astronomer and science popularizer Carl Sagan offered a spiritual vision of contact with extraterrestrials. An epistle from space, written by an older and wiser society, could be detected by our radio telescopes; the aliens might then invite us to join a galactic federation of enlightened peers who communicate in a universal tongue. Sagan thought that translating such a message would be straightforward: "We will share scientific and mathematical insights with any other civilization," he predicted. Wright, by contrast, wonders if humanity's mathematical practices, such as our attachment to prime numbers, might prove to be idiosyncratic. The Caltech workshop had often focused on these sorts of "anthropic" assumptions. No one knows whether, if aliens exist, it will be possible to cross the conceptual gulfs dividing our minds from theirs. The universe may turn out to be more creative than our fantasies. Or it may be, as Wright hopes, that a more structured process of imagination can be a means of transcending our limited ideas.

"We're looking for technology like our own, and so we presume the engineers of that technology will share our principles," he said. "We're looking for kindred spirits that will find interesting what we've found interesting." Contemplating this problem, he regarded the Caltech campus from beneath the shade of a tree.

DEANNA CSOMO McCOOL

Total Eclipse

FROM *Aeon*

Please note: this essay deals explicitly with suicide and may be distressing to some readers.

I STOOD AT ANNA'S bedside, marveling over her porcelain complexion, thick blond hair, and eyelashes so long they'd be the envy of a Maybelline model. The bleached white sheet tucked under her chin covered all but her left hand, which peeked out from underneath.

My seventeen-year-old daughter would cringe and bat my arms away whenever I'd attempt to smooth her hair, which cascaded down her back like a sunlit waterfall until she had it bobbed to her shoulders at age nine, and chopped into a pixie cut at fifteen. Tentatively I reached out to feel it, sweeping every strand from her forehead so I could soak in the tiniest details of her face. Anna, the type of child who would argue that the sky wasn't technically blue, had rarely appeared this calm.

Looking down upon her, I remembered the time she twirled and giggled while jumping to catch fireflies. I remembered how she begged for a puppy and a horse and a younger sibling. For a golden flute. For vanilla ice cream. How she loved birds, and enjoyed trekking through the woods behind our northern Indiana home, notebook clutched in her hand. But I also remembered how her brows seemed permanently furrowed, frozen in a state of unrelenting irritability. I thought about the time, ten years ago, when Anna stood in the emergency room hallway and screamed that her two-year-old sister was faking a febrile seizure. I recalled the moments three years earlier, when her barrage of complaints tainted our family trip to Disney World, the self-proclaimed happiest place on Earth.

Allowed to stroke her hair again, I also thought about her fiery rages, the dark moods that cloaked her adolescence, and the twelve years I spent searching for answers that would ease both. Because of issues ranging from the difficulties in diagnosing children with mental health disorders to a dearth of clinicians and therapy options in some parts of the country, compounded by adolescents' reluctance to follow treatment plans, I had been stuck with the question, just like many other parents: Will my child ever get better?

A belt buckle cracked against the outside of the bathroom door, punctuated only by Anna's wailing. "I hate you!" Anna, then six, screeched during one oppressively hot summer day in 2007. "I wish you would die! I want to die! I'm going to kill myself!"

Drenched in sweat, I cowered on the other side of the door, huddling with my eighteen-month-old, who clung to her green security blanket. My phone was perched on top of the toilet seat, and I couldn't decide whether to call the police, yet again.

The daily rages over anything—or nothing—erupted quickly and lasted for hours. In between, she was constantly irritable. I spent my days feeling like I was carrying TNT, not knowing when a spark would ignite an explosion. The spark could be a smell. The word "no." A neutral glance. Within twenty seconds, my daughter would transform, behaving like a swarm of bees chasing someone into a pond—not letting up until the victim nearly drowned.

The behavior started in kindergarten, and occurred at home, at school, and on weekends. I dutifully drove her to appointments with a therapist and a psychiatrist, who characterized the behavior as a symptom of attention-deficit hyperactivity disorder (ADHD) combined with oppositional defiant disorder (ODD), a behavioral issue some experts contend could stem from permissive parenting or a past riddled with either abuse or neglect. But I wasn't permissive. Anna had never been abused or neglected. Like many seeking answers, I hit the books and kept a notebook about her extreme rages. When I asked Anna's first psychiatrist about her extreme tantrums and outbursts, his warm brown eyes couldn't mask his dismissive body language and cautious remarks that her behavior was likely just an extreme case of ODD. He offered an antipsychotic medication, Zyprexa, to her drug cocktail. But the medication didn't work; the symptoms continued, and Anna's diagnosis remained ADHD and ODD for years.

Our family had become caught in a cycle of issues formed when an unclear diagnosis leads to improper or delayed treatment. Psychologists and psychiatrists point to several reasons for this widespread issue, from the skill and training of the clinician, to the limitations of the way that diagnoses are made, to multiple disorders that exhibit themselves in the same child.

"We also don't have genetic markers yet for any of these illnesses; we don't have blood tests, so a lot of the diagnosis is based on observation and interviews," said Jill Emanuele, a psychologist in New York and senior director of the mood disorders center at the Child Mind Institute. "The other challenge in diagnosing children is that they change really fast, so the presentations of their illness can change pretty quickly." A child brought in to a psychologist at age six with symptoms of inattention or hyperactivity might be diagnosed with ADHD, but the same symptoms might lead to a diagnosis of depression in a thirteen-year-old.

After Anna's psychiatrist retired, another child psychiatrist in our area, whose office hours were limited to one day a week, began seeing her. I continued writing in a behavior diary:

> 10-23-2010: Anna yelled for a half an hour and didn't want to go to her room. Finally got her in her room but she began hitting her arm against her bunk bed. She finally quieted down so I went in to tell her the timeout was over. She was trying to choke herself with her belt.

> 9-22-2011: Anna came home from school and I reminded her to study for her spelling test. She refused, so I told her she would lose computer privileges. I bent down to unplug the laptop and she punched me in the chest. I pretended it didn't hurt because that would make her angrier, but I called the police and drove myself to the doctor.

She had broken my sternum. After a nine-day stint in a mental-health facility, she received new medications, but I received no new answers. Those were still percolating 600 miles away in Bethesda, Maryland, where the psychiatrist Ellen Leibenluft, chief of the Section on Mood Dysregulation and Neuroscience with the National Institute of Mental Health (NIMH), had been researching the problem of severely irritable children for years, and had a possible diagnostic answer for Anna's struggles: disruptive mood dysregulation disorder, or DMDD.

Leibenluft served on the team that recommended DMDD be added to the fifth edition of the *Diagnostic and Statistical Manual of Mental Health Disorders (DSM-V)* in 2013. The *DSM* is the periodically updated handbook used around the world to help professionals diagnose mental illnesses. Children diagnosed with DMDD must meet several criteria: chronic irritability, severe and frequent temper outbursts—more than three times a week—that are disproportionate to their age and situation, and problems functioning in more than one setting. Symptoms, lasting a year or more, must have appeared before age ten.

Each symptom precisely described Anna.

The relatively rare mood disorder, according to a 2018 article in the *Journal of Child Psychology and Psychiatry,* has a prevalence of only about 1 percent of the population; even among those at risk for other mood disorders, it appears only 3 percent of the time. It was added to *DSM-V* to decrease the number of children diagnosed with bipolar disorder and subsequently prescribed powerful medications for it, including the Zyprexa that Anna once took. Some researchers and psychiatrists were concerned about whether DMDD, occurring alongside other disorders in up to 90 percent of cases, is a distinct disorder, or simply a collection of symptoms from other mood or behavioral disorders. But the inclusion of DMDD in the *DSM-V* opened the door for several new studies and clinical trials.

"These kids have a level of irritability and explosivity that's a major functional impairment," said David Rettew, director of child and adolescent psychiatry at the University of Vermont Medical Center. "They're not safe. They're in families where siblings are afraid of these kids; where parents are afraid of setting them off."

Leibenluft and her team traced the dysfunction to the brain in a study published in the *American Journal of Psychiatry* in 2016. There, researchers exposed healthy children, children with bipolar disorder, and children with DMDD to happy, fearful, and angry faces of varying emotional intensity, measuring reaction in the amygdala, the emotion-processing part of the brain, via functional magnetic resonance imaging (fMRI) scans. Notably, all the children were able to label the emotion on each face, but the similarity ended there. The real insight came when comparing children with DMDD with those with bipolar disorder. The children with bipolar disorder showed hyperactivation of the amygdala only in the presence of fearful faces. But the children with DMDD showed hyperactivation—indicating an increase in irritability—across all types of faces, and at every intensity. DMDD was indeed a unique diagnosis, with its own pattern of dysfunction in the brain—and this evidence could be used to double-down, allowing scientists to design new studies for learning still more about this newly recognized psychiatric disease.

I had asked Anna's psychiatrist about DMDD, and he quickly agreed that the mood disorder was most likely her proper diagnosis. When Anna became disillusioned with the talk-therapy portion of her treatment, and I learned in late 2016 about an NIMH study to evaluate children's irritability over time using novel techniques, he encouraged her to participate. Initially, Anna was excited to join the study, saying she wanted to "advance science." Though her tantrums had subsided, depression took the place of rage when she was fifteen, and a stay in a mental health hospital a few months earlier had done little to help. Her grades had slipped. She stopped caring about her appearance, and sunk into online-only friendships. She had felt better during the previous two years, so the depression took us by surprise. Her experience, however, was typical for the disorder—as studies revealed only in recent years. Research has shown that children diagnosed with DMDD often develop severe depression and anxiety as adolescents, even as their tantrums subside.

After several rounds of prescreening phone calls in late 2016, Anna and I were invited to the NIMH campus in February 2017 for the one-day evaluation to determine her eligibility. But by the time we were scheduled to depart for our trip, Anna's mood had sunk even lower, and she ultimately refused to be in the study. She continued to take her medication, but would lie to her psychiatrist about how well it was working. "I hate the world; I hate people," she told me. "I don't want to help anybody. We all just die in the end, anyway. We do a bunch of work, become wage slaves, and die . . . what's the point?"

When Anna was a young child, I could compel her to take her medication and try new ones, or even visit different clinicians. As a teenager, she would still talk with me about some aspects of her mental health, but any suggestion to return to the mental health center was met with anger and threats of suicide. The psychiatrist Kenneth Towbin, chief of clinical child and adolescent psychiatry in the Emotion and Development Branch of the NIMH, suggested that it's common for adolescents to eschew care, whether for mental illness or juvenile diabetes or other chronic medical illnesses. "There are a host of reasons that have to do with the developmental period, features of the disorders themselves, family environment, community culture—peer and neighborhood culture—and societal stigma," Towbin wrote to me. And change is difficult, even in adults, Emanuele noted, so trying to change an adolescent's mind is even more challenging.

Like other parents in my situation, I couldn't get through to Anna, who didn't seem to want help at all. A few months after she decided not to participate in the NIMH study, and five days before the first total solar eclipse visible in North America in decades would darken our sky, Anna walked to a local pharmacy after everyone left the house and bought a box of blister-packaged, over-the-counter sleep aids. When she returned home, she filled our bathtub with water, and swallowed every lavender pill in the box.

As partial paralysis crept over her body, she had second thoughts, and managed to dial 911 before stepping into the tub.

After three days in the hospital and five more in the mental health center, Anna returned home. The psychiatrist who treated her there told me he didn't know how to help her, because she resisted all treatment suggestions and refused to participate in group activities. Therefore, she was released with the same medications. The same suggestions to continue talk therapy. And she felt exactly the same too.

During the following year, I tried to remain hopeful, but I was on edge. Statistics show that a serious suicide attempt often leads to another within six months. But six months passed, and then nine. Anna landed a job at McDonald's for the summer and enjoyed it. Even though she complained about her depression and was unwilling to try the lithium her psychiatrist suggested, she begrudgingly agreed that I could schedule a consultation for electroconvulsive shock therapy, an outpatient procedure proven to ease the symptoms of depression. She earned her driver's license and talked about plans for her senior year—tentatively, but she talked about them.

Maybe she'd make it through this, I thought. I stopped worrying so much when we left her home alone.

But exactly a year since her suicide attempt, and a week before the beginning of her senior year, Anna grabbed her purse and headed out the door, casually telling her twelve-year-old sister that she was picking up dinner at McDonald's. I didn't think anything of it until my husband pointed out that she hadn't returned home after two hours.

"Where are you???" I texted to her at 7:18 p.m. My phone rang within thirty seconds, displaying a number I didn't recognize. When I answered, I heard the squawk of a police scanner, followed by a man's brusque voice.

I envisioned the front of our red Toyota Prius smashed and buckled, the result of a rear-end collision with a car an hour away. I imagined Anna arguing with the police officer about why it wasn't her fault.

"Come to the hospital quick," the police officer urged. "She jumped off a parking garage. Right now she is still alive, but that's all we know."

After ending the phone call, I crumpled into a heap and screamed.

At the hospital, my husband and I were told that someone found Anna, unconscious, in the alley behind the parking garage; no one knew how long she had been there, nor did she have any identification on her. Because police didn't see much blood, they thought perhaps she had overdosed. A closer look showed some bruising and blood, so police then determined she might have been assaulted. But early X-rays revealed a fracture of her calcaneus, or heel bone, which is a common injury sustained after falling from a tall ladder or greater height. The discovery led police to the roof of the parking garage, where they found her purse, paper note, phone, and glasses.

Eventually the trauma doctor, dressed in pristine scrubs, began detailing each of Anna's injuries and issues, pointing to his corresponding body parts as he talked. Unlike her mental health diagnoses, these injury descriptions were assertively precise.

"We tried our very best," the doctor said finally, shaking his head.

"But after a certain amount of time, and doing everything . . . the injuries . . . we knew she would not survive. There was nothing more I could do. She did not survive. I am so very, very sorry."

For me, the jagged pain of her suicide had been partially sanded down before it even happened, smoothed by years of visiting different therapists and psychiatrists, reading about diagnoses, feeling misunderstood, experimenting with different medications, feeling hope, having hope dashed. I'm sure DMDD was a correct diagnosis for Anna's early problems with rage and irritability, but I feel it came too late for us to prepare for the deep depression that would consume her later. Of course, it's possible that the diagnosis wouldn't have made a difference—Emanuele suggests that parents should not become overly concerned with names of diagnoses. No person or pill or label could ease what Anna wrote in her final minutes as a life "without ever feeling happiness or satisfaction," according to a lengthy note she wrote on her iPhone and posted on Reddit before she jumped. Diaries she left behind showed that she had been planning her suicide attempt of August 15, 2018, since May.

"I remember around 12 years of age, I began to have fleeting thoughts of suicide. I never really understood it much back then," she wrote in the note, the link sent to me by one of Anna's online friends. "It's been years since then, and those fleeting thoughts only got worse. Nowadays, I have spent large portions of my time thinking about suicide."

Anna shared in the note how she wished she could have left her mark on the world, but that life was too painful. She couldn't claw her way out of the black hole that enveloped her mind and squeezed away every ray of sunshine. Her hope, she wrote, was that the Universe could be erased, so no being would ever have to suffer again.

On the night Anna died, a social worker led us to a room where we saw her for the final time. Although stricken with a deep sadness, my only reaction was to approach her bed gingerly, and then woodenly stroke her hair. I wanted to know: Why? Why didn't she hold out a little longer? Why couldn't we have made it to the consultation for a different therapy? What more could I have done? But as my thoughts wandered back to her note, I realized her pain was something I could not understand. Despite my own suffering in that moment, I knew that Anna's hope was not my hope.

My hope is that more in this Universe will take mothers of young children seriously when they worry about their child's mental health, and not dismiss their concerns. My hope is that more people enter the field of child psychology and child psychiatry so that there are more treatment and provider options. My hope is that more researchers will advance research into mental health disorders and neuroscience. My most ardent hope, however, is that after years of waiting for a diagnosis and treatment, no other mother is forced to contemplate that her daughter's final, calm expression might have been her most peaceful one ever.

With those hopes in mind, I reached down and stroked Anna's blond hair for the last time.

JON MOOALLEM

"We Have Fire Everywhere"

FROM *The New York Times Magazine*

THE FIRE WAS already growing at a rate of one football field per second when Tamra Fisher woke up on the edge of Paradise, California, feeling that her life was no longer insurmountably strenuous or unpleasant and that she might be up to the challenge of living it again.

She was forty-nine and had spent almost all of those years on the Ridge—the sweeping incline, in the foothills of California's Sierra Nevada, on which Paradise and several tinier, unincorporated communities sit. Fisher moved to the Ridge as a child, married at sixteen, then raised four children of her own, working seventy-hour-plus weeks caring for disabled adults and the elderly. Paradise had attracted working-class retirees from around California since the 1970s and was beginning to draw in younger families for the same reasons. The town was quiet and affordable, free of the big-box stores and traffic that addled the city of Chico in the valley below. It still brimmed with the towering pine trees that first made the community viable more than a century ago. The initial settlement was poor and minuscule—"Poverty Ridge," some called it—until a new logging railroad was built through the town in 1904 by a company felling timber farther uphill. This was the Diamond Match Company. The trees of Paradise made for perfect matchsticks.

Like many people who grow up in small communities, Fisher regarded her hometown with affection but also exhaustion. All her life, she dreamed of leaving and seeing other parts of the world, not to escape Paradise but so that she could return with renewed appreciation for it. But as the years wore on, she worried that she'd missed her chance. There had been too many tribulations and not enough money. She was trapped.

Then again, who knew? That fall, Fisher was suspended in a wide-open and recuperative limbo, having finally ended a five-year relationship with a man who, she said, conned her financially, isolated her from her family, and seized on her diagnoses of depression and a mood disorder to make her feel crazy and sick and insist that she go on disability. "What I thought was love," she said, "was me trying to buy love and him stealing from me." But now, a fuller, bigger life seemed possible. She'd tried community college for a semester. And just recently, she got together with Andy, a big-hearted baker for the Chico public-school system, who slipped out of her bed earlier that Thursday morning to drive down the hill to work. Fisher was feeling grounded again: *happy*. It was odd to say the word, but it must have been true because there she was, getting out of bed at 8 a.m. — early for her — energetically and without resentment, to take her two miniature schnauzers and Andy's lumbering old mutt into the yard to pee.

She stepped out in her slippers and the oversize sweatshirt she slept in. She smelled smoke. The sky overhead was still faintly blue in spots, but a brown fog, forced in by a hard wind, was rapidly smothering it. "I've been here so long, it didn't even faze me," Fisher said. Small wildfires erupted in the canyons on either side of Paradise every year. But then the wind gusted sharply and a three-inch piece of burned bark floated lazily toward her through the air like a demonic moth. Fisher opened her hand and caught it. Bits of it crumbled in her palm like charcoal. She took a picture and texted it to her sister Cindy Christensen. "WTF is happening," she wrote.

Cindy knew about wildfires. In fact, she'd spent every summer and fall fixated on fire since the "fire siege" of 2008, when Paradise was threatened by two blazes, one in each of the canyons alongside it. One morning, as the Humboldt Fire approached from the east, the town ordered more than 9,000 people to evacuate as a precaution, Cindy among them. But when Cindy pulled out of her neighborhood, she instantly hit gridlock. An investigation determined that it took nearly three hours for most residents to drive the eleven miles downhill.

Sitting in traffic that morning, Cindy felt viscerally unsafe. Ever since then, she obsessively tracked the daily indicators of high-fire danger on the TV weather reports and with apps on her phone. "It consumed me," Cindy said. She spent many nights, unable to sleep, listening to the wind plow out of the canyon and batter her roof. Many days, she refused to leave home, worried a fire might blow through her neighborhood before she could return for her pets. She didn't just sign up to get the county's emergency alerts on her phone; she bought her own police scanner.

It pained Tamra to see her sister fall apart every fire season; Cindy seemed irrational—possessed. It was hard to take her seriously. "That's just Cindy," Tamra would say. Now, standing with her phone in one hand and the charred bark in the other, Tamra needed Cindy to be Cindy and tell her what to do.

"Evacuate," Cindy wrote back.

"Answer me!!" Tamra texted again. "It's raining ash and bark." Neither realized that some texts weren't being received by the other. Then the power went out, and Tamra, who had dropped her cellular plan to save money and could only use her phone with Wi-Fi, was cut off from communicating with anyone.

"Leave, T. Paradise is on fire," Cindy was texting her. "Leave!!"

By then, Cindy was almost off the Ridge, bawling in her car from the stress and dread. Forty-five minutes earlier, she learned that a fire had sparked northeast of town, and she immediately didn't like the scenario taking shape. The relative humidity that morning, the wind speed and direction, which would propel the fire straight toward Paradise—it was all very bad. "In my mind, I pictured exactly what happened," she explained. She'd spent years picturing it, in fact. She left right away.

This time, there was no traffic; Cindy says she saw only two other cars the whole way down. Later, she spotted her home in aerial footage of Paradise on the local news. Her aboveground swimming pool was unmistakable. Nearly everything else had burned into a ghostly black smudge.

By the time Fisher got in her yellow Volkswagen, the sky had transformed again: it was somehow both shrouded and glowing. Many other residents had learned to keep a "go bag" packed by the door, with water, medications, and copies of important documents; a woman from the local Fire Safe Council, a volunteer known affectionately as the Bag Lady, held frequent workshops demonstrating how to pack one. But Fisher was indecisive and moving inefficiently. It had taken her nearly forty minutes to commit to leaving, wrangle the dogs, and scramble to grab a few haphazard possessions.

It was now 8:45. So many calls were being placed to 911 that a dispatcher interrupted one man reporting a fire alongside Skyway Road—the busiest street in Paradise and the town's primary evacuation route—with a terse, "Yeah, sir, we have fire everywhere." Officials had started issuing evacuation orders about an hour earlier; Fisher's neighborhood was among those told to clear out first. Her street was plugged with cars. A thick line of them crept forward at the end of her driveway.

There are five routes out of Paradise. The three major ones spread south like the legs of a tripod, passing through the heart of town and continuing downhill toward Chico and the valley below. Fisher lived in the northern part of town, on the easternmost leg of the tripod, Pentz Road; she rented a bedroom from a woman who worked at a nursing home in town. It baffled her to see that all the cars in front of her house were heading north on Pentz, cramming themselves away from the center of Paradise, away from the valley, and further uphill. The opposite lane, meanwhile, was totally empty. It seemed obvious to Fisher that, if the fire was approaching from somewhere in the canyon behind her house, there would be plenty of Paradise left in which to safely wait it out. So she pushed across the traffic, into the empty lane. But she barely went 100 yards before a driver sitting in the jam alongside her rolled down his window and explained that Pentz was blocked up ahead.

"Great," Fisher muttered. As she turned around and took her place in line, she wished the man good luck.

"You too," he said.

She was recording everything on her phone, compelled by some instinct she would strain to make sense of later. She wanted people to know what happened to her and presumed, nonsensically, that her phone would survive even if she didn't. Maybe, too, she wanted someone to be with her while it happened. Her phone created the illusion of an audience; it was the best she could do.

It was suddenly much darker. Everyone had their headlights on. The sky was blood red in places but waning into absolute black. The smoke column was collapsing on them: The plume from the wildfire had billowed upward until, at about 35,000 feet, it froze, became heavier, and fell earthward again. Outside Fisher's passenger-side window, the wind snapped an American flag in someone's yard so relentlessly that it seemed to be rippling under the force of some machine. Then, a mammoth gust kicked up, spattering the street with pine needles. It sounded like a rainstorm and, when it subsided, bright orange embers appeared beside Fisher's car: trails of pinhole lights, like fairies, skittering low over the shoulder, chasing each other out of the dry leaves, then capering off and vanishing in front lawns.

Fisher noticed a minivan struggling to merge just ahead—people weren't letting the driver in. She stopped to let it through, then suddenly screamed: "Oh, my God! There's a fire!" She yelled it again, out her window, as though she worried she were the only one seeing it: the tremendous box of bright, anarchic flame where there used to be a home.

It was 9:13 a.m. Fisher had been in her car for nearly half an hour and traveled altogether nowhere; in fact, the burning house appeared to be only a few doors down from her own. There was a second structure aflame now. The fires were multiplying rapidly.

"I don't want to die!" Fisher shouted. The mood had shifted. People started honking. Fisher honked too. She began to sob and scream, to open her car door and lean her head out, asking what she should do. Later, she felt embarrassed. She would see so many YouTube videos of people calmly piloting their cars through the flames. There was one guy who went viral, singing to his three-year-old daughter as he honked and swerved, commenting on the encroaching inferno as though it were an interactive exhibit at a science museum. ("Be careful with that fire!" the girl says adorably. The father replies, "I'm going to stay away from it, OK?") It didn't make sense to Fisher that she would be the only person screaming. Even the three dogs with her were silent, though two of them were deaf and mostly blind and the third was shivering, eyes locked open, too shocked to make a sound. "I'm scared!" Fisher shouted. "Somebody!"

"OK, calm down," a voice called. The person urged her to turn around again. She did and suddenly, still crying wildly, found herself shooting south again, through the other, wide-open lane of Pentz, following a white truck with a Butte County Fire Department decal on it. She tailed the fireman intently, coasting past one burning house after another. Some were being steadily, evenly devoured; others angrily disgorged flames straight up from their roofs. Fisher knew the people who lived in many of these houses — this was her neighborhood. "This is Pentz Road!" she yelled as she drove. "These are people's homes." Then added: "I'm sorry. I am so sorry!"

When she got to the corner of Pearson Road, a major east–west artery, she saw someone directing cars to take the right turn, where she and the fireman found they could accelerate even more, winding along S-curves through a wooded area that was almost entirely aflame. Fires speckled the slopes along Pearson so that, in the dark, the hillside looked like a lava flow. "It's so hot," Fisher said. "Keep going! Keep going!" But then, they shot around another curve and the fireman's brake lights came on. They had hit a wall of cars, across both lanes.

"No!" Fisher yowled. "What did I do?"

She was silent for a moment. Then something started beeping. It was the low-fuel alert. She was almost out of gas, though it ultimately wouldn't matter. Moments later, her car caught fire.

Afterward, you could feel your mind grinding against what happened, desperate to whittle it down into a simple explanation of what went wrong, who should be blamed, what could be learned. There were many credible answers, specific mistakes to call out. But it was easy to worry that, given the scale of this particular disaster, the principal takeaways might be only humility and terror.

From the start, the Camp Fire was driven by an almost vengeful-seeming confluence of circumstances, many of which had been nudged into alignment by climate change. Paradise had prepared for disasters. But it had prepared *merely* for disasters, and this was something else. In a matter of hours, the town's roads were swamped, its emergency plans outstripped. Nine of every ten homes were destroyed and at least eighty-five people were dead. Many were elderly, some were incinerated in their cars while trying to flee, and others apparently never made it that far.

It was all more evidence that the natural world was warping, outpacing our capacity to prepare for, or even conceive of, the magnitude of disaster that such a disordered earth can produce. We live with an unspoken assumption that the planet is generally survivable, that its tantrums are infrequent and, while menacing, can be plotted along some hazy, existentially tolerable bell curve. But the stability that American society was built around for generations appears to be eroding. That stability was always an illusion; wherever you live, you live with risk—just at some emotional and cognitive remove. Now, those risks are ratcheting up. Nature is increasingly finding a foothold in the unimaginable: what's not just unprecedented but also hopelessly far beyond what we've seen. This is a realm beyond disaster, where catastrophes live. Fisher wasn't just trapped in a fire; she was trapped in the twenty-first century.

By way of analogy, Paradise's emergency-operations coordinator, Jim Broshears, later described giving fire-safety tutorials at elementary schools, back when he was the town's fire chief, teaching second- and third-graders that if there's fire at their bedroom door, they should go out the window, and vice versa. "Inevitably," Broshears told me, "there's the kid who goes, 'What if there's fire at the door *and* the window?'" And no matter what alternative Broshears provided, the kid could always push the story line one step further.

"At some point, they've painted you into a corner and, well, do I tell an eight-year-old kid, 'In that case, you're going to die?' Do you tell a community, 'If this particular scenario hits, a bunch of you are going to die?' Is that appropriate? I don't know the answer." He added, "I think that people are going to conclude that now."

Fisher saw the first flames skitter in the depression where her windshield met the hood. She opened her car door again and leaned her head out. Embers burned tiny holes in her leggings. She was yelling, asking if anyone had water. A contractor in a pickup behind her hollered: "You don't need water. You need to get in my truck." He beckoned her and all her animals over.

Fisher wedged herself among the tools and paperwork scattered on the man's front seat, two dogs on top of her and the largest at her feet. As they inched forward, she took a picture of her burning car and was crushed to realize that she had just abandoned the few possessions she'd managed to save, including the ashes of her big brother, Larry, who, ten years earlier, died suddenly in his sleep.

"I'm Tamra," she told the man driving.

"I'm Larry," he said.

The coincidence was too much: Fisher started crying again.

Larry Laczko wore sleek, black-rimmed glasses and a San Francisco Giants cap and seemed, to Fisher, almost preternaturally subdued, speaking with the slow resignation of a man enduring ordinary traffic on an ordinary Thursday morning. Laczko and his wife lived on the Ridge for fifteen years, then migrated to Chico in 2010, after raising their two kids. For years, Laczko worked at Intel, managing sixty employees, traveling constantly. Then, one Saturday, his wife told him to clean the windows of their home in Paradise—and to clean them *well* this time. Laczko did some research, geeked out a little, and wound up ordering a set of professional-grade tools from one of the oldest window-washing supply companies in the United States. His wife was pleased. Soon, he was washing windows every weekend, toddling around the Ridge with his tools, getting to know his neighbors and friends of friends. "I liked the work, the instant gratification of a dirty window turning clean," Laczko explained, "but it was the interaction with people that I loved." That was sixteen years ago. He quit his job and has run his own window-washing company ever since.

Laczko was on Pearson Road by chance—or because of his own stupidity. In retrospect, he conceded, either assessment was fair. His mother-in-law lived in Quail Trails Village, a nearby mobile-home and RV park. She was eighty-eight and used a walker. Laczko's wife, who was nearby that morning, had already got her out. But Laczko wanted to be helpful. He recently installed an automatic lift chair for his mother-in-law and remembered how, after the 2008 evacuation, many people wound up displaced from the Ridge for days; it would be nice for his mother-in-law to have that chair. So he drove up the hill and cut across on Pearson, only to be turned around by police. Backtracking, he smacked into the traffic that had formed behind him: a blockade of cars, barely moving and every so often, as with Fisher's Volkswagen, suddenly sprouting into flame.

When Fisher climbed into Laczko's truck, the seriousness of his predicament was only beginning to catch up with him. What sounded to Fisher like extraordinary calmness was actually extraordinary focus: he was scanning his surroundings, updating his map of everything that was on fire around him—that tree; the plastic fender of that SUV—while also taking a mental inventory of the back of his pickup, gauging how likely each item was to catch.

"We're getting out of here," Laczko told Fisher. He projected enough confidence that he reassured himself, just slightly, as well.

But clearly he and Fisher were stuck. Thousands of people were, on choked roadways all over the Ridge, each sealed in his or her own saga of agony, terror, courage, or despair. It was like the 2008 evacuations, but far more serious—the gridlock, cinched tighter; the danger, exponentially more acute—and also harder to stomach, given all the focus on avoiding those problems in the ten years since.

After the 2008 fires, the county created a fifth route off the Ridge, paving an old gravel road that wound through mountains to the north. Paradise vigorously revamped and expanded the emergency plans it had in place. The town was carved into fourteen evacuation zones; these were reorganized to better stagger the flow of cars. Paradise introduced the idea of "contraflow," whereby traffic could be sent in a single direction across all lanes of a given street if necessary. Maps and instructions were mailed to residents regularly. There were evacuation drills, annual wildfire-preparedness events, and other, more meticulous layers of internal planning too. Paradise's Wildland Fire Traffic Control Plan identified, for example, twelve "priority intersections" where problems might arise for drivers leaving each evacuation zone and stipulated how many orange cones or human flaggers would ideally be dispatched to each.

"The more you study the Camp Fire," says Thomas Cova, a University of Utah geographer who has analyzed wildfire evacuations for twenty-five years, "the more you think: this could have been way worse. *Way* worse." Cova called Paradise "one of the most prepared communities in the state." A recent *USA Today*–California Network investigation found that only six of California's twenty-seven communities at highest risk for fire had robust and publicly available evacuation plans.

One architect of Paradise's planning was Jim Broshears, who had spent the bulk of his forty-seven-year career as an emergency planner and firefighter struggling to mitigate his community's idiosyncratically high risk of disaster. After the Camp Fire, Broshears confessed that, in his mind, the upper limit of harrowing scenarios against which he'd been defending Paradise was the 1991 Tunnel Fire in the Oakland hills—a wildfire that consumed more than

2,900 structures and killed twenty-five people: "I'll be honest," he told me, "we simply didn't see it being much worse than that." Recently, Broshears showed me a copy of the Traffic Control Plan in a big, thick binder and said, with admirable directness, "It mostly didn't work." Then he clacked the binder shut and insisted, "That is still going to work 98 percent of the time, though."

The *Los Angeles Times* and other newspapers would later dig up many city planning mistakes and communication failures that appeared to compound the devastation on the morning of November 8. The core of the problem was that there just wasn't any time. The fire was moving so astonishingly fast that, only a few minutes after Paradise started evacuating its first zones, it was obvious the entire community would have to be cleared.

There was no plan for evacuating all 27,000 residents of Paradise at once. "I don't think it's physically possible," Paradise's mayor, Jody Jones, told me. For a town that size to build enough additional lanes of roadway to make it possible, she added, would have seemed preposterous and like a waste of taxpayer money had anyone proposed it. Our communities, as they currently exist, were planned and built primarily to be lived in, not escaped. Fully prioritizing evacuation could mean ripping them apart.

Paradise evolved without any genuine planning at all: three adjacent communities just kept expanding until they merged. This produced a town of tangled side streets and poorly connected neighborhoods, often with a single outlet and many dead ends. "In towns all up and down the Sierra, we've got the same pattern," says Zeke Lunder of Deer Creek Resources, which often contracts with the state on wildfire-mapping projects. "I think it's inevitable that this will happen again."

That morning in Paradise, streets were blocked by fallen trees, disabled cars, or even fire blowing crosswise across them. Flaming roadside vegetation slowed or halted traffic on major evacuation routes like Skyway so that many of the cross streets that fed them, like Pearson, backed up, penning other drivers defenselessly into the side streets that fed *them*.

Just ahead of Fisher and Laczko, a woman named Lorena Rodriguez watched flames absorb the space around her car. She reached for her phone to tell her children goodbye, but then she reconsidered, worried the memory of her frightened voice would permit her kids to more vividly imagine her burning alive and keep imagining it for the rest of their lives. This enraged Rodri-guez—that she had been put in a position to have such a thought. So she decided to run, sprinting in a pair of Danskos, threading the lanes of idling vehicles and moving faster on foot than all of them. She kept expecting to find some obstacle blocking the road, a reason for the traffic, but all she saw was more cars.

Rodriguez ran for two and a half miles, all the way west on Pearson until she reached Skyway. She says the street was bumper to bumper most of the way, the vehicles alongside her perfectly still. It was as if time had stopped for everyone but her.

Fisher was thinking about her father, a former fire captain who was protective to the point of pitilessness. To teach his little girls not to play with matches, he showed them gruesome photographs of bodies extracted from houses that burned down.

Those pictures had been flashing through Fisher's mind all morning. Now, on Pearson Road, she sensed she was inside one. She knew there had to be people dying around her and Laczko: good people who wanted to live just as much as she did—surely, who wanted it more.

Fisher inhaled deeply to rein in her crying and told Laczko: "I gotta say something. I've tried to kill myself multiple times, and now, I'm scared." It was true. She felt guilty about it. She also knew, in that moment, that she wanted to live.

It had been all of ten minutes since Laczko waved Fisher into his truck. While some people might have recoiled from a stranger making this kind of admission, Laczko didn't pass judgment or see Fisher as a burden. As a kid, he went to parochial school, though the faith never took; he asked too many questions. Still, he liked the way his wife talked about spirituality, not God so much as a form of godliness that arises whenever two human beings connect. In that moment, he told me, his only thought was, *This person needs to talk, and I can certainly listen.*

After getting turned around on Pearson, Laczko instantly felt deflated—and then, a little foolish too. He was starting to repri-mand himself for driving into a fire. For what? A chair?

Fisher, meanwhile, was exhausted, having so far shouldered the responsibility for her survival alone all morning. "I just wanted to be with somebody," she explained.

For Laczko, "Something clicked—now I had someone to be responsible for."

They were together now, but still trapped, and the windows of Laczko's truck were getting hotter. Until then, the fires blooming erratically around Paradise were spot fires, birthed from embers that the wildfire sprayed ahead of itself as it grew. Now an impregnable riot of heat and flame was cresting the hillside under Pearson Road. This was the fire itself.

There's a dismaying randomness to how a megafire can start: the tire on a trailer goes flat and scrapes against the pavement, producing sparks; the DIY wiring job on someone's hot tub melts. (These were the causes of the 2018 Carr and 2015 Valley Fires, respectively. More than 300,000 acres burned, combined.) But by now, there is also a feeling of predictability: in 2017, for example, seventeen of twenty-one major fires in California were started accidentally by equipment owned by Pacific Gas and Electric (PG&E), which, as California's largest electrical utility, is in the precarious business of shooting electricity through 175,000 miles of live wire, stitched across an increasingly flammable state. Under state law, the company may be liable for damage from those fires, whether or not the initial spark resulted from its negligence. And so, PG&E found itself looking for ways to adapt.

Two days before the Camp Fire, as horrendously blustery and dry conditions began settling on the Ridge and the risk of fire turned severe, PG&E began warning 70,000 of its electricity customers in the area, including the entire town of Paradise, that it might shut off their power as a precaution. This was one of the new tactics that the company had adopted—a "last resort," PG&E called it: in periods of extreme fire danger, if weather conditions aligned to make any accidental spark potentially calamitous, PG&E was prepared to flip the switch, preventively cutting the electricity from its lines. Life would go dark, maybe for days—whatever it took. It was clear that the unforgiving environment in which PG&E had been operating for the last few years was, as the company put it, California's "new normal."

Wildfires have always remade California's landscape. Historically, they were sparked by lightning, switching on haphazardly to sweep forests of their dead and declining vegetation and prime them for new, healthier growth. Noticing this cycle—the natural "fire regimes" at work—Native Americans mimicked it, lighting targeted fires to engineer areas for better foraging and hunting. But white settlers were oblivious to nature's fire regimes; when blazes sprung up around their towns, they stamped them out.

Those towns grew into cities; the land around them, suburbs. More than a century of fire suppression left the ecosystems abutting them misshapen and dysfunctional. To set things right, the maintenance once performed naturally by fire would have to be conducted by state and federal bureaucracies, timber companies, private citizens, and all the other entities through whose jurisdictions that land splinters. The approach has been feeble and piecemeal, says William Stewart, a co-director of Berkeley Forests at the University of California, Berkeley: "Little pinpricks of fuel reduction on the landscape." We effectively turned nature into another colossal infrastructure project and endlessly deferred its maintenance.

Then came climate change. Summers in Northern California are now 2.5 degrees hotter than they were in the early 1970s, speeding up evaporation and baking the forests dry. Nine of the ten largest fires in state history, since record-keeping started in 1932, have happened in the last sixteen years. Ten of the twenty most destructive fires occurred in the last four; eight in the last two. California's Department of Forestry and Fire Protection, known as Cal Fire, expects that these trends will only get worse. It's possible that we've entered an era of "megafires" and "megadisturbances," the agency noted in its 2018 Strategic Fire Plan. And these fires are no longer restricted to the summer and early fall: "Climate change has rendered the term 'fire season' obsolete."

Even deep into last fall, much of the landscape still seemed restless, eager to burn. A bout of heavy rains that spring produced a record growth of grasses around the Ridge—the fastest-burning fuels in a landscape. But then the rain stopped. By the time of the Camp Fire, in November, there hadn't been any significant precipitation since late May, and July had been California's hottest month on record: all that vegetation dried out. "Everything is here," explained a veteran wild-land firefighter named Jon Paul. "All you need is ignition."

The Camp Fire glinted into existence around 6:15 that Thursday morning. Cal Fire hasn't yet released its full investigation, but the available evidence indicates that a hook on a PG&E electrical tower near the community of Pulga snapped, allowing a wire to spring free. The wire flapped against the skeletal metal tower, throwing sparks into the wind, most likely for a fraction of a second before the system's safety controls could have flipped. Still, it was enough: The sparks started a fire; the fire spread.

In the end, PG&E chose not to de-energize its lines. Even with warm, dry air gushing through the canyon early that morning, blowing 30 miles per hour and gusting up to 51, the company claimed that conditions never reached the thresholds it had determined would necessitate a shutoff. "That revealed a failure of imagination on PG&E's part," says Michael Wara, who directs the Climate and Energy Policy Program at the Stanford Woods Institute for the Environment. PG&E was largely forced into the position of having to shut off people's power in the first place, Wara argues, because it failed for decades to invest in the kind of maintenance and innovation that would allow its infrastructure to stand up to more hostile conditions, as climate change gradually exacerbated the overall risk. But now, Wara said, the decision to keep operating that morning suggested that the company still hadn't fully accepted the kind of resoluteness this new reality demanded. Three weeks earlier, PG&E instituted its first, and ultimately only, shutdown of the 2018 fire season, cutting electricity during a windstorm to nearly 60,000 customers in seven counties. It took two days to restore everyone's power; citizens and local governments fumed. "One has to wonder," Wara says, "if the negative publicity and pushback PG&E received influenced decision making on the day of the Camp Fire." ("We will not speculate on past events," a PG&E spokesman said in an email. "The devastating wildfires of the past two years have made it clear that more must be done, and with greater urgency, to adapt and address the issue.")

An even starker truth: it probably wouldn't have mattered. The lines at that particular tower in Pulga wouldn't have been included in a shutoff that morning anyway; PG&E's protocols at the time appeared not to consider such high-voltage transmission lines a severe risk. A shutdown, however, would have de-energized other lower-voltage lines a few miles west of the tower, where, shortly after the first fire started, some vegetation, most likely a tree branch, blew into the equipment and triggered a second blaze.

In a preliminary report, Cal Fire's investigators seemed to regard this subsequent event as negligible, however. Within thirty minutes of igniting, the second fire had been consumed by the first, which was ripping through a fast-burning landscape, powered forward by its own metabolism and pushed by the wind. It had advanced four miles and was already swallowing the small town of Concow. The Camp Fire was moving too fast to be fought.

"It was pretty much complete chaos," Joe Kennedy said. Kennedy is a Cal Fire heavy-equipment operator based in Nevada City, southeast of Paradise. He was called to the Camp Fire at 7:16 that morning and hurtled toward the Ridge with his siren on, in an eighteen-wheeler flatbed with his bulldozer lashed to the back.

Kennedy is thirty-six, a fantastically giant man with a shaved head and a friendly face but the affect of a granite wall; he spoke quietly and, it seemed, never a syllable more than necessary. He had operated heavy equipment his entire adult life, working as a contractor in the same small mountain towns around the Sierra where he grew up, then joined Cal Fire in 2014, just before he and his wife had a child. He claimed his supremely taciturn nature was a by-product of fatherhood; until then, he explained, he was a more reckless adrenaline junkie. But Kennedy loved bulldozers, and he loved the rush of barreling toward a fire in one. "Dozer driver" seemed to be less his job description than his identity, his tribe. "In ten years," he joked, "they'll probably consider it a mental disorder."

Kennedy was dispatched to the Adventist Health Feather River hospital on Pentz Road. By the time he arrived, spot fires were igniting everywhere. The chatter on the radio was hard to penetrate. Now that he was in position, Kennedy couldn't get in touch with anyone to give him a specific assignment, so he fell back on his training and a precept known as "leader's intent": if someone were to give him an order, he asked himself, what would it be?

By then, the hospital staff had completed a swift evacuation of the facility. Nurses later described doing precisely what they practiced in their annual drills but at three or four times the speed: wheeling patients through the halls at a sprint, staging everyone in the ER lobby, then sorting all sixty-seven inpatients into a haphazard fleet of ambulances and civilians' cars arriving outside to carry them away. Many didn't make it far. One ambulance, carrying a woman who had just had a C-section and was still immobilized from the waist down, quickly caught fire in the traffic on Pentz. Paramedics hustled the woman into a nearby empty house. Others took shelter there as well. A Cal Fire officer, David Hawks, mobilized them into an ad hoc fire brigade to rake out the gutters and hose down the roof as structures on either side began to burn.

Kennedy caught snippets on his radio about this group and others hunkered in nearby houses. He'd found his assignment. He climbed into his bulldozer, a colossal Caterpillar D5H that traveled on towering treads like a tank and was outfitted with a huge steel shovel, or "blade." It also had a pretty killer sound system, and as Kennedy turned the ignition, the stereo automatically connected to his phone through Bluetooth and started playing Pantera. Kennedy's technical skill and experience as a heavy-machinery operator was formidable; so was his knowledge of wildland firefighting tactics. But, given the scale of disaster unfolding around him, all that expertise now concentrated into one urgent, almost block-headedly simple directive: "Take the fire away from the houses."

Of course, Kennedy had no idea which houses any of these people were in. All around the hospital lay a sprawl of mostly ranch homes, packed together on small, wooded lots. A great many were already burning, so Kennedy homed in on the others and started clearing anything flammable, or anything already in flames, away from them. Ornamental landscaping, woodpiles, trees—he ripped it all out of the ground, pushed it aside or plowed straight through it, clearing a buffer around each home. He worked quickly, brutally, unhindered by any remorse over the collateral damage he was causing; it's impossible, he explained, to maneuver an eighteen-ton bulldozer between two adjacent houses and not scrape up a few corners.

Before long, Kennedy lost track of exactly where he was; he hadn't even bothered to switch on the GPS in his dozer yet. "It seemed like forever, but it was probably a half-hour," he said. "I think I got eight or nine houses. I made a pretty big mess."

Wildfires are typically attacked by strategically positioned columns of firefighters who advance on the fire's head, heel, or flanks like knights confronting a dragon. If a fire is spreading too rapidly for such an offensive, they instead work to contain it, drawing boundaries around the blaze—a "big box," it's called. Work crews or bulldozers clear vegetation and cut fire breaks to harden that perimeter. Aircraft drop retardants. Everything in the big box can be ceded to the fire; if you have to, you let it burn. But ideally, you hold those lines, and the flames don't spread any farther.

As wildfires get fiercer and more unruly, firefighters aren't just unable to mount direct attacks but are also forced to draw larger and larger boxes to keep from being overrun themselves. "The big box is a lot bigger now," one Cal Fire officer explained. (He asked not to be named, hesitant to publicly concede that "our tactics need to change.") But this strategy breaks down when the fire is racing toward a populated area. The extra space you would surrender to the fire might contain a neighborhood of several hundred homes.

Wildfires aren't solid objects, moving in a particular direction at a particular speed. They are frequently erratic and fluid, ejecting embers in all directions, producing arrays of spot fires that then pull together and ingest any empty space between them. On November 8, the wind was so strong that gusts easily lofted embers from one rim of the Feather River Canyon to the other like a trebuchet, launching fire out of the wilderness into Fisher's neighborhood.

As this swirl of live embers descended, like the flecks in a snow globe, each had the potential to land in a receptive fuel bed: the dry leaves in someone's yard, the pine needles in a gutter. Those kinds of fuels were easy to find. It was November, after all, past the time of year that wildfires traditionally start, and Paradise's trees had carpeted the town with tinder. And every speck of flame that rose up in it had the potential to leap into an air vent and engulf a home. Now it is a spot fire—a beachhead in the built environment, spattering its own embers everywhere, onto other houses, rebooting the entire process.

Within two hours of the first spot fires being reported near Fisher's house, others leapfrogged from one end of Paradise to the other. The progression was unintelligible from any one point on the ground. As one man who was at the hospital later told me, "I thought that the only part of Paradise that was on fire was the part of Paradise we were looking at." And, as happened with Fisher, this generated a horrifying kind of dissonance: scurrying away from the fire only to discover that the fire was suddenly ahead of you and alongside you too.

*

"Take deep breaths," Laczko said.

Fisher had just told him about trying to kill herself. They were barely moving. Embers darted by like schools of bioluminescent fish. Evergreen trees alongside them burned top to bottom. These were the town's famous pines, stressed from years of drought; the pitch inside was heating to its boiling point and, the moment it vaporized, the length of the trunk would flash into flame all at once. This became one of the more nightmarish and stupefying sights that morning on the Ridge: giant trees suddenly combusting.

The topography of that particular stretch of Pearson Road made it a distinctly horrible place to be stranded. Beyond the guardrail to Fisher and Laczko's left, a densely wooded ravine yawned open, with a stream known as Dry Creek Drainage far below. Already, the spot fires and burning trees on either side of the road were casting heat inward. But as the mass of the wildfire moved in, the ravine appeared to create a chimney effect, funneling flames up and over the street—only to be overridden periodically by the prevailing winds, which pushed the flames back. Everyone on Pearson was caught in the middle.

A Cal Fire branch director, Tony Brownell, told me that he was astonished to watch fire doubling back across Pearson, washing over the same land it had just scorched, only the second such immediate "reburn" he witnessed in his thirty-one-year career. This was about fifteen minutes before Fisher's car ignited. Brownell, it turns out, was the fireman in the white pickup truck whom she initially followed into that gridlock from back on Pentz Road. Brownell managed to escape quickly, but as he turned his vehicle around and drove away, he told me, he looked at the flames in his rearview mirror and thought, I just killed that girl.

"You'd think that people would just hurry up and go," Fisher said.

"There's no place to go," Laczko told her. "They're trying. Cal Fire's here to help."

He could see a fire engine a few car-lengths ahead. After fighting to weave forward, it too had been more or less swallowed by the same intractable traffic. Laczko silently made the calculation that if his own truck caught fire, he and Fisher would make a run for it and climb inside to safety.

This would have been a mistake. The Cal Fire captain driving the fire engine, John Jessen, later estimated that the outside temperature was more than 200 degrees, the air swirling with lethally hot gases. Cars were catching fire everywhere, and four drivers fled toward that fire truck and, one after another, crammed themselves into the cab alongside its three-man crew. When two more people came knocking, Jessen turned them away—no more room, he said. "That was probably the worst thing I've ever had to do," Jessen said later. "I don't know if those people made it to another car. I don't know what happened to them."

This was Jessen's twenty-fourth fire season in California. He'd fought five of the ten most destructive fires in state history and was beginning to feel beaten down. "When I started this career twenty-five years ago, a 10,000-acre fire was a big deal," he said. "And it was a big deal if we weren't able to do structure defense and the fire consumed five homes. We took that to heart. We felt like we lost a major battle." Just moments earlier, around the corner on Pentz, Jessen watched fire consume dozens of homes within minutes. He was knocking on the door of another, to evacuate any stragglers, when he saw the actual fire front for the first time. It was already climbing the near side of the canyon, pounding toward town. The wall of flame was 200 feet tall, he estimated, and stretched for more than two and a half miles. That was the moment Jessen scrambled back to his truck and told his crew it was time to move.

Now, marooned on Pearson, Jessen radioed for air support. Later, he would seem embarrassed by this request, chalking it up to "muscle memory": the smoke was too thick for aircraft to fly in. The paint on his hood started burbling from the heat. Inside, the plastic on his steering console was smoking; the stench of its off-gassing filled the cab. The barrel-shaped fuel tanks beneath the doors were splashing diesel around the truck; the brass plugs in their openings got so hot they liquefied.

Jessen, meanwhile, was making a desperate calculation of his own: if their truck caught fire, he decided, they would extinguish it quickly and take off, saving the civilians aboard by pushing other cars out of the way with the front of his fire engine.

Maybe this was the lowest point. The megafire overwhelmed every system people put in place to fight or escape it; now it was scrambling their consciences too. "That's something I never imagined I would be thinking about," Jessen confessed, "pushing people closer to the fire so that I could get out."

Jessen sat there, watching for signs that his truck was about to catch fire. Laczko sat watching his own truck, ready to run for Jessen's. Then someone shouted, "Let's go, let's go, let's go!" Laczko saw a bulldozer churn into view behind him, clobbering one burning car after another.

Joe Kennedy had been mashing through people's landscaping on Pentz when he heard Jessen's distress call. There was no time for the standard, numeric identifiers. "John," Kennedy radioed. "Where you at?"

He switched on the iPad in his dozer and found Jessen's position near the corner of Pearson and Stearns Road. It was more than a mile away. The dozer's maximum speed was 6.3 miles per hour. But Kennedy clipped that distance by disregarding the right angles on his street map and barging his bulldozer through backyards, then eventually barreling down the steep, wooded incline overlooking Pearson and spilling, sloppily, into the middle of the street.

He produced a spectacular ruckus as he pushed the machine down the hill on its treads. From the road, it sounded like trees crashing—and some of it probably was. As Kennedy leveled off, he came upon a group of people, including four nurses from the hospital in scrubs. They were stranded in the middle of Pearson, battered by gusts of embers roaring out of the ravine, buckling over, struggling to breathe and keep walking. One nurse, Jeff Roach, was walking straight at Kennedy's bulldozer, with his arms in the air. Later, Roach explained that he had decided the bulldozer driver would either see him and rescue him and his three friends, or would not see him, keep advancing and crush him under the vehicle's treads. The burning in Roach's lungs was so bad, he said, that he had made his peace with either outcome.

Kennedy stopped. Two of the nurses climbed aboard then scampered to rejoin the others who had piled into a fire engine that appeared behind him. Kennedy began fighting his way up Pearson, toward Jessen, but found cars crammed into both lanes and the shoulder. Some people were idling right beside other vehicles that were expelling fountains of flame. Kennedy turned up the Pantera. He knew what he had to do: take the fire away from the people.

He approached the first burning car and pushed it off the embankment and into the ravine with his dozer blade, then backed up to discover a flaming rectangle of asphalt underneath it. He drove through that, pushed more cars. "I was basically on fire," Kennedy said. A photo later surfaced of an old Land Cruiser shoved so far up the adjacent hillside that it became snared in some sagging power lines. "That was me," Kennedy explained with a noticeable quantum of pride.

At least one of the vehicles Kennedy was shoving around had a body in it: Evva Holt, an eighty-five-year-old retired dietitian who lived at Feather Canyon Gracious Retirement Living, close to Fisher's house. Holt had phoned her daughter that morning to come get her—her daughter and son-in-law lived nearby and frequently came to perform for Holt and the other residents with their choral group—but there was no time. An independent caretaker named Lori LeBoa was readying to leave with a 103-year-old woman, and a police officer put Holt in her Chevy Silverado as well. The three women wound up stuck on Pearson. As the fire curled over Le-Boa's pickup, she jumped out and handed off the older woman to another driver. Turning back for Holt, she saw only fire and two arms reaching out.

Months later, over coffee, I asked Kennedy if he remembered moving that Silverado. He did. The memory seemed painful; he preferred not to talk about it on the record, except to stress that it was clear that he arrived too late to help whoever was inside.

I asked if he knew any details about the woman, if he wanted me to tell him. "I like the story in my head," he said.

Kennedy opened enough space for the stranded drivers on Pearson to maneuver and slowly advance. Moments earlier, one nurse who'd leapt into his dozer accidentally knocked into his iPad, switching his GPS into satellite view. Eventually, when Kennedy looked down at the map again, his eyes locked onto a conspicuous, bare rectangle, free of any vegetation or structures—any fuels to burn. It was a large gravel lot right near Jessen's fire engine; the firefighters just couldn't see it through the smoke. Once Kennedy arrived, the firefighters began herding the entire traffic jam—more than a hundred cars, Jessen says—into that clearing.

"Pull over there," a firefighter hollered at Laczko and Fisher as they crept uphill.

"And then what?" Laczko asked.

"Hunker down and keep your windows rolled up."

"Are you serious?" Fisher erupted. She was hoping for a more sophisticated plan.

"They wouldn't have put us here unless it was safer than where we were," Laczko said.

He eased his truck into place, parallel with the others. Directly in front of them, through the windshield, the frame of a large house burned and burned. For a moment, it was quiet. Then Fisher broke down again, very softly this time. "I don't have anything," she said. "I don't have anything."

Fires are unique among natural disasters: unlike earthquakes or hurricanes, they can be fought, slowed down, or thwarted. And virtually every summer in Paradise, until that Thursday morning, they had been. There was always trepidation as fire season approached but also skepticism that evacuation would ever truly be necessary and worth the hassle. "I confess my sense of denial," said Jacky Hoiland, who had lived in Paradise most of her life and worked for the school district for twenty years. Initially, after hearing about the Camp Fire, she took a look at the sky and then made herself a smoothie.

Still, even before the Camp Fire, many people in Paradise and around California had started to look at the recent succession of devastating fires—the Tubbs Fire, the Thomas Fire, blazes that ate through suburban-seeming neighborhoods and took lives—and intuit that our dominion over fire might be slipping. Something was different now: fire was winning, finding ways to outstrip our fight response, to rear up recklessly and break us down. That morning, in Paradise, there hadn't even been time for that fight response to kick in. And the flight response was failing too. Those who study wildfire have long argued that we need to reshuffle our relationship to it—move from reflexively trying to conquer fire to designing ways for communities to outfox and withstand it. And in a sense, that's what was happening with Laczko and Fisher, though only in a hasty and desperate way: hunkered in that gravel lot, everyone was playing dead.

After the fire, stories surfaced of people retreating into similar so-called temporary refuge areas all over the Ridge: clearings that offered some minimal protection or structures that could be easily defended. One large group sheltered in the Paradise Alliance

Church, which had been scouted and fortified in advance as part of the town's emergency planning. Another group sheltered outside a bar on Skyway and, when it caught fire, scampered, en masse, to an adjacent building and sheltered there. The Kmart parking lot became an impromptu refuge. So did an antique shop called Needful Things. In Concow, one firefighter instructed at least a dozen people to jump into a reservoir as the fire approached.

The group on Pearson wasn't in the gravel clearing long, less than ten minutes, it seems, from videos on Fisher's phone. Eventually, there was a knock on Laczko's window. "We're going to get out of here," a firefighter said, though he didn't specify where they would go. Moments later, another firefighter on a bullhorn shouted, "We're going to go toward the hospital."

"Oh, shit," Laczko blurted.

"We're going back?" Fisher said. She sounded both terrified and incensed. The hospital was on Pentz Road, near where she started. The trauma of the last two hours appeared to be flooding back.

Joe Kennedy led the way in his bulldozer, crawling through the thick smoke on Pearson to batter any obstacles out of their way. The core of the fire had passed, though it had left a kind of living residue everywhere: all the wooden posts of a roadside metal barricade were still burning, and shoals of flames dotted the road where Kennedy had removed burning cars. The cars were still burning too, wherever he had deposited them, belching solid black smoke as the caravan of survivors slowly passed.

"There's my car," Fisher said and turned to film it. Fire spouted from its roof like the plume of a Roman helmet. "It has my Raggedy Ann in it!" she said. The doll was one of the few things she grabbed before evacuating. She had had it since she was six and had expected to be buried with it one day. "Oh, my God," she said. "I'm crying over something so stupid!"

At the hospital, a fire alarm quacked robotically as a small outbuilding, not far from where Laczko and Fisher were parked, expelled smoke from behind a fence. A group of nurses had scavenged supplies from the evacuated emergency room and erected a makeshift triage center under the awning to treat any wounded trickling in. Laczko got out of his truck to see how he could help.

The hospital campus was ringed and speckled with fire. Some of the men were peeing on the little spot fires that danced in the parking lot's landscaped medians. Still, the influx of firefighters that morning had largely succeeded in defending the main building when the fire front moved through. Eventually, a call went out on the radio that the hospital campus was "actually the safest place to be."

Fisher and Laczko's group waited in the parking lot for close to three hours. Then, those lingering fires nearby began to swell and expand, threatening the hospital again. The firefighters were losing pressure in their hoses. The nurses were told to pack everything up. The road out was clear; they had a window in which it was safe to move. Everyone would finally be driving off the Ridge.

As they pulled out of the parking lot, back onto Pentz Road, Laczko noticed his eye-doctor's office burning top to bottom, directly in front of them.

"It's gone," Fisher said.

"It's gone," Laczko said.

"It's gone," Fisher repeated. "That house is gone! And that house is gone!"

They went on gesturing at everything as they drove—or rather, at its absence: all the homes still burning and others that had already settled into static masses of scrap and ash. As happens in any small town, every part of Paradise was overlaid with memories and meanings; each resident had his or her own idiosyncratic map of associations. As Fisher and Laczko coasted down Pentz, they tried to reconcile their maps with the disfigured reality in front of them, speaking the names of each flattened side street, noting who lived there or the last time they had been down there themselves. The iconic home at the corner of Pearson, with the ornate metal fence and sculptures of lions, had been devoured: "It used to be on the garden tour," Laczko said.

"Right here, that was my dog groomer's house."

"My sister is just right up here."

"Are these the people that used to have the Halloween stuff up?"

It was 1:45 p.m. Thirty-nine minutes later, and 460 miles away, a small brush fire would be reported near a Southern California Edison substation north of Malibu. Firefighters wouldn't contain the Woolsey Fire until it had swallowed nearly 100,000 acres and 1,600 structures and charged all the way to the Pacific, where it ran out of earth to consume. This time, as photos surfaced, all of America could find reference points on the map the fire had clawed apart: Lady Gaga evacuated. Miley Cyrus's home was a ruin. The mansion from *The Bachelor* was encircled and singed.

"Oh, God, it's all gone," Fisher said again. She gaped at the east side of Pentz Road, facing the canyon, where there didn't appear to be a single home left: just chimneys, wreckage, the slumping carcasses of cars, everything dun-colored and dead.

Five months after the Camp Fire, at the end of March, the wreckage in Paradise was still overpowering: parcel after parcel of incinerated storefronts, cars, outbuildings, fast-food restaurants, and homes. Patches of rutted pavement, like erratic rumble strips, still scarred Paradise's roadways wherever vehicles had burned. On Pearson Road, I knelt beside one and found a circular shred of yellow plastic, fused into a ring of tar: a piece of Fisher's car. It was startling how similar Paradise looked to when I first came, ten days after the fire. Except that it was spring now: clusters of daffodils were blooming, carefully arranged, bordering what had been fences or front steps.

That week, the city issued its first rebuilding permit, though roughly 1,000 residents were already back, somehow making a go of it, either in trailers or inside the scant number of houses that survived, even as public-health officials discovered that the municipal water system was contaminated with high levels of benzene, a carcinogen released by the burning homes and household appliances, then sucked through the pipes as firefighters drew water into their hoses. Driving around at dusk one evening, letting acre after acre of obliterated houses wash over me, I spotted a lone little boy in what appeared to be the head of a cul-de-sac—it was hard to tell—with heaps of houses all around him. He was standing with his arms raised, like a victor or a king, then he hopped back on his scooter and zipped away.

Jim Broshears, Paradise's emergency-operations coordinator, pointed out that many of the homes still standing tended to be in clusters: "A shadow effect," he called it, where one property broke the chain of ignitions—maybe because its owners employed certain fire-wise landscaping or design features, or maybe just by chance. It showed that, while the destructiveness of any fire is largely random, there are ways a community can collectively lower the odds. "It's really a cultural shift that requires people to look at their home in a different way," Broshears said: to see the unkempt azalea bush or split rail fence touching your home as a hazard that will carry the next fire forward like a fuse, not just to your house but also to the others around it—to recognize that everyone is joined in one massive pool of incalculable and unconquerable risk.

The free market, meanwhile, has continued adjusting to that risk according to its own unsparing logic. Insurance companies have steadily raised premiums or even ceased to renew policies in many fire-prone areas of California, as payouts for wildfire claims will now exceed $10 billion for the second year in a row. Two months after the Camp Fire, PG&E filed for bankruptcy protection. Then it announced, along with two of California's other major utilities, that it would be expanding its Public Safety Power Shutoff program this year. The company is now prepared to preventively cut electricity to a larger share of its infrastructure—high-voltage wires, as well as lower-voltage ones—and across its entire range. Nearly five and a half million customers could be subject to shutdowns at one time or another this summer, "which is all of our customer base," a PG&E vice president, Aaron Johnson, told me: every single one. "With the increasing fire risk that we're seeing in the state," he added, "and the increasing extreme weather, this program is going to be with us for some time to come."

In California, the prospect of life without electricity from time to time—a signature convenience of the twentieth century—has apparently become an unavoidable, even sensible, feature of the twenty-first.

How did it end? With smoke—with colossal shapes of smoke gurgling out of Paradise behind Laczko and Fisher as they glided downhill, and with a stoic figure somewhere inside the smoke, single-mindedly grinding through neighborhoods in his bulldozer, music blaring, chasing after flames as they stampeded uphill, but mostly failing to get ahead of them as he and every other firefighter labored to keep fire away from structures that seemed, in the end, determined to burn.

The houses had revealed themselves: they were just another crop of tightly clustered and immaculately dried-out dead trees, a forest that had grown, been felled and milled, then rearranged sideways and hammered together by clever human beings who, over time, came to forget the volatile ecosystem that spawned that material and still surrounded it now. Some of that wood most likely lived 100 years or more and had been lumber for almost as long: a storehouse of energy that was now bursting open, joining with the burning forests around the Ridge into a single, furious outpouring of smoke—ominous because it was dark and high enough to challenge the sun, but also because it was largely composed of carbon: an estimated 3.6 million metric tons of greenhouse gases that, as seems to happen at least once every fire season lately, was more than enough to obliterate the progress made by all of California's climate-change policies in a typical year.

How did it end? With smoke—with smoke that signaled the world that Fisher knew at the beginning of the day was gone and that surely signaled something just as grave for the rest of us. Within hours, and for nearly two weeks after that, smoke would swamp the lucid blue sky over the valley where Fisher was now heading; where, for weeks, she would be afraid to be left alone and, for months, refuse to drive, terrified by the sensation of slowing down in traffic, even momentarily; where she found herself repeatedly checking the sky to make sure it wasn't black; where she kept showering but swore she still smelled the smoke on her skin. And before long, the smoke had floated all the way to the coast, where it forced the city of San Francisco to close its schools.

How did it end? It hasn't. It won't.

MELINDA WENNER MOYER

Vaccines Reimagined

FROM *Scientific American*

THE HEAT OF the sun, a blazing basketball in the West African sky, was softened by a breeze one afternoon last spring. Every so often the wind whisked a mango off a tree branch and dropped it with a thud on the corrugated iron roof that covered the health center in Bissau, the biggest city in the tiny country of Guinea-Bissau, where the rust-colored ground hadn't felt a raindrop in six months. Inside the building, the air was still and dry, and a line of women and toddlers were sticky with sweat.

An eighteen-month-old named Maria with thick, dark braids studied me nervously as she perched on her mother's lap. (The child's name has been changed to protect her privacy.) Next to them, Carlito Balé, a soft-spoken doctor in a short-sleeved, white button-down shirt, talked with Maria's mother in Portuguese creole, a percussive fusion of Portuguese and African dialects. Balé was telling the mother that Maria was eligible to participate in a clinical trial to test whether an extra dose of measles vaccine prevented not just the measles but many childhood infections that cause serious illness and death.

In the U.S., where life-threatening infections are rare, such a trial might not garner many volunteers. But in Guinea-Bissau, where lives have been scarred by decades of scant resources and poor medical care, families lined up in droves. The nation is one of the world's poorest, and the CIA ranks infant mortality there as the fourth highest among 225 countries. Mothers often wait months to name their babies because one out of every twelve will die before his or her first birthday.

The researchers leading the trial—anthropologist Peter Aaby and physician Christine Benn, whom I had traveled to Guinea-Bissau to meet—have amassed evidence that a few specific vaccines can thwart a multitude of threatening plagues. Over decades they have published hundreds of studies suggesting that live, attenuated vaccines, which are made from weakened but living viruses or bacteria, can stave off not just their target infections but other diseases, such as respiratory infections (including pneumonia), blood infections (including sepsis), and diarrheal infections. In a 2016 review published in the journal *BMJ,* a research team commissioned by the World Health Organization analyzed sixty-eight papers on the topic, many of which came from Aaby and Benn's research. It concluded that the measles and tuberculosis vaccines "reduce overall mortality by more than would be expected through their effects on the diseases they prevent." Some of the research the team evaluated linked the measles vaccine with a whopping 50 percent lower risk of death from any cause.

This notion that live vaccines have what are called "off-target" effects—and powerful ones—has implications that stretch far beyond Africa. In 2017 in the U.S., for instance, researchers at the Centers for Disease Control and Prevention reported that children were half as likely to be hospitalized for non-vaccine-targeted infections between the ages of sixteen and twenty-four months if the last immunization they had received was a live vaccine rather than an inactivated one. New research in immunology suggests that live vaccines can have such wide-ranging effects because they stimulate a part of the immune system that fights a broad-based war against all outside invaders, giving the system a head start on defense. "Although we still need to know much more about the details, I now have no doubt that vaccines do have some off-target effects because of the support from many different types of evidence," says Frank Shann, a pediatrician at Royal Children's Hospital Melbourne in Australia.

Yet other scientists are far less certain. Aaby and Benn's work is, in fact, quite controversial. For one thing, most of the studies from the two Danish researchers do not prove cause-to-effect connections. "Purported effects" is how Paul Fine, an infectious disease epidemiologist at the London School of Hygiene & Tropical Medicine, describes them. Kids who get live vaccines might survive longer for reasons that have nothing to do with immunizations:

the children in those groups might have been healthier to begin with. To address these concerns, Aaby and Benn are now running intervention trials, such as the one Maria was being recruited for. In it, children will be matched for age and basic health, but some will have only the standard single measles shot at nine months, whereas others will get an additional dose as toddlers.

The two investigators also counter that political and pragmatic concerns drive resistance to their ideas far more than do valid scientific critiques. Aaby says that his and Benn's research is inconvenient for public policy because it indicates that live vaccines should be given last in any vaccine series, which upends current immunization schedules and could inadvertently trigger parental worries about safety. Public health scientists "don't want to hear it, and I can understand why they don't want to hear it," Aaby says. And as a result, he claims, many orthodox vaccine researchers "have clearly made me persona non grata." The seventy-four-year-old, who is bespectacled and has a salt-and-pepper goatee, fits the part of the eccentric, obstinate, and misunderstood scientist so well that he has literally become one in a novel: he inspired a character in a best-selling 2013 Danish mystery book, *The Arc of the Swallow*, who gets murdered in the first chapter.

In real life, Aaby and Benn's ideas may be reaching a tipping point. The WHO wrote in a 2014 report that nonspecific vaccine effects seem "plausible and common" and worthy of more attention. Therefore, in April 2017 the agency announced it would oversee the design of two multiyear clinical trials to further test the hypothesis, although those trials have not yet begun. The two researchers, whose professional relationship has evolved into a long-term romantic one, are pushing forward with more of their own trials too. One of them is the study Maria's mother was considering. As I watched in the health center, she decided to enroll her daughter, so Balé picked up a large envelope containing dozens of smaller sealed envelopes and held it open toward her, telling her to pick one—a step that ensured that her daughter would be randomly allocated to either the treatment or control group. Opening her chosen envelope, Balé announced that Maria would get the extra vaccine, and her mother flashed a hopeful smile. She carried her daughter into the next room, where a nurse in a long, white-and-orange tie-dyed dress, black glasses, and a kind smile waited with a needle.

The Measles Clue

In 1979, soon after launching a health surveillance project in Bissau, a young Aaby watched measles kill one out of every four babies in the area. That was the year he saw his first dead body, and he saw a lot more than one.

Back then, childhood vaccines were rare in Africa. The WHO estimates that in 1980, only 6 percent of African children received the first dose of live measles vaccine, and 8 percent got the first inactivated DTP vaccine, which protects against diphtheria, tetanus, and pertussis. It's not as if the vaccine was new; the combination DTP vaccine was licensed in 1949, yet thirty-one years later fewer than one in twelve African children ever received a dose. Indeed, only a handful of childhood vaccines were even available then in Africa. In addition to the DTP and measles vaccines, there was a live tuberculosis vaccine called bacillus Calmette-Guérin (BCG) and a live polio vaccine. In 1980 in the U.S., on the other hand, 86 percent of kids received the live measles vaccine, 98 percent were inoculated with the inactivated DTP vaccine, and 95 percent had gotten live polio vaccines. African children today receive a lot more vaccines than they used to, but they still woefully lag behind the U.S.

In 1978, a year before the historic measles outbreak began, Aaby had been sent to Guinea-Bissau by a Swedish organization to investigate malnutrition. When the epidemic swept into the city, he pulled strings to import measles vaccines and began to inoculate the local children, all the while keeping track of infection and death rates. The move was a bold one: at that time, public health authorities thought that measles vaccine campaigns in Africa were essentially a waste of money and effort. In a 1981 paper published in the *Lancet*, researchers analyzed survival data after undertaking a measles vaccine campaign in Zaire and concluded that in the future, "it may be useful to think twice before allocating already scarce resources to such a programme." Measles took the lives of the weakest children, they argued; even if the vaccine prevented the infection, the spared children would die from something else soon enough.

Aaby's experience didn't support this argument. The before-and-after numbers he saw were staggering: in 1979, the first year of the outbreak, 13 percent of local children between the ages of six months and three years died; in 1980, when the measles vaccine was available, only 5 percent did. Surprisingly, deaths from causes other than measles dropped by one-fifth between 1979 and 1980 too. The trend continued. Even after measles disappeared, immunized children remained more likely than their unvaccinated peers to survive other infections. "It was one of those moments where you can suddenly see something you would never have believed was possible," he recalls. Aaby and his colleagues wrote a letter to the *Lancet* refuting the theory that measles inoculation campaigns in Africa were useless—his first ever publication in a medical journal. After that, he says of the measles vaccine, "I became obsessed."

Aaby has now published more than one hundred studies on this one vaccine. His surveillance program, the Bandim Health Project, a collaboration between Guinea-Bissau's Ministry of Health and the State Serum Institute in Denmark, is one reason why. For more than forty years the project has been registering all pregnancies, births, and deaths in Bissau's urban district of Bandim, as well as in five nearby rural regions. Aaby's team there has monitored the health of more than 500,000 people living in these areas and has collected data on hospitalizations, vaccinations, and health-related choices, such as whether people sleep with mosquito nets. One day during my visit, as I walked around with Aaby, a mother holding a baby said she remembered him from when he visited her as a child some thirty years ago. His colleagues and assistants in the project affectionately call Aaby *Homem Grande*, which translates to "Big Man."

Aaby has always been a bit of a lone wolf—he spends many days working by himself in his home office—but less so during the past fifteen years. While Benn was in medical school in 1992 at Aarhus University in Denmark, she was advised to reach out to Aaby because she wanted to study whether vitamin A supplementation, routinely given with the measles vaccine in developing countries, interacted in any way with the vaccine. "I still have the piece of paper with his number," Benn, who is fifty, tells me as she sits on a bench in Aaby's back garden, her arms hugging her legs. She has been working with Aaby ever since. Benn is now a professor of global health at the University of Southern Denmark and runs the Danish arm of the Bandim Health Project. She is prolific, having published more than 200 papers on issues including the non-specific effects of vaccines and the impact of vitamin A supplementation on infants in developing countries. She calls Denmark home but spends about ten weeks a year in Guinea-Bissau. The two researchers bring to the field, and their relationship, complementary personalities: Benn, effervescent and philosophical; Aaby, serious and precise.

For the most part, Aaby and Benn's work on the measles vaccine has supported Aaby's original observations. In a landmark 1995 *BMJ* paper, they analyzed data from twelve previously published studies—some their own—on the association between measles vaccination and mortality in developing countries. They found that the vaccine was linked to a 30 to 86 percent reduction in overall death risk. In each study, measles itself only killed a small proportion of unvaccinated kids, so the vaccine wasn't just preventing measles; something else was going on. In a 2014 paper published in *JAMA*, Aaby and Benn collaborated with Danish researchers to investigate whether these protective effects extended to high-income countries. They found that Danish children who received the live measles-mumps-rubella (MMR) vaccine as their last inoculation were 14 percent less likely to be hospitalized for any infection than were kids who had most recently received the inactivated DTaP-IPV-Hib vaccine for diphtheria, tetanus, acellular pertussis, polio, and *Hemophilus influenzae* type B. This study inspired the 2017 analysis by the CDC that found live vaccines to be associated with even stronger protection in the U.S.

Aaby and Benn have also linked the BCG vaccine with lower neonatal mortality, and they have studied the live oral polio vaccine (OPV) as well. In a 2018 paper, they reported that child mortality rates were 19 percent lower after OPV campaigns than before them, and a clinical trial they published in 2015 found that OPV given within two days of birth with BCG reduced mortality risk by 42 percent, compared with BCG alone. Based in part on their findings, fifteen scientists wrote a letter to the *Lancet* in 2016 arguing that the global switch from live OPV to IPV, the inactivated polio vaccine, which is part of a plan developed by the international Global Polio Eradication Initiative, could inadvertently increase child mortality.

The two scientists are certain that the evidence they have accumulated points to a clear conclusion: vaccines have more profound effects on the body than we thought. The big mystery they have been grappling with is how, exactly, all this happens.

A Broad Booster

Mihai G. Netea may have an answer. In 2010 Netea, an immunologist at Radboud University in the Netherlands, embarked on a study that he frankly didn't think would be all that interesting. His laboratory was studying how the BCG vaccine affects human immune cells—how it teaches them to recognize and attack the bacterium *Mycobacterium tuberculosis*. To provide an experimental control on one test, lab workers exposed blood samples from vaccinated volunteers to *Candida albicans*, a common yeast. Based on accepted immunology doctrine, which holds that vaccines incite immune responses specific to the targeted pathogen, BCG should have had no effect on the blood's response to *Candida*.

A few weeks later the student running the test approached Netea, concerned. "I think I did something wrong because I see differences with both tuberculosis and with *Candida*," Netea recalls her saying. Perhaps her samples had been contaminated; he suggested that she collect more blood samples and do the experiment over. She did, but the same thing happened. "She came again and said, 'Well, I don't know what to do, but I see precisely the same thing again,'" Netea says. He was flummoxed, so he started reading about BCG and found a handful of surprising animal studies that suggested the vaccine also protected some animals against malaria, influenza, and *Listeria monocytogenes*, a common cause of foodborne illness.

That is when Netea's simple study transformed into a Greek siren, a creature beckoning for his full attention. How could a vaccine against tuberculosis change how the body responds to other pathogens? The idea contradicted established paradigms. Immunizations prime the body to make proteins called antibodies that recognize, attach to, and attack proteins on the pathogens if the body ever encounters them again. This defense is called adaptive immunity, and it acts like a team of snipers that take out only certain targets. Given adaptive immunity's specificity, it didn't make sense to Netea that it could be responsible for BCG's ability to protect against a number of insults.

Another kind of bodily defense—one that researchers histori-cally thought vaccines had little to do with—is known as innate immunity, and it is more like a battalion told to open fire on any-one who edges into its line of sight. It is the rapid-response team, initiating a fight against any new invader. When pathogens invade, innate inflammatory cells get pulled to the infection site. Large white blood cells called phagocytes—particularly a type called macrophages—engulf and destroy the pathogens. They also se-crete immune chemicals called cytokines that draw other immune cells to the scene. The reaction creates proteins that tag pathogens so that they are easier for phagocytes to find.

Given that BCG was increasing protection to multiple patho-gens, it made sense to Netea that the innate immune system might be involved. But conventional thinking held that the innate im-mune system could not "remember" past immunological encoun-ters, such as stimulation from previous vaccines. The thinking has long been that innate immune cells attack whatever they see and then forget about the battle afterward, like a soldier with amnesia. But these assumptions have been woefully incorrect.

In a paper published in 2012 in the *Proceedings of the National Academy of Sciences USA*, Netea's team found that human immune cells primed by BCG produce four times as much of a key cyto-kine called IFN-gamma (IFN-γ) and twice as much of the cytokines TNF and interleukin-1 beta (IL-1β) when later exposed to other pathogens. The cells can initiate these enhanced responses for as long as three months after vaccination, which suggests that the in-nate immune system can, in fact, remember what it learns. More recently, in 2018, the researchers reported that BCG reprograms human immune cells in ways that help them stave off the yellow fever virus.

Netea "has really pioneered a new field within innate immu-nology," says Helen Goodridge, an immunologist at Cedars-Sinai Medical Center in Los Angeles. Studies by other labs also support his theory, showing that the measles vaccine boosts the body's im-mune response to the toxin produced by tetanus bacteria, as well as its response when exposed to *Candida*.

It is unclear how the measles vaccine elicits its broad effects, but Netea's work suggests that BCG trains the innate immune sys-tem by initiating changes in cellular metabolism and by shaping how key immune genes are controlled. After a person gets BCG, little molecular stamps are placed on important immune-related genes, and these stamps later identify the genes so that they can be quickly turned on when another pathogen invades. Why would a live vaccine elicit these effects better than an inactivated one? Researchers theorize that live organisms may stimulate a different reaction simply because they are alive—not just bits and pieces of an organism, as in the inactivated shots. (Real full-on infections, such as measles, do not seem to produce these advantageous effects and can actually suppress immunity.)

While wrapping up his 2012 study in *PNAS*, Netea stumbled across a trial that had just been published by Aaby and Benn suggesting that BCG reduces general neonatal mortality—a finding that was criticized for being biologically impossible. Excited, Netea wrote to Aaby, telling him that he had just discovered a mechanism that made sense of his findings. Since then, the two researchers and Benn have been working together to tease out the immunology behind the Guinea-Bissau data. Vaccines seem to "change the immune system, and they don't just change it in the adaptive, pathogen-specific way," says Tobias Kollmann, an immunologist and infectious disease physician at the University of British Columbia, who sometimes collaborates with Aaby, Benn, and Netea. "They change it in all kinds of different ways."

Trials on Trial

Neal Halsey agrees that Aaby has made important contributions to vaccine research over the course of his career—but his work on off-target effects is not one of them. Halsey, former director of the Johns Hopkins University's Institute for Vaccine Safety, goes back a long way with the Danish scientist. He remembers that in the 1980s, Aaby was the first to identify a potential safety problem with a new, more concentrated measles vaccine introduced in Guinea-Bissau and other developing countries. At first, no one believed him—this appears to be a recurrent Aaby pattern—but then Halsey looked at data he had collected in Haiti and saw the same effects. Based largely on their findings, the WHO withdrew the vaccine from use in 1992.

But today Halsey thinks that Aaby is putting his convictions before the science. At the 2018 World Vaccine Congress in Washington, D.C., Halsey said the data from Guinea-Bissau may be real, but Aaby and Benn have been drawing causal conclusions from it that they shouldn't. Kids who get vaccinated on time are often quite different from those who don't: they can be healthier to begin with, or they can have wealthier parents with the means to drive them to the doctor and take better care of them in general. Concluding that vaccines are responsible for broadly different medical outcomes is too much of a stretch, Halsey says.

A 2017 *BMJ* study from the Netherlands illustrates his point. Researchers analyzed hospitalization rates among toddlers who had received a live vaccine as one of their last shots and then compared them with hospitalization rates among toddlers who had most recently gotten only inactivated vaccines. Scientists found that the live-vaccinated kids were 38 percent less likely than the others to be hospitalized for infections—but those children were also 16 percent less likely to be hospitalized for injuries or poisoning. Vaccines should not affect accident risk; the fact that the researchers found this link underscores the notion that vaccine history aligns with other factors in one's life. The authors concede, though, that the way vaccines are administered in the Netherlands—they are scheduled in advance, and parents usually cancel appointments only if their kids are sick—most likely inflates the "healthy vaccinee" effect, as it is called, and findings from other countries may not be skewed so heavily.

Because it is so difficult to interpret causality from observational studies, Halsey and others have called for Aaby and Benn to conduct more randomized controlled trials, the so-called gold standard for teasing out an intervention's effects. In these studies, children are randomly selected to receive vaccines or placebos and then followed over time. This random allocation eliminates the chance that socioeconomic status or overall health will play a role in vaccine decisions. The problem is that vaccines are already recommended public policy around the world, so it is unethical for researchers to deny children vaccinations to study them. Thus, scientists must get creative—they either have to design trials that provide children with extra vaccines or early ones, or they have to take advantage of natural delays in vaccine receipt.

To undertake a clinical trial in Guinea-Bissau is especially difficult. Aaby and Benn must store vaccines in a refrigerator at their house, where they have a generator, because the electrical grid is so unpredictable (they lost power every day during my visit). Political instability is another problem: one of their attempted trials was disrupted by a devastating civil war in 1998, in which Aaby also suffered a near-fatal wound when he was lanced by a piece of iron left behind by a thief who had looted his house. Some Bissau residents speak only rare dialects, which makes things difficult as well, and many don't have phones.

Despite these challenges, Aaby and Benn are trying randomized trials, such as the one involving Maria. In a few completed tests, the results have not always supported their earlier findings. In a 2018 trial that Aaby and Benn worked on, for instance, researchers found that babies who got the recommended measles vaccine at nine months, plus an additional measles shot between four and four and a half months, were no less likely to be hospitalized or to die than babies who did not get the extra doses. Yet the two are convinced the vaccine effects are real, just not fully understood. Halsey, though, finds their dogged persistence concerning. "Very good objective scientists acknowledge when an initial observation they made is shown not to be true," he says.

Aaby and Benn are unpopular for another reason: they have published studies suggesting that inactivated vaccines, such as DTP, have detrimental effects, particularly for girls. Even though these vaccines protect against their targeted diseases, Aaby and Benn have linked these shots to a higher risk of other infectious diseases. It is unclear why this would happen—perhaps exposure to dead pathogens makes the immune system more tolerant of other future intruders—and critics argue the associations are not just spurious but also dangerous because they could further undermine the public's confidence in vaccines. "Some of them just think that I'm a madman making trouble," Aaby concedes.

A Search for Clarity

His battles, however, are entering a new phase. Although Aaby notes that his own research funds are running short, the WHO says that it will soon step into the arena. Aaby first contacted the agency about his findings in 1997; in 2013 it established a working group to review the data. In 2014 the WHO noted that the issue deserved further attention, and in 2016 and 2017 it discussed plans to oversee additional trials. One trial will investigate the effects on infant mortality of giving BCG vaccination at birth versus a placebo. The other will evaluate the effects of an extra dose of measles vaccine given with DTP between twelve and sixteen months of age.

Aaby and others worry, however, that these trials will yield little clarity. The subjects will be given inactivated vaccines either at the same time as the live vaccines or after them, which, according to Aaby's previous findings, could mute potentially beneficial effects. "We discussed this at length with many experts, and the evidence is clear that those trials will not give the answer," Kollmann says. Shann, the Australian pediatrician, agrees. These trials will be "a scandalous waste of time and money," he says, because "none of those involved really understands the field." And right now it is unclear when the trials will start. WHO spokesperson Tarik Jasarevic says that as of early 2019, the agency has not found financial sponsors for the work.

Ultimately Aaby worries that the WHO is just going through the motions. He suspects the agency wants to appear that it is doing due diligence after its 2014 report on nontargeted effects but that its real goal is to make the issue go away. If nonspecific effects are real and powerful enough to save lives, then public health agencies will have to consider making changes to the vaccine schedule and perhaps even replace some inactivated vaccines with live ones, which would be extremely difficult.

Last year I asked Frank DeStefano, director of the CDC's Immunization Safety Office, what it would take to make such changes in the U.S. "Certainly evidence would have to be stronger that this is a real effect," he said. He noted that the agency had no plans at that time to collect more data on the issue. But even if it had additional evidence, he said, the CDC would have to consider all the possible risks and benefits before making policy changes.

The evening I left Guinea-Bissau I sat in the back garden with Benn, eating Danish cheese that she brought with her from her last trip home, and I thought about the couple's philosophy of science. These researchers are not shy about their beliefs; they are convinced that nonspecific effects are real but so complex that many details remain a mystery, and they are not afraid to say so. To critics, this strength of conviction is a great weakness, a blazing preconception that biases their results. And it may do so. But bias is not unique to them. Scientists are people—people with ideas, and prejudices, and feelings—and every study involves interpretation. How do we know whose interpretations edge closest to the truth? Are those who admit to their beliefs more biased than those who don't? Who should decide when enough evidence has amassed to reach a consensus, particularly when the implications are unexpected, inconvenient, and consequential? Within this small and contentious field, at least, there are no clear answers.

"You have this feeling you are pulling a thread, and you don't know how big the ball of yarn is," Benn said to me. She was referring to the research on vaccines, but she could have been speaking about the scientific process itself. Biology is immensely complicated because our bodies are complex. The practice of science is complicated too, because it is a product of humanity—an endeavor created and shaped by our imperfect minds. If vaccines do what Aaby and Benn think they do—and that is still an open question—it will take a lot more messy unraveling before the world sees things their way.

SIDDHARTHA MUKHERJEE

New Blood

FROM *The New Yorker*

IT MATTERS THAT the first patients were identical twins. Nancy and Barbara Lowry were six years old, dark-eyed and dark-haired, with eyebrow-skimming bangs. Sometime in the spring of 1960, Nancy fell ill. Her blood counts began to fall; her pediatricians noted that she was anemic. A biopsy revealed that she had a condition called aplastic anemia, a form of bone-marrow failure.

The marrow produces blood cells, which need regular replenishing, and Nancy's was rapidly shutting down. The origins of this illness are often mysterious, but in its typical form the spaces where young blood cells are supposed to be formed gradually fill up with globules of white fat. Barbara, just as mysteriously, was completely healthy.

The Lowrys lived in Tacoma, a leafy, rain-slicked city near Seattle. At Seattle's University of Washington hospital, where Nancy was being treated, the doctors had no clue what to do next. So they called a physician-scientist named E. Donnall Thomas, at the hospital in Cooperstown, New York, asking for help.

In the 1950s, Thomas had attempted a new kind of therapy, in which he infused a leukemia patient with marrow extracted from the patient's healthy identical twin. There was fleeting evidence that the donated marrow cells had "engrafted" into the patient's bones, but the patient had swiftly relapsed. Thomas had tried to refine the transplant protocol on dogs, with some marginal success. Now the Seattle doctors persuaded him to try again in humans. Nancy's marrow was faltering, but no malignant cells were occupying it. Would the blood stem cells from one twin's marrow "take" in the other twin?

Thomas flew to Seattle. On August 12, 1960, Barbara was sedated, and her hips and legs were punctured fifty times with a large-bore needle to extract the crimson sludge of her bone marrow. The marrow, diluted in saline, was then dripped into Nancy's bloodstream. The doctors waited. The cells homed their way into her bones and gradually started to produce normal blood. By the time she was discharged, her marrow had been almost completely reconstituted. Nancy emerged as a living chimera: her blood, in a sense, belonged to her twin.

In 1963, Thomas moved to Seattle for good. Setting up his lab first at the Seattle Public Health Service Hospital and then, a dozen years later, at the newly established Fred Hutchinson Cancer Center—the Hutch, as doctors called it—he was determined to use marrow transplantation in the treatment of other diseases, notably leukemia. Nancy and Barbara Lowry were identical twins, and a noncancerous blood disease in one had been curable by cells from the other, a vanishingly rare occurrence. What if a disease involved malignant blood cells, as with leukemia? And what if the donor wasn't a twin? The promise of transplantation had been hindered by the fact that our immune systems are inclined to reject matter from other bodies as foreign; only identical twins, with perfectly matched tissues, can sidestep the problem.

Thomas saw a way around this. First, he would try to eradicate the malignant blood cells with doses of chemotherapy and radiation so high that the functioning marrow would be destroyed, purged of both cancerous and normal cells. That would usually be fatal, but the donor marrow would then replace it, generating healthy new cells.

The next problems arose from trying an "allogeneic" transplant (*allo,* from the Greek word for "other"), using marrow from someone who wasn't an identical twin. The resultant immune response is the consequence of an ancient system for maintaining the sovereignty of organisms. Sponges on the ocean floor use primitive versions of immune systems to reject cells from other sponges that might attempt to colonize them. Good defenses make good neighbors: in nature, chimerism, the fusion of one being with another, is not a new-age fantasy but an age-old threat.

Other pioneers in organ transplantation had learned that these forces of rejection could be blunted if the donor and the host were reasonably well matched. There were now tests to help predict compatibility and to improve the chances that allogeneic marrow cells would engraft. And various immune-suppressing drugs had been developed to further dampen the host's resistance.

Thomas, who won a Nobel Prize for these studies, later described them as "early clinical successes." But for the nurses and the technicians in Seattle who cared for the patients—not to mention the patients themselves—the experience could be harrowing. "Of the hundred patients with leukemia who were transplanted in those early years, eighty-three died within the first several months," Fred Appelbaum, a former student of Thomas's, told me. Sometimes the transplanted marrow failed to take, and the patient died from anemia caused by a lack of red blood cells, or from infections caused by the paucity of white blood cells; sometimes the cancer came back. He added, "What kind of person, with that rate of failure, would perform the hundred-and-first transplant?"

The final cataclysm, in this biblical array of plagues, happened when white blood cells produced by the donor's marrow mounted a vigorous immune response to the patient's body. This phenomenon—called graft-versus-host disease—was sometimes a passing storm, and sometimes a chronic condition; either way, it turned the logic of immunology upside down. Typically, when foreign tissue is transplanted into a body, the fear is that the patient might reject it. But in these bone-marrow-graft cases it's the *transplant* that rejects the patient. The immune cells of the bone-marrow donor—a mutinous crew forced onto an unfamiliar ship—recognize the body around them as foreign. Virtually every major organ system can fall under attack. In some cases, the disease proved fatal; in others, clinicians found ways to manage it with drugs.

In the late 1970s, Appelbaum and his colleagues analyzed the results of allogeneic transplants for leukemia, and found yet another surprise: the patients who had experienced graft-versus-host disease in its chronic form were also the ones whose cancers were least likely to relapse. The imported immune cells were effectively targeting residual cancer cells in the host. What Thomas had achieved with Lowry was akin to a regular organ transplant. (In 1954, in Boston, Joseph Murray had performed the first successful kidney transplant, also between twins.) But the phenomenon observed by doctors at the Hutch suggested that marrow grafts represented a very different kind of medical intervention.

From the start, those findings mesmerized the world of cell therapy. They showed that the human immune system—in particular, the T cell, a type of white blood cell that is central to what is known as "adaptive immunity"—could recognize and attack cancer. Which led to a question: Could T cells be trained to reject cancerous cells but not turn against the host? Could they be the basis of a new class of drug?

At this point, a larger question arises: What is a drug, anyway? A therapeutic substance, you might say. But does it have to be a molecule in its pure form, like aspirin or penicillin? Can it be a mixture of active ingredients—like cough syrup? A toxicologist might quarrel with the notion that certain substances are inherently therapeutic: water is a drug at one dose and a poison at another. Most chemotherapies are poisons even at the correct dose. Galen, the Greco-Roman physician of the second century, argued that all human pathology could be conceptualized as imbalances of humors—black bile, yellow bile, blood, and phlegm. Could a humor, drawn from a patient's body, qualify as a drug?

For most of the twentieth century, the definition of a drug was simple, because drugs were simple: they were typically small molecules synthesized in factories or extracted from plants, purified, and packaged into pills. Later, the pharmacopoeia expanded to include large and complex proteins—from insulin to monoclonal antibodies. But could a living substance be a drug?

Thomas, who saw bone-marrow transplantation as a procedure or a protocol, akin to other organ transplants, would never have described it as a drug. And yet, in ways that Thomas couldn't have anticipated, he had laid the foundation for a new kind of therapy —"living drugs," a sort of chimera of the pharmaceutical and the procedural—which would confound definitions and challenge the boundaries of medicine, raising basic questions about the patenting, the manufacturing, and the pricing of medicines.

In 1971, while Don Thomas was performing his first allogeneic transplants in Seattle, an eighteen-year-old high school senior from the Bay Area named Carl June received news of his draft lottery. He had drawn the number fifty; deployment was virtually certain. So he turned down admission offers from Caltech and

Stanford, and, as he likes to say, chose "the Naval Academy over the paddy fields of Vietnam." June, who is rail-thin and lanky, with the physique of a long jumper, recalls his years at the academy with the ruefulness of an athlete forced to wait on the sidelines. After the Navy paid his way through medical school, at Baylor College, in Houston, he arrived at the Hutchinson Center, where he spent three years in the early 1980s as an oncology fellow, studying marrow transplants in Thomas's research program. He was joining a high-powered group that included a tall, German-born rowing fanatic named Rainer Storb, who focused on tissue typing and transplant therapy; a diminutive, Siberian-born soccer enthusiast named Alex Fefer, who had shown that immune systems could turn against tumors in mice; and Thomas's wife, Dottie, who ran the day-to-day affairs of the lab and the clinic, and whom everyone called "the mother of bone-marrow transplantation."

June became fascinated by early experiments in transferring T cells, but then spent a decade at the Naval Medical Research Institute, in Bethesda, studying infectious diseases, such as malaria and, later, HIV. Finally, in 1999, he moved his lab to the University of Pennsylvania. His personal life, meanwhile, was crosshatched with tragedy: in 1995, his wife, Cindy, was diagnosed with ovarian cancer, and she died six years later. Throughout these years—and especially after Cindy's diagnosis—June kept imagining a new paradigm for cancer treatment, in which living immune cells, rather than drugs, would be mobilized against the disease.

Mature T cells normally come armed with proteins on their surface—called T-cell receptors—which allow them to recognize matching bits of foreign proteins that might be present on the surface of their target cells, such as human cells infected by a virus. These receptors are notably selective: they trigger only when a cell has mounted a protein fragment on its surface and "presented" it to the T cell in the context of certain other proteins—as if they can see a picture only when the frame is right.

Unlike antibodies—Y-shaped proteins that bind like Velcro to a wide range of targets, including free-floating viruses and proteins —T-cell receptors bind to their targets somewhat loosely. The T cell can thus inspect the surface of a cell, alert others, and move on, like a drug-sniffing dog at a security checkpoint, going from one suitcase to another, summoning help where necessary.

For decades, immunologists had reasoned that the T-cell surveillance system might be able to detect and kill cancer cells. But, unlike infected cells, cancerous ones tend to be so genetically similar to normal cells, with such a similar repertoire of proteins, that they're hard for even T cells to pick out of a crowd. A cancer-specific T-cell response could arise only if a gene were mutated or incorrectly regulated in cancer, and if the protein encoded by that gene were fragmented in the right way, and if the fragments were channeled into the cell's system for T-cell detection, and if there were a waiting T cell equipped to sense it as foreign: a graveyard of ifs.

June knew that two researchers at the Hutch—Stanley Riddell, an animated figure with blocky glasses and a mechanical pencil habitually clipped to his shirt pocket, and Philip Greenberg, a man with a dense shag of hair that he had kept since the sixties—had begun to identify T cells that could recognize cytomega-lovirus (a major threat to immunocompromised patients), grow those cells in flasks, and transfuse the increased population of the cells into bone-marrow recipients. In Houston, Malcolm Brenner, Cliona Rooney, and Helen Heslop had done something similar with T cells that targeted tumor cells infected by another patho-gen, Epstein-Barr virus. And at the National Cancer Institute, in Bethesda, a surgical oncologist named Steven Rosenberg tried yet another strategy: he drew native T cells out of malignant tumors, such as melanomas, positing that immune cells that had infiltrated a tumor must have the capacity to recognize and attack the tumor. Rosenberg's team grew these tumor-infiltrating lymphocytes, ex-panding their numbers by a few orders of magnitude, and trans-ferred them back into patients.

There were some potent responses: 55 percent of melanoma patients treated with Rosenberg's transferred T cells saw their tu-mors shrink, and 24 percent experienced a complete regression that they maintained over time. But the responses were also rather hit-and-miss. The T cells harvested from a patient's tumor may have trained themselves to fight it, but they might also be bystand-ers, passive witnesses lingering at a crime scene. They might have become exhausted or inured—"tolerized" to the tumor.

Was it possible to rebuild T cells in order to increase their sensi-tivity to cancerous interlopers? In the late 1980s and early '90s, an Israeli immunologist named Zelig Eshhar, who was a beekeeper in his youth, had set out to create a peculiar hybrid of the two wings of the immune system. Instead of the usual receptor, this T cell would mount a molecular chimera on its surface—a protein that would use the Velcro-like property of an antibody to attach to a cancer cell, combined with the receptor protein that activates the cell to mount an immune response. He called these genetically manipulated entities T bodies. The hope was to bring together the detective skills of a T-cell receptor and the destructive properties of an antibody: these were meant to be drug-sniffing dogs with sharp teeth. But, though Eshhar's cells could detect their targets, they didn't have the long-term potency needed to control cancer.

A crucial breakthrough arrived in the nineties. Michel Sadelain, a postdoctoral researcher at the Massachusetts Institute of Technology, began to work on methods to introduce foreign genes directly into T cells. This gene-delivery technology would soon give rise to a new generation of T cells, able not just to target cancers but also to mount long-term, durable immune responses by amplifying the receptor signals in critical ways. "T cells could die or become exhausted if their signals were not amplified and sustained," Sadelain told me. "The strategy was to activate immunity by genetically weaponizing them." Skeptics questioned the logic of the approach. "Why would you do that?" Sadelain recalls his critics asking. T cells, after all, were *already* capable of recognizing and attacking aberrant cells. Why try to reengineer them with the properties they naturally possess? Wasn't that like forcing remedial Spanish lessons on a Spaniard?

It's true that donor T cells, in marrow-graft patients, could hunt down the host's cancer cells, but they were indiscriminate in their hostilities, in ways that could be lethal. The trick was to get T cells to recognize and respond to cancers both more selectively and more effectually. Merely equipping a T cell with an antibody on its surface wasn't enough. That antibody had to behave as if it were an integral part of the T cell's system of binding, recognition, activation, and memory. Helene Finney, a researcher at the biotech company Celltech, had also begun to design such a receptor for T cells. The result—genetically modified T cells equipped with "chimeric antigen receptors" that were fully integrated into their immune functions—would be termed CAR-T cells, or CAR-Ts. In the course of the nineties, Sadelain and his team perfected the "weaponization" of a T cell into a CAR-T cell. They found that these CAR-T cells could kill cancer cells not only in petri dishes but also in mice carrying human tumors, and that they would persist in the mice even after the tumor had vanished. It was Sadelain who later described them as "living drugs."

But what molecular target should an engineered T cell be instructed to recognize? By 1997, Sadelain's team had come to focus on a molecule called CD19, which is present in certain blood cancers, including many kinds of lymphomas and leukemias, in which a class of white blood cells—B cells—proliferate in a malignant form. Unfortunately, CD19 is not cancer-specific: normal B cells also have CD19 on their surface. The engineered T cells would target those healthy cells too. But biology occasionally grants escape hatches for experimental therapies: B cells are not absolutely required for human survival. There would be a cost to their destruction—without these cells, patients can't generate proper antibody responses, and so become immunocompromised—but patients could be kept alive with transfusions of antibodies.

In December 2003, June began a collaboration with two scientists, Dario Campana and Chihaya Imai, who were working at St. Jude Children's Research Hospital, in Memphis, to craft T cells that would target CD19. (The collaboration, cordial to begin with, spiraled into an acrimonious dispute. St. Jude successfully argued that its researchers weren't properly credited with having designed the receptors for the chimerized cells.) Then June, in the wake of Sadelain's work, grew the modified cells in petri dishes and transferred them into mice, where they seemed to be startlingly active, capable of killing leukemia cells. Sadelain, by then at the Memorial Sloan Kettering Cancer Center, in New York, had devised and was preparing to launch clinical trials to study the effectiveness of an anti-CD19 T-cell therapy. So were Riddell and the oncologist-immunologist Michael Jensen, in Seattle. And so, too, was Steven Rosenberg, at the NCI, in Bethesda.

"Was it a cooperative group?" I asked June. I recalled that Rosenberg's team was the first to publish human data on a CD19-targeting therapy, in July 2010; June and Sadelain followed, in August and November 2011, respectively.

He hesitated, a wary smile inching across his face. He looked like John Malkovich, with his hollow cheeks and arresting intensity. "Yes and no," he said. "We were competing with one another, but we were also writing grants together."

It had taken nearly a decade to perfect the engineering of T cells for human testing. But the biggest hurdle was the amount of tinkering required for their manufacture and production. Working independently, June, Sadelain, and Rosenberg, among other researchers, had to infect a culture of T cells with a virus—which had been disabled so that it couldn't cause disease—that would deliver the chimeric receptors. The engineered strain of cells then had to be multiplied in a special brew of nutrients and growth factors. Technicians and postdoctoral scientists nurtured the cells like a million hungry babies, watching them grow day by day. "We had to set up the virus production and build a cell-therapy facility at Penn," June recalls. "It was not trivial."

By 2010, the first patient at Penn was ready to be treated: a sixty-five-year-old retired corrections officer named Bill Ludwig, who had enrolled in the CAR-T trial that June was leading together with the oncologist David Porter. Ludwig had a relapsed, chemo-resistant form of chronic lymphocytic leukemia, in which malignant B cells proliferate. A previous experimental trial, at the National Institutes of Health, had almost killed him, and his cancerous B-cell counts were rising every day. He had some T cells extracted, and, in ten days, the cells had been infected with the virus and grown seven-hundredfold—enough for several doses.

On August 3, Ludwig was infused with the first dose of his genetically modified T cells. Two more infusions and a few days of waiting followed—and then he fell terrifyingly ill. Every system was failing rapidly—lungs, kidneys, heart—amid a racking fever. Porter was convinced that Ludwig had contracted some unusual infection, but no bacteria or virus could be found. He spent the next week in the ICU.

"But then, all of a sudden, he woke up," June told me. "It was only then that we examined his nodes, and the tumor masses had disappeared. We did a bone-marrow biopsy on day twenty-eight and there was no leukemia. I didn't believe it, so I asked them to do another biopsy at day thirty-one. And, again, no leukemia."

It was weeks before Porter and June realized that this febrile illness—in which Ludwig's core body temperature had climbed to 105 degrees ("The nurses threw the thermometers away, thinking that they had broken," June recalls)—was a result of T cells and their target cells secreting potent inflammatory factors called cytokines. Ludwig had experienced one of the most active inflammatory responses ever witnessed. The infused cells were, in fact, destroying the cancer, slicing apart its membranes, mincing its in-nards. Nearly a month after his infusion, Ludwig recovered from his illness and went into a complete remission. Nine years later, Penn's Patient No. 1 remains alive and cancer-free.

But it was Patient No. 7, treated at the Children's Hospital of Philadelphia (CHOP), who altered the history of T-cell therapy. In May 2010, a five-year-old girl named Emily Whitehead, from central Pennsylvania, was diagnosed with acute lymphoblastic leukemia (ALL). Among the most rapidly progressive forms of cancer, this leukemia generates very immature B cells, and tends to afflict young children. The treatment for ALL ranks among the most intensive chemo regimens ever devised: as many as seven or eight drugs, given in combination, some injected directly into the spine. Although the collateral damage of the treatment can be daunting, it cures about 85 percent of pediatric patients. Emily's cancer, unfortunately, proved treatment-resistant; she relapsed twice, after two brief periods of remission. She was listed for a bone-marrow transplant—the only option for a cure—but her condition worsened in the meantime.

"The doctors told me not to Google it," Emily's mother, Kari, has recalled, of the specific mutation that Emily had. "So, of course, I did right away." Of the children who relapse early, or relapse twice, few survive. Emily arrived at the CHOP in early March 2012, with nearly every organ packed with malignant cells. She was seen by a pediatric oncologist, Stephan Grupp, and then enrolled in a clinical trial for CAR-T therapy.

"We were working against time," June told me. A few hundred feet from where we sat was the cell-manufacturing unit—an enclosed, vaultlike facility with stainless-steel doors, aseptic rooms, and incubators—where Emily's T cells were brought in, infected with the virus, and multiplied. The infusions themselves were largely uneventful: Emily sucked on an ice pop while Grupp dripped the cells into her veins. In the evening, she returned with her parents to her aunt's house, nearby, where she got piggyback rides from her father, Tom. On the second evening, though, she crashed—throwing up and spiking an alarming fever. Her parents rushed her back to the hospital, and things spiraled downward. Her kidneys began to shut down. She drifted in and out of consciousness, verging on multi-organ system failure.

"Nothing made sense," Tom Whitehead told me. Emily was

moved to the pediatric intensive-care unit (PICU), placed on a ventilator, and put into an induced coma. Her parents and Grupp kept an all-night vigil.

"We thought she was going to die," June recalled. "I wrote an email to the provost at the university, telling him the first child with the treatment was about to die. I feared the trial was finished. I stored the email in my out-box, but never pressed Send."

Doctors at CHOP and at Penn worked overnight to determine the cause of the fever. Once again, they found no evidence of infection; instead, they found elevated blood levels of cytokines. In particular, levels of a cytokine known as IL-6 were nearly 1,000 times higher than normal. Ludwig had barely survived his cytokine storm; Emily's was a full-on hurricane.

By a strange twist of fate, June's own daughter had a form of juvenile arthritis, and so he knew about a drug for the condition —approved only recently by the FDA—that blocks IL-6. As a last-ditch effort, Grupp rushed a request to the hospital pharmacy, asking for the off-label use of the new drug. The medication was supplied, and a nurse injected Emily with a dose in the PICU.

Days afterward, on her seventh birthday, she woke up. "Boom," June said, waving his hands in the air. "*Boom*," he repeated. "It just melted away. We did a bone-marrow biopsy twenty-three days later, and she was in a complete remission."

"I have never seen a patient that sick get better so quickly," Grupp told me.

The deft management of what has come to be known as cyto-kine-release syndrome—and Emily's startling recovery—probably saved the field of CAR-T therapy, and helped energize cell therapy in general. She remains in deep remission to this day. No cancer is detectable in her marrow or in her blood.

"If Emily had died," June told me, "it's likely that the whole trial would have been shut down," and perhaps not just at CHOP. (Other hospitals were offering experimental CAR-T therapy too.) He wonders whether, without her recovery, there would be any living drugs.

In August 2017, the FDA approved the use of engineered T cells for chemo-resistant or relapsed ALL in children and young adults. A version of the therapy that June's team pioneered was brought to market by Novartis and sold under the trade name Kymriah, an echo of the word "chimera."

*

Does it really matter that engineered T cells—or gene therapies or genetically modified viruses and microbes—are now defined and marketed as "drugs"? Is this more than a semantic quibble? Throughout the history of medicine, students have distinguished between the history of drugs and the history of procedures, akin to separate royal lineages. In one procession are the discoverers and synthesizers of various antibiotics for infections, chemotherapeutic agents for cancers, corticosteroids for lupus, and the like. In another are the pioneers of various procedures, handcrafted by surgeons and experimental physicians and often named for their inventors: the Halsted mastectomy, Mohs surgery, the Whipple pancreatectomy. Procedures come alive in the tinkering, fussing hands of their operators, who navigate seemingly insurmountable challenges: the bone-marrow transplanter who countenances eighty-three deaths before mastering the method, the surgeon who figures out how best to transfer a piece of liver from a donor to a patient, the cardiologist who learns to maneuver a catheter through an arcing highway of the aorta just so, curving at precisely the right junction to snip a stenotic valve.

What's transmitted—manually, individually, artisanally—to the next generation of surgeons is a process rather than a product, a skill rather than a pill. An apprentice practices the procedure over and over, as if taking lessons in an immensely complicated musical instrument; the teacher looks for the sharpness, the fettle that comes with a hundred attempts. An Emirati surgeon once described the state to me as being "in yarak," referring to the moment when a falcon is fully primed to hunt. Procedures are typically created, nurtured, and perfected in a few hospitals, and they spread as the apprentices gain mastery, move to new places, and promulgate their know-how: see one, do one, teach one.

A drug, in contrast, is a depersonalized entity—perhaps manufactured in New Jersey, packaged in Phoenix, stamped with a name, and dispensed by an anonymous pharmacy on Fourteenth Street. It's hooded in patents, but it's never in yarak. Nor does an antibiotic or an antihistamine leave a patient permanently altered. But the patient who enters the operating room for a mastectomy, or is infused with CAR-T cells, emerges permanently changed, anatomically, physiologically, or genetically. And she is, in a way, a collaborator in the treatment as well as its subject.

We don't entirely know how to regulate, or even conceptualize of, this new generation of drugs. Should the irreversible alteration of a body be governed by different rules from those that are used for conventional pharmaceuticals? Should it be priced through an alternative structure? If your cells are being genetically modified and reinfused into you, who should we say owns them? Once the cellular therapy has been created, could you store it by yourself —in your home freezer, if you chose—for future use? Emily White-head's extra chimerized T cells are frozen inside a steel tank at the Penn hospital. Each freezer has a nickname based on a *Simpsons* character. Hers is called Krusty the Clown.

Perhaps the most immediate implication of the blurring of lines between procedure and drug is the conundrum of price. A single dose of Kymriah for pediatric ALL is priced at $475,000; for Yescarta, a CD19 T-cell therapy designed for certain types of non-Hodgkin's lymphoma, that number is $373,000. These prices rival those of some of the most expensive procedures in American medicine. (A kidney transplant can be priced at $415,000, a lung transplant at about $860,000.) And these price tags don't include the delivery of post-therapy care to CAR-T patients, who typically suffer complications from the infusion. Subsequent hospital stays and supportive care can drive the total costs to a million dollars or more. Merely counting the 7,500 U.S. patients who meet the current FDA indications for Yescarta, the estimated annual expenditure could be $3 billion.

Dozens of labs around the world are now developing CAR-T therapies that work on different targets and different cancers. In May, a multicenter study demonstrated striking response rates for an experimental CAR-T therapy aimed at relapsed multiple my-eloma. My own laboratory, at Columbia, is creating T cells aimed at relapsed cases of acute myelogenous leukemia, for which the survival rates have been dismal. Other teams are testing chime-rized natural-killer cells against glioblastoma and certain lympho-mas. If the number of patients responsive to such therapies in-creased severalfold—as clinical indications expand, and as these therapies go from last ditch to front line in certain patient groups —the expense would dwarf the annual budget of the NIH and could bankrupt the American health care system.

Drug pricing is, of course, at the center of a familiar and inevitably acrimonious debate. The pharmaceutical industry defends high prices as a means to recoup the costs of drug discovery and development. Consumers, insurers, and governments argue that the prices charged for drugs are out of control, and bear no relationship to their real costs. But with cellular therapies the problem isn't merely profiteering—it is that, unlike conventional drugs, cell therapies are inherently expensive to produce. The estimated cost to manufacture a typical CAR-T infusion is close to six figures. In short, even if CAR-T therapy were offered with no margin of profit, it would still rank with some of the most expensive procedures in medicine. Extracting cells from an individual patient, purifying them, genetically modifying them, and expanding their numbers into the millions will never be akin to churning out amoxicillin in a factory.

When Novartis brought Kymriah to market, in 2017, it sought to offset concerns about its daunting price with an extraordinary offer: if the therapy did not work after the first month, treatment centers wouldn't be charged. That's almost unheard of in medicine, and it represents an extraordinary degree of optimism, which may or may not prove justified in the long term. June points out that we don't yet know which patients are likely to respond to the therapy. Ninety-four percent of relapsed and chemo-resistant ALL patients treated at CHOP achieve a complete remission at one month; many, like Emily Whitehead, are likely cured. For a certain class of drug-resistant patients with another form of leukemia, called CLL, the response rate with CAR-T therapy is around 75 percent, to judge from the most recent trial data. Eighty-five percent of drug-resistant patients with multiple myeloma—a malignancy of the blood's plasma cells—have either a complete or a partial response to the therapy, but more than a third of complete responders relapse within a year. (When it comes to yet other cancers, particularly solid tumors, such as pancreatic and ovarian cancer, cellular therapies have yet to produce reliable results.)

"Some of these responses don't last—there's resistance—and it's a big goal in the field to find the cause of resistance," June said. "We still have to run rigorous randomized studies to determine if the therapies are effective, and whether they are cost-effective, and whether they can be delivered at scale. But would you rather push the boundaries of a partially effective cellular therapy, acknowledging all its problems, yet also recognizing its clear responses? Or would you rather pay a million dollars for ineffective chemotherapies, only to pay again for cellular therapy?"

Yet June saw a downside to the fact that cellular therapies were classified as drugs: it could hinder their incremental improvement. "In the current regulatory environment, the FDA approves drugs on a one-by-one basis," he observed. Procedures represent a history of small, iterative improvements. But, if you tweak the substance of a cellular therapy, it's officially a different drug, which has to undergo another gauntlet of trials and agency reviews, a costly and time-consuming process.

I asked June if he foresaw the price of the drugs coming down. "It's all going to be about automation and manufacture," he told me. "If a drug remains out of the reach of the patients who really need it, why even call it a drug?"

It isn't until you witness the production of an individualized cell therapy that you grasp the scale of the challenge. At about eight o'clock on a Tuesday morning last fall, I visited the Hutch and accompanied Bruce Thompson, the scientific manager, and James Adams, the operations head, as they descended two floors, into the cell-processing facility in the E sub-basement. Behind wire-mesh glass, the facility's rooms were painted a fluorescent green. "We all agreed on the color, but now we all agree that we dislike it," Adams told me, ruefully.

I asked Thompson if I could go inside, explaining that I'd been growing human cells in sterile media for more than a decade. Thompson looked at me, unmoved. He is about forty-five, broad-shouldered and soft-spoken, with the gentle but unbending manner of a vault manager at Cartier. "We have very strict anticontamination rules," he said. "And doctors who treat the patients here are *especially* discouraged from walking in and out of the facility."

Instead, I watched through the windows as a technician named Houman Bashiri—in dark-blue scrubs, elastic booties, and a mask —reached into an incubator, took out a flask, and held it to the light. The fluid inside was orange and turbid, with hundreds of thousands of engineered T cells. The cells had been doubling every day, Thompson said. In about a week's time, they would be infused into the patient, where, if all went well, they would multiply even more, kill malignant cells, and then remain in the body, on guard, to survey the tissues and fight any recurrence of cancer.

The facility had thirty-five incubators, eight centrifuges, and six sterile hoods, where the cells are inspected and manipulated. Every time Bashiri added a drop of a chemical—a growth factor, say—he announced the action out loud. A second technician checked the chemical against the protocol and marked it off in a binder, in a maddeningly methodical process meant to guarantee that each action performed on the cells was documented and cross-checked.

I spoke later with Thompson and Adams. "If living cells are to become drugs, they have to be manufactured under standard protocols, like drugs," Thompson said. "This caused tensions between the facility technicians and the doctors—and the tensions still continue." Most of the doctors who ran the studies, or treated patients with the approved cell therapies, had been trained as bone-marrow transplanters. They'd spent much of their careers steeped in the experimental and artisanal nature of the craft. "They were used to looking at their cells every day, and then deciding when to infuse them," Thompson went on. "One of them might come down one afternoon and say, 'Oh, the cells don't look quite ready yet. Why don't we give them another two days and a little squeeze of a growth factor?'"

But each departure from the standard operating practice had the potential of violating a clinical protocol. There has to be a rule, as it were, against exceptions. What's more, untidiness, in this endeavor, can have grave consequences. "Each patient gets his or her own private incubator," Adams said. "That way, we can never contaminate one patient's cells with another's"—a mix-up that could be fatal—"or mistake one for another." When one patient is done, the incubator is sterilized. "The suite is cleaned weekly by a specialized crew," he said. "And once a year we close down the whole facility for a top-to-bottom inspection."

The protocols were rigorous, and yet they could not have been further from the efficiencies of mass manufacture. In this sense, CAR-T still resembles a procedure, like a mastectomy or a liver transplant; it's a matter of painstaking craft. A few months ago, at the Cleveland Clinic, in Ohio, I watched a cardiothoracic surgeon perform a four-hour operation to replace a patient's leaky heart valve. It was a breathtakingly elegant procedure. Each move was meticulously orchestrated and controlled. The surgeon opened a fish-mouth-shaped hole in the aorta and began to stitch in the new valve. Members of the operating team assisted one another in a precise choreography. Whenever someone new entered the room, he or she checked a list to make sure that no protocol had been violated.

For all this precision, however, other aspects of the operation —call them the factory-floor aspects—went undiscussed. I heard no one speak about whether the plastic in the tubing equipment could have been optimized to cut costs. Or whether the team could have worked more efficiently by altering the distance between the hooks where the sterile equipment hung. Or whether the eight-odd minutes it took to put on a gown and scrub hands could have been reduced. Would some intervention in a small, repetitive action have saved a few minutes of operating time so that, added up, the surgeon might be able to operate on one more patient a week?

In medical school in the 1990s, I took classes on the economics of health. I learned about the overuse of medical services, the skyrocketing prices of prescription medicines, and the disparities in access to medical care that such pricing worsened. Distinctions were made between the price of a drug (how much a payer is charged for medicine), its cost (how much it takes to develop and manufacture that medicine), and its value (the actual benefit that a patient receives from a drug or procedure).

But nowhere in these lessons did I encounter the Japanese term *kaizen*—the continuous improvement of a manufacturing process to its leanest, most efficient form. It would have been a worthwhile lesson. Engineers in the world of industrial manufacturing obsess about this. But as doctors, as medical scientists and inventors, we are taught to think about curing deadly diseases or about creating new systems of care. We want to battle the mortal coil, not the plastic coil. We want to close the gaps in access to medical care, not the gaps between hooks in the operating room. We give priority to proofs of principle, not to the particularities of production. Yet, if the newest generations of therapies are to succeed at scale, it may be the small skirmishes that determine the outcome of the larger war. For cellular therapy to reach the masses, its innovators cannot ignore the most trivial-seeming details of the human and material factors of the manufacturing process. Perhaps we need a change in our culture, or even in our vocabulary. In Cleveland, as in operating theaters around the world, the clinicians were in yarak. The new generation of medical care will be enabled by the ceaseless demands of *kaizen*.

A few days after my visit to Cleveland, I flew back to New York. At my laboratory at Columbia, Florence Borot, a postdoctoral scientist originally from Paris, is exploring another way to scale up cellular therapy. A major challenge in the manufacture of CAR-Ts is the exquisitely bespoke nature of their production: right now, every "living drug" has to be made out of a patient's own cells. Borot is trying to engineer T cells so that they might be transferred from a donor to a patient who isn't an immunological match. Borot has a knack for immunological sleight of hand: she hunts through the genome to find factors that enable immune recognition and then, using new genetic technologies, makes them disappear without compromising the functions of the T cells. Variations of this strategy are being attempted by dozens of other scientists, in universities and at biotech companies. The ultimate aim is to create the so-called universal T cell—a cell that has the capacity to engraft in any person's body. These cells could be grown en masse, frozen, and shipped from a central facility to a patient's hospital room.

A second approach creates a drug from a patient's own circulating T cells, but without needing to manipulate and multiply them. An engineered molecule, called a bi-specific T-cell engager (BiTE is the trade name of Amgen's candidate), is designed to tether a T cell to a cancer cell (hence "bi-specific"), and trigger an immune response to the cancer. These molecules would be infused into a patient and engage circulating T cells already present in the patient's blood and lymph nodes. Such T-cell engagers are currently being tested against various cancers in human trials. And there are other strategies for reducing the costly complications of "living drugs." An effort I'm involved in would genetically modify a leukemia patient's noncancerous B cells, or other white blood cells, to shelter them from the effects of CAR-T. If only the cancerous cells were eradicated, the treatment would not damage the immune system, currently its most long-lasting side effect.

The number of cell-therapy researchers, meanwhile, seems to double and redouble week by week. We present our data at conferences dedicated solely to cell engineering. We discuss methods to equip T cells or natural-killer cells with permanent immunological memory, so that they remain on constant guard against relapses of the cancer. We study ways of amplifying the effect of CAR-T therapy by combining it with checkpoint inhibitors, drugs that first became available less than a decade ago and prevent tumor cells from impeding T-cell activity. We analyze mechanisms of resistance —like the occasional appearance of leukemic B cells that don't display CD19—and try to engineer CAR-T cells that will not release the cytokine storms that nearly killed Bill Ludwig and Emily Whitehead.

Through all these exuberant discussions, however, the questions of manufacture and scale linger. Even the most radically innovative methods will need continuous, iterative improvements to make them affordable. We like to imagine medical revolutions as, well, revolutionary—propelled forward through leaps of genius and technological innovation. But they are also evolutionary, nudged forward through the optimization of design and manufacture. There is a fair degree of humility in this knowledge, which a new generation of cell therapists is slowly absorbing.

On a blustery afternoon in May, I attended a conference on cellular therapy, titled "CAR-T and the Rise of Cellicon Valley," at the University of Pennsylvania, which it had co-organized with CHOP. Nearly 1,000 scientists, doctors, and biotech executives converged on a soaring auditorium on Spruce Street, lugging posters in plastic tubes and discussing the next waves of treatment.

Among those in attendance was Emily Whitehead, now fourteen, a year older than my daughter. She has tousled brown hair, and is in her eighth year of remission. "She was happy to miss a day of school," her father told me. She sat in the front row, in a yellow-and-black shirt and dark pants. Emily was eager to take in the latest medical breakthroughs in cellular therapies; she was also looking forward to a celebratory lunch at Pod, a pan-Asian restaurant where the dumplings, apparently, are also a breakthrough.

During a pause in the sessions, Emily and I joined a tour of the medical campus led by Bruce Levine, one of June's colleagues. He is the founding director of the facility at Penn where T cells are modified, quality-controlled, and manufactured, and was among the first people to handle Emily's cells. As in Seattle, the Philadelphia technicians worked singly or in pairs, checking boxes, taking cells out of incubators for observation, sterilizing hands.

The facility may as well have been a small monument to Emily. Photographs of her plastered the walls: Emily at eight, in pigtails; Emily at nine, with a missing front tooth, smiling next to President Obama; Emily at ten, holding a plaque. At a certain point during the tour, I watched Emily look out the window to the hospital across the street. She could almost see into the corner PICU room, where she had been confined for nearly a month. The rain came down in sheets.

I wondered how she felt, knowing that there were three versions of her in the hospital: the one here today, on a break from school; the one in the pictures, who had lived and almost died in the PICU; and the one frozen in the Krusty the Clown freezer next door. A chimeric existence of sorts.

"Do you remember coming into the hospital?" I asked.

"No," she said, looking out into the rain. "I only remember leaving."

DOUGLAS PRESTON

The Day the Dinosaurs Died

FROM *The New Yorker*

IF, ON A certain evening about 66 million years ago, you had
stood somewhere in North America and looked up at the sky,
you would have soon made out what appeared to be a star. If you
watched for an hour or two, the star would have seemed to grow
in brightness, although it barely moved. That's because it was not
a star but an asteroid, and it was headed directly for Earth at about
45,000 miles an hour. Sixty hours later, the asteroid hit. The air in
front was compressed and violently heated, and it blasted a hole
through the atmosphere, generating a supersonic shock wave. The
asteroid struck a shallow sea where the Yucatán peninsula is today.
In that moment, the Cretaceous period ended and the Paleogene
period began.

A few years ago, scientists at Los Alamos National Laboratory
used what was then one of the world's most powerful computers,
the so-called Q Machine, to model the effects of the impact. The
result was a slow-motion, second-by-second false-color video of the
event. Within two minutes of slamming into Earth, the asteroid,
which was at least 6 miles wide, had gouged a crater about 18 miles
deep and lofted 25 trillion metric tons of debris into the atmosphere. Picture the splash of a pebble falling into pond water, but
on a planetary scale. When Earth's crust rebounded, a peak higher
than Mount Everest briefly rose up. The energy released was more
than that of a billion Hiroshima bombs, but the blast looked nothing like a nuclear explosion, with its signature mushroom cloud.
Instead, the initial blowout formed a "rooster tail," a gigantic jet of

molten material, which exited the atmosphere, some of it fanning out over North America. Much of the material was several times hotter than the surface of the sun, and it set fire to everything within 1,000 miles. In addition, an inverted cone of liquefied, superheated rock rose, spread outward as countless red-hot blobs of glass, called tektites, and blanketed the Western Hemisphere.

Some of the ejecta escaped Earth's gravitational pull and went into irregular orbits around the sun. Over millions of years, bits of it found their way to other planets and moons in the solar system. Mars was eventually strewn with the debris—just as pieces of Mars, knocked aloft by ancient asteroid impacts, have been found on Earth. A 2013 study in the journal *Astrobiology* estimated that tens of thousands of pounds of impact rubble may have landed on Titan, a moon of Saturn, and on Europa and Callisto, which orbit Jupiter—three satellites that scientists believe may have promising habitats for life. Mathematical models indicate that at least some of this vagabond debris still harbored living microbes. The asteroid may have sown life throughout the solar system, even as it ravaged life on Earth.

The asteroid was vaporized on impact. Its substance, mingling with vaporized Earth rock, formed a fiery plume, which reached halfway to the moon before collapsing in a pillar of incandescent dust. Computer models suggest that the atmosphere within 1,500 miles of ground zero became red hot from the debris storm, triggering gigantic forest fires. As the Earth rotated, the airborne material converged at the opposite side of the planet, where it fell and set fire to the entire Indian subcontinent. Measurements of the layer of ash and soot that eventually coated the Earth indicate that fires consumed about 70 percent of the world's forests. Meanwhile, giant tsunamis resulting from the impact churned across the Gulf of Mexico, tearing up coastlines, sometimes peeling up hundreds of feet of rock, pushing debris inland, and then sucking it back out into deep water, leaving jumbled deposits that oilmen sometimes encounter in the course of deep-sea drilling.

The damage had only begun. Scientists still debate many of the details, which are derived from the computer models, and from field studies of the debris layer, knowledge of extinction rates, fossils and microfossils, and many other clues. But the overall view is consistently grim. The dust and soot from the impact and the conflagrations prevented all sunlight from reaching the planet's surface for months. Photosynthesis all but stopped, killing most of the plant life, extinguishing the phytoplankton in the oceans, and causing the amount of oxygen in the atmosphere to plummet. After the fires died down, Earth plunged into a period of cold, perhaps even a deep freeze. Earth's two essential food chains, in the sea and on land, collapsed. About 75 percent of all species went extinct. More than 99.9999 percent of all living organisms on Earth died, and the carbon cycle came to a halt.

Earth itself became toxic. When the asteroid struck, it vaporized layers of limestone, releasing into the atmosphere a trillion tons of carbon dioxide, 10 billion tons of methane, and a billion tons of carbon monoxide; all three are powerful greenhouse gases. The impact also vaporized anhydrite rock, which blasted 10 trillion tons of sulfur compounds aloft. The sulfur combined with water to form sulfuric acid, which then fell as an acid rain that may have been potent enough to strip the leaves from any surviving plants and to leach the nutrients from the soil.

Today, the layer of debris, ash, and soot deposited by the asteroid strike is preserved in the Earth's sediment as a stripe of black about the thickness of a notebook. This is called the KT boundary, because it marks the dividing line between the Cretaceous period and the Tertiary period. (The Tertiary has been redefined as the Paleogene, but the term "KT" persists.) Mysteries abound above and below the KT layer. In the late Cretaceous, widespread volcanoes spewed vast quantities of gas and dust into the atmosphere, and the air contained far higher levels of carbon dioxide than the air that we breathe now. The climate was tropical, and the planet was perhaps entirely free of ice. Yet scientists know very little about the animals and plants that were living at the time, and as a result they have been searching for fossil deposits as close to the KT boundary as possible.

One of the central mysteries of paleontology is the so-called "three-meter problem." In a century and a half of assiduous searching, almost no dinosaur remains have been found in the layers three meters, or about nine feet, below the KT boundary, a depth representing many thousands of years. Consequently, numerous paleontologists have argued that the dinosaurs were on the way to extinction long before the asteroid struck, owing perhaps to the volcanic eruptions and climate change. Other scientists have countered that the three-meter problem merely reflects how hard it is to find fossils. Sooner or later, they've contended, a scientist will discover dinosaurs much closer to the moment of destruction.

Locked in the KT boundary are the answers to our questions about one of the most significant events in the history of life on the planet. If one looks at the Earth as a kind of living organism, as many biologists do, you could say that it was shot by a bullet and almost died. Deciphering what happened on the day of destruction is crucial not only to solving the three-meter problem but also to explaining our own genesis as a species.

On August 5, 2013, I received an email from a graduate student named Robert DePalma. I had never met DePalma, but we had corresponded on paleontological matters for years, ever since he had read a novel I'd written that centered on the discovery of a fossilized *Tyrannosaurus rex* killed by the KT impact. "I have made an incredible and unprecedented discovery," he wrote me, from a truck stop in Bowman, North Dakota. "It is extremely confidential and only three others know of it at the moment, all of them close colleagues." He went on, "It is far more unique and far rarer than any simple dinosaur discovery. I would prefer not outlining the details via email, if possible." He gave me his cell-phone number and a time to call.

I called, and he told me that he had discovered a site like the one I'd imagined in my novel, which contained, among other things, direct victims of the catastrophe. At first, I was skeptical. DePalma was a scientific nobody, a PhD candidate at the University of Kansas, and he said that he had found the site with no institutional backing and no collaborators. I thought that he was likely exaggerating, or that he might even be crazy. (Paleontology has more than its share of unusual people.) But I was intrigued enough to get on a plane to North Dakota to see for myself.

DePalma's find was in the Hell Creek geological formation, which outcrops in parts of North Dakota, South Dakota, Montana, and Wyoming, and contains some of the most storied dinosaur beds in the world. At the time of the impact, the Hell Creek landscape consisted of steamy, subtropical lowlands and floodplains along the shores of an inland sea. The land teemed with life and the conditions were excellent for fossilization, with seasonal floods and meandering rivers that rapidly buried dead animals and plants.

Dinosaur hunters first discovered these rich fossil beds in the late nineteenth century. In 1902, Barnum Brown, a flamboyant dinosaur hunter who worked at the American Museum of Natural History, in New York, found the first *Tyrannosaurus rex* here, causing a worldwide sensation. One paleontologist estimated that in the Cretaceous period Hell Creek was so thick with *T. rexes* that they were like hyenas on the Serengeti. It was also home to triceratops and duckbills.

The Hell Creek Formation spanned the Cretaceous and the Paleogene periods, and paleontologists had known for at least half a century that an extinction had occurred then, because dinosaurs were found below, but never above, the KT layer. This was true not only in Hell Creek but all over the world. For many years, scientists believed that the KT extinction was no great mystery: over millions of years, volcanism, climate change, and other events gradually killed off many forms of life. But, in the late 1970s, a young geologist named Walter Alvarez and his father, Luis Alvarez, a nuclear physicist, discovered that the KT layer was laced with unusually high amounts of the rare metal iridium, which, they hypothesized, was from the dusty remains of an asteroid impact. In an article in *Science,* published in 1980, they proposed that this impact was so large that it triggered the mass extinction, and that the KT layer was the debris from that event. Most paleontologists rejected the idea that a sudden, random encounter with space junk had drastically altered the evolution of life on Earth. But as the years passed the evidence mounted, until, in a 1991 paper, the smoking gun was announced: the discovery of an impact crater buried under thousands of feet of sediment in the Yucatán peninsula, of exactly the right age, and of the right size and geochemistry, to have caused a worldwide cataclysm. The crater and the asteroid were named Chicxulub, after a small Mayan town near the epicenter.

One of the authors of the 1991 paper, David Kring, was so frightened by what he learned of the impact's destructive nature that he became a leading voice in calling for a system to identify and neutralize threatening asteroids. "There's no uncertainty to this statement: the Earth will be hit by a Chicxulub-size asteroid again, unless we deflect it," he told me. "Even a three-hundred-meter rock would end world agriculture."

In 2010, forty-one researchers in many scientific disciplines announced, in a landmark *Science* article, that the issue should be considered settled: a huge asteroid impact caused the extinction. But opposition to the idea remains passionate. The main competing hypothesis is that the colossal "Deccan" volcanic eruptions, in what would become India, spewed enough sulfur and carbon dioxide into the atmosphere to cause a climatic shift. The eruptions, which began before the KT impact and continued after it, were among the biggest in Earth's history, lasting hundreds of thousands of years, and burying half a million square miles of the Earth's surface a mile deep in lava. The three-meter gap below the KT layer, proponents argued, was evidence that the mass extinction was well under way by the time of the asteroid strike.

In 2004, DePalma, at the time a twenty-two-year-old paleontology undergraduate, began excavating a small site in the Hell Creek Formation. The site had once been a pond, and the deposit consisted of very thin layers of sediment. Normally, one geological layer might represent thousands or millions of years. But DePalma was able to show that each layer in the deposit had been laid down in a single big rainstorm. "We could see when there were buds on the trees," he told me. "We could see when the cypresses were dropping their needles in the fall. We could experience this in real time." Peering at the layers was like flipping through a paleohistory book that chronicled decades of ecology in its silty pages. DePalma's adviser, the late Larry Martin, urged him to find a similar site, but one that had layers closer to the KT boundary.

Today, DePalma, now thirty-seven, is still working toward his PhD. He holds the unpaid position of curator of vertebrate paleontology at the Palm Beach Museum of Natural History, a nascent and struggling museum with no exhibition space. In 2012, while looking for a new pond deposit, he heard that a private collector had stumbled upon an unusual site on a cattle ranch near Bowman, North Dakota. (Much of the Hell Creek land is privately owned, and ranchers will sell digging rights to whoever will pay decent money, paleontologists and commercial fossil collectors alike.) The collector felt that the site, a three-foot-deep layer exposed at the surface, was a bust: it was packed with fish fossils, but they were so delicate that they crumbled into tiny flakes as soon as they met the air. The fish were encased in layers of damp, cracked mud and sand that had never solidified; it was so soft that it could be dug with a shovel or pulled apart by hand. In July 2012, the collector showed DePalma the site and told him that he was welcome to it.

"I was immediately very disappointed," DePalma told me. He was hoping for a site like the one he'd excavated earlier: an ancient pond with fine-grained, fossil-bearing layers that spanned many seasons and years. Instead, everything had been deposited in a single flood. But as DePalma poked around he saw potential. The flood had entombed everything immediately, so specimens were exquisitely preserved. He found many complete fish, which are rare in the Hell Creek Formation, and he figured that he could remove them intact if he worked with painstaking care. He agreed to pay the rancher a certain amount for each season that he worked there. (The specifics of the arrangement, as is standard practice in paleontology, are a closely guarded secret. The site is now under exclusive long-term lease.)

The following July, DePalma returned to do a preliminary excavation of the site. "Almost right away, I saw it was unusual," he told me. He began shoveling off the layers of soil above where he'd found the fish. This "overburden" is typically material that was deposited long after the specimen lived; there's little in it to interest a paleontologist, and it is usually discarded. But as soon as DePalma started digging he noticed grayish-white specks in the layers which looked like grains of sand but which, under a hand lens, proved to be tiny spheres and elongated droplets. "I think, Holy shit, these look like microtektites!" DePalma recalled. Microtektites are the blobs of glass that form when molten rock is blasted into the air by an asteroid impact and falls back to Earth in a solidifying drizzle. The site appeared to contain microtektites by the million.

As DePalma carefully excavated the upper layers, he began uncovering an extraordinary array of fossils, exceedingly delicate but marvelously well preserved. "There's amazing plant material in there, all interlaced and interlocked," he recalled. "There are logjams of wood, fish pressed against cypress-tree root bundles, tree trunks smeared with amber." Most fossils end up being squashed flat by the pressure of the overlying stone, but here everything was three-dimensional, including the fish, having been encased in sediment all at once, which acted as a support. "You see skin, you see dorsal fins literally sticking straight up in the sediments, species new to science," he said. As he dug, the momentousness of what he had come across slowly dawned on him. If the site was what he hoped, he had made the most important paleontological discovery of the new century.

DePalma grew up in Boca Raton, Florida, and as a child he was fascinated by bones and the stories they contained. His father, Robert Sr., practices endodontic surgery in nearby Delray Beach; his great-uncle Anthony, who died in 2005, at the age of a hundred, was a renowned orthopedic surgeon who wrote several standard textbooks on the subject. (Anthony's son, Robert's cousin, is the film director Brian De Palma.)

"Between the ages of three and four, I made a visual connection with the gracefulness of individual bones and how they fit together as a system," DePalma told me. "That really struck me. I went after whatever on the dinner table had bones in it." His family buried their dead pets in one spot and put the burial markers in another, so that he wouldn't dig up the corpses; he found them anyway. He froze dead lizards in ice-cube trays, which his mother would discover when she had friends over for iced tea. "I was never into sports," he said. "They tried to get me to do that so I would get along with the other kids. But I was digging up the baseball field looking for bones."

DePalma's great-uncle Anthony, who lived in Pompano Beach, took him under his wing. "I used to visit him every other weekend and show him my latest finds," DePalma said. When he was four, someone at a museum in Texas gave him a fragment of dinosaur bone, which he took to his great-uncle. "He taught me that all those little knobs and rough patches and protrusions on a bone had names, and that the bone also had a name," DePalma said. "I was captivated." At six or seven, on trips to Central Florida with his family, he started finding his own fossilized bones from mammals dating back to the Ice Age. He found his first dinosaur bone when he was nine, in Colorado.

In high school, during the summer and on weekends, DePalma collected fossils, made dinosaur models, and mounted skeletons for the Graves Museum of Archaeology and Natural History, in

Dania Beach. He loaned the museum his childhood fossil collection for display, but in 2004 the museum went bankrupt and many of the specimens were carted off to a community college. DePalma had no paperwork to prove his ownership, and a court refused to return his fossils, which numbered in the hundreds. They were mostly locked away in storage, unavailable for public display and enjoyment.

Dismayed by what he called the "wasteful mismanagement" of his collection, DePalma adopted some unusual collecting practices. Typically, paleontologists cede the curation and the care of their specimens to the institutions that hold them. But DePalma insists on contractual clauses that give him oversight of the management of his specimens. He never digs on public land, because of what he considers excessive government red tape. But, without federal support for his work, he must cover almost all the costs himself. His out-of-pocket expenses for working the Hell Creek site amount to tens of thousands of dollars. He helps defray the expenses by mounting fossils, doing reconstructions, and casting and selling replicas for museums, private collectors, and other clients. At times, his parents have chipped in. "I squeak by," he said. "If it's a toss-up between getting more PaleoBond"—an expensive liquid glue used to hold fossils together—"or changing the air-conditioning filter, I'm getting the PaleoBond." He is single, and shares a three-bedroom apartment with casts of various dinosaurs, including one of a *Nanotyrannus*. "It's hard to have a life outside of my work," he said.

DePalma's control of his research collection is controversial. Fossils are a big business; wealthy collectors pay hundreds of thousands of dollars, even millions, for a rare specimen. (In 1997, a *T. rex* nicknamed Sue was sold at a Sotheby's auction, to the Field Museum of Natural History, in Chicago, for more than $8.3 million.) The American market is awash in fossils illegally smuggled out of China and Mongolia. But in the U.S. fossil collecting on private property is legal, as is the buying, selling, and exporting of fossils. Many scientists view this trade as a threat to paleontology and argue that important fossils belong in museums. "I'm not allowed to have a private collection of anything I'm studying," one prominent curator told me. DePalma insists that he maintains "the best of both worlds" for his fossils. He has deposited portions of his collection at several nonprofit institutions, including the University of Kansas, the Palm Beach Museum of Natural History, and Florida Atlantic University; some specimens are temporarily housed in various analytical labs that are conducting tests on them —all overseen by him.

In 2013, DePalma briefly made news with a paper he published in the *Proceedings of the National Academy of Sciences.* Four years earlier, in Hell Creek, he and a field assistant, Robert Feeney, found an odd, lumpy growth of fossilized bone that turned out to be two fused vertebrae from the tail of a hadrosaur, a duck-billed dinosaur from the Cretaceous period. DePalma thought that the bone might have grown around a foreign object and encased it. He took it to Lawrence Memorial Hospital, in Kansas, where a CT technician scanned it for free in the middle of the night, when the machine was idle. Inside the nodule was a broken tyrannosaur tooth; the hadrosaur had been bitten by a tyrannosaur and escaped.

The discovery helped refute an old hypothesis, revived by the formidable paleontologist Jack Horner, that *T. rex* was solely a scavenger. Horner argued that *T. rex* was too slow and lumbering, its arms too puny and its eyesight too poor, to prey on other creatures. When DePalma's find was picked up by the national media, Horner dismissed it as "speculation" and merely "one data point." He suggested an alternative scenario: the *T. rex* might have accidentally bitten the tail of a sleeping hadrosaur, thinking that it was dead, and then "backed away" when it realized its mistake. "I thought that was absolutely preposterous," DePalma told me. At the time, he told the *Los Angeles Times,* "A scavenger doesn't come across a food source and realize all of a sudden that it's alive." Horner eventually conceded that *T. rex* may have hunted live prey. But, when I asked Horner about DePalma recently, he said at first that he didn't remember him: "In the community, we don't get to know students very well."

Without his PhD, DePalma remains mostly invisible, awaiting the stamp of approval that signals the beginning of a serious research career. Several paleontologists I talked to had not heard of him. Another, who asked not to be named, said, "Finding that kind of fossil was pretty cool, but not life-changing. People sometimes think I'm dumb because I often say I don't have the answers—we weren't there when a fossil was formed. There are other people out there who say they do know, and he's one of those people. I think he can overinterpret."

*

After receiving DePalma's email, I made arrangements to visit the Hell Creek site; three weeks later I was in Bowman. DePalma pulled up to my hotel in a Toyota 4Runner, its stereo blasting the theme to *Raiders of the Lost Ark*. He wore a coarse cotton work shirt, cargo pants with canvas suspenders, and a suede cowboy hat with the left brim snapped up. His face was tanned from long days in the sun and he had a five-day-old beard.

I got in, and we drove for an hour or so, turning through a ranch gate and following a maze of bone-rattling roads that eventually petered out in a grassy basin. The scattered badlands of Hell Creek form an otherworldly landscape. This is far-flung ranching and farming country; prairies and sunflower fields stretch to the horizon, domed by the great blue skies of the American West. Roads connect small towns—truck stop, church, motel, houses and trailers—and lonely expanses roll by in between. Here and there in the countryside, abandoned farmhouses lean into the ground. Over millions of years, the Hell Creek layer has been heavily eroded, leaving only remnants, which jut from the prairie like so many rotten teeth. These lifeless buttes and pinnacles are striped in beige, chocolate, yellow, maroon, russet, gray, and white. Fossils, worked loose by wind and rain, spill down the sides.

When we arrived, DePalma's site lay open in front of us: a desolate hump of gray, cracked earth, about the size of two soccer fields. It looked as if a piece of the moon had dropped there. One side of the deposit was cut through by a sandy wash, or dry streambed; the other ended in a low escarpment. The dig was a three-foot-deep rectangular hole, sixty feet long by forty feet wide. A couple of two-by-fours, along with various digging tools and some metal pipe for taking core samples, leaned against the far side of the hole. As we strolled around the site, I noticed on DePalma's belt a long fixed-blade knife and a sheathed bayonet—a Second World War relic that his uncle gave him when he was twelve, he said.

He recalled the moment of discovery. The first fossil he removed, earlier that summer, was a five-foot-long freshwater paddlefish. Paddlefish still live today; they have a long bony snout, with which they probe murky water in search of food. When DePalma took out the fossil, he found underneath it a tooth from a mosasaur, a giant carnivorous marine reptile. He wondered how a freshwater fish and a marine reptile could have ended up in the same

PARK CITY LIBRARY

www.parkcitylibrary.org
435-615-5600

- Checkout Receipt -

Patron Barcode:

Number of items:

Barcode: 87162688
Title: The committed /
Due: 04/29/2021

Barcode: 87162839
Title: The best American Science and
Nature Writing 2020 /
Due: 04/29/2021

04/08/2021 02:57:47 PM

place, on a riverbank at least several miles inland from the nearest sea. (At the time, a shallow body of water, called the Western Interior Seaway, ran from the proto-Gulf of Mexico up through part of North America.) The next day, he found a two-foot-wide tail from another marine fish; it looked as if it had been violently ripped from the fish's body. "If the fish is dead for any length of time, those tails decay and fall apart," DePalma said. But this one was perfectly intact, "so I knew that it was transported at the time of death or around then." Like the mosasaur tooth, it had somehow ended up miles inland from the sea of its origin. "When I found that, I thought, *There's no way, this can't be right*," DePalma said. The discoveries hinted at an extraordinary conclusion that he wasn't quite ready to accept. "I was 98 percent convinced at that point," he said.

The following day, DePalma noticed a small disturbance preserved in the sediment. About three inches in diameter, it appeared to be a crater formed by an object that had fallen from the sky and plunked down in mud. Similar formations, caused by hailstones hitting a muddy surface, had been found before in the fossil record. As DePalma shaved back the layers to make a cross-section of the crater, he found the thing itself—not a hailstone but a small white sphere—at the bottom of the crater. It was a tektite, about three millimeters in diameter—the fallout from an ancient asteroid impact. As he continued excavating, he found another crater with a tektite at the bottom, and another, and another. Glass turns to clay over millions of years, and these tektites were now clay, but some still had glassy cores. The microtektites he had found earlier might have been carried there by water, but these had been trapped where they fell—on what, DePalma believed, must have been the very day of the disaster.

"When I saw that, I knew this wasn't just any flood deposit," DePalma said. "We weren't just near the KT boundary—this whole site *is* the KT boundary!" From surveying and mapping the layers, DePalma hypothesized that a massive inland surge of water flooded a river valley and filled the low-lying area where we now stood, perhaps as a result of the KT-impact tsunami, which had roared across the proto-Gulf and up the Western Interior Seaway. As the water slowed and became slack, it deposited everything that had been caught up in its travels—the heaviest material first, up to whatever was floating on the surface. All of it was quickly entombed and preserved in the muck: dying and dead creatures, both marine and freshwater; plants, seeds, tree trunks, roots, cones, pine needles, flowers, and pollen; shells, bones, teeth, and eggs; tektites, shocked minerals, tiny diamonds, iridium-laden dust, ash, charcoal, and amber-smeared wood. As the sediments settled, blobs of glass rained into the mud, the largest first, then finer and finer bits, until grains sifted down like snow.

"We have the whole KT event preserved in these sediments," DePalma said. "With this deposit, we can chart what happened the day the Cretaceous died." No paleontological site remotely like it had ever been found, and, if DePalma's hypothesis proves correct, the scientific value of the site will be immense. When Walter Alvarez visited the dig last summer, he was astounded. "It is truly a magnificent site," he wrote to me, adding that it's "surely one of the best sites ever found for telling just what happened on the day of the impact."

When DePalma finished showing me the dig, he introduced me to a field assistant, Rudy Pascucci, the director of the Palm Beach Museum. Pascucci, a muscular man in his fifties, was sunburned and unshaven, and wore a sleeveless T-shirt, snakeproof camouflage boots, and a dusty Tilley hat. The two men gathered their tools, got down on the floor of the hole, and began probing the three-foot-high walls of the deposit.

For rough digging, DePalma likes to use his bayonet and a handheld Marsh pick, popularized by the nineteenth-century Yale paleontologist Othniel C. Marsh, who pioneered dinosaur-hunting in the American West and discovered eighty new species. The pick was given to him by David Burnham, his thesis adviser at Kansas, when he completed his master's degree. For fine work, DePalma uses X-Acto knives and brushes—the typical tools of a paleontologist—as well as dental instruments given to him by his father.

The deposit consisted of dozens of thin layers of mud and sand. Lower down, it graded into a more turbulent band of sand and gravel, which contained the heavier fish fossils, bones, and bigger tektites. Below that layer was a hard surface of sandstone, the original Cretaceous bedrock of the site, much of which had been scoured smooth by the flood.

Paleontology is maddening work, its progress typically measured in millimeters. As I watched, DePalma and Pascucci lay on their stomachs under the beating sun, their eyes inches from the dirt wall, and picked away. DePalma poked the tip of an X-Acto into the thin laminations of sediment and loosened one dime-size flake at a time; he'd examine it closely, and, if he saw nothing, flick it away. When the chips accumulated, he gathered them into small piles with a paintbrush; when those piles accumulated, Pascucci swept them into larger piles with a broom and then shoveled them into a heap at the far end of the dig.

Occasionally, DePalma came across small plant fossils—flower petals, leaves, seeds, pine needles, and bits of bark. Many of these were mere impressions in the mud, which would crack and peel as soon as they were exposed to the air. He quickly squirted them with PaleoBond, which soaked into the fossils and held them together. Or, using another technique, he mixed a batch of plaster and poured it on the specimen before it fell apart. This would preserve, in plaster, a reverse image of the fossil; the original was too short-lived to be saved.

When the mosquitoes got bad, DePalma took out a briar pipe and packed it with Royal Cherry Cavendish tobacco. He put a lighter to it and vigorously puffed, wreathing himself in sickly-sweet smoke, then went back to work. "I'm like a shopaholic in a shoe store," he said. "I want everything!"

He showed me the impression of a round object about two inches wide. "This is either a flower or an echinoderm," he said, referring to a group of marine life-forms that includes sea urchins and starfish. "I'll figure it out in the lab." He swiftly entombed it in PaleoBond and plaster. Next, he found a perfect leaf, and near that a seed from a pinecone. "Cretaceous mulch," he said, dismissively; he already had many similar examples. He found three more small craters with tektites in them, which he sectioned and photographed. Then his X-Acto blade turned up a tiny brown bone—a jaw, less than a quarter-inch in length. He held it up between his fingers and peered at it with a lens.

"A mammal," he said. "This one was already dead when it was buried." Weeks later, in the lab, he identified the jaw as probably belonging to a mammal distantly related to primates—including us.

Half an hour later, DePalma discovered a large feather. "Every day is Christmas out here," he said. He exposed the feather with precise movements. It was a crisp impression in the layer of mud, perhaps thirteen inches long. "This is my ninth feather," he said. "The first fossil feathers ever found at Hell Creek. I'm convinced these are dinosaur feathers. I don't know for sure. But these are primitive feathers, and most are a foot long. There are zero birds that big from Hell Creek with feathers this primitive. It's more parsimonious to suggest it was a known dinosaur, most likely a theropod, possibly a raptor." He kept digging. "Maybe we'll find the raptor that these feathers came from, but I doubt it. These feathers could have floated from a long way off."

His X-Acto knife unearthed the edge of a fossilized fin. Another paddlefish came to light; it later proved to be nearly six feet long. DePalma probed the sediment around it, to gauge its position and how best to extract it. As more of it was exposed, we could clearly see that the fish's two-foot-long snout had broken when it was forced—probably by the flood's surge—against the branches of a submerged araucaria tree. He noted that every fish he'd found in the site had died with its mouth open, which may indicate that the fish had been gasping as they suffocated in the sediment-laden water.

"Most died in a vertical position in the sediment, didn't even tip over on their sides," he said. "And they weren't scavenged, because whatever would have dug them up afterward was probably gone." He chipped away around the paddlefish, exposing a fin bone, then a half-dollar-size patch of fossilized skin with the scales perfectly visible. He treated these by saturating them with his own special blend of hardener. Because of the extreme fragility of the fossils, he would take them back to his lab, in Florida, totally encased in sediment, or "matrix." In the lab, he would free each fossil under a magnifying glass, in precisely controlled conditions, away from the damaging effects of sun, wind, and aridity.

As DePalma worked around the paddlefish, more of the araucaria branch came to light, including its short, spiky needles. "This tree was alive when it was buried," he said. Then he noticed a golden blob of amber stuck to the branch. Amber is preserved tree resin and often contains traces of whatever was in the air at the time, trapping the atmospheric chemistry and even, sometimes, insects and small reptiles. "This is Cretaceous flypaper," he said. "I can't wait to get this back to the lab."

An hour later, he had chiseled all the way around the fish, leaving it encased in matrix, supported by a four-inch-tall pedestal of rock. "I'm pretty sure this is a species new to science," he said. Because the soft tissue had also fossilized, he said, even the animal's stomach contents might still be present.

He straightened up. "Time to plaster," he said. He took off his shirt and began mixing a five-gallon bucket of plaster with his hands, while Pascucci tore strips of burlap. DePalma took a two-by-four and sawed off two foot-long pieces and placed them like splints on either side of the sediment-encased fossil. One by one, he dipped the burlap strips in the plaster and draped them across the top and the sides of the specimen. He added rope handles and plastered them in. An hour later, when the plaster had cured, he chiseled through the rock pedestal beneath the fossil and flipped the specimen over, leaving the underside exposed. Back in the lab, he would go through this surface to access the fossil, with the plaster jacket acting as a cradle below. Using the rope handles, DePalma and Pascucci lugged the specimen, which weighed perhaps 200 pounds, to the truck and loaded it into the back. Later, DePalma would store it behind a friend's ranch house, where all his jacketed fossils from the season were laid out in rows, covered with tarps.

DePalma resumed digging. Gusts of wind stirred up clouds of dust, and rain fell; when the weather cleared, the late-afternoon sun spilled across the prairie. DePalma was lost in another day, in another time. "Here's a piece of wood with bark-beetle traces," he said. Plant fossils from the first several million years after the impact show almost no signs of such damage; the insects were mostly gone. The asteroid had likely struck in the fall, DePalma speculated. He had reached this conclusion by comparing the juvenile paddlefish and sturgeon he'd found with the species' known growth rates and hatching seasons; he'd also found the seeds of conifers, figs, and certain flowers. "When we analyze the pollen and diatomaceous particles, that will narrow it down," he said.

In the week that followed, fresh riches emerged: more feathers, leaves, seeds, and amber, along with several other fish, three to five feet long, and a dozen more craters with tektites. I have visited many paleontological sites, but I had never seen so many specimens found so quickly. Most digs are boring; days or weeks may pass with little found. DePalma seemed to make a noteworthy discovery about every half-hour.

When DePalma first visited the site, he noted, partially embedded on the surface, the hip bone of a dinosaur in the ceratopsian family, of which triceratops is the best-known member. A commercial collector had tried to remove it years earlier; it had been abandoned in place and was crumbling from years of exposure. DePalma initially dismissed it as "trash" and decried the irresponsibility of the collector. Later, though, he wondered how the bone, which was heavy, had arrived there, very close to the high-water mark of the flood. It must have floated, he said, and to have done so it must have been encased in desiccated tissue—suggesting that at least one dinosaur species was alive at the time of the impact. He later found a suitcase-size piece of fossilized skin from a ceratopsian attached to the hip bone.

At one point, DePalma set off to photograph the layers of the deposit which had been cut through and exposed by the sandy wash. He scraped smooth a vertical section and misted it with water from a spray bottle to bring out the color. The bottom layer was jumbled; the first rush of water had ripped up layers of mud, gravel, and rocks and tumbled them about with pieces of burned (and burning) wood.

Then DePalma came to a faint jug-shaped outline in the wall of the wash. He examined it closely. It started as a tunnel at the top of the KT layer, went down, and then widened into a round cavity, filled with soil of a different color, which stopped at the hard sandstone of the undisturbed bedrock layer below. It looked as though a small animal had dug through the mud to create a hideout. "Is that a burrow?" I asked.

DePalma scraped the area smooth with his bayonet, then sprayed it. "You're darn right it is," he said. "And this isn't the burrow of a small dinosaur. It's a mammal burrow." (Burrows have characteristic shapes, depending on the species that inhabit them.) He peered at it, his eyes inches from the rock, probing it with the tip of the bayonet. "Gosh, I think it's still in there!"

He planned to remove the entire burrow intact, in a block, and run it through a CT scanner back home, to see what it contained. "Any Cretaceous mammal burrow is incredibly rare," he said. "But this one is impossible—it's dug right through the KT boundary." Perhaps, he said, the mammal survived the impact and the flood, burrowed into the mud to escape the freezing darkness, then died. "It may have been born in the Cretaceous and died in the

Paleocene," he said. "And to think—66 million years later, a stinky monkey is digging it up, trying to figure out what happened." He added, "If it's a new species, I'll name it after you."

When I left Hell Creek, DePalma pressed me on the need for secrecy: I was to tell no one, not even close friends, about what he'd found. The history of paleontology is full of tales of bribery, backstabbing, and double-dealing. In the nineteenth century, Othniel C. Marsh and Edward Drinker Cope, the nation's two leading paleontologists, engaged in a bitter competition to collect dinosaur fossils in the American West. They raided each other's quarries, bribed each other's crews, and vilified each other in print and at scientific meetings. In 1890, the *New York Herald* began a series of sensational articles about the controversy with the headline "Scientists Wage Bitter Warfare." The rivalry has since become known as the Bone Wars. The days of skulduggery in paleontology have not passed; DePalma was deeply concerned that the site would be expropriated by a major museum.

DePalma knew that a screwup with this site would probably end his career, and that his status in the field was so uncertain that he needed to fortify the find against potential criticism. He had already experienced harsh judgment when, in 2015, he published a paper on a new species of dinosaur called a Dakotaraptor, and mistakenly inserted a fossil turtle bone in the reconstruction. Although rebuilding a skeleton from thousands of bone fragments that have commingled with those of other species is not easy, DePalma was mortified by the attacks. "I never want to go through that again," he told me.

For five years, DePalma continued excavations at the site. He quietly shared his findings with a half-dozen luminaries in the field of KT studies, including Walter Alvarez, and enlisted their help. During the winter months, when not in the field, DePalma prepared and analyzed his specimens, a few at a time, in a colleague's lab at Florida Atlantic University, in Boca Raton. The lab was a windowless, wedgelike room in the geology building, lined with bubbling aquarium tanks and shelves heaped with books, scientific journals, pieces of coral, mastodon teeth, seashells, and a stack of .50-caliber machine-gun rounds, dating from the Second World War, that the lab's owner had recovered from the bottom of the

Atlantic Ocean. DePalma had carved out a space for himself in a corner, just large enough for him to work on one or two jacketed fossils at a time.

When I first visited the lab, in April 2014, a block of stone three feet long by eighteen inches wide lay on a table under bright lights and a large magnifying lens. The block, DePalma said, contained a sturgeon and a paddlefish, along with dozens of smaller fossils and a single small, perfect crater with a tektite in it. The lower parts of the block consisted of debris, fragments of bone, and loose tektites that had been dislodged and caught up in the turbulence. The block told the story of the impact in microcosm. "It was a very bad day," DePalma said. "Look at these two fish." He showed me where the sturgeon's scutes—the sharp, bony plates on its back—had been forced into the body of the paddlefish. One fish was impaled on the other. The mouth of the paddlefish was agape, and jammed into its gill rakers were microtektites—sucked in by the fish as it tried to breathe. DePalma said, "This fish was likely alive for some time after being caught in the wave, long enough to gasp frenzied mouthfuls of water in a vain attempt to survive."

Gradually, DePalma was piecing together a potential picture of the disaster. By the time the site flooded, the surrounding forest was already on fire, given the abundance of charcoal, charred wood, and amber he'd found at the site. The water arrived not as a curling wave but as a powerful, roiling rise, packed with disoriented fish and plant and animal debris, which, DePalma hypothesized, were laid down as the water slowed and receded.

In the lab, DePalma showed me magnified cross-sections of the sediment. Most of its layers were horizontal, but a few formed curlicues or flamelike patterns called truncated flame structures, which were caused by a combination of weight from above and mini-surges in the incoming water. DePalma found five sets of these patterns. He turned back to the block on his table and held a magnifying lens up to the tektite. Parallel, streaming lines were visible on its surface—Schlieren lines, formed by two types of molten glass swirling together as the blobs arced through the atmosphere. Peering through the lens, DePalma picked away at the block with a dental probe. He soon exposed a section of pink, pearlescent shell, which had been pushed up against the sturgeon. "Ammonite," he said. Ammonites were marine mollusks that somewhat resemble the present-day nautilus, although they were more closely related to squid and octopi. As DePalma uncovered more of the shell, I watched its vibrant color fade. "Live ammonite, ripped apart by the tsunami—they don't travel well," he said. "Genus *Sphenodiscus,* I would think." The shell, which hadn't previously been documented in the Hell Creek Formation, was another marine victim tossed inland.

He stood up. "Now I'm going to show you something special," he said, opening a wooden crate and removing an object that was covered in aluminum foil. He unwrapped a sixteen-inch fossil feather, and held it in his palms like a piece of Lalique glass. "When I found the first feather, I had about twenty seconds of disbelief," he said. DePalma had studied under Larry Martin, a world authority on the Cretaceous predecessors of birds, and had been "exposed to a lot of fossil feathers. When I encountered this damn thing, I immediately understood the importance of it. And now look at this."

From the lab table, he grabbed a fossil forearm belonging to Dakotaraptor, the dinosaur species he'd discovered in Hell Creek. He pointed to a series of regular bumps on the bone. "These are probably quill knobs," he said. "This dinosaur had feathers on its forearms. Now watch." With precision calipers, he measured the diameter of the quill knobs, then the diameter of the quill of the fossil feather; both were 3.5 millimeters. "This matches," he said. "This says a feather of this size would be associated with a limb of this size."

There was more, including a piece of a partly burned tree trunk with amber stuck to it. He showed me a photo of the amber seen through a microscope. Trapped inside were two impact particles —another landmark discovery, because the amber would have preserved their chemical composition. (All other tektites found from the impact, exposed to the elements for millions of years, have chemically changed.) He'd also found scores of beautiful examples of lonsdaleite, a hexagonal form of diamond that is associated with impacts; it forms when carbon in an asteroid is compressed so violently that it crystallizes into trillions of microscopic grains, which are blasted into the air and drift down.

Finally, he showed me a photograph of a fossil jawbone; it belonged to the mammal he'd found in the burrow. "This is the jaw of Dougie," he said. The bone was big for a Cretaceous mammal —three inches long—and almost complete, with a tooth. After my visit to Hell Creek, DePalma had removed the animal's burrow intact, still encased in the block of sediment, and, with the help of some women who worked as cashiers at the Travel Center, in Bowman, hoisted it into the back of his truck. He believes that the jaw belonged to a marsupial that looked like a weasel. Using the tooth, he could conduct a stable-isotope study to find out what the animal ate—"what the menu was after the disaster," he said. The rest of the mammal remains in the burrow, to be researched later.

DePalma listed some of the other discoveries he's made at the site: several flooded ant nests, with drowned ants still inside and some chambers packed with microtektites; a possible wasp burrow; another mammal burrow, with multiple tunnels and galleries; shark teeth; the thigh bone of a large sea turtle; at least three new fish species; a gigantic ginkgo leaf and a plant that was a relative of the banana; more than a dozen new species of animals and plants; and several other burrow types.

At the bottom of the deposit, in a mixture of heavy gravel and tektites, DePalma identified the broken teeth and bones, including hatchling remains, of almost every dinosaur group known from Hell Creek, as well as pterosaur remains, which had previously been found only in layers far below the KT boundary. He found, intact, an unhatched egg containing an embryo—a fossil of immense research value. The egg and the other remains suggested that dinosaurs and major reptiles were probably not staggering into extinction on that fateful day. In one fell swoop, DePalma may have solved the three-meter problem and filled in the gap in the fossil record.

By the end of the 2013 field season, DePalma was convinced that the site had been created by an impact flood, but he lacked conclusive evidence that it was the KT impact. It was possible that it resulted from another giant asteroid strike that occurred at around the same time. "Extraordinary discoveries require extraordinary evidence," he said. If his tektites shared the same geochemistry as tektites from the Chicxulub asteroid, he'd have a strong case. Deposits of Chicxulub tektites are rare; the best source, discovered in 1990, is a small outcrop in Haiti, on a cliff above a road cut. In late January 2014, DePalma went there to gather tektites and sent them to an independent lab in Canada, along with tektites from his own site; the samples were analyzed at the same time, with the same equipment. The results indicated a near-perfect geochemical match.

In the first few years after DePalma's discoveries, only a handful of scientists knew about them. One was David Burnham, DePalma's thesis adviser at Kansas, who estimates that DePalma's site will keep specialists busy for at least half a century. "Robert's got so much stuff that's unheard of," Burnham told me. "Amber with tektites embedded in it—holy cow! The dinosaur feathers are crazy good, but the burrow makes your head reel." In paleontology, the term *Lagerstätte* refers to a rare type of fossil site with a large variety of specimens that are nearly perfectly preserved, a sort of fossilized ecosystem. "It will be a famous site," Burnham said. "It will be in the textbooks. It is the *Lagerstätte* of the KT extinction."

Jan Smit, a paleontologist at Vrije University, in Amsterdam, and a world authority on the KT impact, has been helping DePalma analyze his results, and, like Burnham and Walter Alvarez, he is a co-author of a scientific paper that DePalma is publishing about the site. (There are eight other co-authors.) "This is really a major discovery," Smit said. "It solves the question of whether dinosaurs went extinct at exactly that level or whether they declined before. And this is the first time we see direct victims." I asked if the results would be controversial. "When I saw his data with the paddlefish, sturgeon, and ammonite, I think he's right on the spot," Smit said. "I am very sure he has a pot of gold."

In September of 2016, DePalma gave a brief talk about the discovery at the annual meeting of the Geological Society of America, in Colorado. He mentioned only that he had found a deposit from a KT flood that had yielded glass droplets, shocked minerals, and fossils. He had christened the site Tanis, after the ancient city in Egypt, which was featured in the 1981 film *Raiders of the Lost Ark* as the resting place of the Ark of the Covenant. In the real Tanis, archeologists found an inscription in three writing systems, which, like the Rosetta stone, was crucial in translating ancient Egyptian. DePalma hopes that his Tanis site will help decipher what happened on the first day after the impact.

The talk, limited though it was, caused a stir. Kirk Cochran, a professor at the School of Marine and Atmospheric Science at Stony Brook University, in New York, recalled that when DePalma presented his findings there were gasps of amazement in the audience. Some scientists were wary. Kirk Johnson, the director of the Smithsonian's National Museum of Natural History, told me that he knew the Hell Creek area well, having worked there since 1981. "My warning lights were flashing bright red," he told me. "I was so skeptical after the talk I was convinced it was a fabrication." Johnson, who had been mapping the KT layer in Hell Creek, said that his research indicated that Tanis was at least forty-five feet below the KT boundary and perhaps 100,000 years older. "If it's what it's said to be," Johnson said, "it's a fabulous discovery." But he declared himself "uneasy" until he could see DePalma's paper.

One prominent West Coast paleontologist who is an authority on the KT event told me, "I'm suspicious of the findings. They've been presented at meetings in various ways with various associated extraordinary claims. He could have stumbled on something amazing, but he has a reputation for making a lot out of a little." As an example, he brought up DePalma's paper on Dakotaraptor, which he described as "bones he basically collected, all in one area, some of which were part of a dinosaur, some of which were part of a turtle, and he put it all together as a skeleton of one animal." He also objected to what he felt was excessive secrecy surrounding the Tanis site, which has made it hard for outside scientists to evaluate DePalma's claims.

Johnson, too, finds the lack of transparency, and the dramatic aspects of DePalma's personality, unnerving. "There's an element of showmanship in his presentation style that does not add to his credibility," he said. Other paleontologists told me that they were leery of going on the record with criticisms of DePalma and his co-authors. All expressed a desire to see the final paper, which will be published next week, in the *Proceedings of the National Academy of Sciences*, so that they could evaluate the data for themselves.

After the GSA talk, DePalma realized that his theory of what had happened at Tanis had a fundamental problem. The KT tsunami, even moving at more than 100 miles an hour, would have taken many hours to travel the 2,000 miles to the site. The rainfall of glass blobs, however, would have hit the area and stopped within about an hour after the impact. And yet the tektites fell into an active flood. The timing was all wrong.

This was not a paleontological question; it was a problem of geophysics and sedimentology. Smit was a sedimentologist, and another researcher whom DePalma shared his data with, Mark Richards, now of the University of Washington, was a geophysicist. At dinner one evening in Nagpur, India, where they were attending a conference, Smit and Richards talked about the problem, looked up a few papers, and later jotted down some rough calculations. It was immediately apparent to them that the KT tsunami would have arrived too late to capture the falling tektites; the wave would also have been too diminished by its long journey to account for the thirty-five-foot rise of water at Tanis. One of them proposed that the wave might have been created by a curious phenomenon known as a seiche. In large earthquakes, the shaking of the ground sometimes causes water in ponds, swimming pools, and bathtubs to slosh back and forth. Richards recalled that the 2011 Japanese earthquake produced bizarre, five-foot seiche waves in an absolutely calm Norwegian fjord thirty minutes after the quake, in a place unreachable by the tsunami.

Richards had previously estimated that the worldwide earthquake generated by the KT impact could have been 1,000 times stronger than the biggest earthquake ever experienced in human history. Using that gauge, he calculated that potent seismic waves would have arrived at Tanis six minutes, ten minutes, and thirteen minutes after the impact. (Different types of seismic waves travel at different speeds.) The brutal shaking would have been enough to trigger a large seiche, and the first blobs of glass would have started to rain down seconds or minutes afterward. They would have continued to fall as the seiche waves rolled in and out, depositing layer upon layer of sediment and each time sealing the tektites in place. The Tanis site, in short, did not span the first day of the impact: it probably recorded the first hour or so. This fact, if true, renders the site even more fabulous than previously thought. It is almost beyond credibility that a precise geological transcript of the most important sixty minutes of Earth's history could still exist millions of years later—a sort of high-speed, high-resolution video of the event recorded in fine layers of stone. DePalma said, "It's like finding the Holy Grail clutched in the bony fingers of Jimmy Hoffa, sitting on top of the Lost Ark." If Tanis had been closer to or farther from the impact point, this beautiful coincidence of timing could not have happened. "There's nothing in the world that's ever been seen like this," Richards told me.

*

One day 66 million years ago, life on Earth almost came to a shattering end. The world that emerged after the impact was a much simpler place. When sunlight finally broke through the haze, it illuminated a hellish landscape. The oceans were empty. The land was covered with drifting ash. The forests were charred stumps. The cold gave way to extreme heat as a greenhouse effect kicked in. Life mostly consisted of mats of algae and growths of fungus: for years after the impact, the Earth was covered with little other than ferns. Furtive, ratlike mammals lived in the gloomy understory.

But eventually life emerged and blossomed again, in new forms. The KT event continues to attract the interest of scientists in no small part because the ashen print it left on the planet is an existential reminder. "We wouldn't be here talking on the phone if that meteorite hadn't fallen," Smit told me, with a laugh. DePalma agreed. For the first 100 million years of their existence, before the asteroid struck, mammals scurried about the feet of the dinosaurs, amounting to little. "But when the dinosaurs were gone it freed them," DePalma said. In the next epoch, mammals underwent an explosion of adaptive radiation, evolving into a dazzling variety of forms, from tiny bats to gigantic titanotheres, from horses to whales, from fearsome creodonts to large-brained primates with hands that could grasp and minds that could see through time.

"We can trace our origins back to that event," DePalma said. "To actually be there at this site, to see it, to be connected to that day, is a special thing. This is the last day of the Cretaceous. When you go one layer up—the very next day—that's the Paleocene, that's the age of mammals, that's our age."

TIM REQUARTH

The Final Five Percent

FROM *Longreads*

WHEN THE MOTORCYCLE accident dealt my brother's brain an irreversible blow, he and his wife were living in their newly purchased farmhouse on the fringes of suburban Chicago. Conway* had been waiting to move out of the city's inner-ring suburbs for years, and each morning on the forested property he woke up exuberant. Shortly after moving in, he built an extraordinary tree house some sixty feet in the air, spanning two trees, with sliding joists under the floor to accommodate sway and a hammock to lie in during sunsets. He loved riding his motorcycle, and before work he'd sometimes take his bike out for a spin on the open roads just a few miles away. His wife, Caroline, loved antiques, and the area was full of shops. They were in their fifties and living in a house they planned to grow old in together. Then, after dinner on a fall day in 2007, Conway hopped on his Harley Softail Classic to go buy ice cream and cigarettes. A drunk driver barreled into him. Conway's left femur snapped and his skull struck the traffic-warmed asphalt, splattering blood all the way to the road's shoulder.

Conway's body was battered, but the real threat, the injury warranting a helicopter ride to the closest hospital with a neurosurgeon on call, was a hemorrhage beneath the subarachnoid membrane, a thin sheath of triple-helixed collagen fibers intertwined with blood vessels that protects the brain's private chemical harbor of cerebrospinal fluid from the open waters of the body's blood.

* Some names have been changed to protect the privacy of individuals

The sons of a doctor ourselves, my brother and I had heard stories about neurosurgeons called in at midnight, and those stories didn't have happy endings.

In the weeks after the accident, I watched Conway wake, recognize familiar faces, and begin to walk. Some signs of progress were cause for celebration; other developments were more worrisome. He'd rarely ever raised his voice at Caroline, but now he called her a "worthless cunt" and a "bitch." He was lewd to the nurses, exposing himself and laughing. When a speech therapist gently reminded him that she would return for another session later that afternoon, Conway retorted, "No you won't, because I'll be fucking you in my van outside!"

At first, the doctors assured us that this inappropriate behavior was a passing recovery phase of traumatic brain injury, or TBI. The lewd remarks eventually subsided, but his behavior took another ominous turn. "He always had a wild streak," Caroline told me. It's true that before the accident, Conway had loved flouting the rules. He'd cut across an empty park on his motorcycle to avoid traffic, or build a towering bonfire in his backyard for kicks. "But there was no violence," she said. After the accident, Conway flew into rages so vicious the hospital staff put a cage over his bed to contain him. When he finally left the hospital, Conway attempted to return to his former life, but he struggled to run his business and pay the bills. He and Caroline's marriage began to fray. Hopes for a full recovery waned, and eventually Conway's neuropsychologist confirmed our fears that the personality change might be permanent. "He's recovered 95 percent brain function," she said. "But the final 5 percent, it might never return."

Conway found himself with a lot of time alone, and the wooded property suddenly felt large and isolating. He started to miss his old suburban block, where he'd been the neighborhood handyman. At the farmhouse, no one came with leaf blowers to fix or chairs to mend. He had no one to show his remarkable tree house to. So one Saturday morning after a heavy snow, Conway drove his pickup truck back to the old neighborhood to plow everyone's driveways, just like he used to do. But there was one neighbor, Dale, whose driveway Conway didn't intend to plow. Years earlier —before the accident, before Conway moved away—their relationship had soured, escalating into a months-long quarrel that involved calls to the police, surveillance cameras (Dale), and Christmas lights in the shape of a giant middle finger (Conway).

Conway told me when he passed Dale's house that day, he thought, "What the hell, I'll let bygones be bygones, and plow his driveway too." But Dale was there, shoveling snow. It's not clear what happened next. According to the police report, Conway didn't plow Dale's driveway; he piled snow in front of it. Dale said Conway then tried to run him over with the snowplow. Dale said he had to grab the top of the plow blade to avoid being knocked over, clinging to it while Conway pushed him several feet through the snow. Dale jumped out of the way but was clipped on the head by the truck's mirror. Conway maintained his truck never touched Dale, but the police must have believed otherwise. Conway was charged with misdemeanor battery.

Time passed, but Conway couldn't move on. If it weren't for the brain injury, Conway later told me, "I wouldn't have done what I was about to do. I would have thought, 'This is over with, I don't care.'" But instead, he climbed up into his tree house and got to thinking about "that motherfucker Dale" and how he was going to "pay him back." Before the accident, Conway had never been violent. But now, all bets were off. "I thought it was right to kill him," he later told me. "He deserved it." Conway climbed down from the tree house, loaded a container of battery acid into the back of his truck, and headed to Dale's.

Dale wasn't home, but his surveillance camera filmed Conway, with his unmistakable limp from the injured femur, pouring acid on Dale's neatly manicured lawn and splashing it on his car, vapor swirling upward as acid reacted with paint. I've asked Conway whether his original intention was to attack Dale with the acid, or just to douse his yard and car. Conway vacillates; one day he would never hurt a person, another day he could. Most of the time, though, he tells me he simply felt compelled. "I both felt it was right," he said, "yet I knew it was wrong. I guess I didn't think too hard about it. I just thought, 'This is what I've got to do,' and did it. It was like I just couldn't stop myself." The next morning Dale called the police, and a week later, Conway was in jail.

When Conway was adopted as an infant by my father and his first wife in late 1955, they were told he was deaf. But then, after a few months in his new home, his mother noticed that he startled when she clapped her hands, something he hadn't done before. To this day, no one can explain why he started to respond to sound a year into his life—or what pre-adoption circumstances caused him to appear deaf in the first place.

Growing up, Conway struggled with school. He assumed the role of class clown, relishing the attention he'd draw every time he gathered a crowd in some muddy spot after a fresh rain to drop wriggling earthworms into his mouth, grinning while the other kids squealed. Conway's outlandishness made him popular with his peers, but teachers were less impressed. They nearly flunked him in every subject, making it clear to him that he was just another cutup with no promise. He managed to graduate from high school, but then drifted from city to city. He worked odd jobs and took some college classes in Idaho toward a nursing degree to prove his teachers wrong and dispel the unspoken suspicion of disability that had haunted him since infancy. Maybe Conway worried that these suspicions were true. Maybe that's why, when he had his first seizure as a young adult and was diagnosed with epilepsy, he wanted to keep it a secret.

Conway worked to get his epilepsy under control and a few years later moved to the small town of Cheney, Washington, to apprentice as a motorcycle mechanic. That's where he had his first motorcycle accident, when he was in his mid-twenties. One day, he was testing out a customer's bike when an elderly woman backed out of her driveway without seeing him. The trunk of her car clipped the motorcycle, catapulting him into the air. He crash-landed in a heap fifty feet down the road, leaving him in a wheelchair for weeks. He also suffered a brain injury that made it more difficult for him to concentrate and possibly worsened his epilepsy but—unlike the later drunk-driver collision that left his brain in shambles—didn't seem to change his personality.

After months of rehab and a full physical recovery, Conway left Washington, eventually moving to Chicago in the early 1980s to try his hand at trading commodities. A friend introduced him to Caroline, who seemed different from the other women he knew. She owned a condo in a tony suburb, had lived in Europe, loved to cook elaborate meals, and was studying commodity trading in her spare time while managing the accounting for a film company. Conway felt he'd hit the jackpot—she didn't treat him like the women who had loved him before, women who had left him because they dismissed him as too wild, too unstable, and too stubborn to change. "Conway was different from the other guys," Caroline told me. "He was fun. He would try anything. I loved dancing and he danced like you wouldn't believe—that's to say, terribly. But it didn't stop him. I loved it." Conway's commodity trading effort failed to get off the ground, so he bought a Snap-on tool franchise—a perfect fit for his automotive know-how and entrepreneurial spirit. Caroline landed a job in the R&D department of a major corporation. The future was bright, and three years later they were married. In Caroline, Conway had finally found someone who realized that his good traits outweighed his bad ones.

When I was a teenager and Conway was in his forties, our father's mind fogged over with dementia and Conway became the closest thing I had to a dad. On a family vacation, he showed me how to drive on country back roads before I turned sixteen (I hit a mailbox). A few years later, he taught me how to ride a motorcycle in a parking lot (this time, a tree). Conway didn't see the point of many social conventions, which as a teenager I found refreshing. When he locked himself out of the house one night, he just shattered one of the door's glass panes and fixed it the next day. He used a circular saw to cut pork roasts. I remember him once crawling under the table at an upscale restaurant to play hide-and-seek with a bored kid. After college, he bought me a motorcycle and we would take weekend camping trips to the northern reaches of Michigan.

By 2006, a year before his personality-shattering collision, Conway and Caroline were twenty years into their marriage, living in a two-story house in the suburbs filled with furniture Conway made after teaching himself carpentry. Conway's business had been decidedly a success—his office walls were decorated with plaques for some of Snap-on's top sales awards—and Caroline was approaching the end of her career. That spring, they bought their nineteenth-century farmhouse and prepared to retire. That's when Conway hopped on his motorcycle one evening to get ice cream and cigarettes and didn't come back.

My first day of neuroanatomy class was just weeks after Conway's accident. While he lay in the hospital in restraints, lashing out indiscriminately, I'd just begun graduate school in neuroscience—a career I was pursuing because I thought it would help me make sense of our father's dementia. And now I thought it would help me make sense of my brother's brain injury. I donned a smock in the chilled air of the basement dissection laboratory and fished a rubbery gray-brown brain out of a bucket of foul-smelling formaldehyde. After placing the brain on a metal table, I ran my gloved hand across the rounded corrugations and traced their grooves, feeling a slight pressure as the clefts parted to allow my finger to pass. I found the precentral sulcus, a deep fissure roughly dividing the prefrontal cortex from the rest of the brain, and followed it forward to the inferior frontal sulcus, a lesser cleft demarcating the prefrontal cortex's outermost third. I paused on this region. It seemed familiar. It was the dorsolateral prefrontal cortex. I had my finger on one of the brain regions damaged when Conway's skull collided with the pavement.

The dorsolateral prefrontal cortex is part of the frontal lobe, a massive chunk of tissue behind our eyes involved in so much of what makes us human: cognition, movement, memory, personality. The frontal lobe is also the brain area injured in one of the most famous cases in neuroscience. In the forested hills of Vermont on a fall day in 1848, twenty-five-year-old Phineas Gage crouched over a hole, holding a thirteen-pound iron rod. The foreman of a team excavating for a railroad, Gage was preparing to blast away rock by filling a hole with an explosive powder, piling on sand, and tamping it down. His three-and-a-half-foot-long iron tamping rod, tapered to a javelin's point, must have hit a rock, sparked, and ignited the exposed powder, sending the rod flying. It sailed through an inventory of body parts I would soon be quizzed on— the zygomatic arch of his left cheek, the left orbit, the cranial vault, the Sylvian fissure—before piercing his frontal lobes and exiting the top of his skull. The rod landed sixty feet away on the forest floor, "greased with the matter of the brain." The exact anatomical damage Gage suffered is difficult to reconstruct (though neuroscientists have tried) and far more extensive than what my brother suffered. But there is little doubt that the iron rod penetrated Gage's frontal lobes, the same region damaged in my brother's brain.

According to his doctor, John Martyn Harlow, Gage had been "a great favorite" with his men and in possession of "a well-balanced mind . . . a shrewd, smart business man." After the accident, he was "fitful, irreverent, indulging at times in the grossest profanity . . . impatient of restraint or advice when it conflicts with his desires . . . at times pertinaciously obstinent, yet capricious and vacillating, devising many plans of future operation, which are no sooner arranged than they are abandoned." His doctor observed that, "The equilibrium . . . between his intellectual faculties and his animal propensities, seems to have been destroyed." His friends simply declared that he was "no longer Gage." Textbooks indicate that Gage then drifted from job to job, including appearances at Barnum's American Museum in New York with his iron rod by his side. He confabulated, brawled, drank, and acted impulsively, showing little concern for the future. About a dozen years later, Gage ended up under the care of his family in San Francisco, and after a series of sudden convulsions at the dinner table, died.

Gage's case has since taken on mythic proportions in neuroscience as the first to link brain damage to personality change. And because Gage became impulsive, his story more specifically suggested that the frontal lobes were the seat of self-control.

As I watched Conway fail to return to his previous life, phrases from Gage's report ticker-taped across my mind ("impatient of restraint . . . capricious and vacillating"). Conway and Caroline's relationship strained because of Conway's volatility ("fitful, irreverent, indulging at times in the grossest profanity"); his once-successful business ("a shrewd, smart business man") slowly fell apart. Conway had always had a devil-may-care attitude, but the brain damage intensified it. He became far more impulsive, making poor decisions even when he could clearly articulate the pros and cons of each choice ("the equilibrium . . . between his intellectual faculties and his animal propensities . . . destroyed"). I foresaw a life, like Gage's, filled with drifting and frustration.

By January 2008, three months after the accident, Conway had come home. He had physically improved and was eager to return to work—with good reason. He hadn't been working during the months of recovery, and as a small-business owner without any employees, that meant no revenue. Then, in the midst of the financial crisis, Caroline's R&D job was eliminated, so she was let go after twenty-four years, just months before she would have been eligible for full retirement benefits. They had to borrow to cover the farmhouse's mortgage payments.

They came up with a plan: Caroline would drive the Snap-on tool truck and accompany Conway on his route. Conway's customers greeted him with cards, packs of cigarettes, *Playboy* magazines. They opened doors when they saw him limping. But the goodwill soon began to fade. Customers would request tools and Conway would forget to order them, or bring the wrong ones. He mixed up accounts, overcharging some customers and forgetting to charge others. When customers would challenge him, Conway didn't handle mistakes the way the old Conway would, with jokes and a little store credit. He became defensive, calling his customers idiots. He would skip stops on his route because of a petty quarrel with a single mechanic in the garage. Some days he never showed up to any stop at all.

Caroline attempted to mitigate the damage by helping out with the bookkeeping and trying to repair his deteriorating relationships, but he was too much to contain and the business too new to her. Soon, almost no one was buying tools from Conway anymore. Increasingly frustrated, he started taking it out on Caroline, often yelling at her in front of his few remaining customers. One night at home, Caroline told me, Conway hit her. It was only a matter of time before his twenty-three-year-old business shuttered. Both Conway and Caroline were now unemployed. Foreclosure threatened.

In June 2008, after a decade of dementia, our father passed away, and Conway's downward spiral accelerated. He began driving his pickup truck and riding a motorcycle again, without a license or insurance. On the way to our father's funeral, he was stopped for going thirty miles per hour over the speed limit with an open bottle of Kahlúa in the car. Later that year, the day after Christmas, he got a DUI. Pre-accident Conway hadn't been a heavy drinker. But over the next several months, Conway drank ferociously and drove recklessly. One night, he came home bloody and belligerent at 2 a.m., his pickup truck abandoned in a nearby field with a broken windshield—events he never could explain. A year after the funeral, almost to the day, Conway was on his way to Dale's with a canister full of acid.

No one questioned that Conway decided to load battery acid into his truck and drive to Dale's. In this strict sense, Conway alone was responsible for his actions. But what ultimately *caused* him to act was a more complicated question, and I found the answer depended on where I decided to look. Was the most recent brain injury responsible? Or did this one compound the effects of the previous brain injury suffered two decades earlier, tipping him over the edge into criminal behavior? Did the neurological toll of a lifetime of epilepsy figure in? What about the circumstances that caused him to appear disabled at birth? Were there any genetic factors? Could you make a case that the lack of support beyond three months in hospital rehab caused the crime? That he wouldn't have done it if the financial crisis of 2008 hadn't led to Caroline's job loss and their foreclosure, stirring up Conway's anger and sense of injustice? It seems futile to sort out these complexities and determine the degree to which an individual is responsible for an action. And yet, this is exactly what the criminal justice system does when assigning blame.

"Blameworthiness should be removed from the legal argot," writes neuroscientist David Eagleman, one of the most vocal proponents of what he calls a "biologically informed jurisprudence." Instead of haggling over the degree of culpability, he continues, "we should focus on what to do, *moving forward,* with an accused lawbreaker." A more humane legal system will "parlay biological understanding into customized rehabilitation, viewing criminal behavior the way we understand other medical conditions such as epilepsy, schizophrenia, and depression—conditions that now allow the seeking and giving of help." By reimagining crime as a form of disease, he proposes "statistically based sentencing," one day using brain scans to confine those most likely to reoffend and rehabilitate those most likely to change.

The neuroscience of crime has flourished in recent years. Some researchers have claimed that psychopaths' brains have defects in what has been called the paralimbic system. Other researchers have claimed that reduced activation in areas of the prefrontal cortex and hypothalamus may contribute to pedophilia. Yet another team concluded that perpetrators of domestic violence had "higher activation in the anterior and posterior cingulate cortex and in the middle prefrontal cortex and a decreased activation in the superior prefrontal cortex." Scientists have posited telltale neural signatures for "intent" and "recklessness." As a graduate student, I felt emboldened by this knowledge and dismissive even of the law's scientific ignorance.

And already, neuroscience had been making its way into the courts. A study by Duke bioethicist Nita Farahany revealed that neuroscience evidence was twice as likely to appear in a judicial opinion in 2008 as compared to just three years earlier. The Supreme Court cited developmental neuroscience to prohibit the death penalty for crimes committed as a juvenile. Mental health courts and veterans courts, which make accommodations for people with brain trauma and PTSD, were cropping up around the country.

While Conway was in court in 2009, I was particularly taken with a pair of new brain-imaging studies suggesting a network of brain regions responsible for self-control. In one study, researchers at the California Institute of Technology placed individuals already on a diet in brain scanners and asked them to choose between a healthy snack like a granola bar and an unhealthy snack, like a cookie. When a dieter refrained from eating junk food, activity in the dorsolateral prefrontal cortex revved up, but when a dieter gave in to temptation, the dorsolateral prefrontal cortex remained conspicuously quiet. The researchers concluded that the dorsolateral prefrontal cortex acted as a taskmaster, tempering activity in more appetitive brain regions so the dieters could exert self-control. These results corroborated another 2009 study observing brain activity in people with borderline personality disorder who also had intermittent explosive disorder. In that study, the individuals performed a laboratory task designed to provoke aggressive behavior while placed in a brain scanner. Impulsive individuals showed increased activation in brain regions involved in emotion and aggression, such as the amygdala, but less activation—again—in the dorsolateral prefrontal cortex. The conclusion of that study was that the dorsolateral prefrontal cortex was the inhibiting brain region, and when it wasn't active enough, impulses went unregulated.

The dorsolateral prefrontal cortex was one of the regions injured in my brother (and likely Phineas Gage), so it struck me as logical to conclude that the inhibitory centers in Conway's brain had become damaged, making it more challenging for him to suppress certain behaviors despite understanding their long-term negative consequences. In other words, Conway's brain damage made him unable to resist committing the crime. It was just a matter of getting a judge or jury to understand. Even if the brain injury could not eliminate Conway's legal responsibility, perhaps it could spare him harsh punishment.

Before Conway's hearing, I offered my amateur legal opinions to his lawyer, along with my materials on the science of self-control. I waxed poetic about how neuroscience was about to revolutionize our legal system, and how we could be a part of that revolution. The lawyer wasn't impressed. "No one will take any of this into account in a case like this," he said matter-of-factly. He instead advised Conway to plead guilty to criminal damage to property, a Class 4 felony, as well as to the misdemeanor battery charge from the snowplow incident, making a case to be released on time served in jail. The stakes were high. If the judge didn't agree to the release, Conway could face prison time.

In court, Conway sat at a bowed wooden table, jumpsuited and shackled, looking a little angry, a little ashamed. Although the lawyer had ignored the stacks of neuroscience evidence I had offered, he'd brought up the brain injury at an earlier competency hearing, arguing that Conway, while not innocent, was "slipping through the cracks" and was "a person who needs all the help the system can afford him." The lawyer felt confident the judge would be lenient since Conway had already spent several months in jail. My jaw dropped when the judge handed Conway a two-year sentence in the state penitentiary. Studies estimate that anywhere from 25 percent to 87 percent of incarcerated people report having suffered a TBI at some point in their lives, as compared to 8.5 percent of the general population. Many of them, like Conway, have attention problems, memory problems, and behavioral problems like impulsivity, irritability, and anger that make it difficult for them to follow orders, get along with other prisoners, and then, after release, to keep jobs, homes, families. But my hard-earned knowledge of the brain appeared to be legally useless, Conway's brain injury legally irrelevant.

Conway's neuropsychologist wasn't surprised he ended up in prison. "It's just horrendous," she said. "But I don't think it's an unusual outcome." Once brain-injury patients finish outpatient rehabilitation at the hospital—which covers basic physical and cognitive therapy—they get little additional support. "It's not good what happens after rehab ends," the neuropsychologist said. "It's like these people fall off a cliff."

If the end of rehab was Conway's cliff, prison was the hard ground at the end of his fall. The guards seemed to mistake his memory and attention problems for defiance. Conway and Caroline told me his outbursts provoked others in the prison. Conway told me he was beaten up, which I could only imagine would worsen his brain injuries. Before prison, Conway had been prescribed an experimental epilepsy drug because it was the only medication that controlled his seizures; he continued taking it even after the revelation of deadly side effects led to an FDA recommendation that it be pulled from the market except to treat the most intractable cases. But the prison physician switched to a cheaper drug over Conway's objections, and he began having seizures—which aren't good for the brain, either. Conway began to break down. One day, in anger, he punched his cell wall so hard it fractured his hand. A few weeks later, he was found wandering the showers, pants around his ankles. He was unresponsive, his eyes staring blankly into space. Later that day he had a five-minute grand mal seizure in his cell. He was placed in an isolation cell for monitoring, where he continued to have seizures. At one point they had to use a defibrillator to reset his heart rhythm. The medical staff's assessment of Conway's nervous breakdown and obliterative, seizure-filled day? "Ineffective coping."

In June 2010, after serving four more months (because of time served in jail), Conway was released on parole; two and a half years after the accident, he seemed more brain-damaged than ever. Caroline was too frightened to pick him up, so he was sent to a homeless shelter. That same day, he had another seizure and was taken to the hospital. He tried to call Caroline, and, on July 4, she finally came to see him at the shelter. They went for a ride in the car, and while heading north on the Edens Expressway, she told him she wanted a divorce. Conway was devastated. According to Caroline, he grabbed the steering wheel and tried to run them off the four-lane highway. She regained control, but Conway opened the door and tried to jump out of the speeding car. Caroline rushed him to the emergency room, where he was committed to the psych ward. Medical records indicate that when released, he said he would commit suicide by throwing himself in front of a train.

I've always wondered what might have become of Conway if, after the injury, he'd had the support he needed, rather than just gradually losing what little stability he had. Near the end of my graduate studies, I learned that Phineas Gage may have recovered more than textbooks had led me to believe. According to Malcolm MacMillan's *An Odd Kind of Fame: Stories of Phineas Gage,* little in the historical record suggests that Gage's impulsivity or aggression lasted for more than a short period following his accident. Only a few years after the injury Gage began working in a New Hampshire livery stable, then moved to Chile to work as a stagecoach driver for seven years. His ability to hold down these jobs is highly inconsistent with the Gage presented in textbooks, and MacMillan speculates that the structured environment of steady work may have helped Gage improve. Gage's real story might not be about losing self-control, but how to regain it. A modern American prison, although technically structured, is probably not the kind of environment MacMillan envisioned.

"The first tragedy was that Conway got hit in the head," Caroline later told me. "The second was the one the system inflicted."

A "biologically informed" legal system as imagined by neuroscientists like Eagleman was the one I had wanted for my brother. It had seemed to me that the law was, at best, slow to adapt to new scientific advances, and, at worst, hopelessly obtuse—and in its ignorance responsible for my brother's fate. But is it a good idea to reduce *all* criminal behavior to misfiring neurons? It's one thing to claim a brain abnormality—such as my brother's TBI—contributed to criminal behavior. It's another thing to say that if someone commits a crime, then it must have been the result of a brain abnormality—which is exactly what scientists like Eagleman are saying when they reimagine crime as a form of neurological disease.

Biological theories of crime have a long and troubling history. In 1876, Cesare Lombroso, sometimes called the father of modern criminology, wrote an influential book called *Criminal Man.* In an account later told by his daughter, he was dissecting a bank robber's brain and noticed a "hollow," like those found in the brains of "the lower types of apes, rodents, and birds." The discovery, she wrote, hit him like "a flash of light": criminals were born, not made. He concluded that the criminal brain "differs essentially from that of normal individuals," strongly resembling that of "primitive races." For many, "primitive races" meant people of color, making it reasonable to assume that anyone who was not white had a higher probability of innate criminality.

And biological theories of crime have an inevitable end point: biological solutions. Lombroso's theory contributed to the scientific rationale for eugenicists to propose the "legal, authorized elimination" of what they viewed as born criminals. In the early to mid-twentieth century the United States government forcibly sterilized at least 60,000 people deemed criminal, "feeble-minded," or sexually deviant (an expansive list that included people who masturbated, queer people, and women who had children while unmarried). People of color, immigrants, and poor women were disproportionately targeted. In 1935, Antonio Egas Moniz performed twenty surgeries destroying the frontal lobes of people "who had previously been violent." His procedure—the lobotomy—transformed them into patients who were "calm, tractable, and generally easier to manage." In 1936, an American named Walter Jackson Freeman II toured the country in what was later dubbed the "lobotomobile," charging $25 to scramble people's frontal lobes with an ice pick inserted through the eye socket. By 1949, when Moniz won the Nobel Prize for his procedure, 10,000 lobotomies had been performed in the United States. As recently as the 1960s, in the midst of nationwide race riots, prominent doctors suggested the civil unrest was caused in part by "brain dysfunction in the rioters" and called for surgical solutions for "the violent slum-dweller." In 1972, it was revealed that the California Department of Corrections had recently turned to neurosurgery to address what it called "the problem of the aggressive, destructive inmate." Using a makeshift metal head restraint built by prison craftsmen, the DOC implanted electrodes in the brains of three prisoners, destroying their amygdalae. I wonder if in another era Conway, as an out-of-control teenager and then a troubled young adult, would have been one of Freeman's patients. If he had been an "urban rioter" in the 1960s, would he have been a candidate for an electrode?

Trapped by the logic of biologizing crime, scientists today also propose biological solutions. Using the example of a pedophile, Eagleman says that rather than reflexively incarcerating people who act on sexual urges toward children, scientists should instead consider neurofeedback treatments to "give more control to neural populations that care about long-term consequences—to inhibit impulsivity, to encourage reflection." Perhaps the most incorrigible offenders should be confined, but with a "prefrontal workout," he claims, in a flourish of neuro-optimism, they can harness "the natural mechanisms of brain plasticity to help the brain help itself. It's a tune-up rather than a product recall."

Eagleman eschews invasive interventions, but others aren't so reticent to relive the past. Researchers have called for deep brain stimulation as "a treatment strategy" to reduce sex drive in people with "abnormalities" in sexual urges who are at "a serious risk of sexual offending." In this case, the troubling twist is these patients would be subjected to the procedure *before* committing a crime. In 2013, researchers inserted probes into the posterior hypothalamic regions of seven men to reduce "aggression and disruptive bouts." Although deep brain stimulation, which can be toggled off, isn't as irreversible as lobotomy or ablation, any biological treatment essentializes criminality to an individual, turning what should be a verb (committing a crime) into a noun (a criminal).

The neuroscientific legal revolution I'd been so enthusiastic about began to make me feel deeply uneasy, and made me wonder if I'd been woefully naive. Because I had wanted courtroom neuroscience to save my brother, I avoided considering its implications. I'd never questioned science's inheritance of what society considered "normal" and "abnormal" behavior. But it's clear that what's "abnormal" or "criminal" shifts over time, culture, and place. Although pedophilia seems inherently criminal to us, men in ancient Greece had socially acceptable sexual relations with adolescent boys. Would they show the same patterns of brain activity as modern-day pedophiles? If they had brain scanners in ancient Greece, would those patterns be declared "normal"?

When it comes to criminal behavior, what brain activity is normal or abnormal is not a biological question. It's a question of social norms, and this is a fatal flaw in the neuroscience of crime. Researchers begin with social definitions of "normal" and "abnormal" behavior, then find distinct patterns of brain activity that match up with those behaviors. They speculate that abnormal brain activity caused the abnormal behavior they defined at the outset. In a circular process, scientists transmute social mores into natural science.

I don't think neuroscientists have bad intentions; I think Eagleman truly believes a "biologically informed jurisprudence" will lead to a more humane justice system. But he fails to grapple with how easily science can absorb prevailing prejudices to justify oppressive forces rather than fight them. After learning more about the troubling history of neuroscience and the law, I had to question not only what I wanted to be true about Conway, but also what I wanted to be true about neuroscience. I realized that many neuroscientists, for all our sophisticated understanding of the electrical properties of neurons, are naive when it comes to how the field might affect complex social problems—and equally naive when it comes to how social norms might shape science. I felt adrift, sensing a fissure in the previously coherent worldview whose explanatory power had given me so much comfort. My experiments became less meaningful; the academic battles over minute details of brain function felt quaint. After a decade of training, I left it all behind.

My most recent visit to Conway, now sixty-five years old, was almost three years ago, nearly a decade after the drunk driver left him mangled on bloody concrete. He and Caroline had gotten back together and were living in a modest house in the Chicago suburbs, where Conway greeted me with a toothy grin and a silver-streaked goatee. As he struggled to open the front door, I noticed his hands —the hands that could fix motorcycles, build furniture, mend windows, the hands that knew when to apply force and when to work delicately. Three fingers were gone, stubs now, his right hand a pincer of thumb and forefinger. He had accidentally chopped them off with a table saw. Following him into the living room, I noticed his limp was much more pronounced. A year earlier, he had accidentally set himself on fire while using a lighter to burn away the frayed ends of the jeans he was wearing; Caroline saw his pants in flames on the lawn and rushed to put them out with a garden hose. Conway's leg was burned so severely that his Achilles tendon was exposed.

Reminders of their former life were scattered about their new home: the wooden hearth from the farmhouse was propped up in the living room, and what was left of Conway's tool collection hung in the kitchen. Although Conway can still lose his temper, that happens less often than it once did. Thanks to powerful medication—its own form of biological intervention—Conway has become a gentler version of himself. That night, he placed a glass of water on the nightstand near my bed, and replaced it with a cup of coffee first thing in the morning. He was friendly with the neighbors, but had trouble following conversations. He filled in memory gaps with fantasy. In quiet moments, which were most of Conway's moments, he was depressed. Sometimes, he contemplated suicide.

For reasons I still can't grasp, Conway—a brain-damaged burn victim with seven fingers—never could qualify for disability. Caroline was managing their day-to-day lives while working a low-wage job as a medical courier, picking up extra shifts when she could to offset Conway's ongoing medical and legal expenses. The family pitched in for housing and other expenses. "No matter what happens, I'll still be there for Conway," Caroline said. "Even if it kills me." She knows that without her constant care, Conway would either return to prison, get himself killed, or both. "I mean, if I leave, I might as well take a gun and shoot him." But she also struggles daily with the injustice of the situation foisted upon her: "This is my prison sentence."

Conway knows his actions contributed to the bear-trap circumstances of their lives. He struggles with where to place the blame. "Some days I'm really mad at the driver, and some days I'm mad that I didn't wear a helmet," he said. "Some days I'm mad at the judge for sending me to prison, and some days I'm mad because I went over to Dale's in the first place." He sighed and took out rolling papers and a pouch of tobacco. With his newly disabled hand, it was difficult for him to position the tobacco in the crease of the paper.

"Mostly I'm just mad that Caroline has to go through all this." He looked at me and shook his head. A pile of fine brown tobacco leaves littered the floor by his feet. "I don't know how to explain it —one moment I think it's my fault for everything, and I get really down. And the next I think it's not my fault for anything, and I get really angry. And then," he laughed, "I just stop thinking at all."

JOHN SEABROOK

The Next Word

FROM *The New Yorker*

I GLANCED DOWN AT my left thumb, still resting on the Tab key. *What have I done?* Had my computer become my cowriter? That's one small step forward for artificial intelligence, but was it also one step backward for my own?

The skin prickled on the back of my neck, an involuntary reaction to what roboticists call the "uncanny valley"—the space between flesh and blood and a too-human machine.

For several days, I had been trying to ignore the suggestions made by Smart Compose, a feature that Google introduced, in May 2018, to the one and a half billion people who use Gmail —roughly a fifth of the human population. Smart Compose suggests endings to your sentences as you type them. Based on the words you've written, and on the words that millions of Gmail users followed those words with, "predictive text" guesses where your thoughts are likely to go and, to save you time, wraps up the sentence for you, appending the AI's suggestion, in gray letters, to the words you've just produced. Hit Tab, and you've saved yourself as many as twenty keystrokes—and, in my case, composed a sentence with an AI for the first time.

Paul Lambert, who oversees Smart Compose for Google, told me that the idea for the product came in part from the writing of code—the language that software engineers use to program computers. Code contains long strings of identical sequences, so engineers rely on shortcuts, which they call "code completers." Google thought that a similar technology could reduce the time spent writing emails for business users of its G Suite software, although it made the product available to the general public too. A quarter of the average office worker's day is now taken up with email, according to a study by McKinsey. Smart Compose saves users altogether two billion keystrokes a week.

One can opt out of Smart Compose easily enough, but I had chosen not to, even though it frequently distracted me. I was fascinated by the way the AI seemed to know what I was going to write. Perhaps because writing is my vocation, I am inclined to consider my sentences, even in a humble email, in some way a personal expression of my original thought. It was therefore disconcerting how frequently the AI was able to accurately predict my intentions, often when I was in midsentence, or even earlier. Sometimes the machine seemed to have a better idea than I did.

And yet until now I'd always finished my thought by typing the sentence to a full stop, as though I were defending humanity's exclusive right to writing, an ability unique to our species. I will gladly let Google predict the fastest route from Brooklyn to Boston, but if I allowed its algorithms to navigate to the end of my sentences how long would it be before the machine started thinking for me? I had remained on the near shore of a digital Rubicon, represented by the Tab key. On the far shore, I imagined, was a strange new land where machines do the writing, and people communicate in emojis, the modern version of the pictographs and hieroglyphs from which our writing system emerged, 5,000 years ago.

True, I had sampled Smart Reply, a sister technology of Smart Compose that offers a menu of three automated responses to a sender's email, as suggested by its contents. "Got it!" I clicked, replying to detailed comments from my editor on an article I thought was finished. (I didn't really get it, but that choice wasn't on the menu.) I felt a little guilty right afterward, as though I'd replied with a form letter, or, worse, a fake personal note. A few days later, in response to a long email from me, I received a "Got it!" from the editor. *Really?*

Along with almost everyone else who texts or tweets, with the possible exception of the president of the United States, I have long relied on spell-checkers and auto-correctors, which are limited applications of predictive text. I'm awful at spelling, as was my father; the inability to spell has a genetic link, according to multiple studies. Before spell-checkers, I used spelling rules I learned in elementary school ("'I' before 'E' except after 'C,'" but with fear-

ful exceptions) and folksy mnemonics ("'cemetery': all at 'E's").
Now that spell-checkers are ubiquitous in word-processing software, I've stopped even trying to spell anymore—I just get close
enough to let the machine guess the word I'm struggling to form.
Occasionally, I stump the AI.

But Smart Compose goes well beyond spell-checking. It isn't correcting words I've already formed in my head; it's coming up with
them for me, by harnessing the predictive power of deep learning,
a subset of machine learning. Machine learning is the sophisticated method of computing probabilities in large data sets, and
it underlies virtually all the extraordinary AI advances of recent
years, including those in navigation, image recognition, search,
game playing, and autonomous vehicles. In this case, it's making
billions of lightning-fast probability calculations about word patterns from a year's worth of emails sent from Gmail.com. (It does
not include emails sent by G Suite customers.)

"At any point in what you're writing, we have a guess about what
the next x number of words will be," Lambert explained. To do
that, the AI factors a number of different probability calculations
into the "state" of the email you're in the middle of writing. "The
state is informed by a number of things," Lambert went on, "including everything you have written in that email up until now, so
every time you insert a new word the system updates the state and
reprocesses the whole thing." The day of the week you're writing
the email is one of the things that inform the state. "So," he said,
"if you write 'Have a' on a Friday, it's much more likely to predict
'good weekend' than if it's on a Tuesday."

Although Smart Compose generally limits itself to predicting
the next phrase or two, the AI could ramble on longer. The trade-
off, Lambert noted, is accuracy. "The farther out from the original
text we go, the less accurate the prediction."

Finally, I crossed my Rubicon. The sentence itself was a pedestrian affair. Typing an email to my son, I began "I am p—" and was
about to write "pleased" when predictive text suggested "proud of
you." I am proud of you. Wow, I don't say that enough. And clearly
Smart Compose thinks that's what most fathers in my state say to
their sons in emails. I hit Tab. No biggie.

And yet, sitting there at the keyboard, I could feel the uncanny
valley prickling my neck. It wasn't that Smart Compose had guessed

correctly where my thoughts were headed—in fact, it hadn't. The creepy thing was that the machine was more thoughtful than I was.

In February, OpenAI, an artificial-intelligence company, announced that the release of the full version of its AI writer, called GPT-2—a kind of supercharged version of Smart Compose—would be delayed, because the machine was too good at writing. The announcement struck critics as a grandiose publicity stunt (on Twitter, the insults flew), but it was in keeping with the company's somewhat paradoxical mission, which is both to advance research in artificial intelligence as rapidly as possible and to prepare for the potential threat posed by superintelligent machines that haven't been taught to "love humanity," as Greg Brockman, OpenAI's chief technology officer, put it to me.

OpenAI began in 2015, as a nonprofit founded by Brockman, formerly the CTO of the payment startup Stripe; Elon Musk, of Tesla; Sam Altman, of Y Combinator; and Ilya Sutskever, who left Google Brain to become OpenAI's chief scientist. The tech tycoons Peter Thiel and Reid Hoffman, among others, provided seed money. The founders' idea was to endow a nonprofit with the expertise and the resources to be competitive with private enterprise, while at the same time making its discoveries available as open source—so long as it was safe to do so—thus potentially heading off a situation where a few corporations reap the almost immeasurable rewards of a vast new world. As Brockman told me, a superintelligent machine would be of such immense value, with so much wealth accruing to any company that owned one, that it could "break capitalism" and potentially realign the world order. "We want to ensure its benefits are distributed as widely as possible," Brockman said.

OpenAI's projects to date include a gaming AI that earlier this year beat the world's best human team at Dota 2, a multiplayer online strategy game. Open-world computer games offer AI designers almost infinite strategic possibilities, making them valuable testing grounds. The AI had mastered Dota 2 by playing its way through tens of thousands of years' worth of possible scenarios a gamer might encounter, learning how to win through trial and error. The company also developed the software for a robotic hand that can teach itself to manipulate objects of different shapes and sizes without any human programming. (Traditional robotic appendages used in factories can execute only hard-coded moves.) GPT-2, like these other projects, was designed to advance technology—in this case, to push forward the development of a machine designed to write prose as well as, or better than, most people can.

Although OpenAI says that it remains committed to sharing the benefits of its research, it became a limited partnership in March, to attract investors, so that the company has the financial resources to keep up with the exponential growth in "compute"— the fuel powering the neural networks that underpin deep learning. These "neural nets" are made of what are, essentially, dimmer switches that are networked together, so that, like the neurons in our brains, they can excite one another when they are stimulated. In the brain, the stimulation is a small amount of electrical current; in machines, it's streams of data. Training neural nets the size of GPT-2's is expensive, in part because of the energy costs incurred in running and cooling the sprawling terrestrial "server farms" that power the cloud. A group of researchers at UMass Amherst, led by Emma Strubell, conducted a recent study showing that the carbon footprint created by training a gigantic neural net is roughly equal to the lifetime emissions of five automobiles.

OpenAI says it will need to invest billions of dollars in the coming years. The compute is growing even faster than the rate suggested by Moore's Law, which holds that the processing power of computers doubles every two years. Innovations in chip design, network architecture, and cloud-based resources are making the total available compute ten times larger each year—as of 2018, it was 300,000 times larger than it was in 2012.

As a result, neural nets can do all sorts of things that futurists have long predicted for computers but couldn't execute until recently. Machine translation, an enduring dream of AI researchers, was, until three years ago, too error-prone to do much more than approximate the meaning of words in another language. Since switching to neural machine translation, in 2016, Google Translate has begun to replace human translators in certain domains, like medicine. A recent study published in *Annals of Internal Medicine* found Google Translate accurate enough to rely on in translating non-English medical studies into English for the systematic reviews that health care decisions are based on.

Ilya Sutskever, OpenAI's chief scientist, is, at thirty-three, one of the most highly regarded of the younger researchers in AI. When we met, he was wearing a T-shirt that said THE FUTURE WILL NOT BE SUPERVISED. Supervised learning, which used to be the way neural nets were trained, involved labeling the training data—a labor-intensive process. In unsupervised learning, no labeling is required, which makes the method scalable. Instead of learning to identify cats from pictures labeled "cat," for example, the machine learns to recognize feline pixel patterns, through trial and error.

Sutskever told me, of GPT-2, "Give it the compute, give it the data, and it will do amazing things," his eyes wide with wonder, when I met him and Brockman at their company's San Francisco headquarters this summer. "This stuff is like—" Sutskever paused, searching for the right word. "It's like *alchemy!*"

It was startling to hear a computer scientist on the leading edge of AI research compare his work to a medieval practice performed by men who were as much magicians as scientists. Didn't alchemy end with the Enlightenment?

GPT-2 runs on a neural net that is ten times larger than Open-AI's first language model, GPT (short for Generative Pretrained Transformer). After the announcement that OpenAI was delaying a full release, it made three less powerful versions available on the Web—one in February, the second in May, and the third in August. Dario Amodei, a computational neuroscientist who is the company's director of research, explained to me the reason for withholding the full version: "Until now, if you saw a piece of writing, it was like a certificate that a human was involved in it. Now it is no longer a certificate that an actual human is involved."

That sounded something like my Rubicon moment with my son. What part of "I am proud of you" was human—intimate father-son stuff—and what part of it was machine-generated text? It will become harder and harder to tell the difference.

Scientists have varying ideas about how we acquire spoken language. Many favor an evolutionary, biological basis for our verbal skills over the view that we are tabulae rasae, but all agree that we learn language largely from listening. Writing is certainly a learned skill, not an instinct—if anything, as years of professional experience have taught me, the instinct is to scan Twitter, vacuum, complete the *Times* crossword, or do practically anything else to avoid having to write. Unlike writing, speech doesn't require multiple drafts before it "works." Uncertainty, anxiety, dread, and mental fatigue all attend writing; talking, on the other hand, is easy, often pleasant, and feels mostly unconscious.

A recent exhibition on the written word at the British Library dates the emergence of cuneiform writing to the fourth millennium BCE, in Mesopotamia. Trade had become too complex for people to remember all the contractual details, so they began to put contracts in writing. In the millennia that followed, literary craft evolved into much more than an enhanced form of accounting. Socrates, who famously disapproved of literary production for its deleterious (thank you, spell-checker) effect on memory, called writing "visible speech"—we know that because his student Plato wrote it down after the master's death. A more contemporary definition, developed by the linguist Linda Flower and the psychologist John Hayes, is "cognitive rhetoric"—thinking in words.

In 1981, Flower and Hayes devised a theoretical model for the brain as it is engaged in writing, which they called the cognitive-process theory. It has endured as the paradigm of literary composition for almost forty years. The previous, "stage model" theory had posited that there were three distinct stages involved in writing—planning, composing, and revising—and that a writer moved through each in order. To test that theory, the researchers asked people to speak aloud any stray thoughts that popped into their heads while they were in the composing phase, and recorded the hilariously chaotic results. They concluded that, far from being a stately progression through distinct stages, writing is a much messier situation, in which all three stages interact with one another simultaneously, loosely overseen by a mental entity that Flower and Hayes called "the monitor." Insights derived from the work of composing continually undermine assumptions made in the planning part, requiring more research; the monitor is a kind of triage doctor in an emergency room.

There is little hard science on the physiological state in the brain while writing is taking place. For one thing, it's difficult to write inside an MRI machine, where the brain's neural circuitry can be observed in action as the imaging traces blood flow. Historically, scientists have believed that there are two parts of the brain involved in language processing: one decodes the inputs, and the other generates the outputs. According to this classic model, words are formed in Broca's area, named for the French physician Pierre

Paul Broca, who discovered the region's language function, in the mid-nineteenth century; in most people, it's situated toward the front of the left hemisphere of the brain. Language is understood in Wernicke's area, named for the German neurologist Carl Wernicke, who published his research later in the nineteenth century. Both men, working long before CAT scans allowed neurologists to see inside the skull, made their conclusions after examining lesions in the autopsied brains of aphasia sufferers, who (in Broca's case) had lost their speech but could still understand words or (in Wernicke's) had lost the ability to comprehend language but could still speak. Connecting Broca's area with Wernicke's is a neural network: a thick, curving bundle of billions of nerve fibers, the arcuate fasciculus, which integrates the production and the comprehension of language.

In recent years, neuroscientists using imaging technology have begun to rethink some of the underlying principles of the classic model. One of the few imaging studies to focus specifically on writing, rather than on language use in general, was led by the neuroscientist Martin Lotze, at the University of Greifswald, in Germany, and the findings were published in the journal *NeuroImage,* in 2014. Lotze designed a small desk where the study's subjects could write by hand while he scanned their brains. The subjects were given a few sentences from a short story to copy verbatim, in order to establish a baseline, and were then told to "brainstorm" for sixty seconds and then to continue writing "creatively" for two more minutes. Lotze noted that, during the brainstorming part of the test, magnetic imaging showed that the sensorimotor and visual areas were activated; once creative writing started, these areas were joined by the bilateral dorsolateral prefrontal cortex, the left inferior frontal gyrus, the left thalamus, and the inferior temporal gyrus. In short, writing seems to be a whole-brain activity—a brainstorm indeed.

Lotze also compared brain scans of amateur writers with those of people who pursue writing as a career. He found that professional writers relied on a region of the brain that did not light up as much in the scanner when amateurs wrote—the left caudate nucleus, a tadpole-shaped structure (*cauda* means "tail" in Latin) in the midbrain that is associated with expertise in musicians and professional athletes. In amateur writers, neurons fired in the lateral occipital areas, which are associated with visual processing.

Writing well, one could conclude, is, like playing the piano or dribbling a basketball, mostly a matter of doing it. Practice is the only path to mastery.

There are two approaches to making a machine intelligent. Experts can teach the machine what they know, by imparting knowledge about a particular field and giving it rules to perform a set of functions; this method is sometimes termed knowledge-based. Or engineers can design a machine that has the capacity to learn for itself, so that when it is trained with the right data it can figure out its own rules for how to accomplish a task. That process is at work in machine learning. Humans integrate both types of intelligence so seamlessly that we hardly distinguish between them. You don't need to think about how to ride a bicycle, for example, once you've mastered balancing and steering; however, you do need to think about how to avoid a pedestrian in the bike lane. But a machine that can learn through both methods would require nearly opposite kinds of systems: one that can operate deductively, by following hard-coded procedures; and one that can work inductively, by recognizing patterns in the data and computing the statistical probabilities of when they occur. Today's AI systems are good at one or the other, but it's hard for them to put the two kinds of learning together the way brains do.

The history of artificial intelligence, going back at least to the fifties, has been a kind of tortoise-versus-hare contest between these two approaches to making machines that can think. The hare is the knowledge-based method, which drove AI during its starry-eyed adolescence, in the sixties, when AIs showed that they could solve mathematical and scientific problems, play chess, and respond to questions from people with a pre-programmed set of methods for answering. Forward progress petered out by the seventies, in the so-called "AI winter."

Machine learning, on the other hand, was for many years more a theoretical possibility than a practical approach to AI. The basic idea—to design an artificial neural network that, in a crude, mechanistic way, resembled the one in our skulls—had been around for several decades, but until the early 2010s there were neither large enough data sets available with which to do the training nor the research money to pay for it.

The benefits and the drawbacks of both approaches to intelligence show clearly in "natural language processing": the system by which machines understand and respond to human language. Over the decades, NLP and its sister science, speech generation, have produced a steady flow of knowledge-based commercial applications of AI in language comprehension; Amazon's Alexa and Apple's Siri synthesize many of these advances. Language translation, a related field, also progressed along incremental improvements through many years of research, much of it conducted at IBM's Thomas J. Watson Research Center.

Until the recent advances in machine learning, nearly all progress in NLP occurred by manually coding the rules that govern spelling, syntax, and grammar. "If the number of the subject and the number of the subject's verb are not the same, flag as an error" is one such rule. "If the following noun begins with a vowel, the article 'a' takes an 'n'" is another. Computational linguists translate these rules into the programming code that a computer can use to process language. It's like turning words into math.

Joel Tetreault is a computational linguist who until recently was the director of research at Grammarly, a leading brand of educational writing software. (He's now at Dataminr, an information-discovery company.) In an email, he described the Sisyphean nature of rule-based language processing. Rules can "cover a lot of low-hanging fruit and common patterns," he wrote. But "it doesn't take long to find edge and corner cases," where rules don't work very well. For example, the choice of a preposition can be influenced by the subsuming verb, or by the noun it follows, or by the noun that follows the preposition—a complex set of factors that our language-loving brains process intuitively, without obvious recourse to rules at all. "Given that the number of verbs and nouns in the English language is in the hundreds of thousands," Tetreault added, "enumerating rules for all the combinations just for influencing nouns and verbs alone would probably take years and years."

Tetreault grew up in Rutland, Vermont, where he learned to code in high school. He pursued computer science at Harvard and earned a PhD from the University of Rochester, in 2005; his dissertation was titled "Empirical Evaluations of Pronoun Resolution," a classic rule-based approach to teaching a computer how to interpret "his," "her," "it," and "they" correctly—a problem that today he would solve by using deep learning.

Tetreault began his career in 2007, at Educational Testing Service, which was using a machine called e-rater (in addition to human graders) to score GRE essays. The e-rater, which is still used, is a partly rule-based language-comprehension AI that turned out to be absurdly easy to manipulate. To prove this, the MIT professor Les Perelman and his students built an essay-writing bot called BABEL, which churned out nonsensical essays designed to get excellent scores. (In 2018, ETS researchers reported that they had developed a system to identify BABEL-generated writing.)

After ETS, Tetreault worked at Nuance Communication, a Massachusetts-based technology company that in the course of twenty-five years built a wide range of speech-recognition products, which were at the forefront of AI research in the nineties. Grammarly, which Tetreault joined in 2016, was founded in 2009, in Kiev, by three Ukrainian programmers: Max Lytvyn, Alex Shevchenko, and Dmytro Lider. Lytvyn and Shevchenko had created a plagiarism-detection product called MyDropBox. Since most student papers are composed on computers and emailed to teachers, the writing is already in a digital form. An AI can easily analyze it for word patterns that might match patterns that already exist on the Web, and flag any suspicious passages. Because Grammarly's founders spoke English as a second language, they were particularly aware of the difficulties involved in writing grammatically. That fact, they believed, was the reason many students plagiarized: it's much easier to cut and paste a finished paragraph than to compose one. Why not use the same pattern-recognition technology to make tools that would help people to write more effectively? Brad Hoover, a Silicon Valley venture capitalist who wanted to improve his writing, liked Grammarly so much that he became the CEO of the company and moved its headquarters to the Bay Area, in 2012.

Like Spotify, with which it shares a brand color (green), Grammarly operates on the "freemium" model. The company set me up with a Premium account ($30 a month, or $140 annually) and I used it as I wrote this article. Grammarly's claret-red error stripe, underlining my spelling mistakes, is not as schoolmasterly as Google Docs' stop-sign-red squiggle; I felt less in error somehow. Grammarly is also excellent at catching what linguists call "unknown tokens"—the glitches that sometimes occur in the writer's neural net between the thought and the expression of it, whereby the writer will mangle a word that, on rereading, his brain corrects, even though the unknown token renders the passage incomprehensible to everyone else.

In addition, Grammarly offers users weekly editorial pep talks from a virtual editor that praises ("Check out the big vocabulary on you! You used more unique words than 97% of Grammarly users") and rewards the writer with increasingly prestigious medallions for his or her volume of writing. "Herculean" is my most recent milestone.

However, when it comes to grammar, which contains far more nuance than spelling, Grammarly's suggestions are less helpful to experienced writers. Writing is a negotiation between the rules of grammar and what the writer wants to say. Beginning writers need rules to make themselves understood, but a practiced writer gives color, personality, and emotion to writing by bending the rules. One develops an ear for the edge cases in grammar and syntax that Grammarly tends to flag but which make sentences snap. (Grammarly cited the copy-edited version of this article for a hundred and nine grammatical "correctness" issues, and gave it a score of 77—a solid C-plus.)

Grammarly also uses deep learning to go "beyond grammar," in Tetreault's phrase, to make the company's software more flexible and adaptable to individual writers. At the company's headquarters, in San Francisco's Embarcadero Center, I saw prototypes of new writing tools that would soon be incorporated into its Premium product. The most elaborate concern tone—specifically, the difference between the informal style that is the lingua franca of the Web and the formal writing style preferred in professional settings, such as in job applications. "Sup" doesn't necessarily cut it when sending in a résumé.

Many people who use Grammarly are, like the founders, ESL speakers. It's a similar situation with Google's Smart Compose. As Paul Lambert explained, Smart Compose could create a mathematical representation of each user's unique writing style, based on all the emails she has written, and have the AI incline toward that style in making suggestions. "So people don't see it, but it starts to sound more like them," Lambert said. However, he continued, "our most passionate group are the ESL users. And there are more people who use English as a second language than as a first language." These users don't want to go beyond grammar yet—they're still learning it. "They don't want us to personalize," he said. Still, more Smart Compose users hit Tab to accept the machine's suggestions when predictive text makes guesses that sound more like them and not like everyone else.

As a student, I craved the rules of grammar and sentence construction. Perhaps because of my alarming inability to spell—in misspelling "potato," Dan Quayle *c'est moi*—I loved rules, and I prided myself on being a "correct" writer because I followed them. I still see those branching sentence diagrams in my head when I am constructing subordinate clauses. When I revise, I become my own writing instructor: make this passage more concise; avoid the passive voice; and God forbid a modifier should dangle. (Reader, I married a copy editor.) And while it has become acceptable, even at *The New Yorker*, to end a sentence with a preposition, I still half expect to get my knuckles whacked when I use one to end with. Ouch.

But rules get you only so far. It's like learning to drive. In driver's ed, you learn the rules of the road and how to operate the vehicle. But you don't really learn to drive until you get behind the wheel, step on the gas, and begin to steer around your first turn. You know the rule: keep the car between the white line marking the shoulder and the double yellow center line. But the rule doesn't keep the car on the road. For that, you rely on an entirely different kind of learning, one that happens on the fly. Like Smart Compose, your brain constantly computes and updates the "state" of where you are in the turn. You make a series of small course corrections as you steer, your eyes sending the visual information to your brain, which decodes it and sends it to your hands and feet—a little left, now a little right, slow down, go faster—in a kind of neural-net feedback loop, until you are out of the turn.

Something similar occurs in writing. Grammar and syntax provide you with the rules of the road, but writing requires a continuous dialogue between the words on the page and the prelinguistic notion in the mind that prompted them. Through a series of course corrections, otherwise known as revisions, you try to make language hew to your intention. You are learning from yourself.

Unlike good drivers, however, even accomplished writers spend a lot of time in a ditch beside the road. In spite of my herculean status, I got stuck repeatedly in composing this article. When I needed help, my virtual editor at Grammarly seemed to be on an extended lunch break.

"We're not interested in writing for you," Grammarly's CEO, Brad Hoover, explained; Grammarly's mission is to help people become better writers. Google's Smart Compose might also help non-English speakers become better writers, although it is more like a stenographer than like a writing coach. Grammarly incorporates both machine learning and rule-based algorithms into its products. No computational linguists, however, labored over imparting our rules of language to OpenAI's GPT-2. GPT-2 is a powerful language model: a "learning algorithm" enabled its literary education.

Conventional algorithms execute coded instructions according to procedures created by human engineers. But intelligence is more than enacting a set of procedures for dealing with known problems; it solves problems it's never encountered before, by learning how to adapt to new situations. David Ferrucci was the lead researcher behind Watson, IBM's *Jeopardy!*-playing AI, which beat the champion Ken Jennings in 2011. To build Watson, "it would be too difficult to model all the world's knowledge and then devise a procedure for answering any given *Jeopardy!* question," Ferrucci said recently. A knowledge-based, or deductive, approach wouldn't work—it was impractical to try to encode the system with all the necessary knowledge so that it could devise a procedure for answering anything it might be asked in the game. Instead, he made Watson supersmart by using machine learning: Ferrucci fed Watson "massive amounts of data," he said, and built all kinds of linguistic and semantic features. These were then input to machine-learning algorithms. Watson came up with its own method for using the data to reach the most statistically probable answer.

Learning algorithms like GPT-2's can adapt, because they figure out their own rules, based on the data they compute and the tasks that humans set for them. The algorithm automatically adjusts the artificial neurons' settings, or "weights," so that each time the machine tries the task it has been designed to do the probability that it will do the task correctly increases. The machine is modeling the kind of learning that a driver engages when executing a turn, and that my writer brain performs in finding the right words: correcting course through a feedback loop. "Cybernetics," which was the term for the process of machine learning coined by a pioneer in the field, Norbert Wiener, in the 1940s, is derived from the Greek word for "helmsmanship." By attempting a task billions of times, the system makes predictions that can become so accurate it does as well as humans at the same task, and sometimes outperforms them, even though the machine is still only guessing.

To understand how GPT-2 writes, imagine that you've never learned any spelling or grammar rules, and that no one taught you what words mean. All you know is what you've read in eight million articles that you discovered via Reddit, on an almost infinite variety of topics (although subjects such as Miley Cyrus and the Mueller report are more familiar to you than, say, the Treaty of Versailles). You have Rain Man–like skills for remembering each and every combination of words you've read. Because of your predictive-text neural net, if you are given a sentence and asked to write another like it, you can do the task flawlessly without understanding anything about the rules of language. The only skill you need is being able to accurately predict the next word.

GPT-2 was trained to write from a forty-gigabyte data set of articles that people had posted links to on Reddit and which other Reddit users had upvoted. Without human supervision, the neural net learned about the dynamics of language, both the rule-driven stuff and the edge cases, by analyzing and computing the statistical probabilities of all the possible word combinations in this training data. GPT-2 was designed so that, with a relatively brief input prompt from a human writer—a couple of sentences to establish a theme and a tone for the article—the AI could use its language skills to take over the writing and produce whole paragraphs of text, roughly on topic.

What made the full version of GPT-2 particularly dangerous was the way it could be "fine-tuned." Fine-tuning involves a second round of training on top of the general language skills the machine has already learned from the Reddit data set. Feed the machine Amazon or Yelp comments, for example, and GPT-2 could spit out phony customer reviews that would skew the market much more effectively than the relatively primitive bots that generate fake reviews now, and do so much more cheaply than human scamsters. Russian troll farms could use an automated writer like

GPT-2 to post, for example, divisive disinformation about Brexit, on an industrial scale, rather than relying on college students in a St. Petersburg office block who can't write English nearly as well as the machine. Pump-and-dump stock schemers could create an AI stock-picker that writes false analyst reports, thus triggering automated quants to sell and causing flash crashes in the market. A "deepfake" version of the American jihadi Anwar al-Awlaki could go on producing new inflammatory tracts from beyond the grave. Fake news would drown out real news.

Yes, but could GPT-2 write a *New Yorker* article? That was my solipsistic response on hearing of the artificial author's doomsday potential. What if OpenAI fine-tuned GPT-2 on *The New Yorker*'s digital archive (please, don't call it a "data set") — millions of polished and fact-checked words, many written by masters of the literary art. Could the machine learn to write well enough for *The New Yorker*? Could it write this article for me? The fate of civilization may not hang on the answer to that question, but mine might.

I raised the idea with OpenAI. Greg Brockman, the CTO, offered to fine-tune the full-strength version of GPT-2 with the magazine's archive. He promised to use the archive only for the purposes of this experiment. The corpus employed for the fine-tuning included all nonfiction work published since 2007 (but no fiction, poetry, or cartoons), along with some digitized classics going back to the 1960s. A human would need almost two weeks of 24/7 reading to get through it all; Jeff Wu, who oversaw the project, told me that the AI computed the archive in under an hour—a mere after-dinner macaron compared with its All-U-Can-Eat buffet of Reddit training data, the computing of which had required almost an entire "petaflop-per-second day"—a thousand trillion operations per second, for twenty-four hours.

OpenAI occupies a historic three-story loft building, originally built as a luggage factory in 1903, three years before the earthquake and fire that consumed much of San Francisco. It sits at the corner of Eighteenth and Folsom Streets, in the city's Mission District. There are a hundred employees, most of them young and well educated, who have an air of higher purpose about them. The staff aren't merely trying to invent a superintelligent machine.

They're also devoted to protecting us from superintelligence, by trying to formulate safety standards for the technology which are akin to the international protocols that govern nuclear materials like yellowcake uranium. What might be the safest course of all —to stop trying to build a machine as intelligent as we are—isn't part of OpenAI's business plan.

Dario Amodei, the research director, conducted the demonstration of the *New Yorker*–trained AI for me, in a glass-walled conference room on the first floor, using an OpenAI laptop. Amodei, thirty-six, has a PhD in computational neuroscience from Princeton and did a postdoc at Stanford. He has boyishly curly hair that he has the habit of twisting around a finger while he talks.

In fine-tuning GPT-2 for the purposes of this article, the neural net categorized distinctive aspects of *New Yorker* prose—the words its writers tended to favor, the magazine's rhythms, its distinctive style of narrative rhetoric, its voice—and the learning algorithm used these data to automatically adjust the neural net's settings, so that its predictions leaned toward *New Yorker* locutions. We were about to find out how well it worked. I had butterflies. It felt as if we were lighting a fuse but didn't know where it led.

The interface on the laptop screen was deceptively simple: a window where you could paste or write in prompts, and four slider controls on the left. Two adjusted the output: how many words the machine wrote each time the user pressed the refresh button. A third was for "generativity"—establishing how jiggy the AI got with its suggestions. The fourth slider adjusted the "nucleus sampling" —the size of the pool of words from which the machine drew in generating text. The refresh button was OpenAI's logo, which looked to me like a mandala, the kind associated with alchemists in the Middle Ages.

I had selected in advance some openings of favorite *New Yorker* articles to prompt the machine. We started by pasting the first paragraph of Lillian Ross's 1950 profile of Ernest Hemingway into the prompt window. It begins:

> Ernest Hemingway, who may well be the greatest living American novelist and short-story writer, rarely comes to New York. He spends most of his time on a farm, the Finca Vigia, nine miles outside Havana, with his wife, a domestic staff of nine, fifty-two cats, sixteen dogs, a couple of hundred pigeons, and three cows.

Amodei allowed me to click the mandala. After a second-long pause, the generator kicked in, and line after line of Robo-Ross's prose began to fill the screen:

> I walked up the path to the fence and saw a plump dog, that had been a common visitor to the Finca Vigía before the war, galloping up a path to the main building, with a tiny cow of the same name standing by her side. There was a puddle of red gravy in the front yard, and Hemingway sat down in a lawn chair.

On first reading this passage, my brain ignored what AI researchers call "world-modeling failures"—the tiny cow and the puddle of red gravy. Because I had never encountered a prose-writing machine even remotely this fluent before, my brain made an assumption —any human capable of writing this well would know that cows aren't tiny and red gravy doesn't puddle in people's yards. And because GPT-2 was an inspired mimic, expertly capturing *The New Yorker*'s cadences and narrative rhythms, it sounded like a familiar, trusted voice that I was inclined to believe. In fact, it sounded sort of like my voice.

I recalled a well-known experiment conducted in 1966 by Joseph Weizenbaum, a German-born professor at MIT who was a pioneer of artificial intelligence. In the experiment, a primitive (by today's standards) chatbot that Weizenbaum named ELIZA —for the George Bernard Shaw ingénue—responded, in writing, to statements by the study's subjects. The bot was programmed to answer in the style of a stereotypical psychotherapist, with questions such as "How does that make you feel?" To Weizenbaum's surprise, the "patients," even when they knew ELIZA was a bot, began revealing intimate details of their lives; his secretary at MIT asked him to leave the room so that she could communicate freely with ELIZA.

I clicked the mandala again, and the machine continued writing its Daliesque version of Ross's profile, using, in addition to the first prompt, the prose it had already generated to generate from:

> He was wearing a tweed suit, over a shiny sweater, and his black hair was brushed back. He had a red beard and wore his waistcoat in an overcoat with the body of a ship, three broad belts of colorful chain-link, a pair of capacious rectangular eyeglasses, and a silk tie. "Gouging my eye," he said, in Italian, saying that he had caused himself that terrible scar, "the

surgeon said it wasn't that bad." When he was very young, he said, he
started smoking but didn't find it very pleasant. The cigarette burns in
his hands and wrists were so bad that he had to have his face covered.

Three chain-link belts? Oddly, a belt does come up later in Ross's
article, when she and Hemingway go shopping. So do eyeglasses,
and cigarettes, and Italy. GPT-2 hadn't "read" the article—it wasn't
included in the training data—yet it had somehow alighted on
evocative details. Its deep learning obviously did not include the
ability to distinguish nonfiction from fiction, though. Convinc-
ingly faking quotes was one of its singular talents. Other things
often sounded right, though GPT-2 suffered frequent world-modeling failures—gaps in the kind of commonsense knowledge that
tells you overcoats aren't shaped like the body of a ship. It was as
though the writer had fallen asleep and was dreaming.

Amodei explained that there was no way of knowing why the
AI came up with specific names and descriptions in its writing;
it was drawing from a content pool that seemed to be a mixture
of *New Yorker*-ese and the machine's Reddit-based training. The
mathematical calculations that resulted in the algorithmic settings
that yielded GPT-2's words are far too complex for our brains to
understand. In trying to build a thinking machine, scientists have
so far succeeded only in reiterating the mystery of how our own
brains think.

Because of the size of the Reddit data set necessary to train GPT-
2, it is impossible for researchers to filter out all the abusive or
racist content, although OpenAI had caught some of it. However,
Amodei added, "it's definitely the case, if you start saying things
about conspiracy theories, or prompting it from the Stormfront
website—it knows about that." Conspiracy theories, after all, are
a form of pattern recognition too; the AI doesn't care if they're
true or not.

Each time I clicked the refresh button, the prose that the machine generated became more random; after three or four tries,
the writing had drifted far from the original prompt. I found that
by adjusting the slider to limit the amount of text GPT-2 generated, and then generating again so that it used the language it
had just produced, the writing stayed on topic a bit longer, but it,
too, soon devolved into gibberish, in a way that reminded me of

HAL, the superintelligent computer in *2001: A Space Odyssey,* when the astronauts begin to disconnect its mainframe-size artificial brain.

An hour or so later, after we had tried opening paragraphs of John Hersey's *Hiroshima* and Truman Capote's *In Cold Blood,* my initial excitement had curdled into queasiness. It hurt to see the rules of grammar and usage, which I have lived my writing life by, mastered by an idiot savant that used math for words. It was sickening to see how the slithering machine intelligence, with its ability to take on the color of the prompt's prose, slipped into some of my favorite paragraphs, impersonating their voices but without their souls.

There are many positive services that AI writers might provide. IBM recently debuted an AI called Speech by Crowd, which it has been developing with Noam Slonim, an Israeli IBM Research Fellow. The AI processed almost 2,000 essays written by people on the topic "Social Media Brings More Harm Than Good" and, using a combination of rules and deep learning, isolated the best arguments on both sides and summarized them in a pair of three- to five-paragraph, op-ed-style essays, one pro ("Social media creates a platform to support freedom of speech, giving individuals a platform to voice their opinions and interact with like-minded individuals") and one con ("The opinion of a few can now determine the debate, it causes polarized discussions and strong feelings on non-important subjects"). The essays I read were competent, but most seventh-graders with social-media experience could have made the same arguments less formulaically.

Slonim pointed to the rigid formats used in public-opinion surveys, which rely on questions the pollsters think are important. What, he asked, if these surveys came with open-ended questions that allowed respondents to write about issues that concern them, in any form. Speech by Crowd can "read" all the answers and digest them into broader narratives. "That would disrupt opinion surveys," Slonim told me.

At Narrative Science, in Chicago, a company cofounded by Kristian Hammond, a computer scientist at Northwestern, the main focus is using a suite of artificial-intelligence techniques to turn data into natural language and narrative. The company's software

renders numerical information about profit and loss or manufacturing operations, for example, as stories that make sense of patterns in the data, a tedious task formerly accomplished by people
poring over numbers and churning out reports. "I have data, and I
don't understand the data, and so a system figures out what I need
to hear and then turns it into language," Hammond explained.
"I'm stunned by how much data we have and how little of it we
use. For me, it's trying to build that bridge between data and information."

One of Hammond's former colleagues, Jeremy Gilbert, now the
director of strategic initiatives at the *Washington Post,* oversees Heliograf, the *Post*'s deep-learning robotic newshound. Its purpose,
he told me, is not to replace journalists but to cover data-heavy
stories, some with small but highly engaged audiences—a high
school football game ("The Yorktown Patriots triumphed over the
visiting Wilson Tigers in a close game on Thursday, 20–14," the
AI reported), local election results, a minor commodities-market
report—that newspapers lack the manpower to cover, and others
with much broader reach, such as national elections or the Olym-
pics. Heliograf collects the data and applies them to a particular
template—a spreadsheet for words, Gilbert said—and an algorithm identifies the decisive play in the game or the key issue in
the election and generates the language to describe it. Although
Gilbert says that no freelancer has lost a gig to Heliograf, it's not
hard to imagine that the high school stringer who once started out
on the varsity beat will be coding instead.

OpenAI made it possible for me to log in to the *New Yorker* AI
remotely. On the flight back to New York, I put some of my notes
from the OpenAI visit into GPT-2 and it began making up quotes
for Ilya Sutskever, the company's chief scientist. The machine appeared to be well informed about his groundbreaking research. I
worried that I'd forget what he really said, because the AI sounded
so much like him, and that I'd inadvertently use in my article the
machine's fake reporting, generated from my notes. ("We can
make fast translations but we can't really solve these conceptual
questions," one of GPT-2's Sutskever quotes said. "Maybe it is better to have one person go out and learn French than to have an
entire computer-science department.") By the time I got home,
the AI had me spooked. I knew right away there was no way the

machine could help me write this article, but I suspected that there were a million ways it could screw me up.

I sent a sample of GPT-2's prose to Steven Pinker, the Harvard psycholinguist. He was not impressed with the machine's "superficially plausible gobbledygook," and explained why. I put some of his reply into the generator window, clicked the mandala, added synthetic Pinker prose to the real thing, and asked people to guess where the author of *The Language Instinct* stopped and the machine took over.

> Being amnesic for how it began a phrase or sentence, it won't consistently complete it with the necessary agreement and concord — to say nothing of semantic coherence. And this reveals the second problem: real language does not consist of a running monologue that sounds sort of like English. It's a way of expressing ideas, a mapping from meaning to sound or text. To put it crudely, speaking or writing is a box whose input is a meaning plus a communicative intent, and whose output is a string of words; comprehension is a box with the opposite information flow. What is essentially wrong with this perspective is that it assumes that meaning and intent are inextricably linked. Their separation, the learning scientist Phil Zuckerman has argued, is an illusion that we have built into our brains, a false sense of coherence.

That's Pinker through "information flow." (There is no learning scientist named Phil Zuckerman, although there is a sociologist by that name who specializes in secularity.) Pinker is right about the machine's amnesic qualities — it can't develop a thought, based on a previous one. It's like a person who speaks constantly but says almost nothing. (Political punditry could be its natural domain.) However, almost everyone I tried the Pinker Test on, including Dario Amodei, of OpenAI, and Les Perelman, of Project BABEL, failed to distinguish Pinker's prose from the machine's gobbledygook. The AI had them Pinkered.

GPT-2 was like a three-year-old prodigiously gifted with the illusion, at least, of college-level writing ability. But even a child prodigy would have a goal in writing; the machine's only goal is to predict the next word. It can't sustain a thought, because it can't think causally. Deep learning works brilliantly at capturing all the edgy patterns in our syntactic gymnastics, but because it lacks a precoded base of procedural knowledge it can't use its language skills to reason or to conceptualize. An intelligent machine needs both kinds of thinking.

"It's a card trick," Kris Hammond, of Narrative Science, said, when I sent him what I thought were some of the GPT-2's better efforts. "A very sophisticated card trick, but at heart it's still a card trick." True, but there are also a lot of tricks involved in writing, so it's hard to find fault with a fellow-mountebank on that score.

One can envision machines like GPT-2 spewing superficially sensible gibberish, like a burst water main of babble, flooding the internet with so much writing that it would soon drown out human voices, and then training on its own meaningless prose, like a cow chewing its cud. But composing a long discursive narrative, structured in a particular way to advance the story, was, at least for now, completely beyond GPT-2's predictive capacity.

However, even if people will still be necessary for literary production, day by day, automated writers like GPT-2 will do a little more of the writing that humans are now required to do. People who aren't professional writers may be able to avail themselves of a wide range of products that will write emails, memos, reports, and speeches for them. And, like me writing "I am proud of you" to my son, some of the AI's next words might seem superior to words you might have thought of yourself. But what else might you have thought to say that is not computable? That will all be lost.

Before my visit to OpenAI, I watched a lecture on YouTube that Ilya Sutskever had given on GPT-2 in March, at the Computer History Museum, in Mountain View, California. In it, he made what sounded to me like a claim that GPT-2 itself might venture, if you set the generativity slider to the max. Sutskever said, "If a machine like GPT-2 could have enough data and computing power to perfectly predict the next word, that would be the equivalent of understanding."

At OpenAI, I asked Sutskever about this. "When I said this statement, I used 'understanding' informally," he explained. "We don't really know what it means for a system to understand something, and when you look at a system like this it can be genuinely hard to tell. The thing that I meant was: If you train a system which predicts the next word well enough, then it ought to understand. If it doesn't predict it well enough, its understanding will be incomplete."

However, Sutskever added, "researchers can't disallow the possibility that we will reach understanding when the neural net gets as big as the brain."

The brain is estimated to contain a hundred billion neurons, with trillions of connections between them. The neural net that the full version of GPT-2 runs on has about one and a half billion connections, or "parameters." At the current rate at which compute is growing, neural nets could equal the brain's raw processing capacity in five years. To help OpenAI get there first, Microsoft announced in July that it was investing $1 billion in the company, as part of an "exclusive computing partnership." How its benefits will be "distributed as widely as possible" remains to be seen. (A spokesperson for OpenAI said that "Microsoft's investment doesn't give Microsoft control" over the AI that OpenAI creates.)

David Ferrucci, the only person I tried the Pinker Test on who passed it, said, "Are we going to achieve machine understanding in a way we have hoped for many years? Not with these machine-learning techniques. Can we do it with hybrid techniques?" (By that he meant ones that combine knowledge-based systems with machine-learning pattern recognition.) "I'm betting yes. That's what cognition is all about, a hybrid architecture that combines different classes of thinking."

What if some much later iteration of GPT-2, far more powerful than this model, could be hybridized with a procedural system, so that it would be able to write causally and distinguish truth from fiction and at the same time draw from its well of deep learning? One can imagine a kind of Joycean super-author, capable of any style, turning out spine-tingling suspense novels, massively researched biographies, and nuanced analyses of the Israeli-Palestinian conflict. Humans would stop writing, or at least publishing, because all the readers would be captivated by the machines. What then?

GPT-2, prompted with that paragraph, predicted the next sentence: "In a way, the humans would be making progress."

JOSHUA SOKOL

Troubled Treasure

FROM *Science Magazine*

ON AN OVERCAST spring morning, a mosaic of life in the heyday of the dinosaurs takes shape piece by piece in this border city [Tengchong, China]. It sprawls across hundreds of tables, on sheets spread by storefronts, and under glass counters in shops. Some vendors hawk jade or snacks, but most everyone is here for the amber: raw amber coated in gray volcanic ash; polished amber carved into smiling Buddhas; egg-size dollops of amber the color of honey, molasses, or garnet. Some browsers seek treasure for their own collections, whereas others act as virtual dealers, holding amber pieces in front of their smartphones and snapping images for distant buyers.

For scientists, this is more than a place to buy pendants or bracelets. One morning in March, paleontologist Xing Lida from the China University of Geosciences in Beijing stops at a table and examines a cockroach in a golf ball–size glob of amber, paused in time from the middle of the Cretaceous period. Its intact limbs curve off a body that looks smaller and narrower than that of today's household pests.

The dealer wants about $900. "It's an okay price," Xing says. But he moves on, hunting rarer, more scientifically valuable game.

Within a few minutes, a stranger notices Xing, shoots video of him, and posts it to social media. With 2.6 million followers on Weibo, a Chinese hybrid of Facebook and Twitter, the baby-faced, hypercharismatic Xing is a celebrity for his studies of dinosaur tracks and other adventures (*Science,* June 23, 2017, p. 1224). Last year, he published twenty-five scientific papers and a dinosaur-related fantasy novel with a foreword by Liu Cixin, the country's superstar science fiction author. But Xing, like a few other Chinese paleontologists, is also lionized for the extraordinary discoveries he has made in this amber: the hatchlings of primitive birds, the feathered tail of a dinosaur, lizards, frogs, snakes, snails, a host of insects. Much as nineteenth-century naturalists collected species from teeming rain forests in far-flung locales, these scientists are building a detailed chronicle of life in a tropical forest 100 million years ago, all from amber mined across the border in Myanmar.

"Right now we're in this frenzy, almost an orgy" of discovery, says paleontologist David Grimaldi, curator of the amber collection at the American Museum of Natural History in New York City. Hundreds of scientific papers have emerged from the amber finds, and Chinese scientists hint that many specimens have yet to be published, including birds, insect species by the thousands, and even aquatic animals such as crabs or salamanders.

But as much as Burmese amber is a scientist's dream, it's also an ethical minefield. The fossils come from conflict-ridden Kachin state in Myanmar, where scientists can't inspect the geology for clues to the fossils' age and environment. In Kachin, rival political factions compete for the profit yielded by amber and other natural resources. "These commodities are fueling the conflict," says Paul Donowitz, the Washington, D.C.–based campaign leader for Myanmar at Global Witness, a nongovernmental organization. "They are providing revenue for arms and conflict actors, and the government is launching attacks and killing people and committing human rights abuses to cut off those resources."

Much of the amber is smuggled into China in a trade that Tengchong officials and traders ballparked at between $725 million and $1 billion in 2015 alone. In China, jewelers, private collectors, and scientists like Xing exchange vast sums of cash through mobile payment apps to compete for prized specimens. The collectors often win the bidding, meaning researchers can study many specimens only on loan.

The mixture of commerce and science "raises new questions that we have not faced . . . in paleontology before," says Julia Clarke, a paleontologist at the University of Texas in Austin who often edits papers on Burmese amber. But given that the amber will be sold even if scientists don't buy in, she says, "What's the other prospective outcome?"

That's what drives Xing to the market. "If we don't get a specimen, it probably becomes cheap jewelry around some young girl's neck."

Some 99 million years before this spring market and about 220 kilometers away in what is now Myanmar, a balmy seaside forest echoed with the calls of strange creatures. The trees bled massive quantities of resin when insects attacked them or storms broke off limbs. The resin puddled and pooled, miring countless creatures "like a mini–La Brea Tar Pits," says paleontologist Ryan McKellar at the Royal Saskatchewan Museum in Regina, Canada. Over time, the resin's frankincense-like gases evaporated; its molecules linked into polymers and hardened into what we now call amber.

Amber excels at preserving fine detail and soft tissue, says Victoria McCoy, a paleontologist at the University of Bonn in Germany. On contact, resin seeps into tissues, protecting the entombed animals and plants from fungus and rot while also drying them out. Later, the resin hardens to form a shell that further protects the fossil inclusions. In the best cases, "cellular- or even subcellular-level details are still preserved," she says.

Amber from other major deposits—specimens that wash up on beaches in Baltic countries or are mined in the Dominican Republic—is far younger. It also rarely traps strong, active creatures, such as dragonflies, or any vertebrates beyond a few lizards.

Burmese amber, in contrast, has revealed a phantasmagoria of creatures, thanks to the vast quantities coming out of the ground and the fact that single pieces regularly approach the size of cantaloupes. As Grimaldi expresses it: imagine giving an entomologist a bigger bug net and allowing them to swing it more times. It's not just insects and other creepy-crawlies. "It's the vertebrates that are absolutely, truly astonishing," says Andrew Ross, head of paleobiology for National Museums Scotland in Edinburgh.

In 2018, scientists reported 321 new species immaculately preserved in Burmese amber, bringing the cumulative total to 1,195. One team recently argued that Burmese amber may boast more biodiversity than any other fossil deposit from the entire reign of the dinosaurs. "You think this can't even be possible," says Philip Currie, a paleontologist at the University of Alberta in Edmonton, Canada, "but it's happening."

Single fossils within that bonanza illuminate how creatures lived and where they fit into the tree of life. Taken together, the finds benchmark the birth of lineages and ecological relationships that still undergird modern ecosystems.

Most of that scientific bounty passes through the bustling market here in Tengchong. And before that, it emerges from a conflict zone.

In 2014, Xing sneaked into Myanmar, hoping to see the source of the specimens that had captivated him. The amber comes from mines near Tanai township in Kachin, where for decades Myanmar's army and the local Kachin Independence Army, an ethnic insurgency, have battled over control of lucrative resources such as jade, timber, and, most recently, amber. Foreigners are not allowed into Tanai. To make his clandestine visit, Xing first traveled across the border some 110 kilometers to Myitkyina, the Myanmar-side hub of the amber trade. When the road seemed safe, a friend smuggled him north dressed in a *longyi*, a traditional Myanmarese wrap skirt.

Xing and other visitors to the mines describe a lush terrain transformed into barren hillsides. Tents cover claustrophobic holes up to 100 meters deep but only wide enough for skinny workers, who say they are responsible for their own medical care after accidents. The miners dig down and, when they hit layers of amber, tunnel horizontally with hand tools to dig it out. They sort finds at night, to avoid publicizing valuable discoveries. Amber with fossil inclusions is the most precious, proof after weeks of uncertainty that a mine will be profitable. Reached by phone through an interpreter, miners say both warring sides demand bribes for the rights to an area and equipment—and then tax 10 percent of the profit.

Xing hasn't yet published his full conclusions from that trip, but he and others suspect the origins of the amber may be more complicated than thought. The oft-quoted age of 99 million years comes from radiometric dating of volcanic ash bought from a miner and published in 2012. But Wang Bo, a paleontologist at Nanjing Institute of Geology and Palaeontology (NIGPAS) in China, thinks the recent wave of amber has a range of ages. He had a friend with Myanmarese citizenship gather more recent samples of volcanic ash, which Wang says show that the amber deposits span at least 5 million years. "It's a period," he says, "not just a point."

Miners and traders aren't concerned with details of geology, however. After the amber is extracted and roughly sorted, scooters, cars, boats, and elephants carry it to dealers either in Myitkyina or straight across the border to Tengchong. Myanmar law explicitly bars exporting fossils without permission—but amber is classified as a gemstone and so is allowed to leave.

China, however, taxes jewelry imports, so dealers here say they smuggle amber in—for example, in the wheel wells of cars. In Tengchong's market that "shadow economy" emerges into broad daylight, wrote anthropologist Alessandro Rippa at the University of Colorado in Boulder in a 2017 anthropological study. Local authorities not only tolerate, but police the market, which has been an economic boon.

Scientists didn't take long to notice. Since the 1920s, a small collection at London's Natural History Museum offered scientists their only glimpse of the diversity of life inside Burmese amber. Then, during a cease-fire in the late 1990s, a small Canadian company started to mine amber in Kachin. It shipped 75 kilograms of raw amber to Grimaldi. He found that each kilogram he acid-washed, cut, and polished contained an average of forty-six organisms. In the early 2010s, the market here started to boom just as amber mines inside China became tapped out. Demand rose for new amber sources—and that trickle of amber fossils from Myanmar turned into a flood.

Before Xing's March visit to the bustling outdoor market, he had already arranged to make a purchase after seeing pictures sent to his phone. Now, in a dimly lit amber jewelry shop, a camera-shy twenty-something broker from Myitkyina delivers today's prize: two lizards in amber. On one, the skin and flesh have vanished in patches, revealing delicate bones. Given the pace of commerce here, a museum, with its bureaucracy and budgeting process, could never compete for that specimen. Xing simply takes out his smartphone and taps a payment app to buy it for a few hundred dollars—a good deal, he says, because this piece is too cloudy and jumbled to make attractive jewelry.

In 2014, Xing began to cultivate a network of buyers here and in Myitkyina and teach them to spot the claws of a Cretaceous bird wing or to count the toes that would tell whether a foot came from a lizard or a dinosaur. Once he gets a tip, he texts a picture to specialists, hoping to figure out whether a specimen's likely scientific importance justifies steep prices. Only then will he decide to buy.

Receiving Xing's texts is "like Christmas every time," McKellar says. Scientists are aware that their identifications can boost prices. Once a specimen has been named as a bird, for example, it might go for tens of thousands or even hundreds of thousands of dollars. Wang adds, "They will use my word to make money."

"In an ideal world, we shouldn't be bartering and buying and selling fossils," says paleontologist Emily Rayfield of the University of Bristol in the United Kingdom, president of the Society of Vertebrate Paleontology, paraphrasing that organization's formal position. "But sometimes there's a need to do that to keep them in, or bring them into, the public trust."

At first, Xing used his own money to buy fossils. Then he persuaded his parents, both doctors, to sell their house in southern China to free up cash. He spent that money by 2016, and he and friends started a nonprofit called the Dexu Institute of Palaeontology (DIP), based in the southern Guangdong province in China, to acquire and house a permanent collection that makes specimens available for other scientists.

Xing has since published papers on enough vertebrates to fill a Cretaceous terrarium, including a baby snake fossil that preserved ninety-seven fragile vertebrae, published in *Science Advances;* the front half of a two-centimeter-long frog, in *Scientific Reports;* and his blockbuster result, a feathered dinosaur tail that appears to contain traces of hemoglobin, in *Current Biology.*

But Xing's first and most sustained success has been with tiny birds. Soon after he had built up his network, a source sent him a picture of the first bird discovered in amber. "The price was about the same as a new BMW, but we still got it," he says. "And we found more, and more, and more after that."

The birds hail from a primitive group called Enantiornithes that went extinct with the other dinosaurs. Amber preserves never-before-seen features of their skin and feathers and may even reveal internal details. "This is a whole new window into avian evolution," Clarke says.

For example, other Chinese bird fossils exhibited flaring tail feathers that had been squished flat inside sedimentary rock. Paleontologists assumed those feathers matched similar ornamental ones in modern birds, which have a central shaft built like a hollow tube. In December 2018, though, Xing published feathers from thirty-one Burmese amber pieces, which revealed an open, superthin central shaft. Given that those flimsy feathers always appear straight in fossils, they must have been able to snap into a rigid state, like a child's snap-on bracelet.

"Now we know, from these 3-D amber specimens, that everything we think we see [from flattened fossils] is wrong," says Jingmai O'Connor, who studies Xing's bird fossils from the Institute of Vertebrate Paleontology and Paleoanthropology in Beijing. In February, the team published another amber discovery: a bird's foot topped with feathers—an expected but previously unseen evolutionary step for modern birds, which later evolved scaly, featherless feet.

The *Jurassic Park* dream of fishing out DNA from amber hasn't yet come true, despite multiple tests in even very young amber, McCoy says. But amber researchers have reported other chemical traces lingering in their fossils: pigments that reveal how creatures shimmered under the mid-Cretaceous sun, and structural molecules such as chitin from arthropod exoskeletons and lignin and cellulose from plants. Last month, McCoy's group reported recovering amino acids from a feather in Burmese amber, bearing a chemical signature that suggested they had still been bound into fragments of proteins before the test. The next step: to actually sequence ancient proteins, which could offer researchers another way to track evolutionary relationships and understand how organisms lived.

But McCoy's experiment involved smashing amber-clad feathers to powder with a hammer. Scientists—and collectors—would prefer other methods to study trapped biomolecules. Researchers have started to experiment with synchrotron imaging, using intense X-rays that cause chemical elements in a sample to fluoresce at distinct wavelengths, for example. "It's going to take a decade for us to figure out how to truly utilize the wealth of information trapped inside these specimens," O'Connor says.

As they examine specimens, scientists stay alert for the products of clever forgers. One specimen marketed as Burmese amber and then subjected to chemical tests contained what would have been the first turtle in amber. "But it was fake," Xing says.

*

Across China at NIGPAS, 2,100 kilometers away inside Nanjing's walled historic center, Wang pours tea. Then he starts to pull out bags of labeled insects in amber. Rare vertebrates may be the charismatic megafauna of Burmese amber, but invertebrates rule in numbers and diversity. Wang, a paleoentomologist, has amassed a 30,000-piece collection of plants and insects in Burmese amber, many bought here with funds from his institution. He still hasn't studied it all. "Eventually, we think maybe four thousand or five thousand species can be found," he says.

His lab employs an array of high-tech imaging systems to peer into specimens without destroying them. In one room, a laser confocal microscope causes delicate structures—like the multifaceted eyes of a fly, now splashed from the scope onto an adjacent monitor—to fluoresce. In another room, a computerized tomography (CT) scanner peers inside fossils to make 3-D models of internal structure.

By applying those techniques, Wang, like his rivals, has unearthed enough 99-million-year-old evolutionary gambits to fill a nature documentary. Take the lacewings, an insect group that today preys on ants and aphids. In one large glob of amber, the extended wing of a butterflylike lacewing shows a decoy eyespot that may have helped misdirect predators. In another, a lacewing larva looks for all the world like a liverwort plant. Still other lacewings have forest floor debris glued onto their backs, a camouflage strategy many modern insects still use.

"It's a pity that most of them became extinct," Wang says, "but we are lucky we found some hidden stories about them."

Some groups have no direct descendants, such as the Haidomyrmecines, nicknamed "hell ants." They evolved near the base of the ant family tree and sported sharp, sickle-shaped tusks that may have slammed upward to impale other insects. Some, the "unicorn" ants, also had a long top horn, probably used to pin prey in place. "These are like the tyrannosaurs of the ant world," Grimaldi says, "that you would never know existed if you studied modern living fauna."

Ancestral spiders offer another surprise. In early 2018, Wang and Huang Diying, a researcher at NIGPAS, separately published specimens in *Nature Ecology & Evolution* with spiderlike bodies trailed by long, scorpionesque tails. Now extinct, those arachnids were holdouts from a very early branch of spider evolution thought to have died out by some 250 million years ago. But in what is now Myanmar, they once crawled alongside the true spiders that persist today. Those proto-spiders also had silk-spinning organs, evidence that even early arachnids had that power.

Of all those riches, the most important may look lackluster: little beetles coated in dots of pollen. They are a clue to a dramatic and quick changeover in life's history that Charles Darwin called "an abominable mystery": the emergence of the flowering plants, which mostly rely on insect visitors to carry their pollen. Other amber specimens from the same ancient forest show pollen from an older group of trees, the gymnosperms—conifers and ginkgoes—which today are pollinated largely by wind. But some of the pollen on the beetles looks too big to be windblown. The amber, it seems, may capture the moment when many insect groups switched their feeding from gymnosperms to flowering plants, touching off the millions of years of coevolution that led to the extraordinary diversity of flowers and their pollinators today.

Studying the evolution of that partnership should help researchers understand why insect groups thrive or fail—a crucial question at a time when entomologists have begun to worry that ongoing climate change could drive a wave of insect extinctions, says paleoentomologist Michael Engel of the University of Kansas in Lawrence. "Burmese amber fits perfectly into this grand, unfortunate, tragic experiment that is going on with the world right now," Engel says.

After perusing the outdoor stalls here, Xing moves from shop to shop, sitting down at one elegant tea table after another to chat with owners. Under jewelry store glass counters, these shops showcase ferns, flowers, scorpions, fearsome spiders, and one tiny pinecone. New specimens emerge from the back in plastic bags. One shop even offers a baby bird, its delicate wing—with its telltale claw—clearly visible. But the dealer is asking about $145,000—too much.

By day's end, Xing's student has a padded backpack full of invertebrates in plastic cases, as well as the lizards. Next, Xing flies to the nearby major city of Kunming, China, to meet with Xiao Jia, a wealthy private collector and online dealer who lent him that first snake in a piece of amber for study.

Along the way, the hustle never stops. After Xiao's driver picks Xing up from the airport, his phone buzzes: a dealer in Myitkyina wants to sell what may be the first fragment of a beehive in amber.

Xing discusses buying it with Xiao. If neither of them grabs that specimen, someone else in the same small, deep-pocketed circle might—like Xia Fangyuan, a collector, dealer, and enthusiastic co-author on about a dozen high-profile papers, who lives across the country in Shanghai, China, and competes with Xing for top specimens. Xia says he spends roughly $750,000 on Burmese amber per year, and grateful scientists like Wang have named species of cockroach, froghopper, parasitoid fly, and caddisfly for him. His vast collection, stored in a bank vault and brought out for visitors at his home, includes a bird, lizards, and a frog. His favorite specimen, he says, is a perfectly preserved insect: a praying mantis he bought for $22,000 that looks like it could cock its head at any moment.

Xia's collection also includes a curious shell bought from a dealer who claimed it was a snail. Suspecting that the specimen was something more, he lent it to Wang, who did a CT scan that revealed the internal chambers characteristic of an ammonite—an extinct marine cephalopod resembling a nautilus. The remarkable seashell must have been caught in resin in a beachside forest, perhaps after it was thrown onto land in a storm. Described in the *Proceedings of the National Academy of Sciences* (*PNAS*) last week, the specimen remains in Xia's private collection.

That arrangement isn't unusual. Chinese collectors hesitate to give specimens to museums outright, Wang says, because China's laws don't offer tax breaks for such donations. But some Western paleontologists are uncomfortable with publishing fossils that remain in private hands. A simple loan of a specimen isn't enough to ensure its long-term preservation or that other researchers can visit and study it for decades and centuries to come. "The whole point of science is that we're generating and testing hypotheses," Rayfield says. "If we're not able to study specimens anymore, then it simply becomes an exercise at taking someone at their word."

And yet *PNAS* is far from the only journal to have published specimens from China's private Burmese amber collections. *Science Advances* (part of the *Science* family of journals) has also published papers on specimens belonging to Xia, as well as on the amber snake, now housed in an exhibit in the back of Xiao's toy store in a Kunming mall. (Xiao and DIP have arranged for the institute to own that specimen, but it is loaned back to Xiao until 2027.)

Pressed on the status of their specimens, both Xiao and Xia —and the scientists with whom they collaborate—say they plan to turn their collections into private museums and that they are committed to accepting requests for study from outside researchers. The *PNAS* paper lists the ammonite specimen, for example, as belonging to the Lingpoge Amber Museum in Shanghai, an institution that Xia says he is preparing. He says he is negotiating with his district-level government for space. Asked whether that situation meets their policies, the *PNAS* editorial board issued a written response: "The authors of this article have assured us that the fossil will be made available to qualified researchers."

Experience leaves some amber researchers wary, however. Engel recalls once asking to visit a published specimen from an amber deposit in Jordan. It was housed in what seemed to be a museum that turned out to be run by a collector. "It was basically his basement," Engel says. "He says, 'Oh yeah, sure you can examine it—for $10,000.'"

Yet the allure of the amber fossils may grow, regardless of ownership—because of scarcity. The supply of amber is far down from its height around 2015, dealers say. As quickly as that window into the Cretaceous opened, it might already be slamming shut.

In June 2017, helicopters from Myanmar's army buzzed over Tanai. According to news reports, they dropped leaflets warning amber miners and other residents to flee. Airstrikes and roadblocks followed, and Myanmar's army has since pried away the amber mining areas from the Kachin Independence Army. A 2018 report by a United Nations investigator indicated that the actions killed four civilians and trapped up to 5,000 people in the area. Citing the army's broader conduct, including in Kachin, another UN fact-finding report called for Myanmar's top generals to be investigated for genocide and crimes against humanity.

Two former mine owners, speaking through an interpreter in phone interviews, say taxes have been even steeper since government troops took control of the area. Both shut their mines when they became unprofitable after the government takeover, and almost all deep mines are now out of business, dealers here corroborate. Only shallow mines and perhaps a few secret operations are still running.

Tracing how revenue from amber funds Myanmar's army and ethnic militias is hard. "As a consumer," says Donowitz, "by increasing the values of those commodities, by participating in those trades, you are part of that conflict."

That's not the only ethical cloud over these specimens. Many fossil-rich nations, including China, Canada, Mongolia—and Myanmar—have written laws to keep unique fossils inside their borders. Myanmar's rules threaten violators with five to ten years in prison, thousands of dollars in fines, or both. As Burmese amber fossils slip through the gemstone loophole, "It's like Myanmar's cultural heritage, paleontological heritage, is just being wholesale ripped out of the ground and distributed around the world," Engel says.

Xing stresses he wants to extract scientific details, not to own specimens. He says he's sensitive to the issue because many Chinese historical objects now sit in foreign museums. "If one day Myanmar gets peace, and they want to build a museum for amber or build a museum for natural history, [Xing's own institute] would love to return all the specimens to Myanmar," he says. "It's not going to come free. But yeah, we'd love to return them."

Some paleontologists also hope to see a Burmese amber collection near the mines or at least within the country's borders. "If Myanmar wanted to build a museum about amber," Grimaldi says, "it would be totally fun to lend my expertise in helping to design and build that. It would be magnificent, and I think it should be done." In recent months, one private amber museum opened in Yangon, Myanmar's largest city. But in addition to education, its English website also offers amber lots for sale, custom jewelry and fossil procurement, and escorted buying tours to amber markets, suggesting the museum is about commerce as well as preservation.

For residents in Tanai, questions about who owns fossils pale in the face of day-to-day security issues. "Right now there is no stability and no rule of law," says one out-of-work miner in a phone call.

But as the formal interview ends, he has a request. He says the miners digging up the amber don't know why scientists care about the insects and other creatures entombed inside it. "If you know," he says, "please share with us?"

JOSHUA SOKOL

The Hidden Heroines of Chaos

FROM *Quanta Magazine*

A LITTLE OVER HALF a century ago, chaos started spilling out of a famous experiment. It came not from a petri dish, a beaker, or an astronomical observatory, but from the vacuum tubes and diodes of a Royal McBee LGP-30. This "desk" computer—it was the size of a desk—weighed some 800 pounds and sounded like a passing propeller plane. It was so loud that it even got its own office on the fifth floor in Building 24, a drab structure near the center of the Massachusetts Institute of Technology. Instructions for the computer came from down the hall, from the office of a meteorologist named Edward Norton Lorenz.

The story of chaos is usually told like this: Using the LGP-30, Lorenz made paradigm-wrecking discoveries. In 1961, having programmed a set of equations into the computer that would simulate future weather, he found that tiny differences in starting values could lead to drastically different outcomes. This sensitivity to initial conditions, later popularized as the butterfly effect, made predicting the far future a fool's errand. But Lorenz also found that these unpredictable outcomes weren't quite random, either. When visualized in a certain way, they seemed to prowl around a shape called a strange attractor.

About a decade later, chaos theory started to catch on in scientific circles. Scientists soon encountered other unpredictable natural systems that looked random even though they weren't: the rings of Saturn, blooms of marine algae, Earth's magnetic field, the number of salmon in a fishery. Then chaos went mainstream with the publication of James Gleick's *Chaos: Making a New Science* in 1987. Before long, Jeff Goldblum, playing the chaos theorist Ian Malcolm, was pausing, stammering, and charming his way through lines about the unpredictability of nature in *Jurassic Park*.

All told, it's a neat narrative. Lorenz, "the father of chaos," started a scientific revolution on the LGP-30. It is quite literally a textbook case for how the numerical experiments that modern science has come to rely on—in fields ranging from climate science to ecology to astrophysics—can uncover hidden truths about nature.

But in fact, Lorenz was not the one running the machine. There's another story, one that has gone untold for half a century. A year and a half ago, an MIT scientist happened across a name he had never heard before and started to investigate. The trail he ended up following took him into the MIT archives, through the stacks of the Library of Congress, and across three states and five decades to find information about the women who, today, would have been listed as co-authors on that seminal paper. And that material, shared with *Quanta*, provides a fuller, fairer account of the birth of chaos.

The Birth of Chaos

In the fall of 2017, the geophysicist Daniel Rothman, co-director of MIT's Lorenz Center, was preparing for an upcoming symposium. The meeting would honor Lorenz, who died in 2008, so Rothman revisited Lorenz's epochal paper, a masterwork on chaos titled "Deterministic Nonperiodic Flow." Published in 1963, it has since attracted thousands of citations, and Rothman, having taught this foundational material to class after class, knew it like an old friend. But this time he saw something he hadn't noticed before. In the paper's acknowledgments, Lorenz had written, "Special thanks are due to Miss Ellen Fetter for handling the many numerical computations."

"Jesus . . . *who is Ellen Fetter?*" Rothman recalls thinking at the time. "It's one of the most important papers in computational physics and, more broadly, in computational science," he said. And yet he couldn't find anything about this woman. "Of all the volumes that have been written about Lorenz, the great discovery —nothing."

With further online searches, however, Rothman found a wedding announcement from 1963. Ellen Fetter had married John Gille, a physicist, and changed her name. A colleague of Rothman's then remembered that a graduate student named Sarah Gille had studied at MIT in the 1990s in the very same department as Lorenz and Rothman. Rothman reached out to her, and it turned out that Sarah Gille, now a physical oceanographer at the University of California, San Diego, was Ellen and John's daughter. Through this connection, Rothman was able to get Ellen Gille, née Fetter, on the phone. And that's when he learned another name, the name of the woman who had preceded Fetter in the job of programming Lorenz's first meetings with chaos: Margaret Hamilton.

When Margaret Hamilton arrived at MIT in the summer of 1959, with a freshly minted math degree from Earlham College, Lorenz had only recently bought and taught himself to use the LGP-30. Hamilton had no prior training in programming either. Then again, neither did anyone else at the time. "He loved that computer," Hamilton said. "And he made me feel the same way about it."

For Hamilton, these were formative years. She recalls being out at a party at 3 or 4 a.m., realizing that the LGP-30 wasn't set to produce results by the next morning, and rushing over with a few friends to start it up. Another time, frustrated by all the things that had to be done to make another run after fixing an error, she devised a way to bypass the computer's clunky debugging process. To Lorenz's delight, Hamilton would take the paper tape that fed the machine, roll it out the length of the hallway, and edit the binary code with a sharp pencil. "I'd poke holes for ones, and I'd cover up with Scotch tape the others," she said. "He just got a kick out of it."

There were desks in the computer room, but because of the noise, Lorenz, his secretary, his programmer, and his graduate students all shared the other office. The plan was to use the desk computer, then a total novelty, to test competing strategies of weather prediction in a way you couldn't do with pencil and paper.

First, though, Lorenz's team had to do the equivalent of catching the Earth's atmosphere in a jar. Lorenz idealized the atmosphere in twelve equations that described the motion of gas in a rotating, stratified fluid. Then the team coded them in.

Sometimes the "weather" inside this simulation would simply repeat like clockwork. But Lorenz found a more interesting and more realistic set of solutions that generated weather that wasn't periodic. The team set up the computer to slowly print out a graph of how one or two variables—say, the latitude of the strongest westerly winds—changed over time. They would gather around to watch this imaginary weather, even placing little bets on what the program would do next.

And then one day it did something really strange. This time they had set up the printer not to make a graph, but simply to print out time stamps and the values of a few variables at each time. As Lorenz later recalled, they had rerun a previous weather simulation with what they thought were the same starting values, reading off the earlier numbers from the previous printout. But those weren't actually the same numbers. The computer was keeping track of numbers to six decimal places, but the printer, to save space on the page, had rounded them to only the first three decimal places.

After the second run started, Lorenz went to get coffee. The new numbers that emerged from the LGP-30 while he was gone looked at first like the ones from the previous run. This new run had started in a very similar place, after all. But the errors grew exponentially. After about two months of imaginary weather, the two runs looked nothing alike. This system was still deterministic, with no random chance intruding between one moment and the next. Even so, its hair-trigger sensitivity to initial conditions made it unpredictable.

This meant that in chaotic systems the smallest fluctuations get amplified. Weather predictions fail once they reach some point in the future because we can never measure the initial state of the atmosphere precisely enough. Or, as Lorenz would later present the idea, even a seagull flapping its wings might eventually make a big difference to the weather. (In 1972, the seagull was deposed when a conference organizer, unable to check back about what Lorenz wanted to call an upcoming talk, wrote his own title that switched the metaphor to a butterfly.)

Many accounts, including the one in Gleick's book, date the discovery of this butterfly effect to 1961, with the paper following in 1963. But in November 1960, Lorenz described it during the Q&A session following a talk he gave at a conference on numerical weather prediction in Tokyo. After his talk, a question came from a member of the audience: "Did you change the initial condition just slightly and see how much different results were?"

"As a matter of fact, we tried that out once with the same equation to see what could happen," Lorenz said. He then started to explain the unexpected result, which he wouldn't publish for three more years. "He just gives it all away," Rothman said now. But no one at the time registered it enough to scoop him.

In the summer of 1961, Hamilton moved on to another project, but not before training her replacement. Two years after Hamilton first stepped on campus, Ellen Fetter showed up at MIT in much the same fashion: a recent graduate of Mount Holyoke with a degree in math, seeking any sort of math-related job in the Boston area, eager and able to learn. She interviewed with a woman who ran the LGP-30 in the nuclear engineering department, who recommended her to Hamilton, who hired her.

Once Fetter arrived in Building 24, Lorenz gave her a manual and a set of programming problems to practice, and before long she was up to speed. "He carried a lot in his head," she said. "He would come in with maybe one yellow sheet of paper, a legal piece of paper in his pocket, pull it out, and say, 'Let's try this.'"

The project had progressed meanwhile. The twelve equations produced fickle weather, but even so, that weather seemed to prefer a narrow set of possibilities among all possible states, forming a mysterious cluster which Lorenz wanted to visualize. Finding that difficult, he narrowed his focus even further. From a colleague named Barry Saltzman, he borrowed just three equations that would describe an even simpler nonperiodic system, a beaker of water heated from below and cooled from above.

Here, again, the LGP-30 chugged its way into chaos. Lorenz identified three properties of the system corresponding roughly to how fast convection was happening in the idealized beaker, how the temperature varied from side to side, and how the temperature varied from top to bottom. The computer tracked these properties moment by moment.

The properties could also be represented as a point in space. Lorenz and Fetter plotted the motion of this point. They found that over time, the point would trace out a butterfly-shaped fractal structure now called the Lorenz attractor. The trajectory of the point—of the system—would never retrace its own path. And as before, two systems setting out from two minutely different starting points would soon be on totally different tracks. But just as profoundly, wherever you started the system, it would still head over to the attractor and start doing chaotic laps around it.

The attractor and the system's sensitivity to initial conditions would eventually be recognized as foundations of chaos theory. Both were published in the landmark 1963 paper. But for a while only meteorologists noticed the result. Meanwhile, Fetter married John Gille and moved with him when he went to Florida State University and then to Colorado. They stayed in touch with Lorenz and saw him at social events. But she didn't realize how famous he had become.

Still, the notion of small differences leading to drastically different outcomes stayed in the back of her mind. She remembered the seagull, flapping its wings. "I always had this image that stepping off the curb one way or the other could change the course of any field," she said.

Flight Checks

After leaving Lorenz's group, Hamilton embarked on a different path, achieving a level of fame that rivals or even exceeds that of her first coding mentor. At MIT's Instrumentation Laboratory, starting in 1965, she headed the onboard flight software team for the Apollo project.

Her code held up when the stakes were life and death—even when a misflipped switch triggered alarms that interrupted the astronaut's displays right as Apollo 11 approached the surface of the moon. Mission Control had to make a quick choice: land or abort. But trusting the software's ability to recognize errors, prioritize important tasks, and recover, the astronauts kept going.

Hamilton, who popularized the term "software engineering," later led the team that wrote the software for Skylab, the first U.S. space station. She founded her own company in Cambridge in 1976, and in recent years her legacy has been celebrated again and again. She won NASA's Exceptional Space Act Award in 2003 and received the Presidential Medal of Freedom in 2016. In 2017 she garnered arguably the greatest honor of all: a Margaret Hamilton Lego minifigure.

Fetter, for her part, continued to program at Florida State after leaving Lorenz's group at MIT. After a few years, she left her job to raise her children. In the 1970s, she took computer science classes at the University of Colorado, toying with the idea of returning to programming, but she eventually took a tax preparation job instead. By the 1980s, the demographics of programming had shifted. "After I sort of got put off by a couple of job interviews, I said forget it," she said. "They went with young, techy guys."

Chaos only reentered her life through her daughter, Sarah. As an undergraduate at Yale in the 1980s, Sarah Gille sat in on a class about scientific programming. The case they studied? Lorenz's discoveries on the LGP-30. Later, Sarah studied physical oceanography as a graduate student at MIT, joining the same overarching department as both Lorenz and Rothman, who had arrived a few years earlier. "One of my office mates in the general exam, the qualifying exam for doing research at MIT, was asked: How would you explain chaos theory to your mother?" she said. "I was like, whew, glad I didn't get that question."

The Changing Value of Computation

Today, chaos theory is part of the scientific repertoire. In a study published just last month, researchers concluded that no amount of improvement in data gathering or in the science of weather forecasting will allow meteorologists to produce useful forecasts that stretch more than fifteen days out. (Lorenz had suggested a similar two-week cap to weather forecasts in the mid-1960s.)

But the many retellings of chaos's birth say little to nothing about how Hamilton and Ellen Gille wrote the specific programs that revealed the signatures of chaos. "This is an all-too-common story in the histories of science and technology," wrote Jennifer Light, the department head for MIT's Science, Technology, and Society program, in an email to *Quanta*. To an extent, we can chalk up that omission to the tendency of storytellers to focus on solitary geniuses. But it also stems from tensions that remain unresolved today.

First, coders in general have seen their contributions to science minimized from the beginning. "It was seen as rote," said Mar Hicks, a historian at the Illinois Institute of Technology. "The fact that it was associated with machines actually gave it less status, rather than more." But beyond that, and contributing to it, many programmers in this era were women.

In addition to Hamilton and the woman who coded in MIT's nuclear engineering department, Ellen Gille recalls a woman on an LGP-30 doing meteorology next door to Lorenz's group. Another woman followed Gille in the job of programming for Lorenz. An analysis of official U.S. labor statistics shows that in 1960, women held 27 percent of computing and math-related jobs.

The percentage has been stuck there for a half-century. In the mid-1980s, the fraction of women pursuing bachelor's degrees in programming even started to decline. Experts have argued over why. One idea holds that early personal computers were marketed preferentially to boys and men. Then when kids went to college, introductory classes assumed a detailed knowledge of computers going in, which alienated young women who didn't grow up with a machine at home. Today, women programmers describe a self-perpetuating cycle where white and Asian male managers hire people who look like all the other programmers they know. Outright harassment also remains a problem.

Hamilton and Gille, however, still speak of Lorenz's humility and mentorship in glowing terms. Before later chroniclers left them out, Lorenz thanked them in the literature in the same way he thanked Saltzman, who provided the equations Lorenz used to find his attractor. This was common at the time. Gille recalls that in all her scientific programming work, only once did someone include her as a co-author after she contributed computational work to a paper; she said she was "stunned" because of how unusual that was.

Since then, the standard for giving credit has shifted. "If you went up and down the floors of this building and told the story to my colleagues, every one of them would say that if this were going on today . . . they'd be a co-author!" Rothman said. "Automatically, they'd be a co-author."

Computation in science has become even more indispensable, of course. For recent breakthroughs like the first image of a black hole, the hard part was not figuring out which equations described the system, but how to leverage computers to understand the data.

Today, many programmers leave science not because their role isn't appreciated, but because coding is better compensated in industry, said Alyssa Goodman, an astronomer at Harvard University and an expert in computing and data science. "In the 1960s, there was no such thing as a data scientist, there was no such thing as Netflix or Google or whoever, that was going to suck in these people and really, really value them," she said.

Still, for coder-scientists in academic systems that measure success by paper citations, things haven't changed all that much. "If you are a software developer who may never write a paper, you may be essential," Goodman said. "But you're not going to be counted that way."

SHANNON STIRONE

The Hunt for Planet Nine

FROM *Longreads*

AT 9,200 FEET, there is 20 percent less oxygen than at sea level, enough to take all the air from my lungs after just three steps. But it didn't stop Mike Brown and Konstantin Batygin from hastily shuffling into the lobby of Hale Pōhaku to check the weather forecast. They stared at the TV monitor, craning their necks, suitcases in one hand, fingers pointing to the screens with the other. "It's Sunday," Brown said, "there's no new forecast until tomorrow. Damn." We were at base camp on the dormant volcano Mauna Kea, on the Big Island of Hawaii. The pair were here to use one of the most powerful telescopes in the world, called Subaru. Tomorrow night, December 3, marked the start of their sixth observing run and their next attempt to find the biggest missing object in our solar system, called—for the moment—Planet Nine.

The Onizuka Center for International Astronomy, located at Hale Pōhaku, looked exactly as you might imagine a Hawaiian dormitory built in the early 1980s would. Each table was covered in an azure nylon tablecloth with salt and pepper shakers. The backs of the chairs depicted scenes from around the island: Mauna Kea, palm trees, snow-capped volcanoes, sandy beaches. It was 7 p.m. when we arrived, and most everyone who lived and worked at these dorms was asleep. (In astronomers' quarters, most people sleep during the day or wake at odd hours of the night to go to work.) The cafeteria was empty. "Oh my god, they have Pop-Tarts! They haven't had Pop-Tarts here for ten years!" said Brown as he unwrapped the shiny foil package to put one in the toaster.

This was a good sign—Pop-Tarts are the nonsuperstitious tradition of astronomical observing—and also dinner.

We would have a snack and go over the game plan for tomorrow night. Brown and Batygin sat down at one of the round tables, laptops out. Brown, a professor of planetary astronomy at the California Institute of Technology in Pasadena, felt optimistic. Batygin, a theoretical astrophysicist and professor of planetary sciences at Caltech, guessed it would take them ten more years of observing. This is their dynamic. If the planet they're looking for exists, it is likely six times the mass of Earth, with an atmosphere made of hydrogen and helium covering its rock-and-ice core. What makes it hard to find is its likely location: at least four hundred times farther away from the sun than our own planet, and fifteen to twenty times farther out than Pluto. As a theorist, Batygin feels that he's already mathematically proven its existence. But it's generally accepted that for a planet to be considered discovered in the field of astronomy, the theory must also be accompanied by a photograph. This is where the Subaru Telescope comes in. They know that Planet Nine is somewhere in between the constellation Orion and Taurus, but that's about as exact as they can get, and they'll need good weather to locate it. Right now the last predicted forecast showed fog. Even at six times the mass of Earth, Planet Nine is so far away that it would appear as a barely visible point of light, even through the lens of the most powerful telescope they could get their hands on.

Though it was only 7 p.m. it was time to settle in for the night. We took a series of wooden bridges faintly illuminated with reddish light to the dorms. (Red light does not affect night vision.) Because of the reduced oxygen, the carry-on-size suitcase I had with me might as well have been the dead body of a weightlifter. We stopped to take a break to catch our breath, and looked up. There is hardly any light at Hale Pōhaku after sundown. An hour away from Kona or Hilo, there are no streetlights, no real building lights, no car lights, it's just dark. What can be easy to forget for anyone that lives in or around a city is that the night sky is not black, but gray. We are drowning ourselves with so much light that we don't realize how much light the darkness really contains. Wherever Planet Nine is—if Planet Nine even is—its surface is touched by the sun's light just like our planet, and as a result some of it is illuminated. The physical particles of light that travel the billions of miles between both bodies also move through space. Their journey begins at the sun, stirring around deep inside the core for thousands of years, moving eventually to the surface where they are finally released. This newly exposed light travels out into the cosmos and to distant unknown worlds. This is why we came, we had to escape the light in order to find it.

We stood there for a moment and as our eyes adjusted, the galaxy turned on. Clusters of stars became the entire sky. Each speck of light had traveled its own distance; traversed its path through the dark void of space, some from the time of the earliest human civilizations, light that left at the dawn of the invention of agriculture and cities, at the time this mountain was last covered in lava. Mike pointed over the hills to a hazy cone of yellow light that shot up like a triangle from the Earth, explaining it was a rare astronomical phenomenon some people wait their whole lives to see: "That is the zodiacal light. It is the sunlight reflecting off of the dust that's floating in the asteroid belt. This is the best I've ever seen it. Wow." Across the sky to the right was the arm of the Milky Way galaxy. It was as though a painter had dipped their brush in starlight and clouds and smeared it ever so carefully across the universe.

With dozens of astronomical discoveries to his name, fifty-three-year-old Mike Brown has the distinction of having found more dwarf planets than any other human in history. Dwarf planets are hundreds of times smaller than Earth, so detecting them when they orbit so far out is extremely tricky. (Pluto, for example, is 500 times less massive than our planet.) In 2001, Brown discovered two dwarf planets called 2001 YH140 and 2001 YJ140. Two years later, using the Palomar Observatory in the mountains outside of San Diego, he caught some light from a distant Kuiper Belt object that no one had ever seen before. It was three times farther away than Pluto, and smaller too. The object was so distant that the view of the sun from its surface could be blotted out with the tip of a pen if held at arm's length. He named it Sedna. Then, in 2005, he found another object—more massive but just a bit smaller than Pluto. He would later name this dwarf planet Eris after the Greek goddess of strife and discord, and oh how much strife this thing caused.

The International Astronomical Union decided that if there

were other "Pluto-size" objects out there then maybe the title "planet" was not a good one for Pluto. Brown became known as the "Pluto Killer"—though mostly by way of his adopted Twitter handle. (Brown said he actually finds Pluto quite interesting, but only admits it under his breath so as not to ruin his bad boy reputation.)

Years later, two astronomers, Scott Sheppard and Chad Trujillo, noticed that a dozen distant Kuiper Belt objects appeared as though they were all operating in concert in the Unknown Regions of space, sharing certain orbital characteristics. Brown was intrigued by their 2014 paper, but thought something wasn't quite right with their hypothesis. That same year Batygin, his former student, was working down the hall. Brown asked Batygin if he wouldn't mind looking at the data with him. Though Brown briefly wondered about the possibility of a planet, he and Batygin quickly pivoted to the idea that enough collective gravity might have put the objects in this orbit. "We tried to examine every hypothesis other than a planet and took it very seriously," said Batygin. "This is not like you come in one day and think a little bit about it then you're done. It takes a lot of time. I made almost complete models for every single other hypothesis before we allowed ourselves to consider the planetary explanation. You have to rule out every other possibility first."

They are not the first to be puzzled by oddities in the outer solar system. Not long after the discovery of Uranus in the eighteenth century, astronomers observed that the planet's orbit wasn't moving at the rate that predictions said it should. The planet appeared to randomly accelerate in its orbit, then decelerate. In 1846, French astronomer Urbain Le Verrier suggested this was the result of another large planet orbiting beyond Uranus that had not yet been found. As in all astronomical observation, an image must be taken in order to consider an object discovered, and no one had ever seen a planet beyond Uranus. Not only did Le Verrier suggest a planet as the cause, he predicted what he thought to be the location. As an expert in mathematics and celestial mechanics, Le Verrier was confident in his claim, so much so that he wrote to German astronomer Johann Galle, who was working at the Berlin Observatory at the time, and told him to look at a specific point in the sky. Galle opened the letter on September 23, 1846, and right away he and his assistant, fellow astronomer Heinrich Louis d'Arrest, took to the telescope. Using Le Verrier's coordinates along with a recently updated star chart, they were able to finally compare this moving object against the tapestry of unmoving stars —they found Neptune less than one hour later.

Planet Nine's Le Verrier is Batygin, who, as 2014 turned into 2015, took to every blackboard and computer simulation he had at his disposal to think over Sheppard and Trujillo's hypothesis using math that only few people in the world understand. He spent more than a year, along with Brown, trying to figure out why these objects were clustered together in space.

Before Planet Nine, Batygin knew little about observing and Brown didn't know much about theory, but Planet Nine cannot be found without both. If anyone knew the theory behind how planetary bodies behaved in space, it was Batygin. By 2014, he was a renowned theoretical astrophysicist, and the following year, was named among Forbes 30 Under 30. He had first distinguished himself at the age of twenty-two, when he proved mathematically that our solar system was unstable—a problem Isaac Newton himself had hoped to solve—and that eventually (a few billion years from now) Mercury could either fall into the sun or collide with Venus, which would result in Mars's ejection from the solar system. Now Brown and Batygin faced a version of the same question Le Verrier asked of himself 169 years ago: what is happening beyond where we can see?

Part of their job was first to try to find a solution less extreme —like a passing star or a galactic anomaly—than a giant undiscovered planet far off in the depths of the solar system, because, a hidden planet? That was absurd. But finally, in the spring of 2015, they both agreed, the only other explanation for this clustering of Kuiper Belt objects was indeed a planet—a big one. On January 20, 2016, they made the announcement proposing that our solar system has a giant planet orbiting far away from everything else. They told all astronomers with access to the most powerful telescopes to go and find it. They wanted to find it too.

Hale Pōhaku. Monday, December 3, 2018. 2:30 a.m.

We met in the cafeteria. It is suggested that all people observing on the summit spend several hours at base camp to adjust to the altitude to prevent dizziness, slurred speech, and death. The summit of the mountain is 13,796 feet and has only 60 percent of the oxygen found at sea level. We were up literally before dawn to begin adjusting to the observing schedule that would now be:

> 10:30 p.m.: Wake up and eat (Breakfast? Dinner?)
> 11 p.m.: Leave for the telescope
> Midnight to 6 a.m.: Observe

Groggy and grunting, both Brown and Batygin dragged their feet down the stairs of the dorm's living room. They do their thinking at base camp and their struggling at the summit. (According to Brown, "Thinking at fourteen thousand feet is not a good idea.") Over Froot Loops and Cheerios, they carefully ran over their own computer simulations with updated search parameters, making inside jokes to each other and giggling. They sometimes debate the location of the planet for hours at a time. At this particular moment, Brown was not only certain that Planet Nine's semimajor axis—that is, the mean distance of the sun along its orbit—was 310, but he was just about willing to stake his life on it. Batygin disagreed: "The reason that we're here right now is because it might not be at 310, it might be at 400." Brown said, looking at me, "Like I said to Konstantin, if we don't get any data, I'm done with this crap, I'm out."

"Yeah, but you say that every time," said Batygin.

To me, "He reminds me that I say that every time."

"It's not like you're doing any actual work."

"I'm actually doing a lot. It actually takes me a long time."

It went on like this. At issue was how many data points they were using in their simulations. Brown had two, but Batygin thought this was wrong, and felt that Brown's room for error (aka, "the wall") was too small. While they consider themselves "regular Caltech nerds," this was also a reference to *Game of Thrones*, since all the distant Kuiper Belt objects are cold and living "beyond the wall." Quick, someone hold the door for this fight:

"You know where else it could be?" said Batygin. "800 AU."

"Pshhh."

"What is the error bar wall? If you try to fit the wall—"

"I don't try to fit the wall."

"*If* you did—"

"*I* don't try to fit the wall. *You* try to fit the wall."

"If you *tried* to fit the wall."

"I wouldn't."

This type of friendly, extremely nerdy, almost-marital bickering is typical of Brown and Batygin, and maybe even expected from two guys who have spent the past few years re-creating the solar system together. They each run simulations that begin at some point in the past four billion years. Since we can't go back in time to see what could have placed Planet Nine where it is or to actually find out *where* it is, they each re-create the growth of the planets over time. Their simulations can take from three days to three months to run, and they start them after all of the large planets have formed, some three to four billion years ago. In 2018 alone they ran more than two thousand Planet Nine parameters with different masses and locations, averaging thirty-eight new solar systems a week. As a result, the slight variations in data are what keep Brown and Batygin bickering and in check.

In order to find their planet, they need to use one of the most powerful telescopes on Earth to capture the light coming from such a great distance. The Subaru Telescope, which was first named the Japanese National Large Telescope, is owned and operated by the National Astronomical Observatory of Japan. Among telescopes its size, Subaru has the largest field of view and magnification available of any Earth-based telescope, which is why this is their only hope of finding the planet. The special camera on Subaru, the Hyper Suprime-Cam, is the real trick. At 10 feet high and 870 megapixels, it is able to focus down to the width of a human hair. The next day, they would try after an entire year without any usable data. This is the search for Planet Nine.

At 4 p.m., we went to bed.

Hale Pōhaku. Monday, December 3, 2018 (still). 11:15 p.m.

Brown speed-walked into the cafeteria, threw his black messenger bag onto one of the chairs of the round table, and with wide eyes whisper-yelled, "HOW IS THE WEATHER AT THE SUMMIT!?" The thirty-second walk from the dorms to the common building was not great. It was raining. There was fog. Batygin and Surhud More, an astronomer and collaborator from the Japanese science team, were prepared with an answer. "Only 10 percent humidity at the summit," More replied, trying to settle Brown's nerves. Over the past three years Brown and Batygin have made five trips to the Subaru Telescope on Mauna Kea. Of the eighteen and a half days they have spent observing, only eight and a half nights have produced useful data. This was no time for fog, almost a four-letter word but not quite.

The parking lot at Hale Pōhaku is paved, while most of the road to the summit is not. A sign at the edge of the parking lot reminds visitors to stop and switch into four-wheel drive for the twenty-five-minute drive up the mountain. This delineation between paved road and unpaved road is a reminder that the journey is dangerous, it takes effort, caution. We must have patience, we must move slowly and remember this is a temporary visit. Our oxygen is about to be reduced by 40 percent, and we will see fewer stars because there is less oxygen in our blood to help our eyes focus. We drove at approximately four miles per hour with just the power of our headlights to prevent us from driving one foot to the right and plummeting down the mountain to our death.

I have been to the tops of mountains, but none like the summit of Mauna Kea. It is not just its meaning and value to the Hawaiian people that might influence the feeling there. When I stepped out of the car, I was grabbed by the wind, encircled, wrapped, and marked—human foreigner. It was cold, below freezing, and it was dark. Nearly the darkest part of any night is around midnight, but after my eyes adjusted, somehow there was a little light. Our bodies' survival mechanisms kick in, pupils are automatically dilated, opened up as wide as possible. In darkness like this we are vulnerable and our animal brains know it. It is the same feeling I imagine I would have if suddenly placed on Mars. This land is not for humans. There is barely any oxygen, there is almost no water in the air. There is no life around, no plants, no birds, nothing—these rocks are the beginning and end of everything. Just enough light from the stars overhead reflected off the bright white paint of the domes. There were no smells. The wind hit me again like a giant palm to my body. Even the sound of the dirt and stone below my shoe was foreign, like stepping on glass but not quite. It was a sound I had never heard. I was not where I had been. I felt reverent and intrusive, almost disoriented. With each crunch of rock under my shoe I was reminded that this is old land. Original land. Volcanoes are monoliths formed from fire and water and air—a million-year-old history cracked and ached below my feet.

The mountain last saw fire from its peak 4,500 years ago. It was toward the end of the Bronze Age. Humans began to use the plow. The world's population was only 25 million, and writing would soon begin in Sumeria and Egypt. I felt suddenly as though I had intruded on the past. Standing there being nearly blown over by the wind and pricked with the cold air felt like being in what in Celtic culture they call a "thin place." The saying goes that the distance between heaven and earth is only three feet apart, but in a thin place, that distance collapses. Oftentimes it is used to describe the moment when a person is about to take their last breath, or right before they take their first. Where heaven meets the Earth —this is Mauna Kea.

For Hawaiians this mountain is sacred. The highest peak in all the Hawaiian islands, it is what they call a *wao akua,* which translates to "home of the gods." The summit of the Mauna, or mountain, is the place where the gods live. Mauna Kea, in English, translates to "white mountain," a nod to the snow-capped peaks, but the full name is Mauna a Wakea, or god of the sky. Traditionally, only religious leaders and Hawaiian royalty were allowed to travel to the top, the place for shrines, burials, and ceremonies. The summit has never been just for anyone—only those with the right could ascend the mountain and be in the presence of the gods. For this reason the use of the summit as a place for large telescopes and observing has been highly contested by the Native Hawaiian community, considering construction on the mountain as a desecration of their most sacred land. Now "science city" dominates it. Whether you believe in god, or the gods, or heaven or hell, or nothing at all, the summit of this ancient mountain and this sacred place felt as though the distance between the unreachable stars and the top of the Earth had collapsed and for as long as we were there, we existed in the thin place.

Mauna Kea, Subaru Observing Control Room.
Tuesday, December 4, 2018. Midnight.

At 14,000 feet Brown's fears of fog no longer mattered. "I can't believe it's so clear!" he said. After taking the elevator up to the third floor where the observing room is, they both nearly ran in, set down their stuff, and immediately got to work. Brown had his laptop open before his jacket was off and Batygin was already on a computer typing in a code that would deliver images to him during the night. They needed to get the telescope calibrated and focused on the patch of sky they would be observing. An engineer and support observer were each at their own computers next to the main screen, which had a countdown clock that read "Time to Completion." In this instance, they were calibrating the telescope. It counted down: 136, 135, 134, 133. One computer screen hung from the top of the room that showed multiple views of various control rooms, one of which was in Tokyo where, every morning, they greet the Japanese team. Brown and Batygin had the last half of the night, midnight to 6 a.m., for observing. They would observe with half-nights for four days, and the last three they would get the run of the telescope from sundown to sunrise.

The countdown reached zero, and the sound of a cuckoo clock went off. This sound marked the end of calibration. They were ready to observe. It also "cuckooed!" every time an exposure finished. Their plan was to capture about one hundred fields on every half-night, weather permitting. The fields functioned like circles on a map, marking the total viewing area of the telescope: around nine full moons' worth. Every exposure lasted sixty seconds, and with each one came a new image of the sky. Batygin's job was to look at random stars in the images to measure their width. The more circular the stars appeared in the camera, the better the seeing was. If he clicked on a star and it appeared jagged, it meant there was upper atmospheric turbulence; if it was slightly oval, the telescope was out of focus; if it appeared washed out, it meant that there was fog. All of this messed with their ability to capture a precise point of light. That's a problem when your entire task is to capture a precise point of light. The windier the conditions, the more the stars' light would smear across what is called an arc second. And to find Planet Nine they needed all arc second readings to be under 2.0, ideally under 1.0. Planet Nine likely travels—at the most—two arc seconds a night, so if the winds are too high in the upper atmosphere, so much that it's smearing the stars into two or three arc seconds wide, the data become unusable. Think of zero arc seconds as being a perfect point in the sky; as the arc seconds creep up, the light gets blurrier, smearing out a little to the sides and blocking whatever possible planet might be hiding behind.

Brown named each field with four numbers in a spreadsheet and kept a log of stars' arc seconds that Batygin randomly clicked on in that field. If the "seeing" was bad, Brown would make a note in the log and they would have to go back and reimage that field. This is where observing becomes less romantic and more like a creepy radio number station. They would wait to take about ten images, and Batygin would then read off the numbers in batches: "4817 is 1.4. 4918 is 0.9. 4919 is 1.05. 5319 is 1.1. 5318 is 1.4," and so on.

Minutes after starting up the cameras, they were collecting data. The weather was holding so spirits were high. Maybe a bit too high? Up at 14,000 feet one can get what is called an "altitude high," which happens when the brain is deprived of oxygen. Some people get cranky, some get sleepy and mellow. Batygin gets happy. More, even, than normal. Every time he comes up to the summit, he has to use oxygen so he knew he was due for some air. There was a first aid cabinet with personal oxygen tanks that you strap around your waist with a belt and prewrapped plastic nose inserts. It was 12:45 a.m. and Batygin had not yet plugged in.

He was in the thick of collecting star data and writing down the next set of numbers to read off to Brown when he opened an image of stars. The sensors on the camera, all 116 of them, collect so much of the sky that as soon as you start to zoom in on any photo, not only do you fill the screen with so many stars that it looks like TV static, but galaxies appear, asteroids, you name it. The screen becomes littered with space stuff. With a black-and-white image open, he pointed to the screen and said, "I think I found Planet Nine!" He was joking, but to Brown's ears, he sounded way too happy. Brown jumped up out of his seat, grumbled "Oh man" under his breath, and walked to the first aid cabinet for a monitor to test Batygin's oxygen. It was below 70. His lips had turned a little purple, and he was way too excited to be up at midnight and working. Brown was worried about him, but Batygin laughed it off, with a facetious dying message to his wife: "Just tell Olga I love her." He unwrapped the plastic tubes that strap around your head and placed them inside his nose. "I'm about to get way less happy,"

Batygin said, half disappointed, half warning us all. He flipped the switch on the oxygen tank, the batteries started up, and he took in one long deep breath.

The control room had more than two dozen computer monitors, most of which have specific readouts: the temperature of the telescope mirror, precipitation, wind speed, etc. Above the computers was a shelf with five speakers that each trace back to a microphone placed on the telescope. Every time the camera's shutter opened and closed it made a sound like Optimus Prime mid-transformation. The volume was up loud so that staff could walk to the break room for coffee and still hear the shutter open and close, which it does every sixty seconds, followed by a cuckoo to mark the successful download of the exposure. Open, sixty seconds, close, "cuckoo!"

Subaru collects a lot of light and from a large swath of the sky. As a result, every night the team's data contained hundreds of asteroids and Kuiper Belt objects, many that have never been seen before. Under normal circumstances, these appearances would warrant follow-up, and even excitement, but there is an urgency to this search. Brown and Batygin don't have time to chase these things night after night, which is what is required to "discover" something. These objects are just light that is collected and discarded. As Batygin and More sorted through images, measuring the seeing in each field, discussing numbers and computer codes, a new image came through and they zoomed in. Against the blue of the computer screen, a massive spiral galaxy appeared. It had a wispy ghostlike body with long, almost jellyfish-like tendrils that stretched around on itself. We leaned over to look at the picture and said, "Oh wow!" which warranted a quick half-joking reply from Brown: "Ugh, galaxies. Those are the worst."

The trouble with looking for one thing in the sky is that our galaxy is full of stars, 100 billion of them, most of which annoy Brown to no end. If Planet Nine exists, it is so faint and so far away that it can easily get overpowered by a regular show-hogging ham of a star. The absolute worst place to look for Planet Nine is into the plane of our galaxy where a lot of those stars live. By 2 a.m., another package of Pop-Tarts had been opened. The numbers were coming in over 1.4—not great. Brown decided they should move the telescope and begin observing on the other side of the galactic plane. They sent the request to the telescope operators to calcu-

late how long the slew would take. They told him that because of
the time of night, to get around the plane of the galaxy would take
forty minutes. "Forty minutes!" Brown exclaimed, "Shit, shit, fuck,
fuck."

Forty minutes is a long time. I was told that it costs a dollar a
second to use this telescope, and forty minutes is a lot of observing time lost when you only have six hours in one night to find
a planet. He decided they would wait a few more hours until the
galactic plane had moved overhead, so the slew that would have
taken forty minutes would only take ten. They would keep observing with the 1.4s until the 4 a.m. slew.

By 4:30, the slew was complete, and the brightness of the galactic plane was out of the way. Brown asked Batygin to read out the
numbers.

"Yep! 7715 is 0.8. 7516 is 1.0. 7515 is 0.7. 7518 is 0.8." They continued coming in under 1, a relief. Joking in the room resumed.
An observer asked Batygin how they process the data after they
return to Caltech, to which he replied, "Well, we have these algorithms—"

Brown interjected: "We have algorithms? Uh, no. I have spent
most of my life writing these programs. This is not stuff you can
get at the App Store."

"You should sell your algorithms on Google Play," joked Batygin.

"Ninety-nine cents," said Brown, with a slight roll of his eyes.
"Give me more numbers!"

At 5:50, we heard another "cuckoo!" The dome began to close
and the team packed up the Pop-Tarts and gear. Despite the 1.4s,
the night marked the first successful collection of data in more
than a year. All anyone could talk about was breakfast. There
wasn't any coffee at the summit, and warm eggs, potatoes, sausage,
and enough coffee to fill a bucket was all that anyone wanted.

The beauty of leaving the summit after 6 a.m. was that it took
around twenty-five minutes to get back to base camp: just enough
time to watch the sun come up. In just under a minute the dark
gray of twilight was swept away. The air was grayish blue, the rocks
I had felt under my shoes earlier were a burnt umber, small and
light. On Mauna Kea, the sun does not just rise, it cracks the sky
open with an almost blinding yellow that is quickly seized and
destroyed by an even brighter orange. Every second new colors

appeared as banded layers of horizontal clouds. What I once understood to be light blue was slightly *more* light blue. It met and danced with lavender that bled like watercolor into mauve, then a soft pink. As we left the parking lot and started to drive down the mountain, other telescopes appeared. They were everywhere. Suddenly white and glossy silver, their towering domes stood atop the reddish soil of the peaks. They were massive. As we drove, the car shook from side to side from the road, like being in a paper airplane played with by the wind. We passed the red mounds of ancient volcanic vents that stood there, markers of lost time. The clouds, like the whitish gray of an old cobblestone street, lingered in the valley below, and suddenly the purple sky began to turn.

Hale Pōhaku. Tuesday, December 4, 2018. 7:30 a.m.

The living room just outside the cafeteria had a Christmas tree and completed jigsaw puzzle that looked like it had been baking in the sunlight since the dorms opened in 1983. There were three couches and cozy green chairs and a fireplace with red and white stockings, hung mostly with care. Batygin spent the day back at the dorm, first trying to figure out if a passing star could have perturbed Planet Nine, placing it into its weird orbit. Brown sorted through data from other telescopes trying to—surprise—find Planet Nine. He has spent nearly every free moment in Hawaii combing through data from the ZTF instrument on Palomar's Samuel Oschin Telescope, the same telescope he used to find the dwarf planets that made him as famous as an astronomer can reasonably expect to be. So far anyway. Lunch was served at 1 p.m., but it would be our dinner. We would go to sleep at 3:30 p.m. and wake up at 11 p.m. to go back to the telescope.

The guys had no idea if they would find Planet Nine that week, and Brown's mood oscillated accordingly. After they got back to Caltech and received the data from the headquarters in Tokyo, they would rely in large part on machine learning to sort through the roughly 160,000 images they'd have. They would take their list of candidates and run it through the computer, and any that came up as possible Planet Nines, as many as 1,000 images, would then be looked at in the old school way: by eye. They would be looking for a tiny speck of moving light. "If ever there were one barely crawling across the screen," Brown told me, "it would be an 'Oh shit, that's it' moment."

This search was different from Brown's previous endeavors. "For my entire career what I feel like what I have been doing is exploring the solar system," he told me. "It never occurred to me that there was more primary exploration left to do. So finding Planet Nine is *the* grandest exploration that can be done of the solar system right now. I wouldn't want to be doing anything else."

"I agree with everything Mike said," added Batygin.

"First time today!" Brown replied.

"Cherish it. It's not going to happen again."

Batygin feels confident that the planet is there. It is not just the evidence of these clustered objects, but after four years of simulations and doing calculations that look like they are in some alien language, he feels that his equations confirm that this *is* a large mass object that is shepherding these objects into place. Planet Nine is doing this. He wants to know that his math is right, and the detection of Planet Nine would do that: "There's a different thrill here for me which is actually the thrill of refutation of confirmation. With theory it's almost like it emerges out of nothing. And really it's only in our heads, it's not something that we have seen before. It is a pure outcome of imagination and there's a thrilling magnetism to that because that imagination might be right. For me that is the most amazing thing, being guided only by mathematics."

"I've never worked on a problem that's taken this long," Brown told me. "It is really difficult to sustain this effort for one singular purpose. It's hard. Sometimes I think, let's just find it so I can do something else, I'm tired of this stupid planet. That's the hardest part for me other than the frustration of not knowing where to find it." Batygin agreed. "There have been a few times in the last few years that I actually stopped working on Planet Nine," he said. "I had moments where I felt like I was getting over-obsessed with this and kind of going in circles so I would make the conscious effort, for the next two months I'm not going to think about Planet Nine, how about magnetic fields of young giant planets or the Schrödinger equation? I took my mind off of things so I could come back with renewed enthusiasm."

"There is only one way to win this survey, and that is to actually find it," Brown continued. "The correct analogy is that there's

this singular somewhere in the ocean and you don't know where
—there is only one giant white whale and you need to go kill it
because it bit your leg off. Sadly, I think that's the right analogy."

Hale Pōhaku. Tuesday, December 4, 2018. 11:15 p.m.

Every morning Brown selects a playlist for the drive to the summit.
It is usually five songs long, which is about how long it takes to get
to the telescope. Brown connected his phone as Batygin, who was
driving, switched the car into four-wheel drive and Cake's 1996 hit
"The Distance" began playing. We climbed the rest of the way up
the mountain listening to Eminem, Kanye West, Lynyrd Skynyrd
(Brown is from Alabama), and Jon Bon Jovi (they attempted the
high notes).

When we arrived at the summit it was windy, much more than
the day before. These were fifty-mile-an-hour gusts, close to the
maximum the telescope could take. The upper atmosphere was
turbulent too. The first batch of numbers came in all over 2.0,
which was very, very bad. While they waited to see if the winds
calmed down, Batygin sketched out a graph and an equation in
Greek. He kneeled on the floor next to Brown and asked for his
help. Despite the fact that when we arrived at the summit we were
warned that the altitude would make it harder to do calculations,
what Batygin had in his notebook was black-belt-level math, he
solved it without seeming to break a sweat. Brown checked the
numbers: "We're getting these 2.6s and 2.9s, and these I declare
to be shit."

"Hold on, I'm still not oxygened up," said Batygin.

"What is 4319?" Brown asked, referring to one of the fields they
had just imaged. "You're showing 1.7, I'm showing 2.2. Can you
check?"

"Yeah," Batygin replied. "It's 2.2. Sorry, got that wrong."

"Please put on your oxygen."

Batygin placed the plastic tubes into his nose and, like putting
on a cool pair of life-saving sunglasses, slipped the rest of the plastic tubing over his ears, and took a deep breath of that "sweet,
sweet oxygen." The control room computers had readout charts
on the screens that showed wind speed and upper atmosphere
turbulence as a red spiky graph, literally off the charts. Because of

Planet Nine's slow pace across the cosmos, these 2.0s and higher were useless data. They were looking for a barely visible point of light; if the stars were blurring out all over the place, Planet Nine would remain hiding. "We are not collecting data that is worthwhile," Brown said as he began putting together a backup plan for his backup plan. In their three years of using Subaru they've had, as Batygin puts it, "pretty shitty luck." Not only has the weather been unpredictable and rainy, but, in May 2018, the nearby volcano Kilauea erupted, destroying more than 700 houses and displacing roughly 3,000 residents. There was concern that sustained seismic activity also meant that Subaru and its camera might be rendered useless for a good portion of the year, leaving the team without an opportunity to observe. Plus, sometimes the weather is so bad on the summit, they can't even go up. "Last December we were sequestered in astronomers' headquarters and hoped that it would stop hailing." Batygin said. "We didn't collect one image that whole run. It was really disappointing."

The team checked on the numbers again, which were climbing beyond 2.5, nearly killing Brown every time. Just short of defeated he said, "Three arc seconds and I'm going to the beach," then requested more numbers.

"Okay, this is a record-breaker, are you ready?" asked Batygin.

Brown, resigned: "Yeah."

"3.3."

The entire room shouted: "3.3!"

"In all my twenty-five years of observing on Mauna Kea I have *never* had three arc seconds," Brown said. Numbers this bad were like turning this gigantic 8.2-meter telescope into a one-meter telescope; it would be impossible to find Planet Nine like this. Brown sat at his computer, arms crossed, and said, "The seeing is crappy, but the good news is clouds are coming in!" Indeed a ghostlike cloud was creeping over the valley and heading straight toward the summit. They waited another twenty minutes or so before Brown asked how it was looking.

Batygin: "Okay, now *this* is a record. Are you ready? 4919 is 3.8."

Entire room: "3.8!"

Brown: "3.8!? 3.8! I think . . . I officially declare failure, which will significantly influence the music mix on the way down."

At 4:10 a.m., Brown and Batygin decided to try the other side of the galactic plane, in the hope that the seeing would be better, and indeed the numbers improved—back down to 1.3s and 1.5s. One of the tricky and interesting things about *if* this planet exists is that *if* they find it, they will have absolutely no idea how it got there. While snacks were consumed and the room filled with a symphony of yawns, Batygin stared into space. He was doing the opposite of what one should do at 14,000 feet—thinking, writing code, and doing some complex math to try to figure out how the movement of our galaxy and passing stars could have affected Planet Nine over time in order to determine the planet's location. By 5:20 a.m. the numbers were staying low, which was just enough to save this batch. At 5:51 a.m. we heard a cuckoo. The morning's drive-down-the-mountain playlist appropriately began with the Rolling Stones' "(I Can't Get No) Satisfaction."

As day broke, the sky filled again with purples and pinks, the colors of dreams. We drove down the road and watched the landscape change: small reddish rocks turned into boulders remaining from the Ice Age, when these mountains were once covered in glaciers. A third of the way down, a random shrub appeared alone next to the road. As we approached Hale Pōhaku, small bee-size yellow wildflowers danced left to right in the breeze, and tall stalk-like plants nestled into the ancient volcanic rock. Anyone would say it was beautiful here, the thick marshmallow clouds hovering in the valley below, always threatening the mental well-being of the astronomers watching out the window.

Back at base camp, around the same round table with the nylon tablecloth, Batygin and Brown reflected on the previous four years. "We had this conversation about a year ago," said Batygin. "We were driving up to Mauna Kea, and Mike was like, 'I think . . . this is kind of weird,' and it is at the end of the day. It is weird because we get on a plane and we go to a beautiful island and instead of spending time like normal people do in Hawaii, we go to the only part of the island that is completely dead, and we stay up all night looking at the sky trying to find something that basically we imagine to be there. It's a strange behavior but man, it's so satisfying."

I left Mauna Kea on Wednesday afternoon, right as the team was due to go to sleep. They observed five more nights and the weather cooperated for all of them. It was the first meaningful collection of data in more than a year. I waited until they both got back home to call and find out how it went. I spoke to Brown first. It had been just over two weeks and all of the images collected from the week of observing had not yet reached his desk at Caltech. "I'm depressed," he said. "I'm in my we're-not-going-to-find-it mode." If they don't find it this time, Brown said, "it's perfectly plausible that we've pointed in the right direction and we've missed it."

Two more weeks passed, a new year arrived, and with it came their data. I asked if they found it but so far, Planet Nine has not made its big debut. They are just starting to sort through their data, though. There is still hope. The trip wasn't exactly their last chance to find Planet Nine. They'll return in February for another round of observing. If they don't find it then? "We will just keep going," Batygin told me, "and by 'keep going' what I mean is wait for LSST." The LSST is the Large Synoptic Survey Telescope, which is being constructed in the Chilean desert. It will be fully operational in 2022; its mirror will be even larger than Subaru and will scan the skies every possible clear night. If Planet Nine is out there, this thing will find it. And at first, it will likely discover hundreds more long-period Kuiper Belt objects that will point the team to the direction of Planet Nine.

"There's a 5 or 10 percent chance anytime you look you'll miss it because there's a star in the way," said Brown, "but you know, it just means—increasingly when you don't find it you have to wonder what the heck is really going on here. I don't think the answer is that there is *no* Planet Nine; certainly the phenomena that Planet Nine does are not going away. I don't think there's any other solution aside from Planet Nine to explain those phenomena so the question is, why are we potentially failing in our prediction of where it is?"

Batygin said that finding Planet Nine is so difficult that it is not just like searching for a needle in a haystack, it is like "you're also looking for it with the lights off and a bunch of fog and your calculations tell you that there should be one more needle in this room somewhere." Can the effort be worth it? According to Brown, yes. "This is like first-level exploration of our solar system. This is like, finding a new continent," he said. "It's hard to imagine that any effort that I could actually put in would be ridiculous if we can actually find this thing that's in our solar system that nobody knows about."

Batygin said, "It's really easy to miss something when you're scanning the sky once, it's true when you're looking for the One Thing. We may or may not find Planet Nine, and of course if we find it, great, if we don't find it then it doesn't really mean anything."

If they *do* find their planet, our daily life will mostly remain the same. Sure, mobiles over children's beds might have nine planets putting them into a peaceful sleep; science textbooks will have to be edited and books about our solar system rewritten. But after the hullabaloo of the news cycle and the introduction of a new planet to all of humankind, things will go back to normal. But for science and the field of astronomy, it will help complete a puzzle and make for many new ones as well. If Planet Nine exists, and if it is found, not only will it serve as a way to understand the bulk of exoplanets that have been discovered around other stars, but it will also help us understand the history of our own solar system; it will help us understand more of how the planets came to be and why they settled where they did. It will be one of the twenty-first century's greatest scientific discoveries. We have no idea what a six-Earth-mass planet looks like. Uranus and Neptune are fourteen and seventeen Earth masses; Mars is ten times less massive than Earth. There is nothing in our solar system that size. Six Earth masses could essentially be a core of a planet like Uranus and Neptune, and if Planet Nine exists that is likely its story. The team thinks that during the early days of the solar system, when the outer planets were forming, there was an additional planetary core, near where Uranus and Neptune were growing. But somewhere in those early days, the third core somehow got flung out by a gravitational interaction with Jupiter or Saturn, and as it was heading out of the solar system, became trapped by the gravity of the sun. Since that time it has been orbiting in the distant solar system, silently sculpting Kuiper Belt objects, marking evidence of its existence. If these objects do in fact point to Planet Nine, it will have been quite the planetary smoke signal, one so unlikely to be found.

And they're not the only ones who've been scooped when searching for something. In January 1613, while observing Jupiter and its moons, Galileo caught a glimpse of what he thought was a "fixed star." He marked a dark spot in his notebook and moved on. He had unknowingly detected the light from Neptune. And just months before Le Verrier predicted its existence, an observatory in England detected it three separate times, noting it as a star.

Batygin takes comfort in facts like these. "When there is one thing you're looking for in the night sky—even the world's best astronomer, which certainly Galileo was really good—you're going to miss it the first twenty-five times," he said.

Many in the scientific community are still skeptical of Planet Nine's existence. Batygin understands their skepticism: "Our firm belief is that only crazy people propose planets beyond Neptune." But he and Brown have now joined the ranks of those throughout history who have said, "But what about a giant planet!" Only this time, they mean it, and they have the math to back it up. Batygin, being the theorist that he is, feels that he has already proven its existence, the same way Le Verrier predicted Neptune's. Sure Galle was lucky that he happened to be using the telescope at the exact right time and that D'Arrest had brought a star chart with him, but even if he hadn't, someone, someday would have found Neptune. For Planet Nine, its discovery day awaits. Until that day comes, if it ever does, they will keep searching.

After the observing run was complete, I asked the pair if they ever felt that trying to find Planet Nine was ridiculous, if the whole notion of a giant missing planet and the efforts they have gone to to find it ever make them feel defeated. They both gave me roughly the same response: no. Their answer brought to mind the French philosopher and writer Albert Camus. He thought a lot about the myth of Sisyphus and plucked his unfortunate mythical backstory away from the root of his actions, the eternal task of pushing a boulder up a mountain only to watch it fall back down again. For Camus, he symbolized the despair that can come from making consistent efforts only to be disappointed again and again with the outcome. However, he saw this phenomenon with humankind. We have an ability to feel joy and find happiness in our tasks before a reward of completion ever arrives, even if it never does. "The struggle itself . . . is enough to fill a man's heart," he wrote.

Despite their constant disappointment and exhaustion, both Brown and Batygin find joy in the process of the search, in the not-knowing, in the wondering, and maybe sometimes even the waiting. "Man's sole greatness is to fight against what is beyond him," Camus said. So why do we bother going to the tops of mountains anyway? To see whatever is below, to understand if we are safe down there? We do it to feel bigger. To feel smaller. To get a new perspective, to do it and say we did it. There are many reasons to make that journey, to see what it is like on the other side, to get to know ourselves better. No one climbs a mountain without searching for an answer to something. So many hero stories begin or end at the top of a mountain. It is an act of completion, a marker of accomplishment, a reminder that one is alive and despite the absurdity of it all we can get ourselves to the top of the sky. Or maybe the attempt to reach the summit is, in itself, enough. Camus said for this reason that "one must imagine Sisyphus happy."

NATALIE WOLCHOVER

A Different Kind of
Theory of Everything

FROM *The New Yorker*

IN 1964, DURING a lecture at Cornell University, the physicist Richard Feynman articulated a profound mystery about the physical world. He told his listeners to imagine two objects, each gravitationally attracted to the other. How, he asked, should we predict their movements? Feynman identified three approaches, each invoking a different belief about the world. The first approach used Newton's law of gravity, according to which the objects exert a pull on each other. The second imagined a gravitational field extending through space, which the objects distort. The third applied the principle of least action, which holds that each object moves by following the path that takes the least energy in the least time. All three approaches produced the same, correct prediction. They were three equally useful descriptions of how gravity works.

"One of the amazing characteristics of nature is this variety of interpretational schemes," Feynman said. What's more, this multifariousness applies only to the *true* laws of nature — it doesn't work if the laws are misstated. "If you modify the laws much, you find you can only write them in fewer ways," Feynman said. "I always found that mysterious, and I do not know the reason why it is that the correct laws of physics are expressible in such a tremendous variety of ways. They seem to be able to get through several wickets at the same time."

Even as physicists work to understand the material content of the universe — the properties of particles, the nature of the big bang, the origins of dark matter and dark energy—their work is shadowed by this Rashomon effect, which raises metaphysical questions about the meaning of physics and the nature of reality. Nima Arkani-Hamed, a physicist at the Institute for Advanced Study, is one of today's leading theoreticians. "The miraculous shape-shifting property of the laws is the single most amazing thing I know about them," he told me, this past fall. It "must be a huge clue to the nature of the ultimate truth."

Traditionally, physicists have been reductionists. They've searched for a "theory of everything" that describes reality in terms of its most fundamental components. In this way of thinking, the known laws of physics are provisional, approximating an as-yet-unknown, more detailed description. A table is *really* a collection of atoms; atoms, upon closer inspection, reveal themselves to be clusters of protons and neutrons; each of these is, more microscopically, a trio of quarks; and quarks, in turn, are presumed to consist of something yet more fundamental. Reductionists think that they are playing a game of telephone: as the message of reality travels upward, from the microscopic to the macroscopic scale, it becomes garbled, and they must work their way downward to recover the truth. Physicists now know that gravity wrecks this naive scheme, by shaping the universe on both large and small scales. And the Rashomon effect also suggests that reality isn't structured in such a reductive, bottom-up way.

If anything, Feynman's example understated the mystery of the Rashomon effect, which is actually twofold. It's strange that, as Feynman says, there are multiple valid ways of describing so many physical phenomena. But an even stranger fact is that, when there are competing descriptions, one often turns out to be more true than the others, because it extends to a deeper or more general description of reality. Of the three ways of describing objects' motion, for instance, the approach that turns out to be more true is the underdog: the principle of least action. In everyday reality, it's strange to imagine that objects move by "choosing" the easiest path. (How does a falling rock know which trajectory to take before it gets going?) But, a century ago, when physicists began to make experimental observations about the strange behavior of elementary particles, only the least-action interpretation of motion proved conceptually compatible. A whole new mathematical language—quantum mechanics—had to be developed to describe particles' probabilistic ability to play out all possibilities and take the easiest path most frequently. Of the various classical laws of motion—all workable, all useful—only the principle of least action also extends to the quantum world.

It happens again and again that, when there are many possible descriptions of a physical situation—all making equivalent predictions, yet all wildly different in premise—one will turn out to be preferable, because it extends to an underlying reality, seeming to account for more of the universe at once. And yet this new description might, in turn, have multiple formulations—and one of those alternatives may apply even more broadly. It's as though physicists are playing a modified telephone game in which, with each whisper, the message is translated into a different language. The languages describe different scales or domains of the same reality but aren't always related etymologically. In this modified game, the objective isn't—or isn't only—to seek a bedrock equation governing reality's smallest bits. The existence of this branching, interconnected web of mathematical languages, each with its own associated picture of the world, is what needs to be understood.

This web of laws creates traps for physicists. Suppose you're a researcher seeking to understand the universe more deeply. You may get stuck using a dead-end description—clinging to a principle that seems correct but is merely one of nature's disguises. It's for this reason that Paul Dirac, a British pioneer of quantum theory, stressed the importance of reformulating existing theories: it's by finding new ways of describing known phenomena that you can escape the trap of provisional or limited belief. This was the trick that led Dirac to predict antimatter, in 1928. "It is not always so that theories which are equivalent are equally good," he said, five decades later, "because one of them may be more suitable than the other for future developments."

Today, various puzzles and paradoxes point to the need to reformulate the theories of modern physics in a new mathematical language. Many physicists feel trapped. They have a hunch that they need to transcend the notion that objects move and interact in space and time. Einstein's general theory of relativity beautifully weaves space and time together into a four-dimensional fabric, known as space-time, and equates gravity with warps in that fabric. But Einstein's theory and the space-time concept break down inside black holes and at the moment of the big bang. Space-time, in other words, may be a translation of some other description of reality that, though more abstract or unfamiliar, can have greater explanatory power.

Some researchers are attempting to wean physics off of space-time in order to pave the way toward this deeper theory. Currently, to predict how particles morph and scatter when they collide in space-time, physicists use a complicated diagrammatic scheme invented by Richard Feynman. The so-called Feynman diagrams indicate the probabilities, or "scattering amplitudes," of different particle-collision outcomes. In 2013, Nima Arkani-Hamed and Jaroslav Trnka discovered a reformulation of scattering amplitudes that makes reference to neither space nor time. They found that the amplitudes of certain particle collisions are encoded in the volume of a jewel-like geometric object, which they dubbed the amplituhedron. Ever since, they and dozens of other researchers have been exploring this new geometric formulation of particle-scattering amplitudes, hoping that it will lead away from our everyday, space-time-bound conception to some grander explanatory structure.

Whether these researchers are on the right track or not, the web of explanations of reality exists. Perhaps the most striking thing about those explanations is that, even as each draws only a partial picture of reality, they are mathematically perfect. Take general relativity. Physicists know that Einstein's theory is incomplete. Yet it is a spectacular artifice, with a spare, taut mathematical structure. Fiddle with the equations even a little and you lose all of its beauty and simplicity. It turns out that, if you want to discover a deeper way of explaining the universe, you can't take the equations of the existing description and subtly deform them. Instead, you must make a jump to a totally different, equally perfect mathematical structure. What's the point, theorists wonder, of the perfection found at every level, if it's bound to be superseded?

It seems inconceivable that this intricate web of perfect mathematical descriptions is random or happenstance. This mystery must have an explanation. But what might such an explanation look like? One common conception of physics is that its laws are like a machine that humans are building in order to predict what will happen in the future. The "theory of everything" is like the ultimate prediction machine—a single equation from which everything follows. But this outlook ignores the existence of the many different machines, built in all manner of ingenious ways, that give us equivalent predictions.

To Arkani-Hamed, the multifariousness of the laws suggests a different conception of what physics is all about. We're not building a machine that calculates answers, he says; instead, we're discovering questions. Nature's shape-shifting laws seem to be the answer to an unknown mathematical question. This is why Arkani-Hamed and his colleagues find their studies of the amplituhedron so promising. Calculating the volume of the amplituhedron is a question in geometry—one that mathematicians might have pondered, had they discovered the object first. Somehow, the answer to the question of the amplituhedron's volume describes the behavior of particles—and that answer, in turn, can be rewritten in terms of space and time.

Arkani-Hamed now sees the ultimate goal of physics as figuring out the mathematical question from which all the answers flow. "The ascension to the tenth level of intellectual heaven," he told me, "would be if we find the question to which the universe is the answer, and the nature of that question in and of itself explains why it was possible to describe it in so many different ways." It's as though physics has been turned inside out. It now appears that the answers already surround us. It's the question we don't know.

ANDREW ZALESKI

The Brain That Remade Itself

FROM *OneZero*

I PUT MY HAND on a bishop and slide it several squares before moving it back. "Should I move a different piece instead?" I wonder to myself.

"You have to move that piece if you've touched it," my opponent says, flashing a wry grin.

Fine. I move the bishop. It's becoming increasingly obvious to me now—I'm going to lose a game of chess to a twelve-year-old.

My opponent is Tanner Collins, a seventh-grade student growing up in a Pittsburgh suburb. Besides playing chess, Collins likes building with Legos. One such set, a replica of Hogwarts Castle from the Harry Potter books, is displayed on a hutch in the dining room of his parents' house. He points out to me a critical flaw in the design: the back of the castle isn't closed off. "If you turn it around," he says, "the whole side is open. That's dumb."

Though Collins is not dissimilar from many kids his age, there is something that makes him unlike most twelve-year-olds in the United States, if not the world: he's missing one-sixth of his brain.

Collins was three months shy of seven years old when surgeons sliced open his skull and removed a third of his brain's right hemisphere. For two years prior, a benign tumor had been growing in the back of his brain, eventually reaching the size of a golf ball. The tumor caused a series of disruptive seizures that gave him migraines and kept him from school. Medications did little to treat the problem and made Collins drowsy. By the day of his surgery, Collins was experiencing daily seizures that were growing in severity. He would collapse and be incontinent and sometimes vomit, he says.

When neurologists told Collins's parents, Nicole and Carl, that they could excise the seizure-inducing areas of their son's brain, the couple agreed. "His neurologist wasn't able to control his seizures no matter what medication she put him on," Nicole says. "At that point, we were desperate . . . His quality of life was such that the benefits outweighed the risks."

Surgeons cut out the entire right occipital lobe and half of the temporal lobe of Collins's brain. Those lobes are important for processing the information that passes through our eyes' optic nerves, allowing us to see. These regions are also critical for recognizing faces and objects and attaching corresponding names. There was no way of being sure whether Collins would ever see again, recognize his parents, or even develop normally after the surgery.

And then the miraculous happened: despite the loss of more than 15 percent of his brain, Collins turned out to be fine.

The one exception is the loss of peripheral vision in his left eye. Though this means Collins will never legally be able to drive, he compensates for his blind spot by moving his head around, scanning a room to create a complete picture. "It's not like it's blurred or it's just black there. It's, like, all blended," Collins tells me when I visit him at home in January. "So, it's like a Bob Ross painting."

Today, Collins is a critical puzzle piece in an ongoing study of how the human brain can change. That's because his brain has done something remarkable: the left side has assumed all the responsibilities and tasks of his now largely missing right side.

"We're looking at the entire remapping of the function of one hemisphere onto the other," says Marlene Behrmann, a cognitive neuroscientist at Carnegie Mellon University who has been examining Collins's brain for more than five years.

What happened to Collins is a remarkable example of neuroplasticity: the ability of the brain to reorganize, create new connections, and even heal itself after injury. Neuroplasticity allows the brain to strengthen or even re-create connections between brain cells—the pathways that help us learn a foreign language, for instance, or how to ride a bike.

The fact that the brain has a malleable capacity to change itself isn't new. What's less understood is how exactly the brain does it. That's where Behrmann's study of Collins comes in. Her research question is twofold: To what extent can the remaining structures of Collins's brain take over the functions of the part of his brain that was removed? And can science describe how the brain carries out these changes, all the way down to the cellular level?

Previous neuroplasticity research has shed light on how the brain forms new neuronal connections with respect to memory, language, or learning abilities. (It's the basis for popular brain-training games meant to improve short-term memory.) But Behrmann's research is the first longitudinal study to look closely at what happens in the brain after the regions involved in visual processing are lost through surgery or damaged due to a traumatic brain injury.

"We know almost nothing about what happens in the visual system after this kind of surgery," she says. "I think of this as kind of the tip of the iceberg."

So far, Behrmann's findings are turning medical dogma on its head. They suggest that conducting brain surgeries in kids suffering seizures shouldn't be viewed as the last available option, as it was for Collins. The surgery he underwent, while successful roughly 70 percent of the time, is still uncommon, which means that many people with similar brain tumors may be suffering unnecessarily. And depending on what Behrmann discovers, we may learn more than we ever have before about the brain's capacity to bounce back.

The first time Collins collapsed because of a seizure, he was four and being minded by a babysitter. Over time, his symptoms grew more varied and more severe. "It's like my brain froze," he says. "I was really confused, and then I'd get really nauseous, throw up, and then I'd be kind of acting normal again."

A daily ritual ensued: Collins would go to school, have a seizure, collapse, and go home. Still, despite the misery, the seizures were a blessing in disguise. They led to the discovery of the tumor slowly enveloping a piece of his brain.

"These are some of the most common tumors we see in children," says Christina Patterson, MD, a pediatric epilepsy neurologist and part of the medical team that prepared Collins for surgery at the UPMC Children's Hospital of Pittsburgh. "Taking out the tumor is ultimately the cure."

The deeper problem with pediatric tumors like the one Collins developed—beyond the nausea, headaches, and confusion that he experienced—is that the seizures they produce can damage the electrical networks of the brain.

"We know that the pediatric brain has plasticity, [and] that we're constantly creating new algorithms in the brain to live life," Patterson says. "But when you have seizures on top of that, those disrupted electrical networks that are the seizures prevent any kind of meaningful remapping."

Inside our brains are about 100 billion neurons. These neurons build thousands of connections with one another and communicate with their cellular brethren by converting electrical signals into chemical neurotransmitters, which are responsible for carrying information between the brain cells. As we master new skills, the brain's neurons form new connections and strengthen old ones that aided in learning that information. Instead of discrete regions carrying out specific tasks, the brain depends on groups of neural networks talking to each other across multiple regions. (Behrmann says a single neuron can communicate with 50,000 other cells.) If the network is damaged, the brain cells can't communicate effectively.

Picture a map of the United States that shows a phone company's LTE network crisscrossing the country, and you have a rough approximation of how the human brain operates. Surgery for Collins, in this case, was akin to repairing a downed cell tower.

Before Collins's surgery to remove the tumor, doctors opened up his head and placed electrodes on the surface of his brain and inside his visual cortex. For seven days, Collins lay in a hospital bed as the electrodes mapped his brain's electrical activity, creating what was essentially a schematic diagram showing doctors where the seizures were originating and which brain areas needed to be cut out.

Collins recognized his parents after the surgery, but he couldn't match their faces to their names. The problem resolved itself in a couple of days, but the episode left Nicole and Carl concerned: how was their son's brain going to function with a missing part?

*

Consider, for a moment, a page from a *Where's Waldo?* book. When your eye focuses on the crowded image, you're actually only receiving two types of feedback: the light that falls on the retina and the color of that light. "That's all your eye can pick up," Behrmann says. "Yet somehow, almost instantaneously, you get an interpretation of the scene."

Patterson put the Collins family in touch with Behrmann, who studies how brain plasticity relates to vision at her lab at Carnegie Mellon. Collins was the ideal candidate for Behrmann's research. Children's brains are young and still developing and therefore have the most potential for neuroplastic change. Because Collins's tumor formed in the part of the brain crucial for visual processing, Behrmann could track his progress over time to determine whether there were any lingering deficits in his ability to interpret images. Because Collins was a child, his brain was also in a critical period of development where it builds the capacity to recognize faces, something that happens gradually and becomes more finely tuned throughout our teenage years.

As University of Toronto psychiatrist Norman Doidge notes in his 2007 book, *The Brain That Changes Itself,* the notion that there is a critical period of brain development is one of the most important discoveries in the area of neuroplasticity—and one for which we have kittens to thank. In the 1960s, as Doidge recounts, scientists David Hubel and Torsten Wiesel mapped the visual cortex of kittens—much in the same way Collins's surgical team mapped his own brain—to learn how vision is processed. Then, in an admittedly grisly procedure, the scientists sewed shut the eyelid of one of the kittens in the study. Upon opening the eyelid, they found that the visual areas of the kitten's brain responsible for processing images from that eye didn't develop, leaving the kitten blind in that eye, even though nothing was biologically wrong with the eye. The researchers discovered that if kittens' brains were to develop normally, they had to be able to see the world around them between their third and eighth weeks of life.

But another discovery from the study proved even more important—and earned Hubel and Wiesel the Nobel Prize. "The part of the kitten's brain that had been deprived of input from the shut eye did not remain idle," Doidge writes. "It had begun to process visual input from the open eye, as though the brain didn't want to waste any 'cortical real estate' and had found a way to rewire itself."

In Collins's case, the question was whether the fully intact left hemisphere of his brain would pick up the functionality of the missing third of his brain, especially the task of facial recognition, which is typically carried out by the right hemisphere.

Starting just before Collins was seven and continuing for three years, Behrmann administered a series of tests roughly every six months. In one challenge, he was shown photos of faces in intervals of roughly thirty seconds. If he remembered a face, he clicked a button. A similar test was administered using photos of houses, and if Collins saw the same photo back to back, he clicked a button. Each test occurred while he was inside a functional MRI machine, which allowed Behrmann to measure the flow of blood and oxygen to different regions of the brain. The more active an area of the brain, the more blood it draws.

Throughout these experiments, Behrmann compared Collins's brain function to a control group of kids his own age without brain abnormalities. The results, published last August in *Cell Reports*, were striking: his neurological function was "absolutely normal," with no subtle delays or deviations in development.

Over coffee in the kitchen of her Pittsburgh home, Behrmann showed me successive scans of Collins's brain that told the tale. "When he was eight, you can see the first glimmerings of face recognition in the brain," she says. "By the time he got to ten, you can see that his left hemisphere looks really like the right hemisphere of the controls."

In scans, Collins's left brain not only looked and performed the way his left brain should; it also looked similar in scans as other kids' intact right brains. That's because the functions of the visual cortex he lost by having one-third of his right brain removed—the ability to see objects and know what they are, and the ability to recognize faces—were subsumed by his left brain. Also fascinating to Behrmann was how the left brain could accommodate two different skills: word recognition, which is the domain of the left brain, as well as facial recognition. Indeed, part of the surprise was that the left brain could keep doing what it normally does in addition to the newly added right-brain activity.

In other words, Behrmann's work revealed that Collins's brain rewired itself, like the brain of the kitten that Hubel and Wiesel studied.

Just how the brain accomplishes this feat remains a central question. By analyzing brain scans using a neuroimaging technique known as diffusion tensor imaging, which shows how water travels along the brain's white-matter tracts, Behrmann has found initial glimmerings that the white matter of the brain—the electrical wiring that underlines communication between multiple neurological regions—actually changes. Areas of the brain that weren't connected before create new links, an example of neuroplasticity in action that may preserve brain functionality. But scientists still don't know what triggers the cells of the white matter to behave in this way.

"When Tanner is twenty, I think we'll know a lot more about the overall wiring," Behrmann says. "The one thing that we will not know in humans, and I don't know how we will ever know it, are the changes that occur at the level of the cells themselves."

Every three to six months, Collins returns to Behrmann's lab to undergo tests and be examined for any visual deficits. Behrmann hopes that following him over time will lead to more definitive answers, not only about how his visual system finally reorganizes itself but also the process by which it does so. "We've got a long way to go, but the work, I think, is really exciting," she says.

In a follow-up study Behrmann conducted with Collins and nine other children—all of whom are missing areas of either their left or right hemisphere—eight of them, including Collins, showed absolutely normal vision function. The two who did not are children whose brain damage from seizures was more severe prior to their surgeries.

This sort of insight is needed to gauge when to perform a brain surgery like the one Collins had. At what age should parents agree to remove a tumor that's causing epileptic seizures? Sometimes, resective surgery that removes brain tissue can make it difficult for a person to use and understand words; it can also, as it did in Collins's case, result in visual impairment.

"Once we have a better picture of exactly what happens after we remove large segments of the brain, we may be able to counsel families more effectively," says Taylor Abel, MD, a pediatric neurosurgeon who specializes in epilepsy surgery and arrived at the

Children's Hospital of Pittsburgh last summer to begin collaborating with Behrmann. "The goal should be to do whatever you can to stop the seizures and get off of medications as early in your life as possible. The sooner you do that, the sooner you can return to a normal developmental trajectory."

It may even be the case, Abel and Behrmann point out, that some of the reorganization that took place in Collins's brain started prior to his scheduled surgery. It's not something Behrmann can prove, since all the research conducted on Collins has taken place post-surgery.

"When you have an abnormality in your brain that's causing seizures, that abnormality can actually cause the brain to reorganize or start reorganizing before the surgery actually takes place," Abel says. "But the other thing that sometimes happens is that the seizures affect the functions in the brain, and the brain doesn't reorganize."

Behrmann says one of the fundamental goals of her research is to study a large enough population of children to determine if there are patterns of optimal recovery based on the age they had their surgery. Reorganization to the degree Collins has experienced is impossible for adults undergoing similar surgery, Behrmann says, as they lack the neuroplasticity seen in children.

For Nicole and Carl, the surgery was unequivocally the right decision. "What was happening before the surgery was pretty awful," Nicole says. "After surgery, the changes were only for the better. Yeah, he has his visual deficits. But everything else was for the better."

In late 2017, a follow-up MRI at the Children's Hospital of Pittsburgh showed that Collins's tumor grew back. This time, though, it was the size of a pea. Two months later, in February 2018, surgeons opened his brain a second time. Collins says the prospect of a second surgery didn't bother him; he just wanted the pea-size tumor out of his head so he wouldn't have to worry about it. (The surgery went well, and he's still tumor-free.)

As we close in on minute 24 of our chess match, I move my king in the corner of the board, still certain of my impending doom. Collins scans his remaining white pieces and then takes a look at where his king sits.

"Mate," he says, looking up at me.

Checkmate for me, I realize, surprised by a victory I did not expect. Collins begins breaking down the moves he made, retracing some of his steps. It seems he forgot about a pawn of mine that was still on the board.

"I like losing," he says. "Obviously, I like winning too. But when you lose, you gain the knowledge."

Even after losing a portion of his brain, Collins is still learning. His brain is still growing, still adapting—and, even if it's not readily apparent, still changing.

Contributors' Notes

Other Notable Science and Nature Writing of 2019

Contributors' Notes

Ross Andersen is deputy editor of *The Atlantic*. He was previously deputy editor of *Aeon Magazine*.

Kelly Clancy is a writer and neuroscientist at University College London.

Daniel Duane is the author of *Caught Inside: A Surfer's Year on the California Coast*. He is at work on a memoir about the Sierra Nevada.

David H. Freedman is a Boston-based science writer. He is a contributing writer for *The Atlantic* and the author of five books, the most recent of which is *Wrong*, about the problems with the published findings of scientists and other types of expertise.

Rivka Galchen, a novelist and essayist, is the author of four books.

Bahar Gholipour is a neuroscientist turned journalist covering biomedicine research, neuroscience, and AI for a wide variety of publications, including *Scientific American, The Atlantic,* the *New York Times, Science, New York Magazine, NBC News,* and the *Daily Beast*. She grew up in Tehran and lives in New York.

Adam Gopnik has been a staff writer at *The New Yorker* since 1987. He has won the National Magazine Award for Essays and Criticism three times, and his books include *At the Strangers' Gate* and *A Thousand Small Sanities*.

Sara Harrison is a freelance journalist who covers science, business, and technology. She is a graduate of the UC Berkeley School of Journalism and Carleton College.

Patrick House received a PhD in neuroscience from Stanford University. His nonfiction writing has appeared in *The New Yorker* online, *Slate,* and the *Los Angeles Review of Books.*

Ferris Jabr is a contributing writer for the *New York Times Magazine.* He has also written for *The New Yorker, Harper's, The Atlantic, Lapham's Quarterly, Wired, Outside, Scientific American,* and *Foreign Policy.* He is currently working on his first book. He lives in Portland, Oregon.

Sarah Kaplan is a *Washington Post* climate reporter covering humanity's response to our warming world. She has reported from the sea ice off Alaska, hurricane-lashed communities in North Carolina, and massive protests on the National Mall, seeking stories of the people most affected by climate change as well as those working hardest to halt it. She previously worked on the *Post*'s science desk, where she wrote about space and the physical sciences.

Adam Mann is a freelance space and physics reporter living in Oakland, California. His work has appeared in many places, including *Wired,* the *New York Times,* the *Wall Street Journal,* and *Scientific American.* In his spare time, he likes thinking about aliens and riding his bike.

Deanna Csomo McCool is a science writer and assistant director of marketing communications in the College of Science at the University of Notre Dame, where she also teaches a course in science journalism. She graduated from Indiana University, earned her master's degree in science writing twenty-five years later from Johns Hopkins University, and has written for a variety of publications. She lives a few miles from Notre Dame with her daughter and a "vicious" rescue dog—a shih-tzu mix.

Jon Mooallem is a writer at large for the *New York Times Magazine* and the author, most recently, of *This Is Chance!,* about the 1964 Great Alaska Earthquake and Anchorage radio reporter Genie Chance.

Melinda Wenner Moyer is a science journalist based in New York's Hudson Valley and a visiting scholar at NYU's Arthur L. Carter Journalism Institute. She is a contributing editor at *Scientific American* magazine and a columnist at *Slate* magazine. She was the recipient of the 2019 Bricker Award for Science Writing in Medicine. Her work has also received first-place awards in the American Society of Journalists and Authors' Annual Writing Awards and the Awards for Excellence in Health Care Reporting.

Siddhartha Mukherjee is the author of *The Emperor of All Maladies,* winner of the 2011 Pulitzer Prize in general nonfiction, and of *The Laws of Medicine*. He is the guest editor of *The Best American Science and Nature Writing 2013*. His latest work, *The Gene*, recounts the quest to decipher the master code of instructions that makes and defines humans and determines the future of our children. Mukherjee is an assistant professor of medicine at Columbia University and a cancer physician and researcher. A Rhodes scholar, he graduated from Stanford University, the University of Oxford, and Harvard Medical School. He has published articles in *Nature*, *The New Yorker*, the *New England Journal of Medicine*, the *New York Times*, and *Cell*. He lives in New York with his wife and daughters.

Douglas Preston is an author and journalist who has published thirty-five books, both nonfiction and fiction. His recent nonfiction book, *The Lost City of the Monkey God*, was named a Notable Book of the Year by the *New York Times*. Preston previously worked as an editor at the American Museum of Natural History and taught nonfiction writing at Princeton University.

Tim Requarth is a freelance science journalist, as well as a lecturer in science and writing at New York University. His writing has appeared in publications such as the *New York Times*, *The Nation*, *The New Republic*, *Slate*, *Foreign Policy*, and *Scientific American*. He received his PhD in neuroscience from Columbia University. He was a 2018 UC Berkeley–11th Hour Food & Farming Journalism Fellow and is a 2019–2020 Brown Institute for Media Innovation "magic grant" recipient.

John Seabrook is the author of *The Song Machine* and other books. He is a longtime staff writer at *The New Yorker*.

Joshua Sokol is a freelance science writer in the Boston area. After working as a data analyst for the Hubble Space Telescope, he attended MIT's Graduate Program in Science Writing, and since 2016 he has won awards from the American Astronomical Society and the Council for the Advancement of Science Writing for his coverage of space and natural history.

Shannon Stirone is a writer whose work has appeared in the *New York Times*, *National Geographic*, *The Atlantic*, and other publications. She covers the intersection of space exploration and society.

Natalie Wolchover is a science journalist based in Queens, New York. She covers the physical sciences as a senior writer and editor for *Quanta Magazine*, with bylines also in *Nature*, *The New Yorker* online, *Popular Science*, and other publications. Her writing was featured in *The Best Writing on Math-*

ematics 2015, and she has won several awards, including the American Institute of Physics' 2017 Science Communication Award.

Andrew Zaleski is a freelance journalist who writes frequently about science, technology, and business. His features and profiles have been published by *Wired, Popular Science, Outside, Men's Health, MIT Technology Review, Bloomberg Businessweek, Elemental,* and *OneZero.* He lives in the Washington, D.C., metro area with his delightful wife and his dog, Finnegan, who is also delightful.

Other Notable Science and Nature Writing of 2019

HAYES BROWN
The End Times Are Here, and I Am at Target. *The Outline.* August 7, 2019

EIREN CAFFALL
Small Wonder: The Challenge of Parenting Through Climate Collapse. *Literary Hub.* December 18, 2019

JAMES S. A. COREY
Dear Dawn: How a NASA Robot Messed Up Our Science Fiction. *National Geographic.* February 8, 2019

MEEHAN CRIST
A Strange Blight. *London Review of Books.* June 6, 2019

THOMAS DAI
Notes on a Metamorphosis. *Conjunctions.* November 26, 2019

LYDIA DENWORTH
What Can Baboon Relationships Tell Us About Human Health? *Scientific American.* January 2019

BRONWEN DICKEY
The Remains. *Esquire.* October 1, 2019

ELIE DOLGIN
The Dappled Dilemma Facing Vitiligo Science. *Knowable.* April 5, 2019

ANN DRUYAN
Dear Voyagers. *National Geographic.* July 10, 2019

MICHAEL ERARD
The Mystery of Babies' First Words. *The Atlantic.* April 30, 2019

TAD FRIEND
Value Meal. *The New Yorker.* September 30, 2019

KATHARINE GAMMON
The Human Cost of Amber. *The Atlantic.* August 2, 2019

SARAH GILMAN
The Rat Spill. *Hakai.* August 13, 2019

HENRY GRABAR
Oh No, Not Knotweed! *Slate.* May 8, 2019

MALCOLM HARRIS
Indigenous Knowledge Has Been Warning Us About Climate Change for Centuries. *Pacific Standard.* March 4, 2019

CJ HAUSER
The Crane Wife. *The Paris Review.* July 16, 2019

MARY HEGLAR
After the Storm. *Guernica.* October 22, 2019

BENJAMIN ALDES WURGAFT
  Animal, Vegetable, or Both? Making Sense of the Scythian Lamb. *Lapham's Quarterly*. August 5, 2019

ED YONG
  The Blue Whale's Heart Beats at Extremes. *The Atlantic*. November 25, 2019
ILANA YURKIEWICZ
  Behind the Scenes of a Radical New Cancer Cure. *Undark*. October 23, 2019

THE BEST AMERICAN SERIES®

FIRST, BEST, AND BEST-SELLING

The Best American Essays

The Best American Food Writing

The Best American Mystery Stories

The Best American Science and Nature Writing

The Best American Science Fiction and Fantasy

The Best American Short Stories

The Best American Sports Writing

The Best American Travel Writing

Available in print and e-book wherever books are sold.

Visit our website: hmhbooks.com/series/best-american